Success Factor Modeling
Volume III

Conscious Leadership and Resilience

Orchestrating Innovation and Fitness for the Future

by

Robert B. Dilts

Design and illustrations by
Antonio Meza

To Jim,
Wishing you
an amazing and FUN
future!

8/7/17

Published by:

Dilts Strategy Group
P. O. Box 67448
Scotts Valley CA 95067
USA
Phone: (831) 438-8314
E-Mail: info@diltstrategygroup.com
Homepage: http://www.diltstrategygroup.com

Library of Congress Control Number: 2016908590

I.S.B.N. 978-0-9962004-4-8

Success Factor Modeling

Volume III

Conscious Leadership and Resilience

Orchestrating Innovation and Fitness for the Future

by

Robert B. Dilts

Design and illustrations by
Antonio Meza

Table of Contents

Table of Contents

Table of Contents

Table of Contents

Dedication

This book is dedicated to my teachers and mentors

Gregory Bateson and *Milton Erickson*

who demonstrated through the example of their lives the quality of awareness and commitment to a higher purpose required for conscious leadership and resilience.

Robert Dilts

With much gratitude I dedicate this book to my parents

Antonio Meza and *Amparo Andrade*

The best examples of conscious leadership and resilience I could have ever wished for

Antonio Meza

Acknowledgements

As with the first two volumes of the *Success Factor Modeling* series, special acknowledgment goes to Antonio Meza for his work on the design of the layout of the book and for his creative and enlightening illustrations. Antonio has been a valued advisor and partner in many other ways as well in bringing this book to publication.

Of course, a major contribution to this book has come from the individuals, groups and organizations that are featured in the Success Factor Case Examples and in the other examples illustrating key principles and success factors. I would like to gratefully honor and acknowledge Elon Musk (SpaceX, Tesla, SolarCity), Steve Jobs (Apple, NeXt, Pixar), Richard Branson (The Virgin Group), Barak Obama (US President), Phil Jackson (Chicago Bulls, LA Lakers), Chesley Sullenberger (US Airways), Jeff Bezos (Amazon.com), Anita Roddick (The Body Shop), Muhammed Yunus (Grameen Bank), Howard Schultz (Starbucks), John Yokoyama (Pike Place Fish Market), William McKnight (3M) and Walt Disney (Walt Disney Productions).

I would like to especially thank Tom Chi (GoogleX), Dr. Lim Suet Wun (Tan Tock Seng Hospital, Singapore), Charles Matthews (Rolls Royce Motors), David Guo (Display Research Laboratories), Jan E. Smith (The Disney Store, Disney Interactive), Vahé Torossian (Microsoft) and Steig Westerberg (Stream Theory) for participating in personal interviews and interactions and generously sharing their experience and knowledge directly with me.

All of these individuals are outstanding examples of next generation entrepreneurship, conscious leadership and resilience.

There are many other leaders and entrepreneurs, too numerous to name, whose experience, reflections and advice are spread throughout this book in the form of quotations and citations. I am deeply appreciative of their inspiration and wisdom.

I also want to express gratitude and appreciation to a number of my colleagues whose collaborations with me have produced important contributions to this book as well as the previous volumes: Miklos (Mickey) Fehrer and his work with me on the SFM Success Mindset Map; Mitchell and Olga Stevko, co-founders with me of the Successful Genius and Conscious Leadership Mastermind group; Stephen Gilligan and our developments on the principles and practices of Generative Change; and Ian McDermott and our work on Intentional Fellowship.

I would also like to thank Glenn Bacon, Michael Dilts and Benoit Sarazin for their time and efforts in reading over the initial draft of this book and offering their feedback and suggestions. Many thanks also go to Amanda Frost for her expert proofreading of this book as well as the first two volumes.

Finally, I would like to deeply acknowledge my brother John Dilts whose fascination with win-win negotiation and meta leadership, along with his love of generative collaboration and his passion for creating a world of visionary entrepreneurs was the foundation and remains the guiding spirit of Success Factor Modeling.

— Robert Dilts

Preface

This three-volume book series on *Success Factor Modeling*™ (SFM™) is the culmination of a dream that began in 1999 when my late brother John Dilts (profiled in Chapter 4 of *SFM Vol. II*, pp. 236-246) and I founded the *Dilts Strategy Group* and began our first explorations with the Success Factor Modeling™ process.

The questions we sought to answer were: "What is the difference that makes the difference between successful and average or poor ventures, teams, leaders and entrepreneurs?" and "What are the critical success factors related to launching or growing a successful and sustainable business."

Many of our discoveries are described in the first two volumes of this work, *Next Generation Entrepreneurs: Live Your Dreams and Create a Better World Through Your Business*, and *Generative Collaboration: Releasing the Creative Power of Collective Intelligence*. These include defining your passion, vision, mission, ambition and role, building a "Circle of Success" by working innovatively and collectively with others. *SFM Volume I*, for instance, captures the spirit and exhilaration (as well as the commitment and skill) related to launching a venture based on your passion and vision. *SFM Volume II* explores the process that John and I called "generative collaboration." It shows how to create the conditions in which people can work creatively and productively with others in order to achieve their dreams and visions.

This book, *SFM Volume III*, is about *Conscious Leadership and Resilience*. This relates to the abilities to inspire others to meaningful action and to withstand challenges and rebound from adversity. The subtitle of the book, *Orchestrating Innovation and Fitness for the Future*, points to the importance of creativity and sustainability as major success factors for creating a thriving and durable venture that contributes positively to the lives of others. This book will help you to track and manage the dynamic interplay between leadership, awareness, resilience, innovation, contribution and sustainable success.

Another theme of this book, and indeed the whole Success Factor Modeling approach, is the intimate relationship between personal and professional growth. A key discovery, and a fundamental premise, of Success Factor Modeling is that, in order to grow our professional career or venture, we must also grow and evolve personally. In order to contribute more, we have to grow more.

Another way of putting this is that, in order to take our professions, our ventures or our lives to the next level, we have to significantly shift and evolve our mindset. That mindset that brought us to where we are today will not take us to the next stage. The pages ahead will offer you many resources for assessing and enhancing your mindset, as well as provide you with roadmaps and tools for rebounding from adversity, "orchestrating innovation," empowering yourself and others, moving from vision to execution and positively influencing others to action through principled persuasion.

When John and I first began sharing our work with SFM, we thought of it as something more than just knowledge about doing effective business, but rather a movement that would help to enrich people's lives and make a better world. It has been almost two decades now that I have been applying the principles, skills and models identified by the Success Factor Modeling approach. In addition to my own ventures, I (and many others) have used the tools of SFM to support a variety of companies and organizations, ranging from fresh start-ups to large multinational organizations with a long history. It has been gratifying to witness this movement gather more and more momentum.

I hope you find this world of Success Factor Modeling and conscious leadership as exciting and rewarding to explore as John and I have. May it bring you much success and satisfaction as you orchestrate innovation and enhance your fitness for the future.

Robert Dilts
June, 2017
Santa Cruz, California

01 Leadership, Consciousness and Fitness for the Future

Leadership means bringing people together in pursuit of common cause, developing a plan to achieve it, and staying with it until the goal is achieved... Leadership also requires the ability to respond to unforeseen problems and opportunities when they arise. [A leader needs] to be able to clearly articulate a vision of where you want to go, develop a realistic strategy to get there, and attract talented, committed people with a wide variety of knowledge, perspectives, and skills to do what needs to be done. In the modern world, I believe lasting positive results are more likely to occur when leaders practice inclusion and cooperation rather than authoritarian unilateralism. Even those who lead the way don't have all the answers.

Bill Clinton

ANTONIO MEZA

Overview of Success Factor Modeling™

Conscious Leadership and Resilience is the third volume in this series of books on Success Factor Modeling™ (SFM). *Success Factor Modeling™* is a methodology originally developed by myself and my late brother John Dilts (see SFM Vol. II, pp. 236-246) in order to identify, understand and apply the critical success factors that drive and support exceptional people, groups and organizations. Success Factor Modeling™ is founded upon a set of principles and distinctions which are uniquely suited to analyze and distinguish crucial patterns of *business practices* and *behavioral skills* used by effective individuals, teams and companies to reach their desired outcomes. The SFM™ process is used to discern key characteristics and capabilities shared by outstanding entrepreneurs, teams and business leaders and then to define specific models, tools and skills that can be used by others to greatly increase their chances of producing impact and achieving success.

The objective of the Success Factor Modeling™ process is to make an *instrumental map*—one supported by a variety of exercises, formats and tools that allow people to apply the factors that have been modeled in order to reach key outcomes within their chosen context. To accomplish this, SFM applies the following basic template:

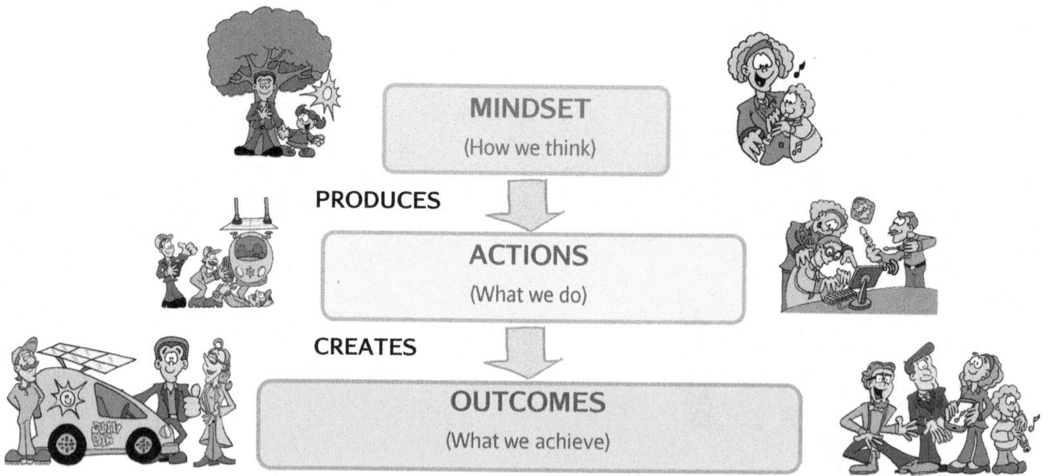

The Basic Success Factor Modeling Template

Our mindset—which is made up of our inner state, attitude and thinking processes—produces outer behavioral *actions*. It is our mindset that determines what we do and the types of actions we take in a particular situation. These actions, in turn, create *outcomes* in the external world around us. A key premise of Success Factor Modeling is that achieving desired outcomes in our environment requires the proper mindset in order to produce the necessary and appropriate actions.

In the first volume in the series, *Next Generation Entrepreneurs: Live Your Dream and Make a Better World Through Your Business*, I applied the Success Factor Modeling process to establish some of the skills and steps necessary to create a "Circle of Success" and build a profitable venture aligned with your life purpose. Volume II, *Generative Collaboration: Releasing the Creative Power of Collective Intelligence*, explored the attitude and practices necessary for people either facilitating or working in teams to increase their capacity to for working together effectively and creatively with others.

Applying Success Factor Modeling to Leadership and Resilience

This book focuses on leadership, innovation and resilience. These are three of the most essential capabilities necessary to achieve robust and sustainable success for any project or venture. *Resilience* is the ability of individuals, teams and organizations to *withstand or recover quickly from difficult conditions* and to maintain a state of equilibrium with respect to both success and adversity. When people are challenged, they can sometimes rise to the occasion. But if the challenge seems too great, they may "crash and burn."

This is where the skills of leadership are an essential resource. Leadership is about ensuring that people (including yourself) are prepared to be their best, meet challenges, overcome obstacles and reach critical goals. *Leadership* is typically described as the ability to "direct the operations, activity, or performance of" (as in "leading" an orchestra), and "to bring to some conclusion or condition" (e.g., "lead" to achieve a goal).

In fact, "leading" and "leadership" come from the Old English word *lithan*, meaning "to go" or "to travel" (as opposed to have power or control). *Lædan* in Old English literally meant "to cause to go". According to Merriam-Webster's Dictionary, leadership means "to guide on a way, especially by going in advance." Thus, leadership is often about "going first," and influencing others as much by one's actions as by one's words.

Clearly then, leadership is intimately tied to motivating and influencing others to take action. In businesses and organizations, "leadership" is often contrasted with "management" *Management* is typically defined as "getting things done through others." In comparison, leadership is defined as "getting others to want to do things." Management is usually associated with improving productivity, establishing order and stability, and making things run efficiently and smoothly. "Leadership" is required to keep moving forward in times of uncertainty, turbulence, social transformation and change.

Success Factor Modeling™ explores the question, "What is the difference that makes the difference?" in order to find the success factors that distinguish between poor, average and remarkable performance.

Leadership, innovation and resilience are essential to achieve success in any venture.

***Leadership** is required to keep moving forward, especially in times of change and uncertainty.*

***Innovation** is necessary to continually adapt to changing conditions and create new possibilities.*

***Resilience** is needed to withstand or recover quickly from difficult conditions and to maintain a state of equilibrium.*

Basic Skills of Leadership

In order to "go" anywhere we minimally need two things: (1) a *direction* and (2) *energy*. Without a direction we wander aimlessly. Without energy, we are trapped in inertia or paralysis. To go somewhere more easily, it also helps to have a *vehicle* to carry us and, if possible, a *path* to follow. In the case of entrepreneurship, the vehicle is the venture. The path is the plan, strategy or "storyboard." In many cases, it is necessary to continue to both create the vehicle and discover the path after the journey has already begun.

> *Leadership is about helping people to go somewhere (generally somewhere new) by providing direction and energy; i.e., expressing a vision and motivating people.*

Thus, the essence of leadership is *providing direction* and *bringing energy*; i.e., expressing a vision and motivating people. As we established in the previous volumes of this series, visions of the future provide guidance and direction for our lives and our work, furnishing the inspiration and impetus for growth and change. Visions that become shared by a number of people form the foundation of effective teamwork and the bases for our ventures; visions that become shared by multitudes constitute the basis for organization, community, culture and ultimately for the progress of civilization.

Leadership, like entrepreneurship, has been a passion of mine for many years. Since the 1980s, I have had the opportunity to observe and interview effective leaders and business executives from around the world. In my book *Visionary Leadership Skills* (1996) I pointed out that, in its broadest sense, leadership can be viewed as the ability to *involve others* in the process of *accomplishing a goal* within some larger *system* or environment. That is, a leader provides an example and influences collaborators towards achieving some end in the context of a bigger system. From this perspective, *leadership* can be summarized as the capability to:

> *In its broadest sense, leadership is the ability to involve others in the process of accomplishing a goal within some larger system.*

1. Express a *vision*
2. *Influence others* to achieve results
3. Encourage *team cooperation*
4. Be *an example*

We can show the relationship between these abilities in the diagram on the following page.

A Leader Provides Direction, Acts as an Example and Involves Others in Reaching Goals Within a System

One of the basic skills of leadership is the capacity to express a vision.

Another important skill of leadership is the ability to encourage team cooperation and "generative collaboration"

In the previous volumes of this series, I have covered some key principles and methods for how to begin to put each of these abilities into practice:

1. Forming and expressing a vision in order to create the future and establish our ventures (see *SFM Vol. I*, pp. 193-213).
2. Knowing ourselves and clarifying our own missions, ambitions and motivations in order be an inspiring example (see *SFM Vol. I*, pp. 172-188 and 213-235).
3. Encouraging team cooperation through collaboration catalysts and creating the conditions for collective intelligence to emerge (see *SFM Vol. II*, pp. 116-127).
4. Motivating and engaging others to join us by creating win-win collaborations and involving them in the success of our ventures (see *SFM Vol. II*, pp. 168-175).

Each of these abilities is equally important for rebounding from adversity and increasing the degree of innovation and resilience of our ventures. In this volume, I will be presenting exercises and practices for deepening and expanding each of these capabilities so that you can learn to maximize the potential of your venture for innovation and resilience, especially during times of challenge and change.

Meeting the Challenges of Change

It is said that things are always changing, but not always *progressing*. During a time of adversity, many challenges will present themselves such as meeting the fear of the unknown and the unfamiliar, dealing with loss, and a general sense of vulnerability. These can plunge us into unhelpful survival strategies – attack, escape or rigidity (fight, flight, freeze) — and may result in some form of regression, inertia, ambivalence, confusion or conflict.

In order to progress through change, it is important to cultivate qualities such as focus, flexibility and stability, balance, connection to our resources and the ability to "let go." It is easy to stay balanced when life moves smoothly, but in order to maintain equilibrium during turbulent times, one must have developed these qualities until they are "in the muscle." Preparing for change requires practice.

In this book you will learn roadmaps and practices, and develop resources and tools designed to help manage various stages of adversity and profound change effectively.

Resilience and Fitness For the Future

Fitness refers to a system's general state of health and readiness to respond to its environment. Fitness is intimately related to longevity. In fact, *fitness for the future* (see *Organizations in Action*, J. Thompson, 1968) is considered one of the most important criteria for the long-term success and survival of any system or venture—much more significant than its past success. This is especially the case in a dynamic and changing environment where what worked in the past may be obsolete.

***Fitness for the future** is essential for the long-term success and survival of any system or venture—especially in a dynamic and changing environment.*

Systemically, "fitness" is related to system theorist Ross Ashby's *Law of Requisite Variety*, which states *that a system needs a sufficient degree of variability in order to effectively adapt to the changes occurring in the world around it.* From this perspective, a system becomes more "fit" by expanding its range of choices and resources. This is typically achieved by increasing the diversity of behaviors, feedback mechanisms and coping strategies available to the system. Thus, innovation is a key requirement for fitness for the future.

Both physical and mental fitness, for instance, involve developing a degree of flexibility and stamina. These are achieved through consistent exercise and practices rather than through techniques or one-time interventions. Thus, fitness relates more to the ongoing behavior patterns or "life style" of the individual or culture of the organization than to particular events or interventions.

Fitness for the future involves the abilities to adapt to changes and take advantage of opportunities that arise, in many cases unexpectedly or spontaneously, as a person, group or venture moves into the future. As science fiction author Arthur C. Clarke so eloquently pointed out, *"The Future just isn't what it used to be."*

Fitness for the future requires innovation in order to have the flexibility necessary to quickly and effectively adapt and rebound in response to changes in the world around us.

There is an old and wise saying that "an ounce of prevention is worth a pound of cure." When resources are developed and in place ahead of time, a person or organization is able to rise to the challenge instead of scrambling to deal with unnecessary problems. Fitness for the future involves being prepared for problems, goals and situations to come that we have not yet anticipated or even imagined. Having resources already in place reduces the need for "crisis management."

Sustainable development is a key concern for next generation entrepreneurs and "zentrepreneurs."

Fitness for the future is intimately connected with sustainable development. Sustainable development is one of the most fundamental issues facing today's generation of entrepreneurs and organizations. *Sustainable development* is defined as *"development which seeks to produce sustainable economic growth while ensuring future generations' ability to do the same by not exceeding the regenerative capacity of nature."* In other words, it is about "enabling development that meets today's needs without prejudicing the ability of future generations to meet their own needs." Broadly, it is the principle of stewardship and responsibility in the use and management of resources and achieving a balance between economic growth, technological developments and environmental considerations. Successful sustainable development is a key concern for next generation entrepreneurs and "zentrepreneurs" (see *SFM Vol. I*, pp. 66-73).

***Sustainable development** involves the capacity to "meet today's needs without compromising the ability of future generations to meet their own needs."*

Truly sustainable development involves moving beyond simply surviving to fully engage the capacity to thrive as an individual, team or organization. To *survive* is defined as "to continue to live or exist in spite of an accident or ordeal" or "to manage to keep going in difficult circumstances." The implication is that, when we are in survival mode, we are struggling to maintain "business as usual," but we are not necessarily growing or prepared to grow. To *thrive* is defined as to "grow or develop well or vigorously; to prosper or flourish." Thus, in order to thrive, we need to dynamically adapt to our environment in a way that uses resources wisely and that also makes us fit for the future.

Integrating the mindset necessary to foster fitness for the future and support sustainable development with the skills of leadership creates a new type of leadership that can be called "conscious leadership."

In order to move from a survival mode to one in which we are thriving, our mental maps of who we are and what is possible in the world must become broader, and we must perceive old limitations in a completely new way. This requires that we break through our old mindset and "get outside of the box," learning at the level of what anthropologist Gregory Bateson called *Learning IV*—the creation of something "completely new." Such a generative state both "includes and transcends" our previous knowledge and awareness, and is a key part of our ability to be resilient and stay fit for the future. Integrating this shift in mindset with the skills of leadership elevates leadership to a new level that can be called "conscious leadership."

Conscious Leadership

Conscious leadership involves building a sustainable venture and guiding yourself and your team from a state of centered presence, accessing multiple intelligences and living your highest values in service to a larger purpose for the benefit of all stakeholders. In addition to the basic skills of leadership, conscious leadership requires being:

- Authentic
- Emotionally intelligent
- Purposive
- Responsible

As we will explore in this book, achieving competence in conscious leadership involves important practices such as:

1. Formulating and communicating a meaningful and inclusive vision for all stakeholders.
2. Focusing on higher purpose.
3. Influencing through inspiration.
4. Balancing self-interest and the common good, in themselves and others.
5. Respecting and integrating multiple perspectives.
6. Leading by example (walking your talk).
7. Exercising mindful self-leadership and reflecting thoughtfully on the lessons gained from experience.

Qualities of Conscious Leadership

Success Factor Case Example:
Elon Musk:
Founder of PayPal, SolarCity, Tesla Motors and SpaceX

"Constantly think about how you could be doing things better and keep questioning yourself"

Elon Musk

A good example of conscious leadership, innovation and resilience in today's business world is entrepreneur Elon Musk. Musk founded his first company (**Zip2** – a website that provided online content publishing software for various news organizations) at the age of 23 and sold it in 1999 for $300 million. His next venture was the online payment platform **PayPal** which allows users to safely buy and sell online. PayPal was acquired by eBay in 2002 for $1.5 billion in stock, of which Musk received $165 million. Since then, Musk has shifted the focus of his vision to affordable solar energy for the public through his company **SolarCity** (established in 2006), and has made the dream of an electric car possible and inexpensive with **Tesla Motors** (incorporated in 2003). Beyond that, his **SpaceX** space travel company (launched in 2002) created the first privately funded liquid-fuelled vehicle to put a satellite into Earth orbit and became the first commercial company to launch and dock a vehicle to the International Space Station.

Musk, who is clear about his determination to transform the way people live today, has clearly focused his vision on ventures that support "fitness for the future" and sustainable development. He consciously and intentionally chose things that he believed would most positively affect the future of humanity: the Internet; clean energy; and space exploration. He then sought to discover how he could make thriving businesses out of them. As he describes it:

> *It's really kind of like a relevance optimization: What do I think is going to make the biggest difference to the future of humanity – and then I try to see if I can have the value of the output be greater than the cost of the input, which is necessary for any ongoing enterprise. But it's definitely not from the perspective of "this is the best return on investment" or anything like that. If one were to rank order return on investment and the amount of effort required, I think Space and Cars would be really low on the list... So it's just from the standpoint of, "am I working on things that I think will have the biggest impact on the future?" And then making the economics work is necessary just because if you don't make the economics work then you're not going to have any effect on the future.*

Elon Musk's notion of "relevance optimization" involves balancing contribution to humanity with financial return and economic viability.

It is revealing that Musk's passion for creating positive change emerged as a result of an existential crisis he experienced as a teenager. Musk grew up in Apartheid South Africa. Not only did he witness first hand the effects of prejudice and the discrimination of one population toward another, Musk himself was frequently ruthlessly bullied because he was "nerdy" and different. These experiences along with the difficult divorce of his parents left him deeply depressed by the lack of answers to the large questions of life, such as the purpose of existence. Instead of becoming cynical or retreating into addictive behaviors like many others would have, Musk transformed his depression into a profound commitment to the expansion of global consciousness and the achievement of "collective enlightenment." He became convinced that if global consciousness could be expanded, perhaps in the future mankind would be able to ask the right questions. As he put it:

> *I came to the conclusion that we should aspire to increase the scope and scale of human consciousness in order to better understand what questions to ask. Really, the only thing that makes sense is to strive for greater collective enlightenment.*

Musk's passion for creating positive change by striving for collective enlightenment emerged as a result of his experience growing up in Apartheid South Africa and being bullied as a child.

Such aspirations to "increase the scope and scale of human consciousness" and the desire to "make a positive difference in the future of humanity" are at the core of all conscious leadership. The visions of conscious leaders for their ventures always serve a higher purpose that benefits the maximum number of stakeholders.

Rather than simply make cars, for instance, Tesla's deeper mission is to "help accelerate the advent of sustainable transport" by putting out the best electric cars they can make, demonstrating that electric cars are feasible, profitable and desirable – and *helping* the *other* car companies transition faster to electric vehicles. In fact, in 2014 the company took the unusual step of an "open source" approach for its technology, suspending the enforcement of its more than 200 patents in order to encourage development of electric cars. "Tesla will not initiate patent lawsuits against anyone who, in good faith, wants to use our technology," Musk announced. "When I started out with my first company, Zip2, I thought patents were a good thing and worked hard to obtain them," he says. "And maybe they were good long ago, but too often these days they serve merely to stifle progress, entrench the positions of giant corporations and enrich those in the legal profession, rather than the actual inventors... Tesla Motors was created to accelerate the advent of sustainable transport. If we clear a path to the creation of compelling electric vehicles, but then lay intellectual property landmines behind us to inhibit others, we are acting in a manner contrary to that goal."

Perceiving his role as being a "catalyst for change," Musk has taken an unprecedented "open source" approach for the technologies developed at Tesla Motors.

Similarly, the ultimate core goal of SpaceX is not just to make rocket ships but to serve a much bigger purpose which is to pave the way to humanity "becoming a multi-planet species."

In Elon Musk's bigger vision, the Internet can serve as a global nervous system, renewable energy can expand the timeframe within which mankind can try to ask the right questions before running into economical or ecological collapse, and space exploration can serve as a backup for life itself. Musk considers becoming a spacefaring civilization as an important step in evolution itself, akin to life first crawling onto land. In Musk's words:

> *My goals are to accelerate the world's transition to sustainable energy and help make humanity a multi-planet civilization, a consequence of which will be the creation of hundreds of thousands of jobs and a more inspiring future for all.*

Elon Musk's generative vision of better and more sustainable future continues to spawn new products and ventures.

A Generative Vision

It is clear that Elon Musk's vision and mission for his ventures comes more from the perspective of being a part of something much bigger than himself rather than from the perspective of an isolated individual focusing on self-benefit. His vision emerges from a deep passion, intention and commitment to change things for the better. Vision of this type is inherently *generative*. This means that it continues to create specific new future scenarios as the territory in which we are operating changes and evolves. It is not rigidly fixated upon the details or contents of any particular context or circumstances.

This type of vision does not focus on any one specific destination. Rather, its purpose is to provide a direction from which any number of new specific ventures and products may emerge. Musk's passion and intention to "increase the scope and scale of human consciousness," "strive for greater collective enlightenment" and make a positive impact on the future of humanity have spawned a series of successive projects and ventures, and new ones continue to emerge and evolve as the world continues to change.

In August 2013, for instance, Musk unveiled a concept for a "Hyperloop" between Los Angeles and San Francisco. The vision is of a high-speed transportation system incorporating reduced-pressure tubes in which pressurized capsules ride on an air cushion driven by linear induction motors and air compressors. Musk's design would make travel cheaper than any other mode of transport for such long distances.

In December 2015, Musk announced the creation of OpenAI, a not-for-profit artificial intelligence (AI) research company. *OpenAI* aims to develop artificial general intelligence in a way that is safe and beneficial to humanity. By making AI available to everyone, Musk wants to "counteract large corporations who may gain too much power by owning super-intelligence systems devoted to profits, as well as governments which may use AI to gain power and even oppress their citizenry."

The scope of Musk's vision ranges from renewable energy to artificial intelligence to sustainable transport and ultimately space travel.

In late 2016, Musk announced plans to produce "solar shingles," designed to replace a traditional roof and generate electricity at the same time. Musk claims that Tesla's shingles would be more durable and last longer than ordinary roof tiles, while generating electricity at the same time. Moreover, the new solar shingles would actually be cheaper than a normal roof. "So the basic proposition will be: Would you like a roof that looks better than a normal roof, lasts twice as long, costs less and—by the way—generates electricity?" said Musk. "Why would you get anything else?"

Early in 2015 Musk introduced a home battery called the *Powerwall*, with the aim of making more consumers less dependent on big power companies. The battery is intended as a means of storage for solar power, such as that provided by solar panels and solar shingles; though Musk points out it will also work for non-solar consumers in cases of power outage. "It provides security, freedom and peace of mind," Musk says. The most recent generation of the Powerwall battery for instance can power an average two-bedroom home for a full day. "Our goal is to fundamentally change the way the world uses energy," Musk claims. "It sounds crazy, but we want to change the entire energy infrastructure of the world to zero carbon." He adds that "all we need" is to roll out 2 billion Powerwalls to meet the energy needs of the entire world, and that the poorest communities with no power lines will benefit the most. "That seems like a crazy number," Musk admitted of the 2 billion figure, "but it's comparable to the number of cars and trucks on the road [around the world] — and they get completely refreshed every 20 years."

Musk's desire to "increase the scope and scale of human consciousness" and make a positive difference in the future of humanity has transformed into the vision of electric cars, solar energy, reusable rockets and humans as an "multi-planet species."

To support the development of the Powerwall and to produce the batteries necessary for Tesla's line of cars, Musk is building a 5-million-square-foot *Gigafactory* in Nevada. The multi-billion dollar facility will, of course, be powered by solar panels. "The factory itself is a product," explains Musk, "It's the machine that builds the machines and demands more problem solving than the product it makes . . . The factory has far more potential for innovation than the product itself."

In March of 2017, Musk announced the launch of a new venture known as *Neuralink*, whose purpose is to create a direct link between the human brain, computers and artificial intelligence. Using what Musk calls a "neural lace," the vision of the company is to create devices that can be implanted in the human brain so people could directly upload or download their thoughts to or from a computer.

Musk's plans to start a human colony on Mars as early as 2023 in order to ensure the survival of our species is a clear example of fostering fitness for the future.

Musk's most ambitious venture is to colonize Mars. Musk is designing a multi-stage launch and transport system, including a reusable booster rocket — which SpaceX has already successfully tested. The booster, with an "interplanetary module" on top of it, would be nearly as long as two Boeing 747 aircraft. It could initially carry up to 100 passengers. Musk has already said he wants to launch the first unmanned trip to Mars before 2018. He wants to send the first humans to Mars in 2022, with the spacecraft touching down in 2023. His ultimate purpose for this is to ensure the continuation of life as we know it. "If we stay on Earth forever," he asserts, "there will be an inevitable extinction event . . . The reason I am personally accruing assets is to fund this. I really have no other purpose than to make life interplanetary."

Task Significance and Teamwork

This type of bigger vision and purpose creates a great amount of what is termed "task significance" (*see SFM Vol. II*, pp. 56-57). *Task significance* relates to the perception that one's work and actions affect others in an important and meaningful way. Research shows that the perception of task significance has a marked influence on motivation and performance. Knowing that their work has a positive impact on others significantly increases people's level of energy and effort, fostering a strong sense of *mission* which can be defined as *"a strongly felt aim or calling"* to serve something beyond oneself (see *SFM Vol. I*, pp. 45-47). This has a tremendous impact on motivation, team cooperation and resilience. As Elon Musk points out, "Putting in long hours for a corporation is hard. Putting in long hours for a cause is easy."

Elon Musk's mission to accelerate the world's transition to sustainable energy and help make humanity a multi-planet civilization has made it possible for him to attract some of the most talented people in the world and direct their efforts toward solving some of the most important problems facing the human race.

Elon Musk's ability to identify and prioritize worthy challenges and problems has made him a leader that some of the most talented people in the world are willing to follow. The high degree of task significance present in his ventures allows Musk to surround himself with many of the world's leading professionals and experts. He then directs their efforts towards solving some of the most ambitious and exciting problems currently faced by the human race. This leads to extremely motivated teams, driven by their belief that the work they are carrying out right now might be the most important contribution of their lives to humankind's advance. As Musk points out:

> *If you can get a group of really talented people together and unite them around a challenge, and have them work together to the best of their abilities, then a company will achieve great things.*

And it is undeniable that Musk and his teams have achieved some great things. Within ten days after launch of the Powerwall in early 2105, for example, the company sold out of the battery until mid-2016—translating into $800 million worth of reservations. It became one of the few products to rival the sales of the iPhone.

Just a week after announcing its more affordable Model 3 all-electric vehicle in April 2016, Tesla had received more than 325,000 pre-orders from potential customers—each of whom put down $1,000 to reserve a car—making it the single biggest one-week launch of any product ever. The achievement was all the more remarkable considering that the company did not advertise or pay for any endorsements. Instead, the interest spread completely organically, driven by the passion of current and future customers who believed so strongly in what the company was trying to achieve. At the time of this writing, less than five years after selling its first Model S, Tesla had become the most valuable automobile manufacture in America.

Musk and his teams have been responsible for some of the biggest and most successful sales launches in history.

Resilience and Feedback

Of course, Musk's journey has not always been easy. In fact, it has required incredible resilience. As a so-called "serial entrepreneur" (one who has started a number of different ventures) Musk is not just a dreamer. He is very conscious of the challenges involved in launching a start-up. He claims:

> *Starting a company is a very tough thing . . . you should certainly expect that it's going to be very hard. It's going to be harder than getting a job somewhere by a pretty good margin, and the odds of you losing the money that you invested or your friends invested are pretty high.*
>
> *I mean, those are just the basic facts. So if you don't mind things being really hard and high risk, then starting a company is a good idea. Otherwise, it's probably unwise. It will certainly stress you out. So I think you have to be pretty driven to make it happen. Otherwise, you will just make yourself miserable.*

Elon Musk's focus on higher purpose has allowed him take bigger risks than others are willing to and to develop a remarkable capacity for resilience.

This underscores the importance of "task significance" and vision as a necessary support to one's passion and entrepreneurial ambitions. As I have pointed out in the previous volumes of *Success Factor Modeling* (see *SFM Vol. I*, pp. 41-44), a key characteristic of the vision of successful next generation entrepreneurs and leaders is that it is always directed outward beyond themselves. That is, it is about what they want to see more of or different in the world – it is about "creating a world to which people want to belong." As Musk advises:

> *Focus on something that has high value to someone else, be really rigorous in making that assessment, because our natural human tendency is wishful thinking, so the challenge to entrepreneurs is telling what's the difference between really believing in your ideals and sticking to them as opposed to pursuing some unrealistic dream that doesn't actually have merit.*

According to Elon Musk, it is vital for entrepreneurs to be able to know the difference between "really believing in your ideals and sticking to them as opposed to pursuing some unrealistic dream that doesn't actually have merit."

When our sense of passion and ambition are linked to a strong experience of vision and mission, it creates a powerful motivation. This is what drives next generation entrepreneurs and conscious leaders to take big risks and do what appears impossible to others. As Musk claims, "If something is important enough, even if the odds are against you, you should still do it."

This intense degree of motivation is required to get through the difficult periods that are inevitable in any project or venture. As Musk explains it:

> *When you first start the company, things seem optimistic and rosy and exciting. I think for the first six months to one year, things seem pretty good and then things start to go wrong . . . And you make mistakes, you encounter issues you didn't expect, you step on land mines . . . it's just bad. Years two through five are usually quite difficult. You've got to be prepared to do whatever it takes, work whatever hours. No task is too menial. I think that's the right attitude for CEO of a start-up.*

Dealing with Crisis and Transition with Tenacity, Innovation and Determination

Elon Musk is an authentic example of his own advice. Running three major ventures at the same time, he has had to overcome major obstacles, and is known to work 80-100 hours a week.

Musk demonstrated incredible resilience following the global financial crisis of 2008 when all 3 of his companies began collapsing simultaneously.

Just after the global financial crisis of 2008, for example, Musk faced the biggest challenge of his career so far. All 3 of his companies began collapsing simultaneously. Trying to get Tesla's first car, the Roadster, up and running, and launch SpaceX's rockets safely into space, Musk had personally put almost all of the money he'd earned from EBay's acquisition of PayPal into the two companies. To deal with the crisis, Musk had to lay off almost 1/3 of his staff and close Tesla's branch in Detroit. SolarCity also began staggering. The bank that had backed their leases, pulled out of the deal. In addition, Musk was going through a difficult and very public divorce.

With only a week's worth of cash left in the bank, things looked bleak. "I remember waking up the Sunday before Christmas in 2008 and thinking to myself, 'man, I never thought I was someone who could ever be capable of a nervous breakdown,'" he says. "I felt this is the closest I've ever come. Because it seemed pretty, pretty dark."

Then, almost miraculously, on Dec. 23, 2008, NASA awarded SpaceX a $1.6 billion contract to haul at least 20 metric tons of cargo to the international space station over 12 planned flights. "NASA called and told us we won a $1.5 billion contract," Musk recalls. "I couldn't even hold the phone. I just blurted out, 'I love you guys!'" About three months earlier, on Sept. 28, 2008, after four years of trying and three previous failures, SpaceX's Falcon 1 rocket had finally lifted off delivering a dummy payload to orbit. "We were running on fumes at that point," Musk says. "We had virtually no money... a fourth failure would have been absolutely game over. Done." Since then, his cargo capsule has successfully docked multiple times with the space station and returned to land safely back on Earth.

Two days after the NASA call, on Christmas Eve, Tesla's investors decided to put more money into the company. Musk's dreams were saved in a period of three days having been just inches away from complete failure. Had he broken down and given up earlier, of course, the recovery would have never happened.

Clearly one of Musk's major success factors is his willingness to risk everything, especially when confronted with multiple failures. When asked by an interviewer, "When you had that third [rocket launch] failure in a row, did you think, 'I need to pack this in'?" Musk replied, "Never . . . I don't ever give up. I mean, I'd have to be dead or completely incapacitated."

This type of extreme determination is not something that can be expected from the top executives of the large multinational public companies Musk competes with. Typical corporate leaders are paid to minimize risks and maximize returns to stockholders. Musk's mission is essentially to change the world or fail trying, while corporate CEOs usually aim for slightly above average returns while minimizing the potential downside and most of all avoiding failure. However, as Musk claims:

> *Failure is an option here. If things are not failing, you are not innovating enough . . . I think it's really a mindset. You have to decide, "We're going to try to do things differently." Well, provided that they're better.*

Key to Elon Musk's remarkable resilience is his extreme determination and willingness to risk everything especially when confronted with multiple failures.

You shouldn't do things differently just because they're different. They need to be different or better. But I think you have to sort of decide, "Let's think beyond the normal stuff and have an environment where that sort of thinking in encouraged and rewarded and where it's okay to fail as well." Because when you try new things, you try this idea, that idea . . . well a large number of them are not going to work, and that has to be okay. If every time somebody comes up with an idea it has to be successful, you're not going to get people coming up with ideas.

Elon Musk's unique mindset, tenacity and determination have alowed him to bounce back from the brink of disaster and achieve things that seemed impossible.

As a result of his unique mindset, tenacity and determination, Musk has been able to bounce back from the brink of disaster and make huge steps forward. Within four years after the crisis of 2008, for instance, Tesla produced the Model S sedan, which even skeptics in Detroit hailed as possibly the best car ever built. SpaceX docked a rocket with the International Space Station, and SolarCity went public. Musk had been on the verge of total catastrophe and then pulled off one of the greatest entrepreneurial comebacks in history.

Elon Musk summarizes the essence of his mindset with the following advice:

Constantly think about how you could be doing things better and keep questioning yourself . . . Be very rigorous in your self-analysis, certainly be extremely tenacious, and just work like hell. Put in 80-100 hours every week. All these things improve the odds of success.

Musk advises entrepreneurs and leaders to have "a feedback loop, where you're constantly thinking about what you've done and how you could be doing it better," and to "take as much feedback from as many people as you can."

Musk's recommendation to "constantly think about how you could be doing things better and keep questioning yourself" encapsulates one of the most important practices of conscious leaders: exercising mindful self-leadership and reflecting thoughtfully on the lessons gained from experience. "I think it's very important to have a feedback loop, where you're constantly thinking about what you've done and how you could be doing it better," Musk says. "Take as much feedback from as many people as you can about whatever idea you have. ... Seek critical feedback. Ask them what's wrong. You often have to draw it out in a nuanced way to figure out what's wrong."

In addition to getting external feedback, Musk claims that it is essential to keep questioning yourself and examining your own beliefs, mental maps and assumptions through accurate self-analysis. As he explains:

Accurate self-analysis. It's difficult to do so, since you're too close to yourself by definition. People do not think critically enough. People assume too many things to be true without sufficient basis in that belief. It's very important that people closely analyze what is supposed to be true, and build it up, analyze things by the first principles, not by analogy or convention,

Gratitude and Generosity

In *Success Factor Modeling Volume I* (pp. 131-132) I pointed out that truly successful people have the inner experience of feeling both grateful and generous. They are grateful for what they have received and achieved and, at the same time, they are able to generously share what they have with others. That is, successful people have enough of what they need and feel that they want give something back. As a successful entrepreneur and conscious leaders, Elon Musk is an excellent example of this.

In addition to being highly motivated and ambitious, Musk is also immensely generous. He is chairman of the Musk Foundation, for example, which focuses its philanthropic efforts on science education, pediatric health and clean energy. He is also a trustee of the X Prize Foundation, promoting renewable-energy technologies. He sits on the boards of The Space Foundation, The National Academies Aeronautics and Space Engineering Board, The Planetary Society, and Stanford Engineering Advisory Board. Musk is also a member of the board of trustees of the California Institute of Technology.

Musk's charitable acts and philanthropic efforts demonstrate a high level of gratitude and generosity characteristic of truly successful people.

He began a program through his foundation in 2010 to donate solar-power systems for critical needs in disaster areas. The first such solar-power installation was donated to a hurricane response center in Alabama that had been neglected by state and federal aid. To make it clear that this was not serving Musk's commercial interests, SolarCity noted that it had no present or planned business activity in Alabama. In a 2011 visit to Soma City in Fukushima, Japan, which had been devastated by tsunami, he donated a solar power project to the city valued at $250,000.

Musk joined The Giving Pledge (see *SFM Vol. I*, p. 129) in April 2012, offering an ethical commitment to donate the majority of his fortune to philanthropic causes. Musk became a member of the campaign first popularized by Warren Buffett and Bill Gates, joining more than 81 of the world's most financially successful people to pledge at least half of their wealth to humanitarian efforts.

Conclusion

Elon Musk epitomizes a number of success factors supporting conscious leadership, innovation and resilience. Musk's unprecedented successes, despite the many challenges he has faced, are a clear illustration of how our mindset is ultimately the most important factor in launching a project or venture and moving from surviving to thriving. Musk's mental attitude clearly produces ongoing innovation, tenacious determination and continual improvement. This has allowed him and his ventures to make a meaningful contribution while achieving financial robustness, growth and resilience.

Elon Musk's ability to bounce back and thrive, despite the many challenges he has faced, is a clear illustration of how mindset is ultimately the most important factor in launching a project or venture and achieving sustainable success.

As a leader, Elon Musk certainly demonstrates all of the basic skills of leadership identified earlier in this chapter:

1. He expresses a rich and powerful vision of what the future could be like.
2. He *influences others* to achieve results by inspiring them with the belief that the work they are carrying out right now might be the most important contribution of their lives to humankind's advance.
3. He encourages *team cooperation* by aligning team members around worthy challenges and creating a culture that supports innovation and makes room for failure.
4. He leads by *example*, taking the biggest risks and working as much or as hard as anyone else to achieve the mission.

Musk's capacity for persistence and his tolerance for risk are driven by his focus on a higher purpose, and his belief in what he is doing and in the ability of his team and himself to achieve it.

Clearly, much of Musk's success is a result of his capacity for persistence and resilience. It is equally clear that his tolerance for risk, his ability to "stay the course" and his capacity to rebound from potential disasters are driven by his focus on a higher purpose, and his belief in what he is doing and in the ability of his team and himself to achieve it. It also seems evident that Musk's emphasis on a higher purpose, combined with his balancing of self-interest and the common good, spawn a vision and ventures that seek to produce sustainable development and "fitness for the future."

Another key aspect of Musk's mindset is his dedication and resolve to "try to do things differently and better." Musk clearly understands and embraces Ashby's Law of Requisite Variety – that in order to survive and thrive, a system needs a sufficient degree of variability in order to effectively adapt to the changes occurring in the world around it. In fact, all of his actions seem dedicated to the principle that innovation is the foundation for any sustainably successful venture or species.

In summary, Elon Musk's example provides us with a powerful prototype of all of the key characteristics of conscious leadership listed earlier:

1. The success and range of impact of his three major ventures, along with his other projects, demonstrate an ability to *formulate and communicate meaningful and inclusive visions benefiting all stakeholders.*
2. His aspirations to "increase the scope and scale of human consciousness" and the desire to "make a positive difference in the future of humanity" reflect a *strong focus on higher purpose.*
3. His ability to convey to people the belief that the work they are carrying out right now might be the most important contribution of their lives to humankind's advance is a powerful illustration of the use task significance to *influence through inspiration.*
4. Musk's capacity for "relevance optimization" in which he balances contribution to humanity with financial return and economic viability is an example of how he consistently seeks to *balance self-interest and the common good.*
5. His advice to "take as much feedback from as many people as you can about whatever idea you have" illustrates his strong capacity to *respect and integrate multiple perspectives* by seeking feedback from many sources.
6. Musk's formidable work ethic and willingness to assume the brunt of the risk for his ventures epitomize the practice of *leading by example* (walking one's talk).
7. His commitment to continually question himself and his emphasis on "accurate self-analysis" display a determination to *exercise mindful self-leadership and reflect thoughtfully on the lessons gained from experience.*

Elon Musk's example provides a powerful prototype of the key characteristics of conscious leadership.

Of course, it is important to realize that nobody can ever be perfect or perfectly "conscious." Elon Musk also has his shortcomings and "blind spots." The fact that he has been divorced (twice from the same woman) is an indication that there are important areas in which he could bring more attention and balance in his personal relationships, professional relationships and in his own self-care. The path to conscious leadership, innovation and resilience is a life-long journey.

It is also important to keep in mind that nobody can ever be perfect or perfectly "conscious," and that the path to conscious leadership, innovation and resilience is a life-long journey.

In fact, a major goal of this book is to provide a number of principles, tools, practices and disciplines that support all of us in the movement to a more conscious and creative life. These processes will address several different levels of success factors.

Elon Musk's example provides a powerful prototype of the key characteristics of conscious leadership.

Key Levels of Success Factors

In the previous volumes of Success Factor Modeling I have presented a number of different levels of success factors associated with the effective performance of individuals, teams and organizations. These levels have been defined in depth in the first two volumes of this work and in other books that I have written (see *From Coach to Awakener*, 2003 and *NLP II: The Next Generation*, 2010)

- **Environmental factors** determine the external opportunities and constraints that a person, team or organization must recognize and to which they must react. Environmental factors involve the state of the external context in which we are living and acting—*where* and *when* our actions are taking place. The goals and outcomes of individuals, teams and organizations are invariably defined and measured with respect to some type of environmental production or impact; e.g., manufacture an electric car, reduce carbon emissions, send a rocket into space, etc. The primary feedback for our actions comes from the concrete environment around us.

  Clearly, sustainable success and fitness for the future are grounded in our ability to understand our influence on our environment and to respond effectively, flexibly and ecologically to changes and uncertainties in that environment. Elon Musk provides a good example of the ability of a conscious leader to take environmental factors into account as a key part of his ventures and business strategy, looking at both long and short term consequences of his actions and seeking to maximize his positive impact while adapting flexibly to challenges and changes.

The example of Elon Musk also illustrates a number of the key levels of success factors associated the effective performance of individuals, teams and organizations.

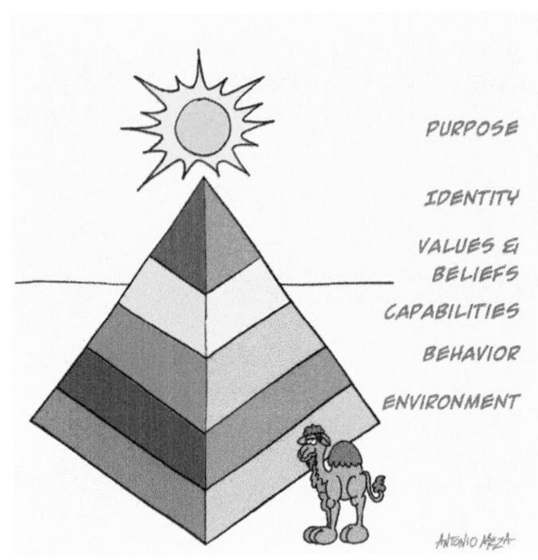

Similar to a pyramid, the various levels of success factors are grounded in the concrete aspects of behavior and the external environment—*where*, *when* and *what* to do.

Behavioral factors relate to the specific action steps taken in order to respond effectively to the environment and reach desired outcomes. They involve *what*, specifically, must be done and accomplished in order to take advantage of opportunities or respond to change in the environment. The "behavioral" level of leadership has to do with the specific behavioral activities that the leader, his or her collaborators and his or her venture must engage in order to rebound from adversity and pursue their goals and outcomes. The specific behaviors that people actively participate in, such as tasks and interpersonal interactions, serve as the primary means for achieving organizational goals: raising money, declaring bankruptcy, etc., determine what an entrepreneur achieves, or does not achieve. Thus, the actions we take create the outcomes we reach. As Elon Musk pointed out, "If other people are putting in 40 hours in a week, and you're putting in 100, you will achieve in four months, what it takes them a year to achieve." All leadership is ultimately grounded in action.

Like the rungs on a ladder, our capabilities, beliefs and values allow us to adapt, refine and align our actions with our higher purpose by clarifying *how* and *why* to do what we need to do.

- **Capabilities** refer to the mental maps, plans, strategies and other methodologies that lead to innovation, resilience and success. They direct *how* actions are generated, selected and monitored. A key question relating to rebounding from adversity and achieving success is not simply how much action to take, but *which* actions to take. Achieving success is not so much about working harder as it is about working "smarter." As the example of Elon Musk has shown, our mindset determines our actions. "Capabilities" have to do with the mental strategies and processes leaders and their collaborators develop and apply in order to guide and give direction their specific behaviors. Simply prescribing behaviors does not ensure that tasks will be accomplished and goals reached. The function of the level of capabilities is to provide the perception and direction necessary to select and, if necessary, to create the appropriate actions needed to achieve particular objectives.

Leadership at the level of capabilities is essentially thought leadership. It involves influencing people's minds and mindset. Elon Musk's advice to "constantly think about how you could be doing things better and keep questioning yourself" is clearly directed to the level of developing capabilities. Musk's notion of "relevance optimization" in which he balances contribution to humanity with financial return and economic viability is another example of a key capability of conscious leadership. It guides which actions are selected and implemented.

- **Beliefs and values** provide the motivation and reinforcement that support or inhibit particular capabilities and behaviors. They relate to *why* a particular path is taken and to the deeper motivations which drive people to act or persevere. Leadership at the level of "beliefs and values" involves influencing people's hearts as much as their minds. In addition to developing behavioral skills and capabilities, an effective leader must also address the beliefs and values of his or her customers, collaborators, stakeholders and partners. The degree to which some product, service or task fits (or does not fit) into the personal or cultural value systems of one's customers, collaborators and stakeholders will determine the degree to which they embrace or resist it.

  Beliefs and values make up one of the most important aspects of a conscious leader's mindset. Entrepreneur Cindana Turkatte (profiled in SFM Vol., pp. 163-171) maintains that the success of a venture begins with people's "commitment and empathy" for what they are doing. "You can't give up," she says. "You have to believe in what you are doing. If you don't believe in what you are doing, you should be doing something else." Elon Musk, as we have seen, is able to inspire people with the belief that the work they are carrying out right now might be "the most important contribution of their lives to humankind's advance."

Beliefs and values make up one of the most important aspects of a conscious leader's mindset, providing the motivation and reinforcement that support or inhibit particular capabilities and behaviors

- **Identity factors** relate to people's perception of their mission, role and position with respect to others. These factors are a function of *who* a person or group perceives themselves to be. The "identity" level has to do with the unique, distinguishing characteristics that define an individual, group or organization. It is the foundation for the "brand" and "image" of an individual, group or venture.

  The level of identity is in many ways an integration and synthesis of all of the other levels: values, beliefs, capabilities and behaviors. It is one of the reasons that being an example is such an important aspect of leadership and especially conscious leadership. At the level of identity, we lead through our "being." As Gandhi so clearly put it, "You must *be* the change you want to see in the world." When something reaches the level of identity, it is part of our "DNA." Elon Musk's declarations, "I don't ever give up," and that "I'd have to be dead or completely incapacitated," are an indication that his goals and intentions are at a level of mission and identity. Identity level motivations are even more profound than beliefs and values.

Like the bullseye on a target, our sense of identity and purpose provide a clear and compelling direction for our behavior by defining *who* we are and *for whom* and *for what* we are dedicating our actions.

Our sense of purpose comes from the perception of belonging to and serving something bigger than ourselves.

- **Purpose** relates to people's experience of contributing to the larger system of which they are a part. These factors involve *for whom* or *for what* a particular action step or path has been taken. Our sense of purpose comes from our perception of being a part of larger and larger systems surrounding us. It determines the overall direction and meaning behind the actions, capabilities and identity of an individual, team or organization.

  Purpose is perhaps the strongest of all motivations. It is why "task significance" has such a major affect on effort and performance. People are willing to make bigger sacrifices and take bigger risks for the sake of something bigger than themselves than they are for their own self-benefit. The focus on and commitment to a higher purpose is one of the hallmarks of all conscious leadership. It is clear that this the primary emphasis of leaders like Elon Musk in his dedication to "increase the scope and scale of human consciousness" and desire to "make a positive difference in the future of humanity." .

Holons, Holarchies and Conscious Leadership

As I have pointed out in *SFM Vol. I* (pp. 22-23) and *SFM Vol. II* (pp. 54-55) our sense of purpose comes from the perception that we are "holons" and part of an interconnected "holarcy." It is an intriguing reality of our existence that, on the one hand, we are whole and independent beings. On the other hand, we are also part of systems that are bigger than us. Arthur Koestler used the term *holarchy* to describe the dynamics of this relationship. In *The Act of Creation* (1964, p. 287) Koestler explained:

> *A living organism or social body is not an aggregation of elementary particles or elementary processes; it is an integrated hierarchy of semi-autonomous sub-wholes, consisting of sub-sub-wholes, and so on. Thus the functional units on every level of the hierarchy are double-faced as it were: they act as whole when facing downwards, as parts when facing upwards.*

It is an intriguing reality of our existence that, on the one hand, we are whole and independent beings. On the other hand, we are also part of systems that are bigger than us.

So something that integrates parts on the level below into a larger whole becomes a part itself for the level above it. Water, for instance, is a unique entity that emerges from the integration of hydrogen and oxygen. Water itself, however, can become a part of many other larger entities from orange juice to oceans to the human body. Thus, water is both a whole made up of smaller parts and a part of other larger wholes.

In *A Brief History of Everything* (1996) transformational teacher and author Ken Wilber described this relationship in the following way:

> *Arthur Koestler coined the term "holon" to refer to an entity that is itself a whole and simultaneously a part of some other whole. And if you start to look closely at the things and processes that actually exist, it soon becomes obvious that they are not merely wholes, they are also parts of something else. They are whole/parts, they are holons.*
>
> *For instance, a whole atom is part of a whole molecule, and the whole molecule is part of the whole cell, and the whole cell is part of a whole organism, and so on. Each of these entities is neither a whole nor a part, but a whole/part, a holon.*

The notions of "holon" and "holarchy" describe the fact that everything that exists is both made up of successively smaller wholes and part of successively larger wholes.

According to Wilber, each new whole *includes* yet *transcends* the parts on the level below it. It is important to point out that, in a holarchy, if a lower level of such a system is not present the levels above it will not be able to be fully expressed. The lower levels are the necessary components of all higher levels.

Each person is a whole, made up of wholes (cells, organs, psychological states, etc.) and part of a greater whole (e.g. family, group, community, etc.).

Each of us, then, is a holon. We are made up of whole atoms, which make up whole molecules, that combine to create whole cells, which join together to make whole organs and a whole interconnected nervous system from which our whole body is formed. We in turn are part of progressively larger wholes: a family, a professional community, the whole system of living creatures on this planet which is, in turn, part of our solar system and ultimately the whole universe.

To conscious leaders, the notions of "holon" and "holarchy" are not merely interesting intellectual concepts, they are organizing principles for one's life and professional activity. As is clearly illustrated in the case of Elon Musk, conscious leaders perceive themselves to be a contributing member of a much larger holarchy. The scope of Musk's consciousness and vision includes the entire planet and even reaches into the solar system with his plans for humanity to become an interplanetary species.

The primary measure of the "consciousness" of a conscious leader is how much of the larger holarchy he or she is able to hold in awareness as he or she is planning for the future, making decisions and taking action.

Thus, we can say that the primary measure of the "consciousness" of a conscious leader is how much of the larger holarchy he or she is able to hold in awareness as he or she is planning for the future, making decisions and taking action. The more conscious one is, the more of the holarchy one is able to take into consideration in order to create multiple win-win results (or at least not win-lose results). And, of course, the larger the holarchy one is addressing, the greater the number of stakeholders there will be. This is the major challenge of conscious leadership and, indeed, the major challenge for humanity today.

Where do we define the edges of the holarchy of which we are a part? Where do we put the borders and the walls? Do we place the limit of the holarchy at ourselves, our family, business, community, country, continent, planet?

Each person is a whole, made up of other wholes (cells, organs, psychological states, etc.) and part of a greater whole (e.g. family, group, community, etc.).

Dealing with the Limitations of Consciousness

When our consciousness of the holarchy is limited, we will take actions that create a "win" for one part of the system which is achieved at the expense of another part. This creates imbalances that can become major crises.

It is the limitations of our consciousness in this regard that are responsible for the majority of the problems we see in the world today. When our consciousness is limited, a "win" for one part of the holarchy is achieved at the expense of another part. We may end up sacrificing our family or our personal lives for our professional success; or sacrifice the health of the planet for the success of our business; or sacrifice the health of our bodies for our duty to our family or community; or sacrifice one community, culture or country for the success of another.

As an example, I have a colleague who was founding partner in a company in the UK that grew quickly and was financially very successful. However, within two years after the company started, two of the seven founders had been divorced, two others had gotten cancer and my colleague had a breakdown. This was clearly neither a sustainable nor thriving situation.

I have come across situations and stories such as this countless times in my coaching and consulting work. A person's attempts to achieve success in one area of the holarchy leads the abandonment and break down of another.

It is common sense that if we don't take care of our heart, we can get a heart attack. If we don't take care of our family or marriage, the family or marriage can suffer. If we don't take care of our venture, it begins to fall apart. If we don't take care of our communities, those communities begin to decay. If we don't take care of our environment, it can become contaminated and unstable.

Creating sustainable success is a matter of consciousness and balance with respect to every part of the system—the microcosm and the macrocosm.

Creating sustainable success is a matter of consciousness and balance with respect to every part of the system. There is an old saying that advises us to "think globally and act locally." From the perspective of conscious leadership, it is also equally important to consider the microcosm as well as the macrocosm. I have long expressed the goal of conscious leadership as "to create a world to which people want to belong" —including ourselves. The way we care for ourselves and our family is an expression of the same consciousness and values that we apply to our team members, customers and community. As my teacher and mentor Gregory Bateson (a key figure in modern systems theory) used to point out, "Everything is a metaphor for everything else." Authenticity, responsibility and alignment are about bringing conscious leadership to every level of the holarchy. Like a tree, the roots must go as deep and as wide as the branches which reach out for the sky.

Even intentionally conscious leaders like Elon Musk struggle with the challenge of creating sustainable wins for all parts of the larger holarchy, as is reflected in his multiple divorces and inconsistent attention to his diet and physical health.

Expanding the Scope of Consciousness

This brings up the importance of somatic intelligence, collective intelligence and the ability to tune into the "field" (see *SFM Vol. II*, pp. 350-353) as key skills of conscious leadership. Cognitive understanding alone is not sufficient to achieve the level of consciousness needed to hold all of the dimensions of the holarchy necessary to make harmonious and sustainable decisions. We also need to be able to tap into what I referred to as the "creative unconscious" in previous volumes of *Success Factor Modeling* (see *SFM Vol. I*, p. 44 & pp. 202-205 and *SFM Vol. II*, pp. 176-179 & p. 352). The creative unconscious is a form of awareness that extends beyond the limitations of our cognitive mind and increases our capacity for wisdom.

Cognitive understanding alone is not sufficient to achieve the level of consciousness needed to hold all of the dimensions of the holarchy necessary to make harmonious and sustainable decisions.

Steve Jobs (profiled in SFM Vol. I, pp. 252-280) acknowledged the importance of having other forms of awareness as a leader when he claimed:

> *I began to realize that an intuitive understanding and consciousness was more significant than abstract thinking and intellectual logical analysis. Intuition is a very powerful thing, more powerful than intellect, in my opinion. That's had a big impact on my work.*

Intuition and access to "the creative unconscious" are essential to conscious leadership, innovation and resilience.

Advising people to "have the courage to follow your heart and intuition," Jobs purposely took steps to expand his own conscious awareness as is attested by his comments about experimenting with LSD as a young man. "Taking LSD was a profound experience, one of the most important things in my life," he reported. "LSD shows you that there's another side to the coin, and you can't remember it when it wears off, but you know it. It reinforced my sense of what was important – create things instead of make money, putting things back into the stream of history of human consciousness as much as I could."

Though Jobs himself was clearly flawed in may ways, as evidenced by his untimely early death and the "horror stories" told by some of his co-workers, he also demonstrated many of the characteristics of conscious leadership in other areas of his personal and professional life. And it is undeniable that Jobs achieved a very high degree of success in many of the areas where he did demonstrate conscious leadership. As he put it:

We're here to make a dent in the universe. Otherwise, why even be here? We're creating a completely new consciousness, like an artist or a poet. That's how you have to think of this. We're rewriting the history of human thought with what we are doing . . .

We try to use the talents we do have to express our deep feelings, to show our appreciation of all the contributions that came before us, and to add something to that flow. That's what's driven me.

Israeli Prime Minister Golda Mier claimed that she never made any important decision *"without first consulting at least two people—my great-grandmother, who is no longer alive, and my great-granddaughter, who is not yet born."*

Job's comments about "putting things back into the stream of history of human consciousness," "rewriting the history of human thought" and showing "appreciation of all the contributions that came before us, and to add something to that flow" bring up the important dimension of time for conscious leadership. The larger holon we are a part of is not only a matter of space. It is also a matter of time. We are part of a legacy that extends from our ancestors on to the generations that will follow us. Golda Mier, the first female Prime Minister of Israel (1969-1974), is reported to have said that she never made any important decision "without first consulting at least two people — my great-grandmother, who is no longer alive, and my great-granddaughter, who is not yet born."

Meir's statement reflects the Native American notion of *seven generation stewardship* which advises people to remember seven generations in the past and consider seven generations in the future when making critical decisions. The principle of "seven generation stewardship" originated with the Great Law of the Iroquois. According to the principle it is important to think seven generations ahead (about 150 years into the future) when making decisions today in order to be sure that those decisions would benefit our children seven generations into the future.

Conscious leadership, then, requires expanding the scope of consciousness in multiple dimensions. This is clearly a challenging but important step in our evolution and in our capacity for resilience and survival. The call to greater consciousness is perhaps nowhere better expressed than in the following statement by the great scientist Albert Einstein.

> *A human being is a part of the whole called by us universe, a part limited in time and space. He experiences himself, his thoughts and feeling as something separated from the rest, a kind of optical delusion of his consciousness. This delusion is a kind of prison for us, restricting us to our personal desires and to affection for a few persons nearest to us. Our task must be to free ourselves from this prison by widening our circle of compassion to embrace all living creatures and the whole of nature in its beauty.*

How do we widen our circle of consciousness and compassion? What prevents us? How do we free ourselves from the prison created by the "delusion" of our consciousness that we are separated from one another? What influence does that have on the decisions we make for our lives and our ventures?

These are some of the key questions we will be practically addressing in the coming chapters of this book.

Albert Einstein maintained that "*a human being is a part of the whole called by us universe,*" but that, because we are "*limited in time and space*" we experience ourselves and our thoughts and feelings as something "*separated from the rest.*" According to Einstein, our task must be to "*widen our circle of compassion to embrace all living creatures and the whole of nature.*"

What process, trigger or reference experience automatically connects you to the felt sense of a larger self beyond your identity as separate individual?

Tom Chi
Co-Founder GoogleX

Finding Your Connection to the Larger "Holarchy"

Experiencing a connection to the larger holarchy of which we are a part helps us to regain a sense of purpose, focus and commitment. There are certain natural triggers or reference points that can immediately connect us to or remind us that we are part of something bigger than ourselves. Prayer, icons, rituals, etc., are examples of that. Certain people, stimuli and other phenomena can also became anchors that connect us the awareness that we are part of something greater.

A fascinating example is provided by Tom Chi, co-founder of Google's development lab Google X; a division of Google that is responsible for developing paradigm-pushing innovations such as:

- Google Glass
- Autonomous self-driving vehicles
- Contact lenses that monitor glucose through tears
- Balloons in the stratosphere that provide internet to the world

Chi, who was also a participant in my Silicon Valley Conscious Leaders Mastermind group, shared that one of his practices to expand his consciousness and connect to the larger holarchy was to simply choose any object in his environment and begin to imagine "all of the hands responsible for it being there."

For example, let's say you look at a glass of water on the table near you. There are the hands that filled the glass and the hands that placed the glass on the table. There are the hands that took the glass from the cupboard that stored it. There are the hands that placed it in the cupboard. There are the hands that washed the glass before it was put in the cupboard; the hands that drank from the glass before it was washed; the hands that unpacked it in its current location; the hands that shipped it there, the hands that packed it for shipment; the hands that transported it to the packers; the hands that took it off the machine that made it; the hands that made that machine; the hands that designed the machine; the hands that designed the glass; the hands that harvested the raw materials from which the glass was made; the hands that designed the glass that inspired the design for that particular glass; and so on.

Chi recounts that one of the triggers that immediately reminds him that he is part of something bigger than himself is the memory of a serious illness that he suffered early in his career. The treatment of the illness required that he receive a series of emergency blood transfusions that replaced almost all of the blood in his body. As he was recovering, Chi suddenly realized "most of me is someone else." It dawned on him that "I am alive because of the generosity of at least 10 people who I will never meet." He made the commitment to be grateful to what he called the "invisible generosity" of so many people "that is holding you up."

This also stimulated in him some fundamental questions such as: "How must we think in order to have the world that we want?" and the question at the foundation of Google's so-called Moonshots: "How do we positively change a billion lives?" It was these types of question that inspired him to co-found GoogleX.

Today Chi is an proponent of "rapid prototyping" which he sees as a means to accelerate the innovations that will create the world of tomorrow.

Tom Chi's realization that he was "alive because of the generosity of at least 10 people" whom he would never meet stimulated in him fundamental questions as: "How must we think in order to have the world that we want?" and the question at the foundation of Google's so-called Moonshots: "How do we positively change a billion lives?

Pick any object in your immediate environment and ask yourself, "how many hands were involved in it being there?"

Ego and Soul

Our "ego" is our sense of being a separate self, individual identity and separate whole.

Our "soul" emerges from our experience of being part of someting bigger than ourselves as an integrated holon.

In summary, conscious leadership must take into account the motivations arising from two complementary aspects of our reality: those emerging from (1) our existence as a separate, independent whole and those arising from (2) our existence as a part of a larger whole (e.g., family, profession, community, etc.). The part of our existence that we experience as an *individual whole* we typically call our *ego*. The part of our existence that we experience as a *holon* (part of a larger whole) can be referred to as our *soul*.

From the perspective of Success Factor Modeling, both of these aspects, ego and soul, are necessary for a healthy and successful existence. The primary questions relating to our *ego* are about what we want to achieve for ourselves in terms our *ambition* and *role*: "What type of life do I want to create for myself?" and "What type of person do I need to be in order to create the life I want?" These are about living out our dreams for ourselves. The primary questions with respect to the *soul* are those related to our *vision* and *mission* for the larger systems of which we are a part: "What do I want to create in the world through me that is beyond me?" and "What is my unique contribution to bringing that vision into expression?"

In the SFM approach, these distinctions of *ego* (one's self as an independent whole) and *soul* (ourselves as holons that are a part of a bigger system) are combined together with the various levels of success factors, as shown in the following diagram.

Our highest level of performance and greatest satisfaction come when we balance and align the motivations of our ego and our soul; embracing the dual realities that we are simultaneously separate wholes and integrated holons.

The complementary dimensions of ego and soul tend to bring out a different emphasis for each level of success factors. The ego side accentuates ambition, role, the importance of permission, strategy and appropriate reactions to constraints and potential dangers in the environment. The soul side puts priority on vision, mission, inner motivation and activating the energy and emotional intelligence needed to proactively take advantage of environmental opportunities.

Research with Success Factor Modeling indicates that the highest levels of performance of an individual, team or organization occur when the levels of success factors related to both ego and soul are balanced, aligned and integrated. Conscious leadership is not just about creating value for shareholders. It is creating value for all "stakeholders," including those that do not yet exist.

Clarifying and aligning one's vision, mission, ambition and role are an essential part of achieving this balance and integration. These four guideposts are the foundations of a successful entrepreneurial mindset and form the basis for the projects and ventures we undertake as entrepreneurs.

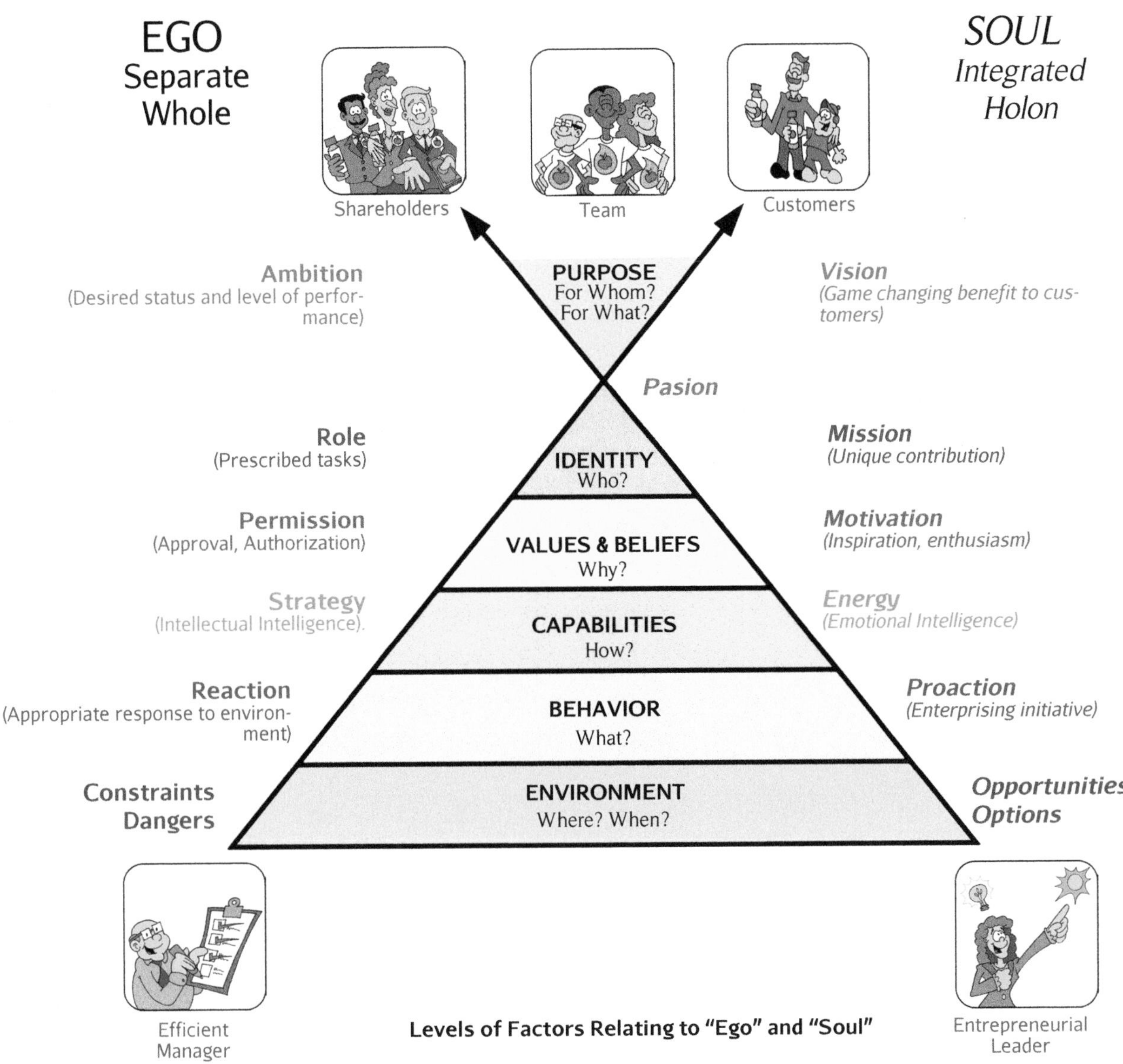

Levels of Factors Relating to "Ego" and "Soul"

Developing Wisdom

For conscious leadership, we must add another dimension to the four guideposts listed above. In addition to vision, mission, ambition and role, another significant factor related to the mindset needed to create a successful and sustainable venture that is "fit for the future" is a certain degree of wisdom. *Wisdom* is defined in the dictionary as "the ability to think and act using knowledge, experience, understanding, common sense, and insight." These aspects of "mindset" are applied to attain "an optimum judgment as to what actions should be taken." Thus, wisdom is about having a broad and balanced perspective that allows a person or group to make better and more ecological choices and decisions.

Wisdom involves having a broad and balanced perspective that allows a person or group to make better and more ecological choices and decisions.

In his November 2013 LinkedIn article *How to Think like a Wise Person*, author and Wharton University professor Adam Grant (see *SFM Vol. II*, pp. 56-57 & p. 294) outlines the following steps to develop greater wisdom:

1. Reflect thoughtfully on the lessons gained from experience.
2. See the world in shades of grey, not black and white.
3. Balance self-interest and the common good.
4. Challenge the status quo.
5. Aim to understand, rather than judge.
6. Focus on purpose over pleasure.

These steps are clearly aligned with the practices characterizing conscious leadership. We can easily say that conscious leaders are wise leaders, and that wise leaders are conscious leaders.

Greater wisdom is a natural consequence of conscious leadership.

In the coming chapters of this book, I will be providing principles, models and tools that will help you to develop the key capacities of conscious leadership; in particular in the context of being an entrepreneur. Our goals will be, in the words of Elon Musk, to "increase the scope and scale of human consciousness" in order to "make a positive difference in the future of humanity." There is perhaps nothing more important that we can be doing for ourselves, our world today and for our future.

Chapter Summary

Success Factor Modeling™ is a methodology whose purpose is to identify the critical success factors—the "differences that make the difference"— shared by outstanding entrepreneurs, teams and organizations, and then to define specific models, tools and skills that can be used by others to greatly increase their chances of producing impact and achieving success. To do this, SFM™ examines the relationship between mindset, actions and outcomes to search for the most important and reproducible patterns of *business practices* and *behavioral skills* used by effective individuals, teams and companies to reach their desired outcomes.

This book, *Success Factor Modeling Volume III*, focuses on leadership, innovation and resilience. *Resilience* is the ability of individuals, teams and organizations to withstand or recover quickly from difficult conditions and to maintain a state of equilibrium with respect to both success and adversity. Accomplishing this requires both innovation and leadership.

Effective *leadership* involves providing direction and bringing energy; i.e., expressing a vision and motivating people. It also involves encouraging team cooperation and being an example. A good leader provides direction, acts as an example and inspires others to work together effectively in order reach meaningful goals.

Good leaders must also ensure that their ventures are *"fit for the future."* That is, that they are able to adapt and respond effectively to the challenges and change that will inevitably occur. This requires sufficient flexibility and innovation in order to expand their range of choices and resources.

Fitness for the future goes hand-in-hand with *sustainable development*, which is about "enabling development that meets today's needs without prejudicing the ability of future generations to meet their own needs." This requires the creative and responsible use and management of resources and achieving a balance between economic growth, technological developments and environmental considerations.

Achieving all of these things together demands *conscious leadership* – the ability to "build a sustainable venture and guide yourself and your team from a state of centered presence, accessing multiple intelligences and living your highest values in service to a larger purpose to the benefit of all stakeholders." Conscious leaders are authentic, emotionally intelligent, purposive and responsible.

Conscious leadership involves the ability to "build a sustainable venture and guide yourself and your team from a state of centered presence, accessing multiple intelligences and living your highest values in service to a larger purpose to the benefit of all stakeholders."

Elon Musk provides a good example of all of the key characteristics of conscious leadership. The visionary founder of companies like PayPal, SpaceX, Tesla Motors and SolarCity, Musk aspires to "make a positive difference in the future of humanity" by "increasing the scope and scale of human consciousness" and "striving for greater collective enlightenment." Through his ventures, his stated goals are to "accelerate the world's transition to sustainable energy and help make humanity a multi-planet civilization, a consequence of which will be the creation of hundreds of thousands of jobs and a more inspiring future for all."

Making this happen has required an incredible amount of tenacity, determination and innovation. Musk has had to deal with numerous setbacks and survive a crisis in which three of his companies were about to fail. He was able to pull off one of the greatest entrepreneurial comebacks in history due to his dedication to a higher purpose and his capacity for innovation and self-reflection. His advice to other leaders and entrepreneurs is "Constantly think about how you could be doing things better and keep questioning yourself."

Elon Musk's example reveals key elements on a number of different *Levels of Success Factors* identified by Success Factor Modeling: environment, behavior, capabilities, beliefs and values, identity and purpose. It also illustrates the importance of the ability of conscious leaders to perceive themselves as a contributing member of a larger "holarchy"—an integrated system of parts and wholes that extends from sub-atomic particles to the universe.

According to the notion of *holarchy*, we are made up of whole atoms, which make up whole molecules, that combine to create whole cells, which join together to make whole organs and a whole interconnected nervous system from which our whole body is formed. We in turn are part of progressively larger wholes: a family, a professional community, the whole system of living creatures on this planet which is, in turn, part of our solar system and ultimately the whole universe. The primary measure of the "consciousness" of a conscious leader is how much of the larger holarchy he or she is able to hold in awareness as he or she is planning for the future, making decisions and taking action. The more conscious one is, the more of the holarchy one is able to take into consideration in order to create multiple win-win results.

Thus, one of the goals of this volume of Success Factor Modeling is to help leaders and entrepreneurs practically expand their "scope and scale of consciousness." A starting point is to *find your connection to the larger holarchy.* This can be done by reflecting on what process, trigger or reference experience automatically connects you to the felt sense of a larger self beyond your identity as separate individual. People like Steve Jobs (co-founder of Apple), Golda Meir (first woman Prime Minister of Israel) and Tom Chi (co-founder of GoogleX) provide interesting examples of how this connection can be made and why it is important.

Perhaps one of the most significant success factors relating to conscious leadership, innovation and resilience is balancing issue related to *ego* (our existence as a separate, independent whole) and *soul* (our existence as a part of a larger whole). The highest levels of performance of an individual, team or organization occur when the various levels of success factors related to both ego and soul are balanced, aligned and integrated.

Ultimately, achieving fitness for the future, sustainable development, innovation and resilience require a certain degree of wisdom. *Developing wisdom* requires that we reflect thoughtfully on the lessons gained from experience; see the world in shades of grey versus black and white; balance self-interest and the common good; challenge the status quo; aim to understand, rather than judge; and focus on purpose over pleasure.

All of these issues, capabilities and success factors will be expanded upon in the coming chapters of this book.

References:

- Bill Clinton On Leadership, Fortune Magazine, April 7, 2014.
- Elon Musk: Tesla, SpaceX and a Quest for a Fantastic Future, Vance, Ashlee, HarperCollins Publishers, New York, NY, 2015.
- http://vator.tv/news/2010-12-23-elon-musk-work-twice-as-hard-as-others
- http://www.inc.com/jana-kasperkevic/google-hangout-advice-elon-musk-richard-branson.html
- http://www.mindvalleyinsights.com/how-tom-chi-co-founder-of-google-x-innovates-like-crazy/

02 Rebounding From Adversity – Developing Resilience

If you can keep your head when all about you Are losing theirs and blaming it on you; If you can trust yourself when all men doubt you, But make allowance for their doubting too;

If you can wait and not be tired by waiting, Or, being lied about, don't deal in lies, Or, being hated, don't give way to hating, And yet don't look too good, nor talk too wise;

If you can dream – and not make dreams your master; If you can think – and not make thoughts your aim; If you can meet with triumph and disaster And treat those two imposters just the same;

If you can bear to hear the truth you've spoken Twisted by knaves to make a trap for fools, Or watch the things you gave your life to broken, And stoop and build 'em up with worn out tools;

If you can make one heap of all your winnings And risk it on one turn of pitch-and-toss, And lose, and start again at your beginnings And never breath a word about your loss;

If you can force your heart and nerve and sinew To serve your turn long after they are gone, And so hold on when there is nothing in you Except the Will which says to them: "Hold on";

If you can talk with crowds and keep your virtue, Or walk with kings – nor lose the common touch; If neither foes nor loving friends can hurt you; If all men count with you, but none too much;

If you can fill the unforgiving minute With sixty seconds' worth of distance run – Yours is the Earth and everything that's in it, And – which is more – you'll be a [conscious leader – RD]!

Rudyard Kipling

ANTONIO MEZA

Developing the Discipline to Rebound

As the example of Elon Musk clearly illustrates, the ability to anticipate and deal with adversity is a crucial success factor for both entrepreneurs and leaders. Musk warns that "starting a company is a very tough thing . . . you should certainly expect that it's going to be very hard." He cautions that, when launching a new venture, it is inevitable that you will "make mistakes," "encounter issues you didn't expect" and "step on land mines." As he points out, "You've got to be prepared to do whatever it takes."

Successful entrepreneurs and conscious leaders are well aware that resilience, fitness for the future and sustainability (especially during challenging times) require a high degree of discipline. Discipline is a function of ongoing exercise and practices rather than "quick-fix" techniques or one-time interventions.

In his groundbreaking work *The Fifth Discipline* (1990), Peter Senge claimed there were **five disciplines** which need to be practiced by everyone in a venture in order for it to truly become a sustainable entity or "learning organization". These five disciplines can be considered the foundations for resilience, fitness for the future and sustainable development:

1. Attaining and encouraging personal mastery.
2. Awareness and examination of mental maps and assumptions.
3. Developing vision and creating the future.
4. Encouraging team learning.
5. Developing the ability for systemic thinking.

Even though it has been more than 25 years since Senge initially formulated these five disciplines, they are just as relevant for today's individuals, teams and organizations. In fact, they are remarkably parallel to the "three jewels" of Zentrepreneurship identified in *SFM Volume I* (pp. 70-71) – Dharma, Buddha and Sangha:

- Pursuing personal mastery and increasing awareness of mental maps and assumptions are about working to achieve our highest expression and attaining the best version of ourselves ("Buddha").
- Developing vision, creating the future and practicing systems thinking are about authentically living our life paths and fulfilling our purpose in harmony with our environment ("Dharma").
- Encouraging team learning relates to developing a community of peers, mentors, sponsors and collaborators who are using the same methods and working towards the same goals ("Sangha").

The previous volumes of *Success Factor Modeling* have presented a number of tools, models and methods which support Senge's five disciplines and make resilience, fitness for the future and sustainable development more practical and attainable. This volume will continue to explore the skills, tools and practices that help to put all of these five disciplines into practice in order to promote fitness for the future and the capacity for resilience on both an individual and organizational level.

We will begin with an exploration of emotional intelligence and personal mastery.

The Importance of Emotional Intelligence

In the definition of conscious leadership I gave in the previous section, I identified emotional intelligence as one of the key abilities characterizing conscious leaders. Certainly, developing greater emotional intelligence is an essential success factor for achieving resilience, sustainable success and fitness for the future.

Emotional Intelligence (EQ) is considered to be a type of socially oriented intelligence distinct from traditional abstract, rational intelligence (IQ). According to author Daniel Goleman, emotional intelligence involves "the ability to monitor one's own and others' emotions, to discriminate among them, and to use the information to guide one's thinking and actions."

Thus, emotional intelligence refers to the capacity for recognizing our own feelings and those of others, for motivating ourselves, and for managing emotions in us and in our relationships. These abilities are distinct from, but complementary to, academic intelligence or the purely cognitive capacities measured by IQ.

A number of studies indicate that traditional intelligence (IQ) is only one of the factors that determine life success. Compelling research indicates that EQ (emotional intelligence) is *twice as important as IQ and technical skills* for outstanding performance. Correlation of IQ test scores with how well people perform in their careers indicates that IQ accounts for only about 25% of an individual's success. The remainder is EQ.

Most elements of emotional intelligence are considered learnable competences that are essential for effective leadership, teamwork and collaboration. Developing emotional intelligence helps us to be personally prepared to be our best, meet challenges, overcome obstacles and stay focused on our desired state.

A key goal of this volume of *Success Factor Modeling* is to provide skills and tools which help entrepreneurs and leaders to improve their emotional intelligence along the two dimensions of: (1) personal EQ – the ability to understand one's own feelings and motivations, and (2) social EQ – the ability to understand the feelings and intentions of others.

Personal EQ is the capacity to recognize and manage our own emotional responses.

Social EQ includes the ability to understand and respond to the feelings and intentions of others.

The Five Components of Emotional Intelligence

When an inner situation is not made conscious, it appears outside as fate.
– **Carl Jung**

According to Goleman, emotional intelligence includes five fundamental components:

Self-Awareness

- Emotional self-awareness
- Accurate self-assessment (the skill of "meta position")

Self-Regulation

- Self-control and internal state management
- Behavioral Flexibility
- Personal alignment

Self-Motivation

- Self-discipline
- Perseverance
- Accountability

Knowledge is only a rumor until it is in the muscle.
— **New Guinea proverb**

Empathy

- Social sensitivity (enriching the skill of "second position")
- Adopting multiple perceptual positions

Social Skills

- Establishing rapport
- Interpersonal influence (the skill of "pacing and leading")
- Adapting one's communication style

The following table summarizes some of the key capacities and characteristics of emotional intelligence that we will be exploring in this chapter and the sections to come.

	Definition	Characteristics	
Self-Awareness	Ability to recognize and understand your moods, emotions and drives as well as their effects on others.	Self-Confidence, Realistic Self-Development, Authentic	
Self-Regulation	Ability to manage or redirect disruptive impulses and moods. Propensity to suspend judgment - to reflect before acting.	Trustworthiness and integrity, Comfort with Ambiguity, Openness to change	
Self-Motivation	A passion to work for reasons that go beyond money or status, Ability to balance self-interest with common good	Disciplined, Optimism in the fact of failure, Accountable	
Empathy	Ability to understand the emotional makeup of other people, Skill in treating people according to their emotional reactions	Expertise in building and retaining talent, Cross-cultural sensitivity	
Social Skills	Ability to find common ground and build rapport, Proficiency in managing relationships and building networks	Effectiveness in leading change, Persuasiveness, Expertise in building and leading teams	

It is interesting to note that these components align well with the findings of the Google study on "collective IQ" that I cited in *SFM Vol. II* (pp. 300-301). In the study, Google researchers discovered that the members of the best and most effective teams in the company displayed high degrees of empathy and social skills. These included *"social sensitivity"*—i.e., perceiving how others feel based on their tone of voice, facial expressions and other nonverbal cues—and *"psychological safety"* —a team climate characterized by interpersonal trust and mutual respect in which people were comfortable being themselves. Clearly, EQ (emotional intelligence) is foundational component for "collective IQ."

Emotional intelligence is also one of the major success factors that we have discovered in effective entrepreneurs and leaders, especially when they are dealing with adversity and need to maximize resilience. Throughout the remainder of this book, we will be providing insights and exercises to help you develop a greater level of emotional intelligence for your own feelings and the motivations and feelings of others.

Developing Emotional Intelligence

Intelligence, in general, is defined as: *The ability to interact successfully with one's world, especially in the face of challenge or change.* Webster's Dictionary defines intelligence as "the capacity to know or understand," and to have "good judgment."

Emotional intelligence, then, involves the ability to interact successfully with emotions by understanding them, having good judgment with respect to them and selecting appropriately between them. Developing effective emotional intelligence involves applying these competences with respect to (a) *ourselves*, (b) *others* and (c) *groups*.

Effective leadership requires emotional intelligence and the ability to inspire resourceful emotional states and to manage difficult emotional states in oneself and others.

The primary areas involved in applying emotional intelligence as a leader or entrepreneur are:

(1) dealing with difficult emotional states and

(2) stimulating or eliciting resourceful emotional states.

Emotional reactions are typically considered to be the "juice" which brings energy into a particular situation or interaction. Emotional responses themselves, however, can be perceived as either "positive" or "negative." Positive emotions are associated with motivation and enthusiasm. Negative emotions are associated with problems and limitations. Usually, though, emotions themselves are not the problem. It is the behavior produced by the emotion, and the effects of that behavior on others, that determines whether a particular emotion is a problem or a resource.

Emotions themselves are neither "positive" or "negative" but can be expressed in helpful or unhelpful ways.

According to Grolier's Encyclopedia:

> *An emotion is a condition that affects the entire organism and influences how successfully it interacts with its environment. Emotions are reactions to important life issues, such as being confronted by danger or a rival, competing for food or jobs, finding a mate, or losing a parent. Such reactions help the individual with problems, that is, by fighting, by running away, by falling in love, or by calling for help. Although emotion represents a change in a person's inner state, it is also a change in behavior; most importantly, the behavior is designed to have an effect on the people or events around the person.*

Emotions are a person's inner reactions to perceived important life issues that stimulate behaviors whose purpose is to have an effect on the people or events around that person.

Thus, emotions are complex states having both an internal and external manifestation. The internal, subjective aspects of emotions are described in terms such as "happy," "sad," "angry," "disgusted," etc. The external manifestations of emotions are referred to in behavioral terms, such as "smiling," "frowning," "crying," "embracing," "hitting," "running away," etc.

Skills for Dealing with "Negative" Emotions

Dealing with "negative" emotions in an emotionally intelligent way involves (a) acknowledging that they have survival value, (b) seeking and understanding the positive intention behind them, and (c) adding more behavioral alternatives, given the intention and the specific context related to the emotional response. Viewed from the perspective of Success Factor Modeling, the *what* (the behavior) associated with the emotional response should be separated from the *why* (the beliefs, values, and intention) which are the sources of the emotional response. The intention behind an emotional reaction is the meaning or purpose of that emotion. The *positive intention* of "fear," for instance, may be "protection." The positive intention of "anger" may be motivation to "act," or "set boundaries."

Dealing effectively with emotions, especially "negative" emotions, involves identifying the underlying purpose or intention of the feeling state and connecting that intention to an appropriate behavioral response.

Once the intention has been identified, appropriate choices of behavior can be explored and connected with the intention behind the emotion. Rather than behaviorally responding with violence when angry, for example, a person can learn other choices which satisfy the intention of the anger: i.e., talking about his or her feelings, taking a walk, focusing on a project, etc. This involves the development of a number of key competences including:

1. *Recognizing* (calibrating) the presence of a particular emotional state
2. *Acknowledging* the presence of the state without judgment
3. *Holding* the emotional state in an environment of "equanimity" (making space for it)
4. *Understanding* the emotional state and its function (positive intention)
5. *Resourcing* the emotional state by connecting it to other complementary emotions and states
6. *Transforming* or refining the expression of the emotional state to be more harmonious and productive with respect to its positive intention
7. *Integrating* the emotional state as a contributing part of a larger system

Self-Awareness

Self-Regulation

In this chapter we will explore how to develop and apply these competences with respect to yourself and others in order to rebound from adversity and become more fit for the future.

Coordinating Head, Heart and Gut

Clearly emotional intelligence requires that we utilize more than just our cognitive intellect. EQ involves access to somatic knowledge and information. We have to bring the brains in the belly and in the heart online with those in the head. We are generally not taught how to use these other brains in school, but they are the foundation for emotional intelligence.

The Brain in the Belly

The *enteric nervous system* in our gut, for example, consists of some 500 million neurons –five times as many as the one hundred million neurons in the human spinal cord, and about 2/3 as many as in the whole nervous system of a cat. In fact, the enteric nervous system is frequently called the "second brain" of the human body.

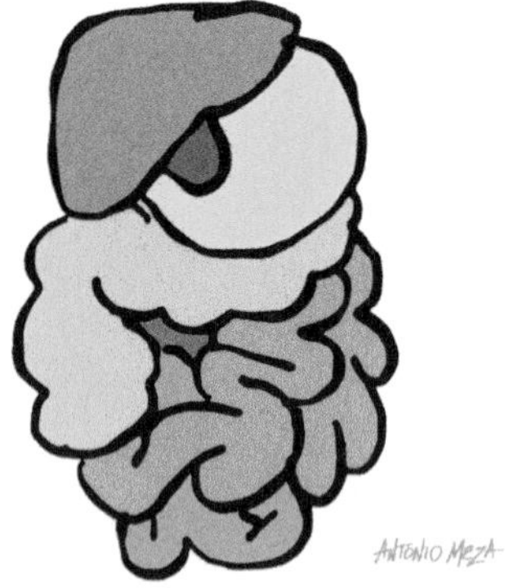

The enteric nervous system, with almost as many neurons as the brain of a cat, is considered the "second brain" of the human body.

Biologists believe that, as mammals evolved, the enteric nervous system was too important to reside inside the head of a newborn with long connections going down to the belly. Babies need to eat and digest food from birth. Therefore, the process of evolution seems to have preserved the enteric nervous system as an independent circuit. It is only loosely connected to the central nervous system and can mostly function alone, without control by the brain in the head

Just like the one in our head, the "brain in the belly" sends and receives impulses, records experiences and responds to emotions using the same neurotransmitters as the brain cells in our heads. The enteric nervous system is located in the sheaths of tissue lining the esophagus, stomach, small intestine and colon. Considered a single entity, it is a network of neurons, neurotransmitters and proteins that pass messages between neurons, forming a complex circuitry that enables it to act independently, learn and remember producing "gut feelings."

When the central nervous system encounters a threatening situation, for example, it releases stress hormones that prepare the body to fight or flee. The enteric system contains many sensory nerves that are stimulated by this chemical surge – hence the experience we call "butterflies."

For this reason, the brain in the gut is generally associated with intuition and evaluation..

The Brain in the Heart

In addition to the brain in the belly, there is also a growing body of research illustrating that your heart is much more than a mechanical pump. The developing field of *neurocardiology* is demonstrating that the heart is, in fact, a highly complex, self-organized information processing center with its own functional "brain" that communicates with and influences the brain in our heads via the nervous system, hormonal system and other pathways. These influences profoundly affect brain function and most of the body's major organs, greatly impacting our internal state and ultimately our quality of life.

Similar to the enteric nervous system, the heart's elaborate circuitry enables it to act independently of the brain in the skull – to learn, remember, and even feel and sense. The heart's nervous system contains around 40,000 neurons, called sensory neurites, which detect circulating hormones and neurochemicals and sense heart rate and pressure levels.

Various groups, most notably the Institute of HeartMath, in Boulder Creek, CA, have been working on ways to tap into the intelligence of "the brain in the heart." Contending that "the heart is the most powerful generator of rhythmic information patterns in the human body" researchers at the HeartMath Institute claim that "as a critical nodal point in many of the body's interacting systems, the heart is uniquely positioned as a powerful entry point into the communication network that connects body, mind, emotions and spirit."

It is no wonder that people subjectively associate the heart with connection and passion.

Clearly, conscious leaders need to use their heads and their cognitive intelligence, but they need more than that. Conscious leadership requires more than "brain and spreadsheet." Conscious leaders are also emotionally intelligent "heart and gut" leaders that use the holarchy of their entire nervous system—head, heart and gut—to make decisions and inspire others.

Learning to use all three brains together is a key part of mastering emotional intelligence and what is known as the "Inner Game."

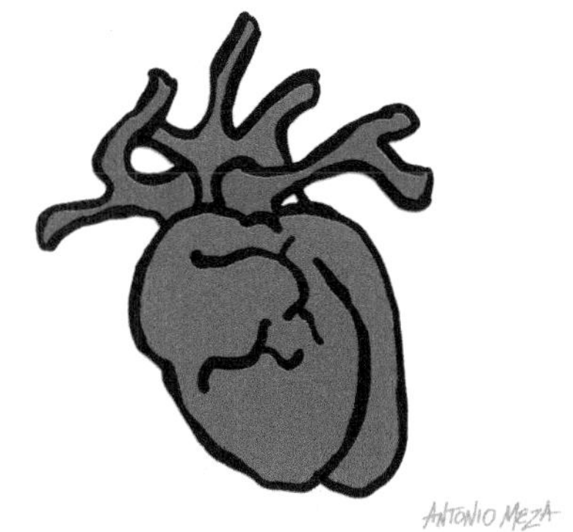

There is also a brain in the heart, which creates a communication network that connects body, mind, emotions and spirit.

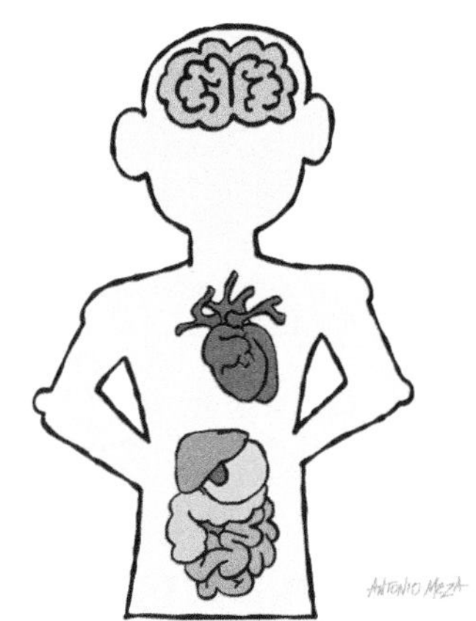

Conscious leaders align head, heart and gut to make decisions and inspire others.

Resilience and the "Inner Game"

> *In every human endeavor there are two arenas of engagement: the outer and the inner. The outer game is played on an external arena to overcome external obstacles to reach an external goal. The inner game takes place within the mind of the player and is played against such obstacles as fear, self-doubt, lapses in focus, and limiting concepts or assumptions. The inner game is played to overcome the self-imposed obstacles that prevent an individual or team from accessing their full potential.*
>
> —Timothy Gallwey

Timothy Gallwey
Author and Creator of the "Inner Game"

To be effective, leaders and entrepreneurs must learn to master their "inner game."

Key to resilience, fitness for the future and conscious leadership is mastering our "inner game." The *Inner Game* has to do with mobilizing our inner resources, overcoming self-imposed obstacles and being true to our values and purpose. As every successful athlete, leader and performer knows, to win the outer game, we must first succeed in the inner game. Emotional intelligence is a key part of mastering the inner game.

It is probably self-evident to most of us that if, in our attempt to achieve an outer goal, we meet an inner obstacle, it is going to be much more difficult to accomplish that outer goal. If we meet an outer obstacle with inner resources, we will approach it as a challenge and give our best to succeed (like Elon Musk). When an inner obstacle meets an outer resource, we are "lucky" and will probably feel supported. If we meet an outer obstacle with an inner obstacle, however, we have most likely created an unsolvable problem. In other words:

- When an *outer obstacle* is met by an *inner obstacle*, the result is an unsolvable problem.
- When an *outer obstacle* is met by *inner resources*, the result is an achievable challenge.
- When an *inner obstacle* is met by *outer resources*, the result is a lucky break.
- When *inner resources* are met with *outer resources*, the result is magic!

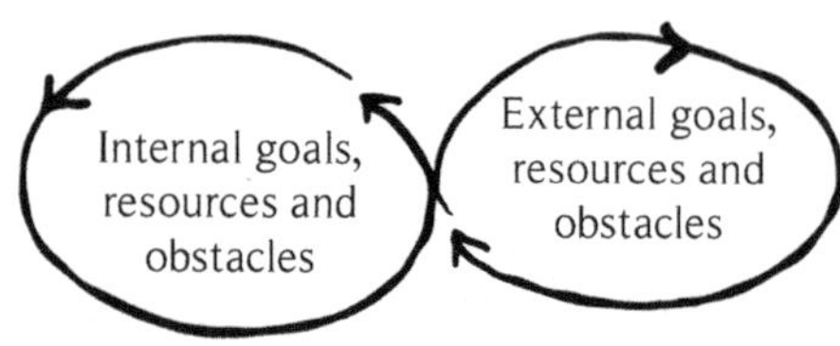

The state of our inner game determines how effective we are in the outer game.

Learning to master your "Inner Game" is a key to successful performance under any circumstances and the foundation of *personal mastery*. The "Outer Game" of any activity has to do with its behavioral and environmental aspects. In sports, this involves the physical aspects related playing the game and using the equipment (tennis racket, skis, ball, bat, mitt, etc.). In a business environment, this has to do with applying the tools and implementing the procedures necessary to accomplish mission critical tasks and compete effectively in the marketplace.

The *Inner Game* has to do with your mental and emotional approach to what you are doing. This includes your attitude, belief in yourself and your team, your ability to concentrate effectively, to deal with mistakes and pressure, and so on. The concept of the "Inner Game" was developed by Timothy Gallwey (1974, 2000) as a way of helping people to achieve excellence in various sports (e.g., tennis, golf, skiing, etc.), music and also business and management training. Success in any area of performance involves using your mind and emotions as well as your body. Preparing yourself mentally and emotionally to perform well is the essence of your inner game.

Outer game

Fundamental to the inner game is our ability to stay in an optimal performance state when confronted with difficult circumstances. During a time of adversity or crisis, we have a choice. Either we find our "inner zone of excellence" and re-energize ourselves by connecting to our higher purpose and inner resources, or we give up or give in to the challenges and obstacles we face.

Indeed, as Elon Musk warned, many challenges will present themselves in our ventures: fear of the unknown (i.e., what will happen tomorrow?), dealing with loss (i.e., a job, a member of the team, a home, etc.) and a general sense of vulnerability (i.e., how can I succeed in the face of unfavorable circumstances?). These can plunge us into unhelpful survival strategies such as aggression, escape or rigidity.

Inner game

When we are able to ground in our "inner zone," however, actions flow with a type of effortless excellence that is called, "playing in the zone." Some indicators that you are focused and in "the zone" are:

- A sense of "humble authority" – self-confidence without arrogance a feeling of confidence and the absence of anxiety and self-doubt
- A focus on performing beautifully and excellently
- A state of relaxed readiness in the body and focused spaciousness in the mind
- Performance comes without effort and without having to think about it

The opposite of this state—anxiety, lack of confidence, low energy, fear, stress, mental and emotional paralysis—are responsible for many difficulties and failures. To put it another way, *limitations in people limit their performance, which limits the venture.*

Skills for Mastering Your Inner Game

Mastering your inner game and increasing your resilience is a function of developing key self-management skills.

Self-Awareness

Self-Regulation

Emotionally intelligent entrepreneurs and leaders know how to recognize when they are in their inner "zone of excellence" and when they are out of that zone. They also know what to do in order to get back "in the zone" if they need to. This requires practice.

Physical practice is what builds the skills of your outer game and puts them into "muscle memory" so you don't have to think about it while performing. Similarly, there are mental and somatic skills and exercises can help you to improve your inner game. Some key inner game skills include:

- *Self-Awareness* – Increasing your awareness of the key cognitive and somatic elements making up and influencing your inner state and mindset
- *Self-Calibration* – Assessing the current state of those key elements with respect to their optimum values
- *Self-Adjustment* – Adjusting the key elements to produce a more appropriate or optimum expression and exploring the new options that this creates
- *Self-Anchoring* – Finding cues and triggers that will help you to remember and solidify and optimum expression of your mindset and inner state

In relation to achieving self-mastery and maintaining an optimal mindset, these processes are typically applied in the following sequence:

1. Bringing new *awareness* to the emotional state or problematic mindset that is triggered by or contributing to some current problem state or situation where you have lost your connection to your "inner zone of excellence." This involves becoming conscious of its deeper cognitive and somatic structure.
2. *Calibrating* the current state of your mindset in relationship to its optimum state. This makes it possible to begin identifying the key factors influencing your mindset; i.e., the "differences that are making a difference."

3. *Adjusting* the ongoing magnitude of intensity or activity of the key factors in order to bring them to a more appropriate or effective level. Exploring the impact that this adjustment makes on the emotions, behavior and situation associated with the problem state in order to discover what new choices are possible. It is important to keep in mind that the optimum level is not always the maximum level.
4. *Anchoring* a particular degree of intensity or activity of a set of key factors in order to maintain them at an optimum level, especially in changing and challenging situations.

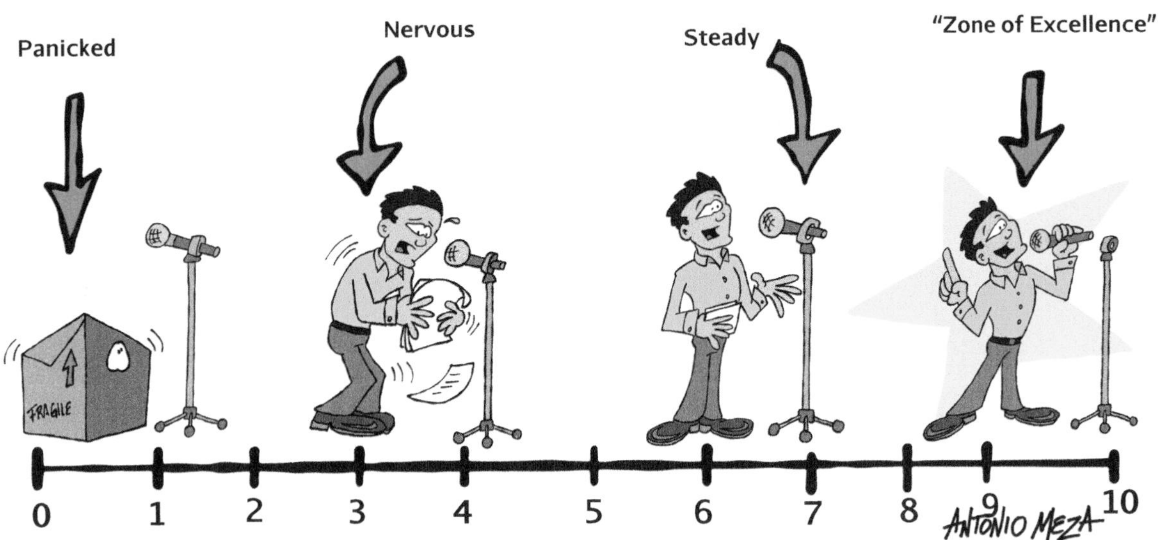

Learning to calibrate and adjust your inner state is an important skill for self-mastery.

Creating Resource Anchors

Anchoring refers to the process of associating a particular internal response with some environmental cue or trigger, so that the response may be quickly, reaccessed. Anchoring is a process that is similar to the "conditioning" technique used by Pavlov to create a link between the hearing of a bell and salivation in dogs. By associating the sound of a bell with the act of giving food to his dogs, Pavlov found he could eventually just ring the bell and the dogs would start salivating, even though no food was given.

An important skill for mastering your inner game, increasing resilience and remaining in your "zone of excellence" is creating resource anchors.

You can use the process of anchoring to help you remember and access your inner resources. A certain object, for instance, may become an anchor for a positive internal state. An article of clothing can become an anchor for a feeling of confidence, for example. A piece of music may become an anchor for a state of excitement or determination. Some of these types of associations are spontaneous and natural. You can also consciously choose to establish, strengthen and re-trigger positive associations. In this way, an anchor becomes a tool for mastering your inner game.

Anchoring is a process for creating cues or triggers to remind yourself of your goals and your inner resources. People have all the resources they need to make positive changes and get what they want. Frequently, though, they forget those resources at times when they need them most. Sometimes you need a trigger or "anchor" to get in touch with them. Anchoring can be a very useful tool for helping to establish and reactivate the internal states associated with purpose, creativity, learning, concentration and other important inner resources.

A resource anchor is an object, image or some other stimulus that helps to remind you of and reconnect you with internal resources.

The basic steps for creating a resource anchor are:

1. Remember a time when you experienced the resourceful experience strongly. See what you saw, hear what you heard and feel what you felt as vividly as you can.
2. Find something to use as an anchor to trigger to help remind you of and reconnect you to the resourceful experience. (Object, picture,article of clothing, key word, gesture, etc.)
3. Put yourself back into the resourceful experience. See what you saw, hear what you heard and feel what you felt as vividly as you can. Connect the memory of this experience to your anchor by shifting your attention momentarily to the cue or trigger.
4. Clear your mind and change your state for a moment. Do something to distract yourself.

5. Put your attention on your anchor. You should immediately get the resourceful feeling. If you don't, repeat steps 3 and 4 a few more times until the association is automatic.

In my Conscious Leaders Mastermind group (see *SFM Vol. II*, pp. 69-71), we jokingly say that "whoever has the most anchors wins." By "winning" in this case, we don't mean making someone else lose but rather being able to maintain an optimal mindset and remain in one's zone of excellence no matter what happens. Having many resource anchors ensures that you will be able to the best of yourself in any situation.

Former US president Barak Obama carries resource anchors in the form of keepsakes that remind him of his higher purpose.

As a good example of this, in a January 16, 2016 interview, former US president Barak Obama revealed that, for inspiration, he always carried with him some of the keepsakes people had given him since he started running for office. He maintained that they helped him cope on a bad day because they reminded him that "somebody gave me this privilege to work on these issues that are going to affect them." This connected him to his higher purpose, giving him the energy and motivation to "get back to work."

When asked for an example, Obama pulled an intriguing assortment of objects from his right pants' pocket including rosary beads from Pope Francis, a tiny Buddha, a metal poker chip he said came from a bald biker with a handlebar mustache he met in Iowa in 2007, a Coptic cross from Ethiopia and a statuette of God Hanuman. He claimed that when felt tired or discouraged, reaching into his pocket could help him get over it. While Obama has too many of the mementos to carry all of them around, he remarked "I'll pick out a few things...to remind me of all the people I've met along the way and the stories they told me."

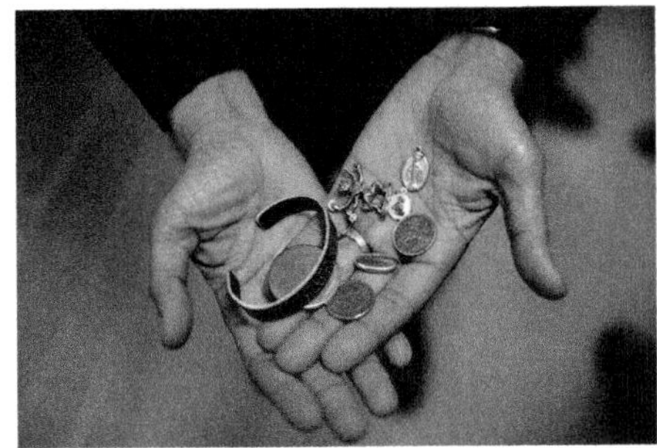

Obama claims that these anchors help him cope with difficult situations by reminding him of "all the people I've met along the way and the stories they told me."

Like Obama, I myself have many resource anchors that I use constantly. Some are meaningful mementos; others are portraits of key mentors that I have drawn, photographs, post cards, awards, etc. One of my favorites is an Albert Einstein "action figure" that is solar powered. When light shines on the solar battery, his right arm starts pointing to the right side of his head. This reminds me of the importance of the imaginative "right brain" in addition to the logical "left brain."

Managing Your Energy

Managing your energy and knowing how to recover or reset your inner energy level is another important inner game capability for leaders and entrepreneurs.

In addition to having a rich assortment of resource anchors, self-mastery and success in your inner game require practices that help you to manage your inner level of energy effectively in order to stay within your "inner zone of excellence." As an example, some years ago I was facilitating a leadership development project for very high-level managers in a well-known international technology company. This group made up the most profitable division of the organization, worldwide. As we explored the "differences that made a difference" in effective leadership, the man who was in charge of this division made the point that, to him, in addition to providing vision and direction, leadership was essentially the process of bringing proactive energy into his interactions. Regardless of whether it was his team, his organization or a particular meeting, he saw his job as being to bring positive, proactive energy. And of course to do that, he also needed to deal with the inevitable drops or disturbances of energy that can emerge.

One of the things this leader did as an ongoing practice was that, every morning before work, he would bring his attention into his body and feel his inner level of energy. Then, he would make the commitment to come home to his family with the same amount of energy at the end of the day.

Identifying and utilizing personal "energy catalysts" can be helpful in order to establish and recover a good level of energy whenever you need it.

This required that he be very in tune with his own level of energy throughout the day. If it dropped, he had ways of increasing it. If it became disturbed he had strategies for correcting it. If it became blocked he had methods to unblock it or "reset" it. These are what we could call "energy catalysts".

One of his modalities for dealing with disturbed or negative energy, for instance, was to sing (and he was not a naturally talented "singer"). He related a humorous example of how, when he was going from a particularly difficult meeting to another appointment, he had to warn the taxi driver that he would be singing during the drive because he did not want to begin the next meeting feeling tense and angry.

This top manager's ability to sense, set, and sustain a positive level of body energy requires a special type of somatic and emotional intelligence. Managing our energy is a key part of our inner game. Explore some of your own "energy catalysts" through the following reflections:

1. Tune into your internal level of energy right now. How strong is it? What type of quality does it have? Develop your own way of sensing and measuring your level and quality of energy.
2. Identify several situations where you need to maintain a good level and quality of energy, but sometimes find it difficult or challenging.
3. What are some ways in the past that you have increased, corrected, unblocked or reset your level of energy (i.e., your past energy catalysts)? How could you use them to improve your energy that you feel now and in the challenging situations you have identified?
4. What are some other ways that you can use your body, voice or other levels of internal success factors (behaviors, thoughts, beliefs, sense of identity, connection to your purpose, etc.) to increase and improve the level and quality of energy you feel now or in the challenging situations you have identified?

Self-Awareness

Self-Regulation

Conscious Leadership requires the ability to tune into yourself and the level and quality of your energy, and to have ways of correcting, unblocking or resetting your level of energy if it gets disturbed.

The Power of Presence

Developing a greater capacity to be present in your body and in the moment is another key success factor for entering your inner "zone of excellence" and mastering your inner game.

Presence is another important element of the "inner game" for entrepreneurs and leaders. Merriam-Webster's dictionary defines *presence* as "a quality of poise and effectiveness that enables a performer to achieve a close relationship with his or her audience." The ability to be poised, effective and achieve a close connection to those with whom we are interacting is an essential quality to be successful as an entrepreneur or leader.

As the definition above implies, poise and connectedness come from the capacity to be present, centered in yourself and in relationship with those around you—i.e., in contact with the larger "holarchy." The quality of presence is frequently the "difference that makes the difference" in our ability to enjoy life, collaborate generatively and contribute to the growth and transformation of others. Presence is associated with feelings of aliveness, connection, creativity, satisfaction and flow. When we are not present and are disconnected, we can feel empty, out of control, distant and unavailable.

My colleague, transformational teacher Richard Moss, points out that *the distance between ourselves and others is the same as the distance between ourselves and ourselves.* This implies that the way we relate to others and to the world around us is a mirror for how we relate to ourselves. It is from this fundamental relationship with ourselves that our relationships with others and the external world emerge. This self-to-self relationship is frequently limited by those feelings that we don't know how to meet, accept and integrate in ourselves.

Phil Jackson
Head Coach of
11 NBA Title Winning Teams

When people are both connected to themselves and present with each other, the natural feelings that emerge are compassion, empathy, genuine interest in each other, spontaneity, authenticity and joy. These feelings are the foundation for all effective personal and professional relationships.

Consider the following comments about the power of presence by Phil Jackson, widely considered one of the greatest coaches in the history of the National Basketball Association (NBA). His reputation was established as head coach of the Chicago Bulls from 1989 through 1998; during his tenure, Chicago won six NBA titles. His next team, the Los Angeles Lakers, won five NBA titles from 2000 to 2010. In total, Jackson has won 11 NBA titles as a coach. He is the winner of the most championships in NBA history as a player and a head coach.

According to Jackson, presence is the gateway to our inner zone of excellence. As he put it:

> *Like life, basketball is messy and unpredictable. It has its way with you, no matter how hard you try to control it. The trick is to experience each moment with a clear mind and open heart. When you do that, the game—and life—will take care of itself.*
>
> *Winning is important to me, but what brings me real joy is the experience of being fully engaged in whatever I'm doing.*
>
> *In basketball—as in life—true joy comes from being fully present in each and every moment, not just when things are going your way. Of course, it's no accident that things are more likely to go your way when you stop worrying about whether you're going to win or lose and focus your full attention on what's happening right this moment.*

Winning NBA basketball coach Phil Jackson maintains that "being fully present in each and every moment" and experiencing each moment "with a clear mind and open heart" enhances both satisfaction and performance.

Jackson confirms the principle that mastering the inner game is the key to success in the outer game.

Explore the power of presence for yourself:

- *What is it like when you are present and fully engaged in what you are doing?*
- *How do you stay present in your body "with a clear mind and open heart" in situations of adversity?*
- *What types of outer disturbances and inner responses challenge your ability to stay "fully present in each and every moment?" What helps you to refocus "your full attention on what's happening right in this moment?*

Self-Regulation

COACH Versus CRASH

In a CRASH state you are contracted, emotionally reactive, mentally paralysed, separated from others and from your own resources, and feeling hostile and hurt.

As we said before, things are always changing, but not always progressing. During times of intense adversity it is possible that we can collapse into an inner stuck state that can be summarized by the letters in the word CRASH:

- **C**ontraction
- **R**eaction
- **A**nalysis Paralysis
- **S**eparation
- **H**ostility, Hurt or Hatred

When we "CRASH" we are out of our "inner zone of excellence" and everything becomes more difficult. We no longer perceive ourselves as a holon in connection with the larger holarchy and lose our connection to our "soul." When we confront an outer obstacle from the CRASH state, we experience it as an unsolvable problem.

In order to progress through change, it is important to cultivate qualities such as flexibility and stability, balance, connection to something bigger than ourselves and the ability to let go. This comes from being centered and in our "inner zone of excellence" and connected with something beyond the confines of our individual egos. These processes are characterized by what we call the COACH state (see *SFM Vol. I*, pp. 34-35 and *SFM Vol. II*, p. 15 & pp. 74-75):

- **C**entered and present in our bodies
- **O**pen to possibilities and to others
- **A**ware and mindful
- **C**onnected to ourselves, our purpose and others around us
- **H**olding whatever is happening from a state of resourcefulness, curiosity and hospitality

These five qualities are the pillars of self-mastery and the key to personal resilience and the ability to remain within our inner zone of excellence in challenging circumstances.

In a COACH state you are centered and present in your body, open to receive and to give, mentally alert and aware, fully connected to yourself and others and able to hold whatever is happening within you or around you from a state of resourcefulness.

The COACH state is the basis of a successful mindset and the foundation for emotional intelligence and mastering your inner game. The COACH state is essentially an internal state of presence, resourcefulness, curiosity and receptivity.

The reason for putting ourselves into the COACH state is to "open our channel," as it were, and connect to the experience of being both an individual whole and part of something bigger than ourselves that gives us purpose and energy. Achieving and maintaining this state is the cornerstone for any successful performance. Making the COACH state one's baseline performance state is one of the most important success factors for conscious leadership and resilience.

The five qualities of the COACH state are the pillars of self-mastery and the key to personal resilience and the ability to remain within our inner zone of excellence in challenging circumstances.

As I pointed out in *SFM Volume II* (p. 73), a good analogy for entering the COACH state is putting your laptop, tablet or smart-phone "online" and connected to a wireless network of some sort. This gives the device access to the "cloud" which makes it a type of "holon" in that it is able to access its own inner programming and data and at the same time is connected to a larger field of "collective intelligence." When online and connected to the cloud, a tablet or smart-phone can receive information about real time events from other parts of the world. It can even download new apps that expand its versatility and performance. It can also transmit information to other devices and the cloud through the wireless network. Once on the cloud, that information and knowledge can be accessed and utilized by many other devices.

If our tablet or smart-phone is "offline," however, it is limited only to previously existing data and applications that are currently in its memory.

Our nervous systems are in some ways like these devices. Our nerve cells form a type of circuitry that runs various programs or applications. In the COACH state we have full access to all of our personal applications and data, and we are also online and have the potential to connect to the "cloud" of knowledge in the field of collective intelligence around us. In other states, we have more limited access to our own resources and to the knowledge and ideas coming from others. In the CRASH state, for instance, where we are contracted, reactive, stuck in our own analysis paralysis, separated and hostile, we have access to only a small portion of our potential intelligence and resources.

Entering the COACH state is like putting your nervous system "online" and connecting it to the "cloud" and a larger field of "collective intelligence."

Practicing The COACH State:

Finding Your "Inner Zone of Excellence"

Just like mastering performance in the outer game, mastering your inner game requires practice.

Practicing the COACH state helps to make it your natural default response to whatever is going on in your outer game.

Self-Awareness

Our capacity for both resilience and innovation comes from being centered and in our "inner zone of excellence" and connected with something beyond the confines of our egos. These processes are characterized by what we have referred to as the COACH state:

It is important to have practices that help to create and strengthen the COACH state so that we can stay in our zone of excellence and bring the best of ourselves into whatever we do. It is easy to stay resourceful when life moves smoothly, but in order to maintain equilibrium during turbulent times, one must have developed these qualities until they are "in the muscle".

1. Sit or stand in a comfortable position with both feet on the floor and your spine erect but relaxed (i.e., "in your vertical axis"). Check that your breathing is regular and from the belly. (Short, rapid breathing from the chest would indicate that you are in a stressed mode.)
2. Bring your attention to the soles of your feet (i.e., put your "mind" into your feet.). Become aware of the universe of sensations in the bottoms of your feet. Feel the surface of your heels, toes, arches and the balls of your feet.
3. Begin to expand your awareness to include the physical volume (the 3-dimensional space) of your feet and then move your awareness up through your lower legs, knees, thighs, pelvis and hips. Become aware of your *belly center*, breathe deeply into it and say to yourself: "I am here." "I am present." "I am centered."
4. Continuing to stay aware of your lower body, expand your awareness up through your solar plexus, spine, lungs, rib cage and chest. Bring awareness to your *heart center* in your upper chest, breathe into your chest and say to yourself: "I am open." "I am opening."

5. Now continue to expand your awareness up through your shoulders, upper arms, elbows, lower arms, wrists, hands and fingers, and up through your neck, throat and face. Be sure to include all of the senses in the head: the eyes, ears, nose, mouth and tongue. Bring your awareness to the skull, brain and your *head center*. Breathe as if you are breathing into your head center, bringing oxygen and energy, and say to yourself: "I am awake." "I am aware." "I am alert and clear."
6. Staying in contact with the ongoing physical sensations in your body, starting from your feet and including all three centers (belly, heart and head), become aware of all of the space below you, going into the center of the Earth; all the space above you, reaching into the sky; all of the space to your left; all of the space to your right; all of the space behind you; all of the space in front of you. Feel a deep sense of connection to your feet and the centers in your belly, heart and head, and to the environment and field (holarchy) around you. Be aware of the vast array of resources available to you within yourself and in the field around you. When you can experience a connection to this sense of a larger Self, say to yourself, "I am connected."
7. Keeping your awareness on your body and simultaneously on the space around you, sense a type of field or holding environment in which you can hold all of the resources, strength, intelligence and wisdom available to you as well as disturbing energies such as fear, anger, sadness, etc. Feel the sense of courage and confidence to face whatever comes your way as you stay centered and present with all of yourself and open to your environment. Say to yourself, "I am ready."

We are what we repeatedly do. Excellence, then, is not an act, but a habit.

—Aristotle

Practice means to perform, over and over again in the face of all obstacles, some act of vision, of faith, of desire. Practice is a means of inviting the perfection desired.

We learn by practice. Whether it means to learn to dance by practicing dancing or to learn to live by practicing living, the principles are the same. One becomes in some area an athlete of God.

—Martha Graham

Self-Regulation

Rehearsing Resilience

Practicing the skills of the inner game is also necessary for increasing your capacity for personal resilience.

Of course, it is one thing to find your zone of excellence while contemplating it from a calm and neutral position. It is another to maintain an optimal mindset under physically and emotionally challenging conditions. This is where practice and discipline become essential success factors. It could literally save your life and the lives of others (both figuratively and literally).

Practicing the following set of steps regularly will allow you to empower yourself and greatly enrich your repertoire of options for resilience in all areas of your life.

Self-Awareness

Self-Regulation

1. *Self-Awareness:* Think of a challenging situation where it is difficult for you to stay in your "zone of excellence" – i.e., where you have a tendency to CRASH. Put yourself into that experience using memory or imagination. Bring your attention to your inner state and inner game. What are you aware of? (Images, sounds, feelings, sensations, etc.)
2. *Self-Calibration:* On a scale of 0 to 10 (0 meaning not at all and 10 meaning completely), how fully do you experience your COACH state as you think of being in that situation?
3. *Self-Adjustment:* What can you simply and easily adjust in order to increase your COACH state just a little bit more? (i.e., take a breath, adjust your posture, say something to yourself, visualize something resourceful, remember a positive reference experience, think of a good role model, act "as if" you were in your COACH state, etc.)
4. When you make the adjustment, what level does your COACH state move to? What difference does it make? How does it affect your creative energy? Your resourcefulness? Your relational availability? What becomes possible now? How does it affect your outer game?
5. *Self-Anchoring:* How could you "anchor" this level of resourcefulness so that it is available to you the next time you are in that situation? What image, gesture, object, etc., will help you to remember/hold this level?

Developing resilience involves the self-awareness to be able to calibrate your internal state and make adjustments to bring yourself back into your inner "zone of excellence."

This being human is a guest house
Every morning a new arrival.
A joy, a depression, a meanness,
some momentary awareness comes
as an unexpected visitor.
Welcome and entertain them all!
Even if they are a crowd of sorrows,
who violently sweep your house
empty of its furniture,
still treat each guest honorably.
He may be clearing you out for some new delight.
The dark thought, the shame, the malice,
meet them at the door laughing,
and invite them in.
Be grateful for whoever comes,
because each has been sent
as a guide from beyond.
– **Rumi**

Recovering from a CRASH: Gathering the Resources Necessary to Hold Difficult Feelings

In spite of how well we prepare, in some cases we will be unable to avoid a complete CRASH. Instead of making adjustments to our inner state, we will need to "reset" our whole inner game and transform whatever is creating the CRASH state. A key aspect of self-mastery and success in one's inner game is the ability to acknowledge and transform inner obstacles and interferences with one's "zone of excellence"; these frequently come in the form of difficult feelings that create "neuromuscular lock."

In order to reset our state and transform the obstacles in our way we need to be able to connect "beneath" them (to something deeper in ourselves) and connect "beyond" them (to something bigger than ourselves). In *SFM Vol. I* (p. 158), for example, entrepreneur Mark Fizpatrick talked about the importance of developing the ability to "just to keep grounded and to keep it all in perspective." He talked about prayer, which is a way of connecting to something bigger than oneself. These comments reflect an obvious parallel to Elon Musk's ability to connect to his higher purpose as a way to make it through the period in 2009 when all three of his companies were failing.

Creating a "Guest House" for Difficult Feelings

The larger frame or psychological field in which we hold difficult feelings generally determines the impact or influence they have upon us. Family therapy innovator Virginia Satir, for instance, used to frequently ask her clients two questions when they were caught in a CRASH state, struggling with some life challenge. The first question was, "How do you feel?" A client might respond to this question by answering that he or she felt angry, sad, afraid, guilty, or some other type of difficult feeling. Then Virginia would ask a second question: "How do you feel about feeling that way?"

The answer to this second question is quite significant and determines a lot about the impact and meaning the answer to the first question will have. It makes quite a difference if someone feels calm or curious about feeling angry rather than feeling guilty, helpless or frustrated about feeling angry. It is these second feelings that determine the ease and quality with which we are able to stay centered and resourcefully hold the first set of feelings. As my colleague Richard Moss likes to ask, "Is your fear safe inside of you?"

Our inner response to our feelings and emotional states reflects the relationship we have with them and determines whether those feelings will be a problem or not.

In the generative coaching work that I developed with my colleague Stephen Gilligan, we use several statements, or "mantras" as we call them, as a way to create a positive and emotionally intelligent inner holding environment (a "guest house" in the words of the Rumi poem) for feelings that usually create some form of CRASH. The four fundamental statements are:

1. "That's interesting."
2. "I'm sure it makes sense."
3. "Something needs to be heard, held or healed."
4. "Welcome...."

Emotional intelligence requires viewing and responding to emotional states with curiosity and compassion. This takes self-awareness and practice.

The statement "That's interesting" reminds us that there is something to be learned or better understood regarding the situation; that it too is an area where we can potentially evolve and grow. The affirmation "I'm sure it makes sense" acknowledges the fact that there is most likely some positive intention behind the response, even if we do not understand what it is yet; i.e., that it is a "guide from beyond" in Rumi's languaging. The assertion that "Something needs to be heard, held or healed" brings the awareness that whatever is happening is part of a larger holarchy and deserves to be recognized, treated respectfully and can benefit from receiving our resources. The declaration "Welcome" means that we are intentionally giving it a place and not trying to "get rid" of it.

We have found practicing these statements with ourselves and others to be quite powerful. They often bring an almost immediate relaxing of the CRASH state and a marked lessening of inner turmoil. This allows people to begin to connect to their resources and to the larger holon of themselves.

Holding Difficult Feelings

Inspired by Virginia Satir's work, I developed the following exercise to help myself and others discover and apply the resources needed to keep from CRASHing when faced with strong and difficult or "negative" emotions, so that the causes of those feelings could be identified and transformed. As you will see, it requires using your somatic intelligence (through body movement and gestures) as much as or more than intellectual reasoning.

1. Identify a situation in which you experience a difficult feeling that you are not able to hold resourcefully and which consequently creates an obstacle or drags you into some form of the CRASH state. Put yourself into that experience using memory or imagination. Bring your attention to your inner state and inner game. Repeat to yourself the four statements "That's interesting," "I'm sure it makes sense," Something needs to be heard, held or healed," Welcome." Bring awareness to the feeling and allow your body to naturally express it in a gesture and movement (e.g., clenching fists).
2. Now take a step back from the location in which you were experiencing this difficult feeling. From this new physical location, reflect upon the you who is experiencing the difficult feelings. How do you feel about those difficult feelings? How do you feel about yourself for feeling them? What is your relationship with those feelings and with yourself when you are feeling them? It is more than likely that you will experience some other form of unhelpful or unresourceful feelings such as frustration, helplessness, self-judgment or despair. Again, with respect to the second feeling, repeat the four statements "That's interesting," "I'm sure it makes sense," Something needs to be heard, held or healed," Welcome." Find the gesture or movement that expresses this second feeling (e.g., hands pushing away).
3. Now step back to a third location and put yourself into a resourceful state in which you are centered, open, awake (the COACH state) and connected to the larger holarchy. Recall the process, trigger or reference experience that you discovered in the previous section that automatically connects you to the felt sense of a larger self beyond your identity as separate individual. What resources (e.g., trust, acceptance, curiosity, strength, etc.) could help you to "keep grounded and to keep it all in perspective?" What resource(s) would allow you to hold both sets of feelings from your larger Self rather than become stuck in them or in conflict with them?
4. Bring the resources you have identified fully into your body and your inner game. (If you need to, you can facilitate this by finding reference experiences for these resources and reliving them as fully as you can.) Find a gesture and movement that expresses this resource and brings it present in your body (e.g., arms open above your head).
5. Step back into the second location bringing the resources and gesture from step 4. Don't attempt to change anything. Just hold the feelings and responses associated with the second location within the larger field of the resource. Make the gesture and movement associated with the resource you have chosen. Notice what shifts in your perception and attitude toward the difficult feelings and the "you" who is feeling them in the challenging situation.
6. Now return to the location in which you placed the situation in which you experience the difficult feelings and bring the resources you have identified with you. Again, don't attempt to change anything. Just hold the feelings and responses associated with the second location within the larger field of the resource. Make the gesture and movement associated with the resource you have chosen. How do you feel now about those difficult feelings? What changes in your ability to hold those difficult feelings? What becomes possible?

Learning to hold difficult feelings involves creating a "guest house" for them through a connection to your higher purpose and the larger holarchy.

Transforming "CRASH" States

Once you are able to hold difficult feelings and welcome them into your "guest house" it becomes possible to understand them, transform them and integrate them. Earlier in this chapter I identified seven skills for dealing with "negative" emotions:

1. *Recognizing* (calibrating) the presence of a particular emotional state
2. *Acknowledging* the presence of the state without judgment
3. *Holding* the emotional state in an environment of "equanimity" (making space for it)
4. *Understanding* the emotional state and its function (positive intention)
5. *Resourcing* the emotional state by connecting it to other complementary emotions and states
6. *Transforming* or refining the expression of the emotional state to be more harmonious and productive with respect to its positive intention
7. *Integrating* the emotional state as a contributing part of a larger system

In order to transform difficult feelings and CRASH states it is necessary to understand their positive intentions and connect them with complementary resource states.

The Holding Difficult Feelings process applies the first three skills of recognizing, acknowledging and holding the problematic emotional response in a resourceful way. To transform and integrate the response, it is necessary to understand its positive intention and connect it to other complementary states. You can do this with the difficult feeling you were working with in the previous exercise by going through the following steps.

Self-Awareness

1. Associate into the difficult feeling that you were working with in the previous exercise that was creating a "CRASH" state. Repeat the gesture or movement that is associated with or represents that feeling state (e.g., clenching fists) paying close attention to how it affects your inner game. Notice in what way that movement leads you away from your COACH state. (It most likely increases some form of "neuro-muscular lock.")
2. Now go back to the resource state you identified in the third step of the previous exercise and make the gesture and movement associated with that state (e.g., arms open above your head).

3. Staying in the COACH state, move slowly back to the movement associated with the difficult feeling. Repeat the movement (e.g., clenching fists) several times *very* slowly, staying centered and with heightened awareness. As you do, consider the *positive intention* of the movement and associated emotional state. What is it trying to do or accomplish for you?
4. Keeping the positive intention of the movement and the feeling in mind, slowly return to the gesture associated with the resource state (e.g., arms open above your head). Become aware of how this resource can support the positive intention of the difficult feeling.
5. Remaining in the COACH state, practice moving back and forth between the two gestures, slowly, gracefully and mindfully. Notice how there are many combinations and variations of expression between the two gestures and movements. Find a way of blending the two gestures and movements into a single gesture and movement. What becomes possible in both your inner and outer game as a result of the integrated movement?

Self-Regulation

You can repeat these same steps with the second feeling in the previous exercise.

Just like calisthenics and physical exercise can improve the health and fitness of your body, and studying and mental practice can improve your cognitive functioning, practicing exercises like the ones in this chapter can strengthen your emotional intelligence and your capacity for resilience. This capacity is crucial as you navigate the challenging outer game of launching, growing and sustaining a successful venture.

In the same way that calisthenics and physical exercise are needed to improve the health and fitness of your body, it takes practice to strengthen your emotional intelligence and your capacity for resilience

Sometimes when you're in the middle of one of these crises, you're not sure you're going to make it to the other end. But we've always made it, and so we have a certain degree of confidence, although sometimes you wonder.

I think the key thing is that we're not all terrified at the same time.

Steve Jobs

Collectively entering the COACH state can create a strong and rich sense of interconnection and resourcefulness.

Practicing Holding Difficult Feelings in a Group

As the adjacent comment by Steve Jobs' implies, one of the keys to handling crisis and rebounding from adversity is creating a "field" of confidence and resourcefulness so that team members can support one another in times of doubt and fear. One of the primary ways to do this is as a leader is to ground ourselves in our COACH state and support others to do the same. When we can do this we create a field of resources between ourselves and others that helps to bring out the best in each other. In fact, it could be said that the true leader in a challenging situation is the person who is able to resourcefully hold the most difficult feelings.

We refer to this special relationship and the field it produces as the *COACH Container*. Creating a strong and rich COACH Container with collaborators is essential for strengthening the ability to deal with challenge and uncertainty and increases the potential to rebound from adversity.

In SFM Volume II (pp. 73-75) I presented a simple process for Creating a COACH Container in a group that involved the following steps:

1. Sit or stand facing each other in a relaxed, aligned and balanced posture.
2. Bring your awareness into your body and your breath and become present.
3. Go through the steps of the Practicing the COACH State exercise (presented on pages 66-67) together.
4. As each group member senses that he or she is fully present and in his or her COACH state he or she says aloud to the others, "I am here" (as in a roll call) or "I am ready."
5. A nice additional step is for group members to look around the group and, as they make eye contact with one another, say aloud to each other, "I see you. Welcome."

When done with authenticity and presence, this should create a strong and rich sense of mutual rapport and resourcefulness. This is what we call the field or "container." It is often useful to share with each other how you sense the "container" or field of your relationship. You may prefer to use a metaphor or symbol. It can also help to create an anchor together (a movement, verbalization, symbol, etc.) that you can use to return to the full experience of the COACH Container that you have created more quickly. Sports teams, for example, will often go through a brief ritual or cheer before starting a game to bring all of the players into a collective "zone of excellence."

The purpose of this practice is to ensure that all participants begin their interaction from the best version of themselves, in order to get the most from the interaction. Just as athletes have warm-up practices that allow them to be the best of themselves during competition or practice, the COACH Container prepares collaborators in teams and groups to get the best from one another.

Creating a shared "anchor," such as a collective movement or gesture, can help members of a group to quickly return to a resourceful state.

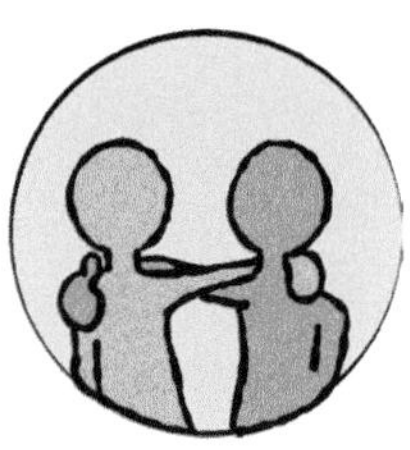

Empathy

Welcoming Difficult Feelings in a Group

By applying the principles and practices of emotional intelligence to groups, collaborators can learn to make space for emotional responses that may arise from their interactions.

When emotions can be non-judgmentally recognized, acknowledged and their positive intentions understood, it becomes possible to find the resources that either allow the emotions to simply pass or become transformed and integrated as a productive part of the group experience.

Resilience and dealing effectively with crisis, challenge and uncertainty require the acceptance and integration of many different emotions and inner states. The field of the group needs to welcome and acknowledge all of these inner states and energies in order to be authentic and productive. Whatever is withheld becomes a type of "shadow" that weakens the field.

Similar to developing the skill of holding difficult feelings as part of our inner game, it is important for groups of collaborators to be able to make space for emotional responses that may arise from their interactions, especially in times of adversity and uncertainty. When emotions can be recognized, acknowledged, held from a larger space of non-judgmental equanimity and their positive intentions understood, it becomes possible to find the resources that either allow the emotions to simply pass or become transformed and integrated as a productive part of the group experience.

The following exercise can be done with a group of collaborators in order to practice acknowledging and welcoming difficult feelings that may emerge within the group.

1. Create a strong "COACH Container" by going through the steps in the previous exercise.
2. One of the group members begins by recalling an experience of a difficult feeling such as:
   - Anxiety/Fear
   - Stubbornness/Resistance
   - Neediness
   - Hostility

   When the person is able to feel authentically some degree of the presence of the difficult feeling, he or she acknowledges it by saying, "I feel . . ." and names the state. (There is no need to try to justify or explain the feeling.)
3. The other group members are to create a space for the difficult feeling using the statements, "That's interesting," "I'm sure it makes sense," "Something needs to be heard, held or healed," "Welcome."
4. Group members remain in the COACH state and open their attention to the larger holarchy and sense of common purpose. (Individuals may do

this by recalling a process, trigger or reference experience that automatically connects them to the felt sense of a larger self beyond their identity as separate individual as explored in the previous chapter.)

5. Tuning in to their hearts and guts, group members are to become curious about what resources could help the person sharing their difficult feeling to "keep grounded and to keep it all in perspective?" Rather than attempt to figure something out cognitively or rationally, group members are instead to use their emotional intelligence and "let something come" to them intuitively. It could come in the form of words, an image, a symbol, a gesture or some other feeling.

6. Each group member then in turn shares the resource that has emerged with the rest of the group by saying aloud, "The resource that comes to me is . . ." and expresses the words, image, symbol or gesture.

7. After all of the group members have shared their resources, the person with the difficult feeling describes what has shifted with respect the feeling and in his or her inner game.

Helping others find resources for dealing with difficult feelings creates a positive field of support and helps to develop social EQ.

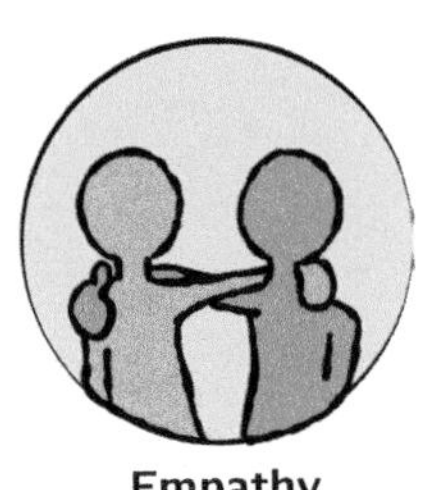

Empathy

The process is repeated until each member of the group has had an opportunity to share a difficult feeling.

This, of course, is a highly ritualized procedure whose purpose is to give people the opportunity to practice specific skills of emotional intelligence in an atmosphere of psychological safety. It is only one of many possible structures that can help to improve team cooperation and resilience. I have presented other exercises and practices of this type in *Success Factor Modeling Volume II* such as:

- *Applying Intervision to Promote Generative Collaboration for Problem Solving* (pp. 124-127)
- *Shifting from CRASH to COACH State* (pp. 304-305)
- *Transforming Potential Conflicts Through the Tetra Lemma* (pp. 306-309)

As we shall see in the chapters ahead, there are also many other procedures and forms through which people can express and address difficult feelings in a group, such as "town hall" meetings and "clearing the air" sessions. The value of having such structures in place is that when the inevitable and unexpected challenges do come, the leader and team members are ready to respond quickly and resourcefully.

The following Success Factor Case Example provides a good illustration of this and a number of other principles we have covered the first two chapters.

Success Factor Case Example:
Dr. Lim Suet Wun – CEO Tan Tock Seng Hospital

Singapore's "Ground Zero" for the SARS Epidemic of 2003

Dr. Lim Suet Wun

When Dr. Lim Suet Wun became CEO of Tan Tock Seng Hospital in Singapore there was nothing that could have prepared him for the crisis he would face when the SARS (Severe Acute Respiratory Syndrome) outbreak hit the country in early 2003. Tan Tock Seng Hospital is where the first case of the deadly and virulent SARS disease showed up in Singapore. As a result, it became the hospital responsible for disease containment—the "Ground Zero" for combating the SARS epidemic in the country.

As a result of a government decision, all staff and patients were quarantined at the hospital for months. They were not allowed to leave and risk the possibility of the further spread of the disease. People were forced to live together in tight quarters, facing an unknown, deadly and highly infectious disease. It was a "life and death situation," and almost half the people infected were hospital staff and health care workers, including senior doctors. In fact, hospital workers were the group most likely to contract the illness. In addition, all of the new cases of patients with the disease in the country were sent to the hospital, increasing the chances of contamination to the workers and other patients already there. In the beginning, nobody knew for sure what caused the disease, how it spread or how to protect people from contracting it. "It was a crisis complicated by uncertainty," explains Wun.

Dr. Lim Suet Wun demonstrated many of the skills of emotional intelligence as CEO of Tan Tock Seng Hospital in Singapore during the SARS outbreak in 2003.

Reflecting on how he met the crisis, Dr. Wun identified three key success factors:

1. *Getting and filtering the information necessary to make decisions.*

   This was essential for Wun to achieve effective "rumor control." It has been said that "it is human nature to expect the worst" when the situation is dangerous and uncertain. "Rumors are like a cancer in this situation," says Dr. Wun. He was fortunate that he had already taken steps to ensure that appropriate communication infrastructures and processes were already in place—e.g., "town hall" meetings, clear points of contact, cascading message protocols, etc. "The crisis essentially intensified structures already in place," he explains. An even greater crisis was averted because people were familiar with communication channels and "trusted the process."

Social Skills

2. *Disseminating the information and decisions and ensuring cooperation.*

   "The main thing is that everyone needed to work together and cooperate as a team," explains Wun. To accomplish this, it is paramount to make sure that everyone, at all levels of the organization is "on the same page." As Wun put it, "The people in the boiler room need to know where the ship is heading." Adherence and accountability regarding decisions were also extremely important. In such a life and death situation this required, in Wun's words, a few "public hangings"; meaning individuals were publicly reprimanded or disciplined. He quipped that, for some people, you have to "shoot them in the tail and they will catch up."

3. *Demonstrating confidence and belief in decisions through example.*

   The most difficult challenge was dealing with how the uncertainty affected the emotional states of the team members. There was a sense of anxiety and fear that could have easily turned into panic and other types of CRASH states. Crisis situations are those where "actions speak louder than words." As a powerful example, in the early days of the SARS epidemic, some staff members worried about whether wearing masks and gloves was adequate protection. As a result of his commitment to his mission as a doctor and a leader, Wun made it a point to visit all of the hospital staff and patients everyday and shake their hands wearing this equipment. In other words, by his actions he was saying, "I believe in our mission and our decisions enough to risk my life" and "I am the first one to adhere to the consequences of our decisions." This is the epitome of "walking your talk." Wun's walking around and visibility also had the effect of building and enhancing connection and trust with both staff and patients.

Embodying Leadership and Emotional Intelligence

Dr. Wun's calm demeanor and congruent actions created a "field" of calm, resourcefulness and cooperation making it possible to contain the disease effectively. This helped to avert what could have become a major disaster in a small and densely populated country like Singapore.

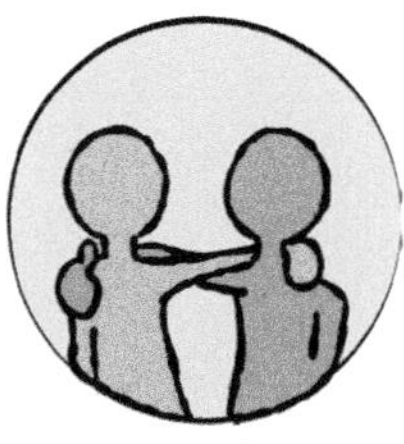

Empathy

Self-Motivation

Dr. Wun's mastery of his inner game and his calm demeanor and congruent actions as a leader in a situation of uncertainty with the potential for great anxiety and fear created a "field" of calm, resourcefulness and cooperation making it possible to contain the crisis and avoid disaster.

Dr. Wun's successful handling of the SARS crisis at the Tan Tock Seng Hospital demonstrates the importance of: (1) preparation and practice; (2) a sense of mission and higher purpose that connects one to a larger Self beyond the individual ego; and (3) the creation and nurturing of a resourceful "field" of support (a "COACH Container").

The success of Dr. Wun and his handling of the situation at the Tan Tock Seng Hospital demonstrate the importance of:

1. Preparation and practice – Having cooperative structures and protocols in place.
2. A sense of mission and higher purpose that connects one to a larger Self beyond the individual ego – Dr. Wun's commitment to his mission as a doctor and a leader.
3. The creation and nurturing of a resourceful "field" of support (a "COACH Container") – Shaking the hands of each staff member and patient every day.

Dr. Wun's case is a clear demonstration of the fundamental leadership abilities to 1) express a clear direction (so the "The people in the boiler room need to know where the ship is heading."), 2) influence and inspire others to appropriate action, 3) encourage team cooperation and 4) be an example. Dr. Wun's actions also demonstrated an intuitive grasp of all five components of emotional intelligence: Self-Awareness, Self-Regulation, Self-Motivation, Empathy and Social Skills.

One of his major challenges was to acknowledge and address very intense and difficult feelings. His example illustrates the abilities to:

- recognize and understand emotions and drives and their effects on others
- manage and redirect disruptive impulses and moods
- work for reasons that go beyond money or status
- balance self-interest with common good
- understand the emotional makeup of other people
- treat people according to their emotional reactions
- find common ground and build rapport
- manage relationships and enhance trust

These competences helped transform a crisis into a success story.

Chapter Summary

The ability to anticipate and deal with adversity is an essential success factor for both entrepreneurs and leaders. The capacity for resilience is developed through practice and discipline. Peter Senge's *five disciplines* of a learning organization—personal mastery, examination of mental maps and assumptions, visioning and creating the future, team learning and systems thinking—provide a powerful roadmap for enhancing resilience and fitness for the future.

Another essential skill for conscious leaders and next generation entrepreneurs is *emotional intelligence* which refers to the capacity for recognizing our own feelings and those of others, for motivating ourselves, and for managing emotions in us and in our relationships. According to author Daniel Goleman, there are five fundamental components of emotional intelligence: Self-Awareness, Self-Regulation, Self-Motivation, Empathy and Social Skills.

The primary areas involved in applying emotional intelligence as a leader or entrepreneur are: (1) dealing with difficult emotional states in oneself and others and (2) stimulating or eliciting resourceful emotional states. Dealing with "negative" emotions in an emotionally intelligent way involves (a) acknowledging that they have survival value, (b) seeking and understanding the positive intention behind them, and (c) adding more behavioral alternatives, given the intention and the specific context related to the emotional response.

Emotional intelligence requires that we utilize more than just our cognitive intellect. It involves access to somatic knowledge and information. Recent neurological research has confirmed that there is a substantial level of intelligence in the belly (the enteric nervous system) and the heart as well in the head. While the brain in our head is primarily associated with reason and planning, the brain in the gut is generally connected with intuition and evaluation, while the heart is linked with interpersonal connection and passion. Conscious leaders must learn to use all three brains—head, heart and gut—to make decisions and inspire others.

Another key to resilience, fitness for the future and conscious leadership is mastering our "inner game." The *inner game* has to do with mobilizing our inner resources, overcoming self-imposed obstacles and being true to our values and purpose. The inner game has to do with your mental and emotional approach to what you are doing. This includes your attitude, belief in yourself and your team, your ability to concentrate effectively, to deal with mistakes and pressure, and so on.

Mastering the inner game involves identifying and grounding in your "*inner zone of excellence*," a state characterized by a sense of humble authority and effortless performance. Achieving this requires certain fundamental skills such as Self-Awareness, Self-Calibration, Self-Adjustment and Self-Anchoring.

Success in the inner game is supported by the ability to create *resource anchors*. Anchoring is a process for creating cues or triggers to remind yourself of your goals and your inner resources. Having many resource anchors ensures that you will be able to the best of yourself in any situation.

Managing your energy is another core capacity for mastering your inner game. The ability to bring positive, proactive energy to ourselves and others is essential for leaders and entrepreneurs. Being able to recognize our internal level and quality of energy, and deal with the inevitable drops or disturbances of energy that can emerge, is crucial to our success. Developing practices that help to increase, correct, unblock or reset your level of energy is another important discipline for conscious leadership.

Another vital characteristic of conscious leadership is presence. *Presence* can be defined as "a quality of poise and effectiveness that enables a performer to achieve a close relationship with his or her audience." The ability to be poised, effective and achieve a close connection to those with whom we are interacting is an essential quality to be successful as an entrepreneur or leader. When people are both connected to themselves and present with each other, the natural feelings that emerge are compassion, empathy, genuine interest in each other, spontaneity, authenticity and joy. These feelings are the foundation for all effective personal and professional relationships.

Practicing the COACH *state* is a way of discovering and strengthening your inner zone of excellence, increasing your capacity to manage your energy and enhancing the power of your presence. The COACH state involves being 1) Centered in our deeper Selves, 2) Open to possibilities, 3) Aware and alert, 4) Connected to ourselves, our purpose and a larger field of support, and 4) able to Hold whatever is happening from a state of resourcefulness, curiosity and hospitality.

The opposite of the COACH state is a state of *CRASH*: Contracted, Reactive, caught in Analysis paralysis, Separated from ourselves and others, and Hostile. When we CRASH we are out of our "inner zone of excellence" and everything becomes more difficult. When we confront an outer obstacle from the CRASH state, we experience it as an unsolvable problem.

Rehearsing resilience involves learning to detect when you are leaving your inner zone of excellence and losing your COACH state and knowing what adjustments to make to recover. Doing this regularly will support you to greatly enrich your repertoire of options for resilience in all areas of your life.

In spite of our best preparations, there will be situations in which we are unable to avoid a complete CRASH. Instead of making adjustments to our inner state, we will need to "reset" our whole inner game and transform whatever is creating the CRASH state. Recovering from a CRASH involves Creating a *"Guest House" for Difficult Feelings* and learning to hold those feelings in a resourceful way by connecting "beneath" them (to something deeper in ourselves) and connecting "beyond" them (to something bigger than ourselves).

Transforming "CRASH" States is a function of and integrating the response that is creating the CRASH by understanding its positive intention and connecting it to other complementary resource states. This is best done by activating our somatic intelligence through gestures and movement as well as using our cognitive abilities.

In times of challenge and crisis it is important for leaders to be able to ground themselves in their "inner zone of excellence," or COACH state, and support others to do the same. This serves to create a field of resources between themselves and others that helps to bring out the best in one another *Practicing holding difficult feelings in a group* is a way to implement specific skills of emotional intelligence in an atmosphere of psychological safety in order to create a "field" of confidence and resourcefulness so that team members can support one another in times of doubt and fear. To do so requires creating a strong and rich *COACH Container* similar to the way that sports teams will often go through a brief ritual or cheer before starting a game to bring all of the players into a collective "zone of excellence."

Resilience and dealing effectively with crisis, challenge and uncertainty require the acceptance and integration of many different emotions and inner states. The field of the group needs to welcome and acknowledge all of these inner states and energies in order to be authentic and productive. Whatever is withheld becomes a type of "shadow" that weakens the field. Similar to developing the skill of holding difficult feelings as part of our inner game, it is important for groups of collaborators to be able to make space for emotional responses that may arise from their interactions, especially in times of adversity and uncertainty. The practice of *Welcoming Difficult Feelings in a Group* allows challenging emotions to be recognized, acknowledged, held from a larger space of non-judgmental equanimity and their positive intentions understood. It then becomes possible to find the resources that either allow the emotions to simply pass or become transformed and integrated as a productive part of the group experience.

The value of having such practices and structures in place is that when the inevitable and unexpected challenges do come, the leader and team members are ready to respond quickly and resourcefully.

Dr. Lim Suet Wun's success at managing the highly charged situation at Singapore's Tan Tock Seng Hospital during the deadly SARS Epidemic of 2003 is a powerful example of how the principles and capabilities of conscious leadership and emotional intelligence and be applied in a "life or death" situation in order to get through crisis and rebound from adversity.

In the coming chapters, we will be returning to these principles and skills as we explore the mindset and actions necessary to launch a sustainable venture and to deal with the constraints dangers and opportunities that arise as you seek to bring your vision into action.

References and Related Readings:

- *The Fifth Discipline*; Senge, P.; Doubleday, New York, NY, 1995.
- *Emotional Intelligence: Why It Can Matter More Than IQ;* Goleman, D.; Bantam Books, New York, NY, 1995.
- *The Inner Game of Tennis,* Gallwey, T., Random House, New York, NY, 1974.
- *The Inner Game of Work: Focus, Learning, Pleasure and Mobility in the Workplace,* Gallwey, T., Random House Trade Paperbacks, New York, NY, 2000.
- *What Does Obama Carry In His Pocket? Hanuman Statue Among Lucky Charms,* Associated Press, January 16, 2016.

  http://www.ndtv.com/world-news/what-does-barack-obama-carry-in-his-pocket-find-out-on-youtube-1266454
- *Next Generation NLP: The Inner Game* (audio CD), Dilts, Robert and Bacon Dilts, Deborah, Journey to Genius, Santa Cruz, CA, 2011. www.journeytogenius.com
- *Next Generation NLP: Holding Difficult Feelings* (audio CD), Dilts, Robert and Bacon Dilts, Deborah, Journey to Genius, Santa Cruz, CA, 2011. www.journeytogenius.com

03
Conscious Leadership and Next Generation Entrepreneurship

The leaders we revere and the businesses that last are generally not the result of a narrow pursuit of popularity or personal advancement, but of devotion to some bigger purpose. That's the hallmark of real success. The other trapping of success might be the by product of this larger mission, but it can't be the central thing.

Barack Obama

The moment one definitely commits oneself, then providence moves too. All sorts of things occur to help one that would never otherwise occurred. A whole stream of events issues from the decision, raising in one's favor all manner of unforeseen incidents and meetings and material assistance which no man could have dreamed would have come his way.

Goethe

ANTONIO MEZA

Key Characteristics of Next Generation Entrepreneurs

Success Factor Modeling Volume I presented the skills needed to become a successful "next generation entrepreneur." I defined a *next generation entrepreneur* as someone who creates a sustainable business or project in order to live his or her own dream, while delivering a product or a service that makes a positive difference in the world and also stimulates his or her personal growth (see *SFM Vol. I*, pp. 64-71). A next generation entrepreneur, or "zentrapreneur," is a person who is committed to:

A next generation entrepreneur is someone who creates a sustainable business or project in order to live his or her own dream, while delivering a product or a service that makes a positive difference in the world and also stimulates his or her own personal growth.

- Living his or her dream; i.e., is passionate about something more than money
- Making a positive difference in the world
- Establishing a venture that is economically robust and sustainable (if not growing)
- Delivering something new, meaningful and innovative

Thus, next generation entrepreneurs want to create both a successful *and* purposeful business or career; combining ambition with contribution and mission with the desire for personal growth and fulfillment. They also desire to attract and collaborate with others who share the same vision, mission and ambition. Like conscious leadership, next generation entrepreneurship involves *creating a world to which people want to belong.*

Next generation entrepreneurs want to create both a successful and purposeful business or career; combining ambition for achievement with the determination to contribute and the desire for personal growth and fulfillment.

As I pointed out in *SFM Vols. I & II*, successful next generation entrepreneurs accomplish this through the following five key practices:

- Growing personally and spiritually
- Contributing to society and the environment
- Building a successful and sustainable venture and career
- Supporting the emotional and physical well-being of oneself and others
- Sharing visions and resources with a community of peers, igniting new possibilities

These practices can be summarized in the following diagram:

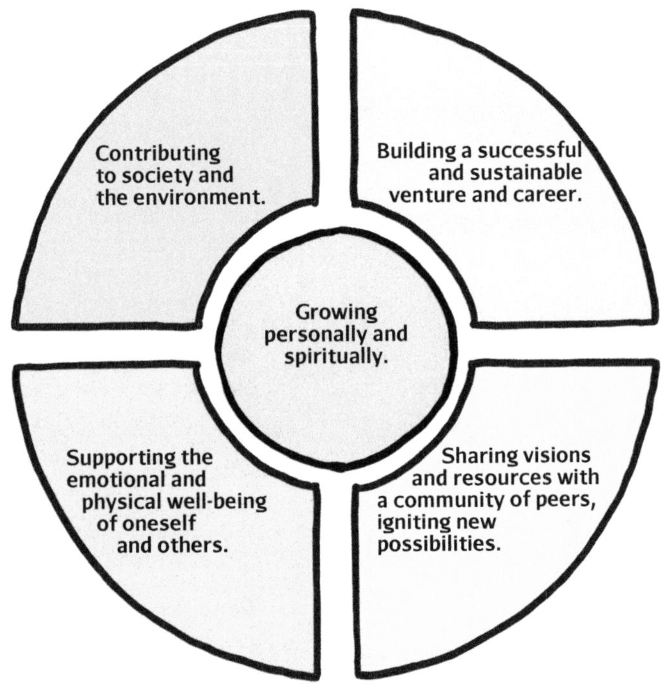

Key Practices Relating to Authentic Success and Creating a World to Which People Want to Belong

Clearly, these five practices of next generation entrepreneurs are equally important for conscious leaders. Research with Success Factor Modeling has shown that, in order to turn these five keys to authentic success into a project or venture, next generation entrepreneurs create what we call the *SFM Circle of Success*™ (see *SFM Vol. I*, pp. 76-95 & SFM Vol. II, pp. 18-26).

The SFM Circle of Success™

A "Circle of Success" is constructed by bringing together the outcomes, actions and mindset needed to build a successful venture. The five practices of authentic success defined previously translate naturally into five *core outcomes* to be achieved to make a truly next generation venture. Those five core outcomes are:

1. *Personal Satisfaction* that comes from growing personally and spiritually
2. *Meaningful Contribution* that results from making a positive difference for society and the environment
3. *Financial Robustness* that is a consequence of building a successful and sustainable venture and career
4. *Innovation and Resilience* that is a result of supporting the emotional and physical well-being of oneself and others
5. *Scalable Growth* that is supported by sharing visions and resources with a community of peers, igniting new possibilities

In order to achieve these outcomes, we have observed that the founders of successful ventures divide their focus of attention and their actions in a balanced way between five fundamental perspectives: 1) themselves and their sense of purpose and motivation for what they are doing, 2) their customers and their products or services, 3) their investors and stakeholders, 4) their team members or employees and 5) their strategic partners and allies.

In other words, in order to achieve the five core outcomes for a successful next generation venture, entrepreneurs need to engage in a number of critical actions directed toward key people and groups. These *critical actions* include:

1. *Connecting* with **themselves** and their *purpose and motivation* for the venture.
2. *Developing products and services* for their **customers** and *generating enough interest and revenue* to support their enterprise — establishing both sufficient "mind share" and market share.
3. Growing a team of competent **team members** by *creating alignment* with respect to the mission of the venture and continuing to *increase their competency* as the business matures.
4. *Raising funds and securing other essential resources* needed to support the venture to reach its ambition, then continuing to *expand the business and create value* for **stakeholders and investors.**
5. *Building win-win relationships* and establishing alliances with strategic **partners** that allow all parties to *enrich and leverage resources* in such a way that they can increase visibility and expand their roles in the marketplace.

As the name "circle of success" implies, we represent the relationship between these critical actions and the core outcomes they create as a circle, with oneself and one's purpose and motivation in the center surrounded by four quadrants of customers/market, team members/employees, stakeholders/ investors and partners/alliances.

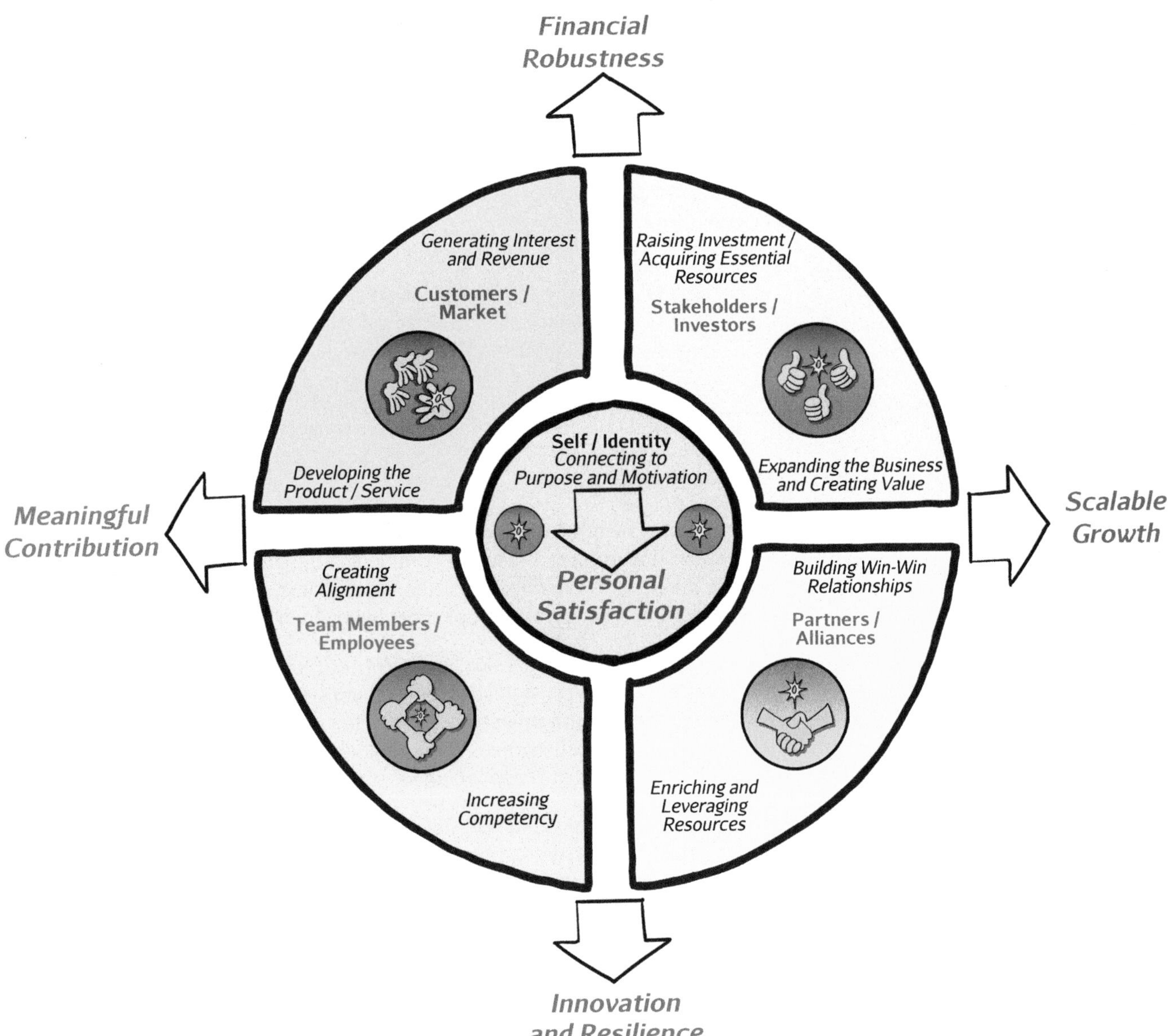

The SFM Circle of Success™

Establishing an Entrepreneurial Mindset

Creating a successful venture is founded upon an entrepreneurial mindset that is founded on a person's capacity to understand and share his or her passion, in the form of a vision, mission, ambition and role.

Our Success Factor Modeling studies have shown that creating a successful venture is ultimately founded upon an *entrepreneurial mindset* that produces and encourages the actions necessary to reach core outcomes. This mindset is a function of an entrepreneur's capacity to share his or her *passion*, in the form of *vision*, *mission*, *ambition* and *role*, with respect to the key perspectives defined by the Circle of Success.

- Personal ***passion*** comes from connecting fully with one's **self** and one's deepest **identity** and discovering what brings us enthusiasm and energy. It involves exploring the question: *What do you really love to do?*

- The entrepreneur's ***vision*** is a function of his or her personal passion expressed outward toward **customers and the market** in order to make a contribution. It is the answer to the question: *What do you want to create in the world?*

- The alignment of **team members and employees** working together to reach the vision is a result of communicating and sharing one's passion in the form of the ***mission*** of the venture. It is a result of answering the question: *What is your unique contribution to the vision?*

- The entrepreneur's passion in the form of his or her ***ambition*** to build a successful and sustainable venture and create value is what motivates **stakeholders and investors** to offer the resources and take the risk to join the venture. It involves being clear about the answer to the question: *What do you want to accomplish for yourself?*

- The entrepreneur's passion for applying his or her area of excellence in the form of a ***role*** and building win-win relationships with peers that enrich and leverage resources is what forms the basis for effective **partnerships and alliances**. This requires clarifying: *Who do you need to be in order to fulfill your mission and ambition?*

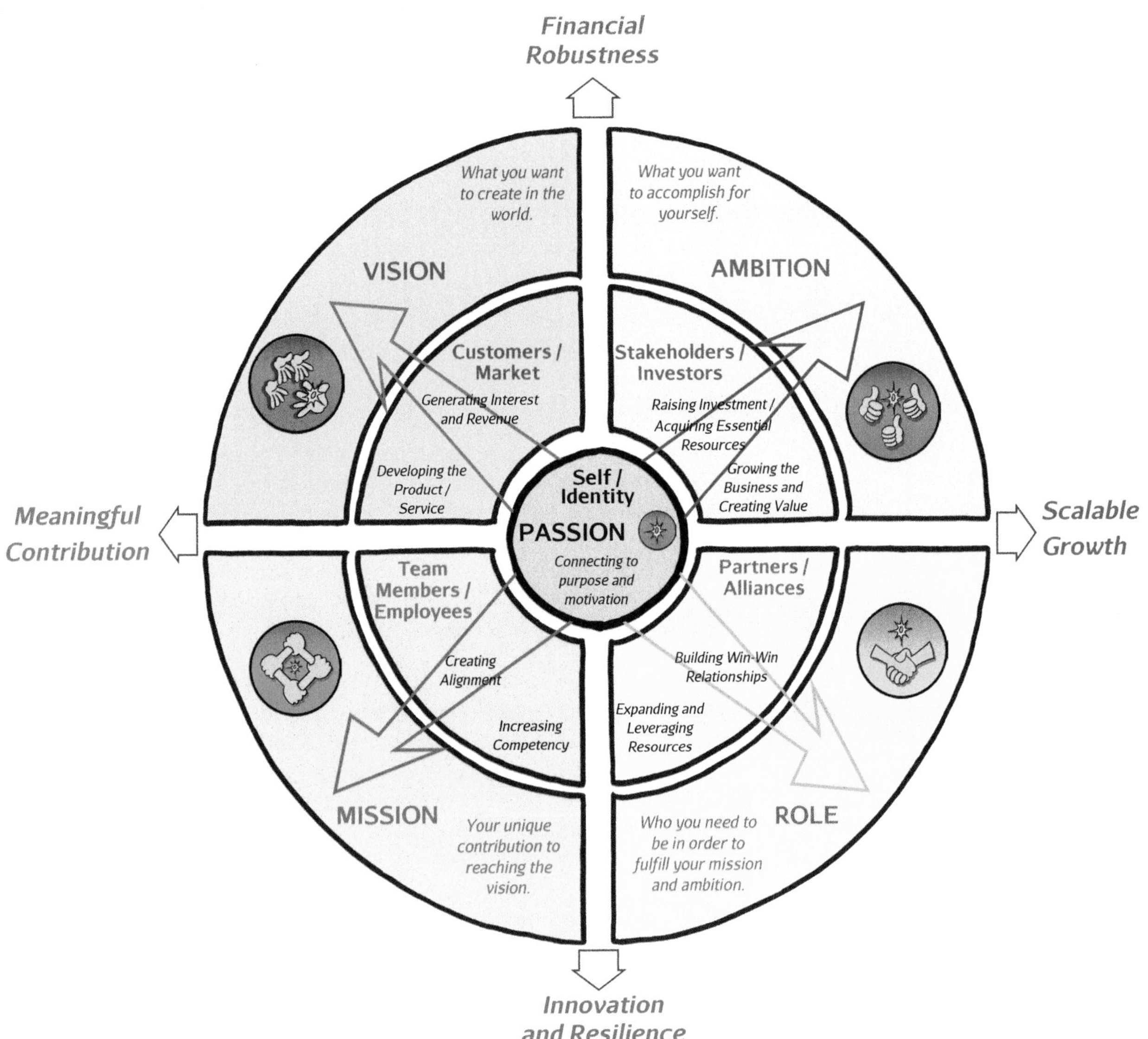

Vision, Mission, Ambition and Role, and the SFM Circle of Success™

Example: Elon Musk's Circle of Success

Elon Musk's uncanny ability to create game changing innovations and turn them into sustainable businesses provides a clear example of the potential of an entrepreneurial mindset and the importance of knowing how to build a Circle of Success.

A good illustration of how to build a Circle of Success is the example of Elon Musk presented in Chapter 1. Musk's early passion for "collective enlightenment" and desire to change things for the better were the foundation for a generative vision to "increase the scope and scale of human consciousness" and "make a positive difference in the future of humanity." That bigger vision manifested in specific products such as electric cars, solar energy panels and reusable rocket ships.

The unprecedented interest in products such as the Powerwall and the Tesla Model 3, in spite of little or no advertising, illustrate how interest and revenue can be generated by the passion ignited in current and future customers who believe strongly in the vision a venture is attempting to reach.

Musk's mission to "accelerate the world's transition to sustainable energy and help make humanity a multi-planet civilization" and his ability to identify and prioritize worthy challenges and problems has allowed him to surround himself with teams made up of the world's the leading professionals and experts. His capacity to unite them around a challenge, and have them "work together to the best of their abilities" has allowed his ventures to make meaningful contributions and "achieve great things." As Musk explains:

> *I think it's important that everyone understands exactly what the mission is, what the goal is and that when they join the company, they be brought into that overall goal. As long as that goal is clearly defined and understood and people are saying "yes," they agree with that goal when they join the company—so, they are not just joining for a salary but they believe in what the company is doing—then you can go back to them and if their activity is not aligned with the company, you can say: "Hey, you need to change your behavior in this particular way." And then they usually do. On rare occasions when somebody does not, then you have to be prepared to let them go from the team.*

Musk's ambition to create "hundreds of thousands of jobs and a more inspiring future for all" has allowed him to attract and acquire investment and other essential resources with which to pursue his vision. His ability for "relevance optimization" and balancing contribution to humanity with financial return and economic viability has made it possible for him to expand his business and create value for investors and other stakeholders.

Musk's powerful strategy of "relevance optimization" brings together vision and contribution to humanity with ambition and profitability for investors and other stakeholders.

Musk's role as a catalyst for change and "open source" approach for technology has opened the door to a number of important win-win partnerships that allow him to move his ventures forward at an accelerated pace. His is company Open AI, for instance, has major partnerships with Microsoft, Y Combinator and others. Tesla has established a partnership with potential competitor BMW to develop battery technology. Solar City has partnered with Nest to install "smart" thermostats that improve energy use. In addition to NASA, SpaceX has partnerships with airline companies like Boeing and has recently established a key partnership with Google to launch satellites that would provide worldwide Internet coverage.

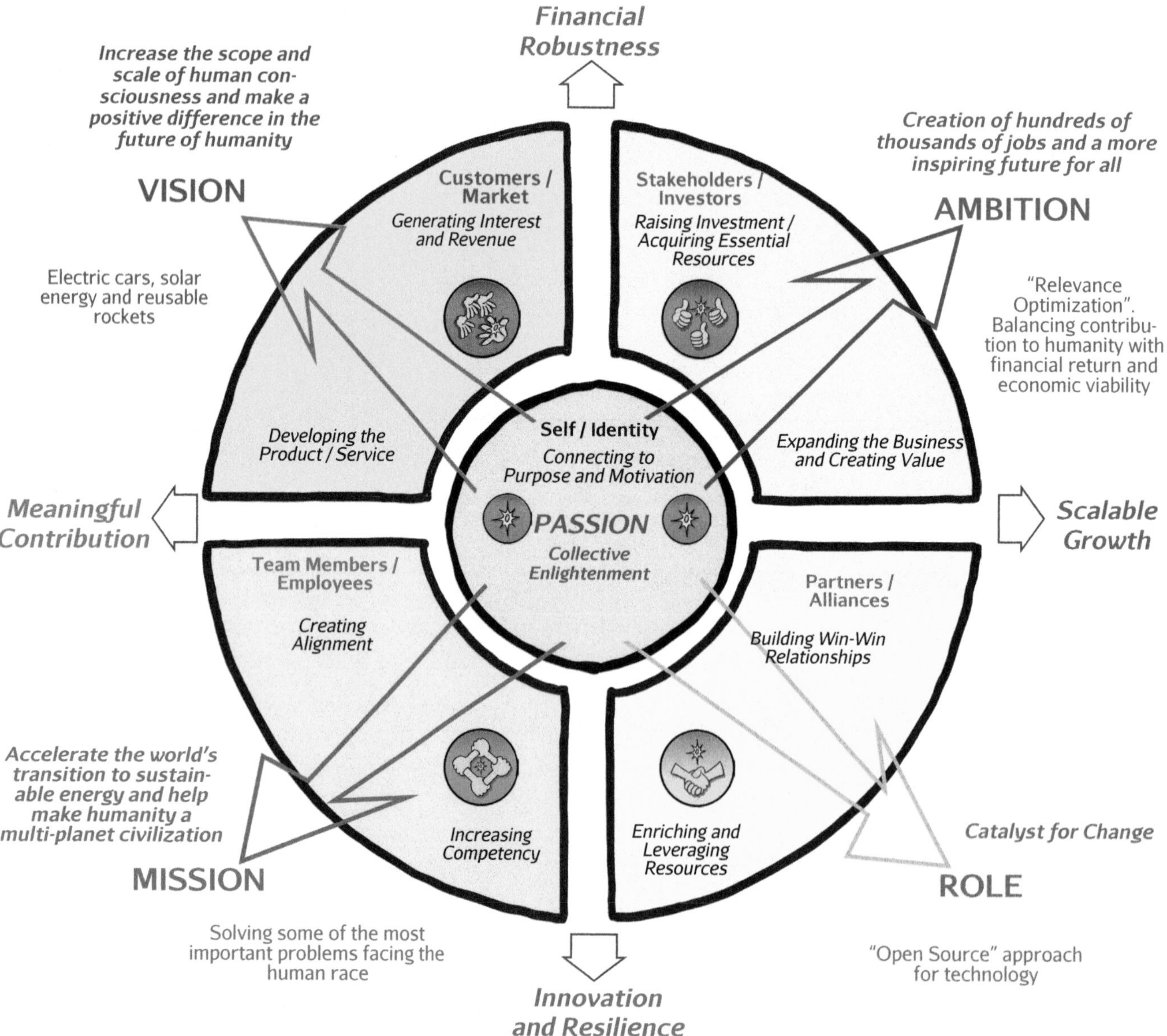
Elon Musk's Circle of Success
Financial Robustness
Increase the scope and scale of human consciousness and make a positive difference in the future of humanity
VISION
Electric cars, solar energy and reusable rockets
Creation of hundreds of thousands of jobs and a more inspiring future for all
AMBITION
"Relevance Optimization". Balancing contribution to humanity with financial return and economic viability
Customers / Market
Generating Interest and Revenue
Stakeholders / Investors
Raising Investment / Acquiring Essential Resources
Developing the Product / Service
Self / Identity
Connecting to Purpose and Motivation
Expanding the Business and Creating Value
Meaningful Contribution
PASSION
Collective Enlightenment
Scalable Growth
Team Members / Employees
Creating Alignment
Partners / Alliances
Building Win-Win Relationships
Accelerate the world's transition to sustainable energy and help make humanity a multi-planet civilization
MISSION
Increasing Competency
Enriching and Leveraging Resources
Catalyst for Change
ROLE
Solving some of the most important problems facing the human race
"Open Source" approach for technology
Innovation and Resilience

ELON MUSK'S CIRCLE OF SUCCESS
VISION
Customers / Market
INCREASE THE SCOPE AND SCALE OF HUMAN CONSCIOUSNESS AND MAKE A POSITIVE DIFFERENCE IN THE FUTURE OF HUMANITY.
* ELECTRIC CARS, SOLAR ENERGY AND REUSABLE ROCKETS
AMBITION
Stakeholders / Investors
CREATION OF HUNDREDS OF THOUSANDS OF JOBS AND A MORE INSPIRING FUTURE FOR ALL
* RELEVANCE OPTIMIZATION". BALANCING CONTRIBUTION TO HUMANITY WITH FINANCIAL RETURN AND ECONOMIC VIABILITY
MISSION
Team Members / Employees
ACCELERATE THE WORLD'S TRANSITION TO SUSTAINABLE ENERGY AND HELP MAKE HUMANITY A MULTI-PLANET CIVILIZATION
* SOLVING SOME OF THE MOST IMPORTANT PROBLEMS FACING THE HUMAN RACE
ROLE
Partners / Alliances
CATALYST FOR CHANGE
* "OPEN SOURCE" APPROACH FOR TECHNOLOGY
Self / Identity - Passion
COLLECTIVE ENLIGHTENMENT

The SFM Success Mindset Map™

The SFM Success Mindset Map™ identifies three main areas of a successful mindset: Meta, Macro and Micro.

A major mission of Success Factor Modeling is to help entrepreneurs and conscious leaders of all kinds build an effective Circle of Success like Elon Musk. As part of this mission, my colleague Mickey A. Feher—an international entrepreneur and coach—and I, with the support of SFM illustrator Antonio Meza, have developed what we call the *SFM Success Mindset Map™*.

To create the map, we have applied the distinctions of Success Factor Modeling to analyze well-known entrepreneurs such as Elon Musk, Steve Jobs of *Apple Inc.*, Richard Branson of the *Virgin Group*, Jeff Bezos of *Amazon.com*, Howard Schultz of *Starbucks*, Muhammed Yunus of *Grameen Bank*, Anita Roddick of *The Body Shop*, and many others. In addition to the key elements of entrepreneurial mindset listed earlier—passion, vision, mission, ambition and role—we have established a number of other specific patterns of mindset, behaviors and habits that support Next Generation Entrepreneurship and Conscious Leadership.

In fact, the SFM Success Mindset Map™ identifies three main areas of a successful mindset:

1. *Meta Mindset* – Big-picture clarity
2. *Macro Mindset* – Habits of success
3. *Micro Mindset* – Ongoing priorities

Mindset Maps International has created an App that allows you to assess your strengths in the various areas of the SFM Success Mindset Map™. (Available at *http://www.mindsetmaps.com.)*

Our **Meta Mindset** has to do with our fundamental attitude toward our work, our world and our place in that world. Meta Mindset relates to success factors at the levels of *purpose* and *identity*. Our Meta Mindset is essentially made up of our sense of passion, vision, mission, ambition and role. These provide the "*big-picture clarity*" with regard to our project or venture.

Macro Mindset relates to the mental disciplines and practices required to bring focus to the big-picture of our venture and begin to put it into action. These practices and disciplines involve success factors at the level of *capabilities* such as managing our energy and focus, seeking honest and frequent feedback, scanning for opportunities, dealing effectively with risks and adversity, and recharging and balancing ourselves. In this sense, our Macro Mindset defines our *habits of success*.

Our **Micro Mindset** produces and guides the specific actions necessary build a sustainable venture. Micro Mindset focuses on success factors at the level of *behaviors*. It determines our *ongoing priorities* such as clarifying purpose and motivation, developing our product or service, generating interest and revenue, growing and aligning an effective team, acquiring necessary resources, expanding our business, creating value for stakeholders and building win-win partnerships that enrich and leverage available resources.

These three areas of mindset may be integrated together to make up what we call the "SFM Mindset Compass." The fundamental notion of a **Mindset Compass** is that particular aspects of mindset are more needed to achieve the various core outcomes defined by the Circle of Success than others. Securing financial robustness, for instance, would require a different combination of Meta, Macro and Micro Mindset attributes than would be necessary for, say, increasing innovation and resilience. Thus, similar to a literal compass, the SFM Mindset Compass shows which course to take if you want or need to move your project or venture in a certain direction.

In summary, the Mindset Compass specifies which elements of the three areas of mindset, Meta, Macro and Micro, are most important and relevant for achieving the various core outcomes defined by the Circle of Success. Depending upon your *Meta Goal* or *current focus* for your venture, that outcome could be enhancing personal satisfaction, making a meaningful contribution, securing financial robustness, increasing innovation and resilience or achieving scalable growth. The Mindset Compass helps you to identify your particular aptitudes and tendencies and to know which ones you need to prioritize and strengthen in order to take your project or venture to the next level.

The SFM Mindset Compass specifies which elements of the three areas of mindset, Meta, Macro and Micro, are most important and relevant for achieving the various core outcomes defined by the Circle of Success.

In the remainder of this chapter, you will have a chance to explore each of these areas of your own mindset and to reflect upon your strengths and areas for development. I will provide more in-depth information on each of the mindset areas and you will have the opportunity to do some of the accurate self-analysis that Elon Musk has claimed is so crucial for success. Let's begin this exploration with Meta Mindset.

Meta Mindset - Big picture clarity

As we have established, *Meta Mindset* relates to success factors at the levels of *purpose* and *identity* and has to do with our fundamental attitude toward our work, our world and our place in that world. To help clarify and enrich each element of Meta Mindset, Mickey Feher and I have selected a well-known entrepreneur who typifies each aspect of Meta Mindset to serve as a type of role model.

Starting a new venture is also very much like the journeys taken by the early explorers. They needed to have a certain mindset and tools in order to arrive at their desired destinations. We have thus also chosen to use a number of legendary explorers, navigators and leaders, such as Ulysses, Earnest Shakleton, Christopher Columbus, Sir Francis Drake, Admiral Horatio Nelson and Noah, to symbolize key aspects of the Meta Mindset of Next Generation Entrepreneurs and Conscious Leaders.

The Meta Mindset of successful entrepreneurs and leaders is made up of the following six elements.

Meta Mindset - Big picture clarity

1. Know what you really love to do (Know what you are passionate about).

Passion is an intense desire or enthusiasm for something. It is a relentless inner drive to find what it is that you care deeply about and for which you have talent and pursue it with all of your heart. Our symbol for passion is the **spark** that ignites the fire of your enthusiasm, determination and energy for making a difference.

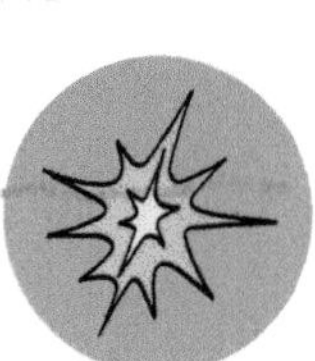

You need passion and energy to create a truly successful business. There is no greater thing you can do with your life and your work than follow your passions—in a way that serves the world and you.

Richard Branson – *The Virgin Group*

We have chosen entrepreneur **Richard Branson** as the role model for passion in business. Acknowledged as a passionate and inspiring leader, Branson is best known as the founder of Virgin Group, which comprises more than 400 companies. Of starting his businesses, Branson claimed, "My interest in life comes from setting myself huge, apparently unachievable challenges and trying to rise above them ... from the perspective of wanting to live life to the full, I felt that I had to attempt it."

We have selected the famous mythical traveler **Ulysses** as our other role model for passion. In the works of Homer, Dante and Tennyson, Ulysses is depicted as a passionate voyager who "lusts for adventure." In the *Odyssey* Homer's Ulysses fervently states "*The journey is the thing*." Claiming that "Each man delights in the work that suits him best," Ulysses declares: "*Let me not then die ingloriously and without a struggle, but let me first do some great thing that shall be told among men hereafter*."

Ulysses

According to Tennyson's Ulysses, "*I cannot rest from travel: I will drink Life to the lees [the sediment at the bottom of the bottle]; all times I have enjoy'd greatly, have suffer'd greatly, both with those that loved me, and alone.*" He claims that he is driven by the desire "*to strive, to seek, to find and not to yield.*"

Passion for what you are doing is the foundation for a success mindset.

To explore this aspect of your Meta Mindset, reflect upon how clearly you are able to answer the following questions:

- *What do you really love to do?*
- *What are you excited about?*
- *What is interesting and compelling for you?*
- *What brings you a deep sense of enthusiasm and energy?*

2. Know what you want to help create in the longer term future (Are clear about your destination; and your longer term vision)

A vision is "a mental image of what the future will or could be like" that focuses on how people's lives could be improved in some way.

Vision can best be defined as "a mental image of what the future will or could be like." The creative vision of successful entrepreneurs has to do with this ability to imagine and focus on longer-term possibilities that improve our lives in some way. It involves the ability to see beyond the confines of the "here and now" and imagine future scenarios. It also involves the capacity to set and stay focused on longer-term goals, adopting long-term plans and a holistic view. Our symbol for this type of vision is a **map** that shows the destination you are attempting to reach.

We are stubborn on vision. We are flexible on details... Amazon.com strives to be the e-commerce destination where consumers can find and discover anything they want to buy online.

Jeff Bezos – *Amazon.com*

Jeff Bezos, founder of the Internet e-commerce giant Amazon, is our role model for vision. Bezos claims he left his "well-paying job" at a New York City hedge fund to when he "learned about the rapid growth in Internet use" in the United States. He saw this as a major opportunity for people to have easier access to products (initially books) and pay less because they did not have to pay taxes on online purchases. He launched Amazon.com in 1994 after making the cross-country drive from New York to Seattle, writing up the Amazon business plan on the way. Like other budding entrepreneurs, he initially launched his vision from his garage. By 2014, Amazon had become the world's largest on-line retailer.

I made a vow to myself that some day I would go to the region of ice and snow and go on and on till I came to one of the poles of the earth, the end of the axis upon which this great round ball turns.

Ernest Shackleton

Sir Ernest Henry Shackleton was a polar explorer who led three British expeditions to the Antarctic. As a result of his relentless pursuit of his of his vision, Shackleton was the first person to see and travel on the South Polar Plateau. Shackleton's self-sacrificing leadership and determination to reach his destination against all odds made him one of the principal figures of the period known as the Heroic Age of Antarctic Exploration.

To explore this aspect of your Meta Mindset, reflect upon how clearly you are able to answer the following questions:

- *What do you want to create in the world through you that is beyond you?*
- *What new possibilities do you want to see in the world?*
- *What is the world to which you want to belong?*

3. Are clear about your direction, regardless of whether or not you know the ultimate destination.

A vision for the future is sometimes more about a particular direction than a specific goal or destination.

Vision is about looking into the future to see what you want to create in the world through your venture. When we look far away, however, we cannot always see the final result so clearly. Sometimes an entrepreneur has a direction in mind, but *not* a specific end-goal or destination. Entrepreneurs like Jeff Bezos were very clear on their destination. Others like Anita Roddick knew their direction but not the ultimate destination.

We have chosen a **compass** to represent this type of vision; in which you know which direction you want to go, but not necessarily where you will end up.

Anita Roddick was a British businesswoman, human rights activist and environmental campaigner, best known as the founder of *The Body Shop*—a cosmetics company producing and retailing natural beauty products that shaped ethical consumerism. The company was one of the first to prohibit the use of ingredients tested on animals and one of the first to promote fair trade with third world countries.

Roddick, however, initially just wanted to create a livelihood for herself and her daughter. She also believed that the world needed to "Go Green," as she put it. Based on her early travels around the world she kept asking herself "Why waste a container when you can refill it?" "What if you could build a venture that is based on a green philosophy and fair trade?" Roddick claimed that she had no clue how she built a corporation that: "is a multi local business with over 2,045 stores serving over 77 million customers in 51 different markets in 25 different languages and across 12 time zones." She clearly had the "compass" but not the Map with the exact destination.

You can create an honorable livelihood, where you take your skills and use them and you earn a living from it, it gives you a sense of freedom and allows you to balance your life the way you want.

Crazy people see and feel things that others don't. But you have to believe that everything is possible. If you believe it, those around you will believe it too.

Anita Roddick – *The Body Shop*

Christopher Columbus is the iconic example of a traveler who was clear about his direction, but had no real idea of exactly where it would lead him and his crew. Convinced that the Earth was spherical and that he could reach the East Indies by sailing West long enough, Columbus used a compass to stick to his (magnetic) westward course for weeks at a time. By doing so, he ended up discovering a whole new world, unknown to Europeans of the time, and launched the beginning of the European exploration and colonization of the American continents.

I am not solicitous to examine particularly everything here, which indeed could not be done in fifty years, because my desire is to make all possible discoveries.

Christopher Columbus

To explore this aspect of your Meta Mindset, reflect upon how clearly you are able to answer the following questions:

- *What do you want to see better or different in the world?*
- *What do you want to see more of and less of in the future?*

The mission of an individual or organization has to do with their contribution to a purpose and vision that is bigger than themselves.

4. Know your purpose — know what you stand for and why you are doing what you are doing. Are clear about your mission — the unique contribution you want to make through your venture.

The *mission* of an individual or organization has to do with their contribution to manifesting a particular vision. The word comes from the Latin *missio*, which means "the act of sending." In fact, mission is defined in the dictionary as "an important assignment carried out for political, religious, or commercial purposes." Mission relates to the unique gift and contribution that you bring to the table as you set on your journey to realize your vision. The mission of individual within an organization has to do with his or her contribution to that organization and its vision. Similarly, an organization's mission will be with respect to the larger system of its customers and their needs.

We have selected a **barrel** as the symbol for purpose and mission as it represents the cargo you are bringing to others in order to make a positive difference in their lives.

Making money is a happiness. And that's a great incentive. Making other people happy is a super-happiness.
Muhammed Yunus – *Grameen Bank*

Muhammed Yunus is a powerful role model for the sense of purpose and mission. He is the founder of *Grameen Bank* which pioneered the concept of micro-credit for supporting entrepreneurs in developing countries (see *SFM Vol. I*, pp. 66-67). Yunus' vision emerged when he discovered that very small loans could make a huge difference for people who had scarce economic resources. In his native country of Bangladesh, for instance, Yanus observed that village women who made bamboo furniture struggled to keep their small businesses going and were often taken advantage of when they tried to borrow money. Traditional banks did not want to make loans to poor people due to what they perceived as the high risk of default. Yunus, however, was convinced that, given the chance, the women would be more than willing to repay the money and a reasonable amount of interest. Yunus lent $27 of his own money to 42 women in the village and made a small but significant profit on every loan. This validated his vision and reinforced his belief that microcredit was a viable business model that could positively transform the lives of people living in poverty.

On 1 October 1983, Yunus launched a full-fledged bank for poor Bangladeshis named Grameen Bank ("Village Bank"). By July 2007 Grameen had issued $6.38 billion to 7.4 million borrowers. In 2006, Yunnus and Grameen Bank received the Nobel Peace Prize for these efforts, the success of which has inspired similar programs throughout the world.

Noah is the Biblical character who built a gigantic vessel (an Ark) in order to save the animal species of the earth (gathering them two-by-two) from being wiped out as a result of a vast flood. Clearly, Noah represents a traveler with no particular direction or destination but rather has a strong mission and purpose – the preservation of terrestrial life on earth. As a role model, Noah diligently accepted his calling to serve something bigger than himself and never wavered from it.

A great flood is coming. The waters of the heavens will meet the waters of earth. We build a vessel to survive the storm. We build an Ark.

Noah

To explore this aspect of your Meta Mindset, reflect upon how clearly you are able to answer the following questions:

- *What is your service to the bigger system and vision?*
- *What is your unique contribution to making the vision happen?*
- *What are the special gifts, resources, capabilities and actions that you bring to the larger system in order to help reach the vision?*

5. Are clear about your ambition — what you want to become and achieve in the next two to five years.

Ambition is a result of the desire and determination to achieve success and recognition for oneself. Ambition is defined as "a strong desire to do or to achieve something, typically requiring determination and hard work" that brings us personal benefit. Our ambitions in the form of dreams and aspirations for our lives arise from a healthy ego and come from the drive for growth and mastery. Ambitions arise from our personal dreams, desires, drives and needs. In addition to making a reasonable or good living from our endeavors, for example, we may have a desire for growth, a drive for achievement or a need for recognition and approval.

Ambition is a function of the desire for achievement and acknowledgment. It arises from the drive for growth and mastery.

We have chosen a **timer** as the symbol for ambition for two reasons. Firstly, it represents a type of "race against time"; an attempt to achieve something within a defined period. Secondly, it indicates the notion that, as Steve Jobs pointed out, our "time is limited" and it is important to stay focused on our goals and aspirations.

We're here to put a dent in the universe. Otherwise why else even be here? Our goal is to make the best devices in the world, not to be the biggest.

Your time is limited, so don't waste it living someone else's life.

Steve Jobs – *Apple Inc.*

Disturb us, Lord, when we are too pleased with ourselves, when our dreams have come true, because we dreamed too little, when we arrived safely. Because we sailed too close to the shore.

Disturb us, Lord, to dare more boldly, to venture on wilder seas where storms will show Your mastery; where losing sight of land, we shall find the stars.

Sir Francis Drake

The role of a person or organization is a result of the place they have and the purpose they serve with respect to others.

In many ways, **Steve Jobs** is the epitome of entrepreneurial ambition (see *SFM Vol. I*, pp 252-280). Jobs founded Apple Computer with Steve Wozniak in a garage in "Silicon Valley" in the San Francisco Bay Area, California in 1976 at the age of 21. When the company went public in 1980, it generated more capital than any stock market launch since the Ford Motor Company in 1956, and created 300 new millionaires overnight. By the time of Jobs' death in October 2011, Apple had become the largest technology firm in the world with revenue for the year of $127.8 billion in sales. In March 2012 its stock market value had reached $500 billion.

Sir Francis Drake is a vivid role model for a bold and ambitious adventurer. An English sea captain, privateer, navigator and politician of the Elizabethan era, Drake carried out the second circumnavigation of the world in a single expedition, from 1577 to 1580. His incursion into the Pacific also initiated an era of privateering and piracy against the Spanish on the western coast of the Americas. He was second-in-command of the English fleet that defeated the Spanish Armada in 1588. The most renowned British seaman of his time, Drake was awarded knighthood in 1581 by Elizabeth I.

To explore this aspect of your Meta Mindset, reflect upon how clearly you are able to answer the following questions:

- *What type of life do you want to create for yourself?*
- *What do you want to accomplish? What type of status and performance do you want to achieve with respect to yourself and others?*
- *What would you like to be recognized and/or remembered for? What would like to be able to add to your resume or biography?*

6. Are clear about your role – the position you have with respect to others in your market/environment.

Role is defined as "the function assumed or part played by a person in a particular situation." Thus, roles are related to both "function"—which is based upon competency—and "the part played"—which is determined by one's position or status. So, on one hand, a role reflects personal skills, abilities, and effort. It is related to what a person does (or is expected to do). In fact, people are most successful in roles that are "compatible with their personal characteristics and skills." On the other hand, role reflects "status"; i.e., who we are in relation to others. In other words, role is an intersection of both the position a person occupies with respect to others, and the expected capabilities and behaviors attached to that position.

We have selected a **flag** as the symbol for role as flags themselves are most often used as potent symbols representing role, status or identification with a particular function or identity.

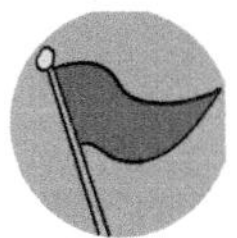

Starbucks has become ubiquitous around the world as a brand that represents a particular role known as "coffeehouse culture." Dating back to the 14th century, coffeehouses in Western Europe and the Eastern Mediterranean were traditionally social hubs, as well as artistic and intellectual centers. **Howard Schultz** had a vision to bring the role and tradition of the Italian coffeehouse to the United States, making it "a place for conversation and a sense of community; a third place between work and home." Embracing this role, Schultz set out to make Starbucks a different kind of company. One that not only celebrated coffee and the rich tradition, but that also brought a feeling of connection. Today Starbucks is considered the main representative of "second wave coffee" and operates 23,768 locations worldwide in more than 70 different countries.

Starbucks has a role and a meaningful relationship with people that is not only about the coffee.

Howard Schultz – *Starbucks*

Lord Horatio Nelson was one of Britain's greatest naval commanders. He had a long and distinguished career, in which he gained a reputation as a master tactician and for great personal bravery. Nelson is a compelling example of someone who has found and embraced his or her role. At the age of only 12, Nelson joined the navy as an apprentice working in the lowest naval ranks. However his aptitude and enthusiasm for his job saw him rapidly rise through the ranks, until he was given his own ship and made a captain at only 20 years old. Over the years, Nelson developed a reputation as a very good commander, who was daring, bold and – when necessary – willing to disobey orders. He would lose his right arm and the sight in one of his eyes in the fulfillment of his post. Nelson's crowning moment came at the Battle of Trafalgar, where Britain's decisive victory over Napoleon's fleet ended the threat of a French invasion of England. It also cost Nelson his life. Shortly before his death, he was heard to murmur – "Thank God I have done my duty."

Recollect that you must be a seaman to be an officer and also that you cannot be a good officer without being a gentleman.

Duty is the great business of a sea officer; all private considerations must give way to it, however painful it may be.

Admiral Horatio Nelson

To explore this aspect of your Meta Mindset, reflect upon how clearly you are able to answer the following questions:

- *What type of person do you need to be and role do you need to have in order to create the life you want as well as succeed in your ambition? Mission? Vision?*
- *What is your position with respect to others in your environment/market.*
- *What are the core competences necessary to be the type of person you need to or to achieve and remain in the necessary position or status?*

Assessing Your Meta Mindset

Assess your Meta Mindset by rating the following six statements on a scale of 0–10 (where 10 is the most true for you and 0 is not true for you at all).

1. **I know what I really love to do (I know what I am passionate about).**

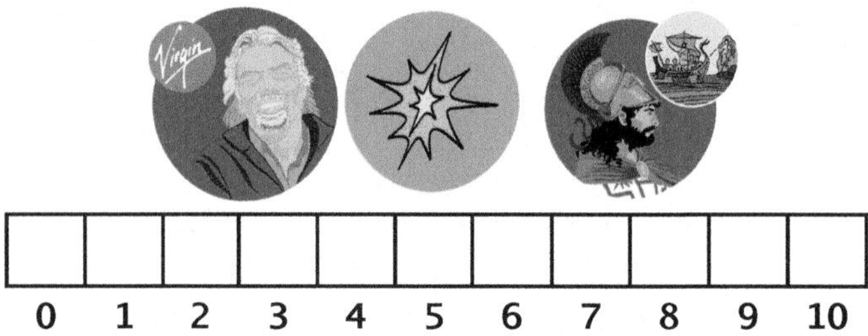

2. **I know what I want to help create in the longer term future (I am clear about my destination; and my longer term vision)**

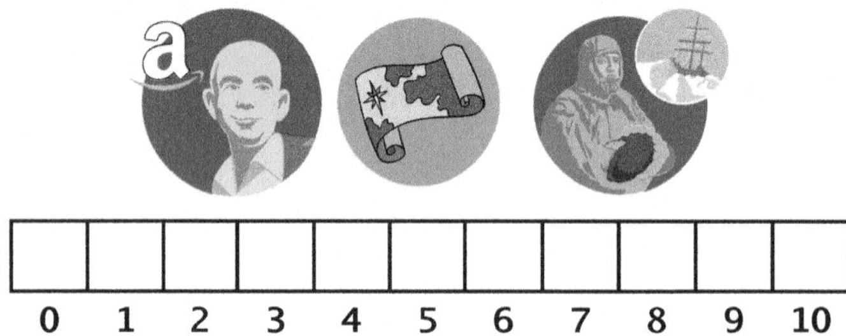

3. **I am clear about my direction, regardless of whether or not I know the ultimate destination.**

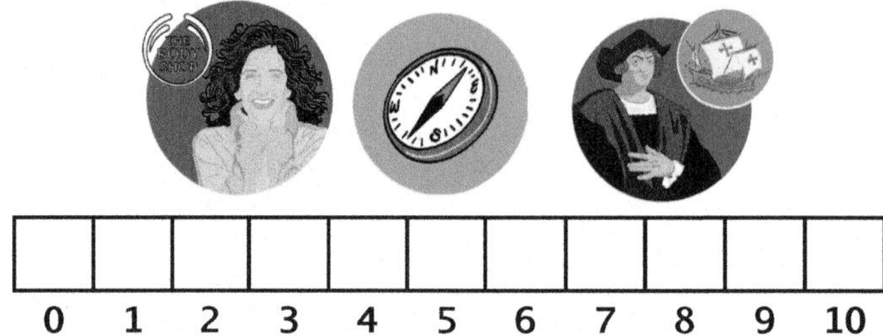

4. **I know my purpose - I know what I stand for and why I am doing what I am doing. I am clear about my mission - the unique contribution I want to make through my venture.**

5. **I am clear about my ambition - i.e., what I want to become and achieve in the next two to five years.**

6. **I am clear about my role - i.e., the position I have with respect to others in my market/environment.**

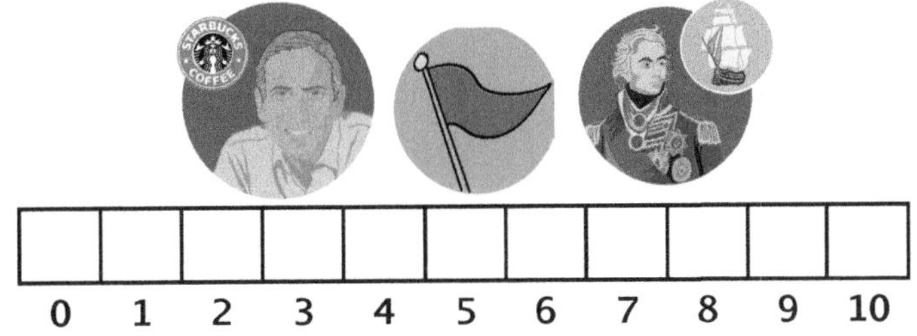

Now, reflect on the answers that you have given above. Which ones are below a rating of 7? These are areas for potential improvement. They may even be essential areas for improvement depending upon your goals for your project or venture as we shall see.

Over the course of the rest of this book, I will be providing tools and exercises to help you to develop these various aspects of your Meta Mindset. There are also some important and useful exercises in *Success Factor Modeling Volume I.*

- Clarifying your passion: pp. 175-179
- Clarifying your long-term vision and destination: pp. 200-201
- Clarifying your direction (even if the destination is not clear): pp. 206-207
- Clarifying your mission and contribution: pp. 213-216
- Clarifying your ambition: pp. 222-228 and 233-235
- Clarifying your role: pp. 236-237

Macro Mindset - Habits of success

Macro Mindset - Habits of success

As stated previously, Macro Mindset relates to the mental disciplines and practices required to bring focus to the big-picture of your venture and begin to put it into action. Like lifting barbells, such practices strengthen the mental discipline necessary for sustainable success. These involve such capabilities as managing your energy and focus, seeking honest and frequent feedback, scanning for opportunities, dealing effectively with risks and adversity, and recharging and balancing yourself.

The Macro Mindset of successful entrepreneurs and leaders is made up of the following five "habits of success." I have selected quotes from a number of successful entrepreneurs to help define and clarify the significance and purpose of each practice.

It's very rewarding when you work on something that you think is going to make a big difference. Yes, it's a little bit harder, but I think the passion one might bring with it brings so much more energy to that that you are more likely to succeed.

Sergey Brin – Google

1. **Do what you are passionate about and invest a lot of energy and focus into making what you want happen.**

   We have chosen the symbol of the **sail** for this aspect of mindset as it indicates that you have the energy and motivation for your venture and are ready to go "full sail" for what you want. This is an essential attribute needed to begin or complete any entrepreneurial endeavor.

   You have to have an emotional investment in what you are doing. If you don't love what you are doing, failure is pretty much guaranteed. Success is not guaranteed by any means, but failure is much more likely if you don't love what you are doing.
   — **Biz Stone** – Twitter

Constantly seek out criticism. A well thought out critique of whatever you are doing is as valuable as gold. And you should seek that from everyone you can, but particularly your friends.

Elon Musk – Tesla, SpaceX, Solar City`

2. **Seek feedback and have established ways to get honest and frequent feedback.**

   We have chosen the symbol of the **Telescope** or "**Spyglass**" for this aspect of mindset as it indicates that you have the means to get ongoing and relevant feedback. Getting honest and frequent feedback is an important habit of success in order to avoid problems and obstacles and make necessary course corrections.

   What you really need to do is think, "What is the smallest possible test that I can run for this idea, for this concept, for this theory?" Get it out there and get customers using it, because your customers are going to be the ones to tell you if its really working or not. — **Leah Busque** – TaskRabbit

3. **Constantly scan for opportunities and invest time to create them.**

We have chosen the symbol of the *Crow's Nest* for this aspect of mindset as it indicates that you have the habit in place to consistently scan your horizon for possibilities and "weak signals" that may indicate important opportunities. This is a key characteristic of all successful entrepreneurs.

So, when we are coming up with ideas, we always ask ourselves, "What kind of new market is this creating?" And then also, "What part of my day and what problem is it solving?" And so I've gone as far as taking an entire catalog of my day from the moment I open my eyes and writing down every single thing that I do. And then asking myself, "Is there something here?" —**Kevin Rose** – Digg

One of the things that I do is that I question a lot of things. And you can do that in a good way and a bad way. But hopefully you get people to examine why they are doing something and the way they are thinking.

The worst thing you can end up with is a situation where you get told, "Well, this is the way its always been." That's the worst ever. That's a non-answer. Instead, ask yourself, "Given everything we have today, is there a way we can make this better?"

Daniel ek – Spotify

4. **Are internally grounded and resourceful and have your ways of re charging and balancing yourself and practice them on a daily basis.**

We have chosen the symbol of the *Hammock* for this aspect of mindset as it indicates that you have the means and the discipline to be able to take care of yourself and not become overly stressed or burned out. Having practices that keep you grounded, balanced and recharged is an essential property of sustained and healthy success.

If you don't love it, you won't make it through the long period of pain that is inevitable. So make sure that you take care of yourself during the process, make sure you take care of your mental health, your physical health while you are doing it, because it is a long road. —**Emmett Shear** – Twitch

I've had to deal with lots of mentally challenging situations, like when my world sailing record attempts failed. That's why I keep fit. If your body is sharp, your brain will be sharp.

I run every day. It keeps me fit, keeps the endorphins going and keeps the brain functioning well. I can definitely achieve twice as much in a day by keeping fit.

Richard Branson – The Virgin Group

5. **Are aware of risks and potential problems and don't get discouraged or distracted in the face of adversity and negative feedback.**

We have chosen the symbol of the *Steering Wheel* or *"helm"* for this aspect of mindset as it indicates that you have the tools and resources to remain in control under challenging and changing conditions. Being able to remain focused and "stay the course" is one of the most important attributes of successful entrepreneurs. It is necessary to know how to "take the helm" and steer through stormy waters.

So just go and do it, try it, learn from it. You will fail at some things. That's a learning experience that you need so that you can take it on to the next experience. And don't let people who you may respect, and who you believe know what they are talking about, don't let them tell you it can't be done, because often they will tell you it can't be done, but that 's because they just don't have the courage to try it. —**Pierre Omidyar** – eBay

So many things go wrong when you are starting a company. And people often ask, "What mistakes should you avoid making?" And my answer to that question is, "Don't even bother to try to avoid making mistakes because you are going to make tons of mistakes. The important thing is to learn quickly from whatever mistakes you make and not giving up. There are things that every single year of Facebook's existence could have killed us or made it so that it seemed like moving forward or making any progress just seemed intractable. But you kind of bounce back and you learn. Nothing is impossible. You have to just keep running through the walls.

Mark Zuckerberg – Facebook

Assessing Your Macro Mindset

Assess your Macro Mindset by rating the following five statements on a scale of 0–10 (where 10 is the most true for you and 0 is not true for you at all).

1. **I am doing what I am passionate about and invest a lot of energy and focus into making what I want happen.**

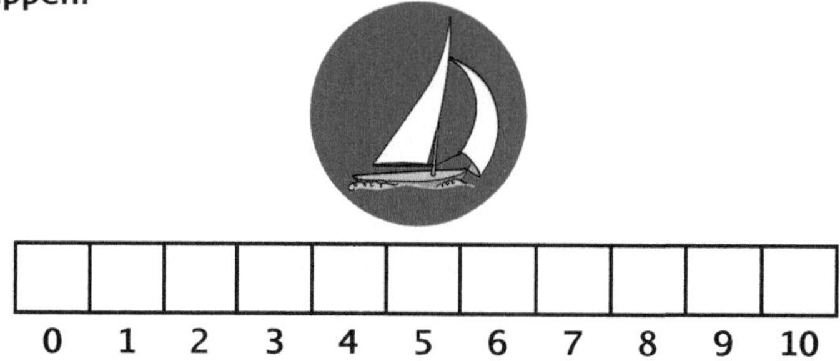

2. **I seek feedback and have established ways to get honest and frequent feedback.**

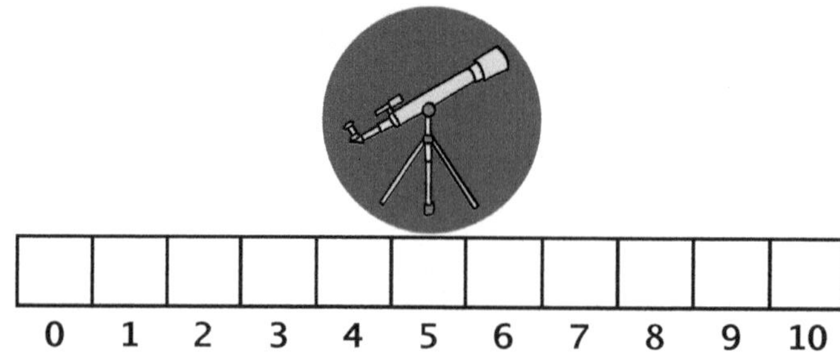

3. **I am constantly scanning for opportunities and invest time to create them.**

4. I am internally grounded and resourceful and have my ways of recharging and balancing myself and practice that on a daily basis.

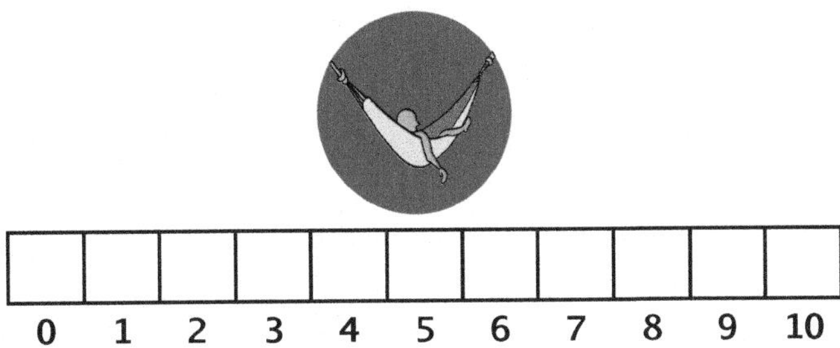

5. I am aware of risks and potential problems and don't get discouraged or distracted in the face of adversity and negative feedback.

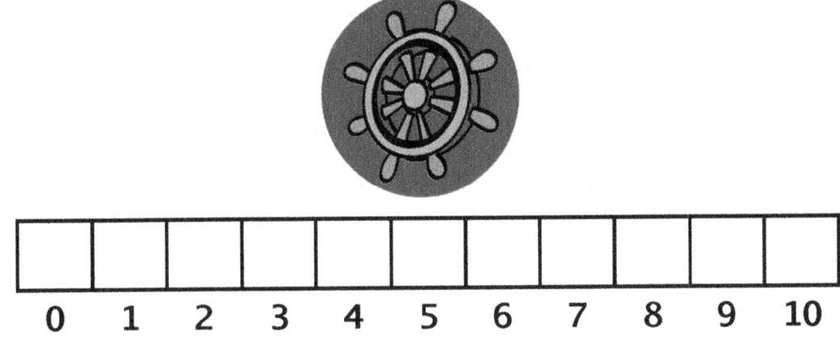

Again, reflect on the answers that you have given above. Which ones are below a rating of 7? These are areas for potential improvement. And, as with the various elements of your Meta Mindset, they may even be essential areas for improvement depending upon your goals for your project or venture. Make note of the ones that have lower ratings. In the coming chapters, you will have an opportunity to develop these various aspects of your Macro Mindset.

Micro Mindset — Ongoing Priorities

Do something you're very passionate about. And don't try to chase what is kind of the "hot passion of the day."

Jeff Bezos – Amazon.com

It is not just about doing focused groups. It is not just about double-checking your vision. It is really about his concept of testing our ideas rigorously throughout the product development process; throughout the marketing process even as we scale up.

Eric Ries – The Lean Startup

Micro Mindset — Ongoing Priorities

As we have established, our *Micro Mindset* produces and guides the specific actions necessary to build a sustainable venture. The Micro Mindset of successful entrepreneurs and leaders is a function of identifying their ongoing priorities.

The Micro Mindset of successful entrepreneurs and leaders is defined with respect to nine critical actions. As with the disciplines of Macro Mindset, I have selected quotes from a number of successful entrepreneurs to help define and clarify the significance and purpose of each practice.

1. **SelfMotivator:** Setting aside the time to explore and reconnect with what you love to do, what is important to you and what you are good at doing — i.e., your passion, your sense purpose and your excellence.

The focus of the SelfMotivator is to keep an ongoing connection to your purpose, passion and motivation in order to live true to yourself and your identity.

I think people who look for great ideas to make money aren't nearly as successful as those who say, "Okay, what do I really love to do? What am I excited about? What do I know something about? What is interesting and compelling?

Michael Dell – Dell

2. **MarketMaker:** Creating opportunities for ongoing dialog with customers and prospects.

The focus of the MarketMaker mindset is to open and maintain dialog with multiple customers and customer representatives in order to generate interest and revenue.

Most startups that fail do it ultimately because they did not make something that people wanted. They made something that they thought people would want, but they were either in denial about whether it was actually any good or somebody else came along and made something that people wanted even more.

Paul Graham – Y Combinator

3. **ProductCreator:** Brainstorming, generating and implementing products, solutions and services that anticipate and fulfill customer needs.

The *ProductCreator* mindset aims to anticipate and fulfill customer needs and desires by developing innovative and empowering solutions (products and services).

> *What this all comes down to is doing something exceptional for your users. Whether its in community, whether its in connection or whether it in design. This is our big advantage as a start up; that we can actually get away with doing that. We can make this the core part of why we are doing business.*
>
> **Alexis Ohanian** – Reddit, Hipmunk

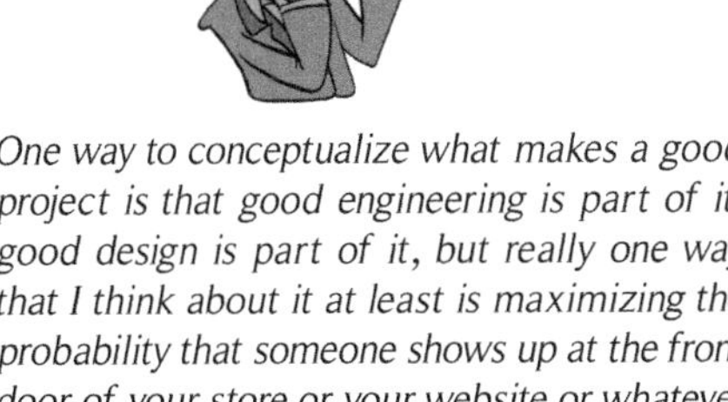

> *One way to conceptualize what makes a good project is that good engineering is part of it, good design is part of it, but really one way that I think about it at least is maximizing the probability that someone shows up at the front door of your store or your website or whatever it is and ends up with a solved problem.*
>
> **Drew Houston** – DropBox

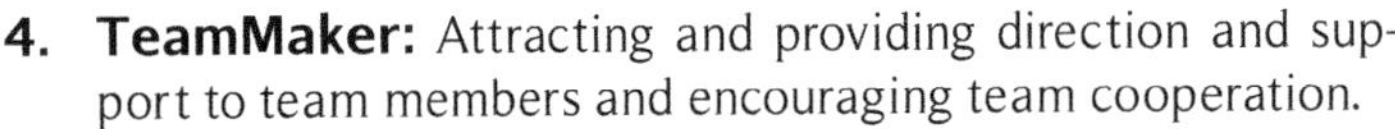

4. **TeamMaker:** Attracting and providing direction and support to team members and encouraging team cooperation.

The emphasis of the *TeamMaker* mindset is to attract and give direction to people who support the mission of the venture (its products and services) by fostering synergy, complementarity and alignment.

> *The hardest thing is to start. You have all these ideas and everyone has an idea, but its really about executing the idea and building the idea and attracting other people to help you work on the idea. That is the biggest challenge. But the way to begin is to get the idea out of your head, draw it out, talk about it, program it if you are a programmer or make it if you building something.*
>
> **Jack Dorsey** – Twitter, Square

> *You don't have to be the best, but you have to be "dangerous." You have to learn just enough to be dangerous to build an idea, concept it and show it to the world. And then it turns out there are lots of other people, including all 170 employees who work at Instagram who are much better at doing all that stuff than I am. But you need to find people that will be drawn to the idea that you build, and then they end up taking it and making it even better.*
>
> **Kevin Systrom** – Instagram

I often half-jokingly say to a lot of people that my job is basically to be the assistant for the rest of the company. My job is to make sure that you have everything that you need to "kick ass." If you don't have that then let me know, because I am not doing my job.

Andrew Ljung – Soundcloud

5. **CompetenceBuilder:** Encouraging and providing opportunities for team members to learn and grow.

The primary attention of the *CompetenceBuilder* mindset is on providing opportunities and resources necessary for team members to grow and to increase competency.

> *I think you should be spending your money on teaching and on sharing. So that might mean hiring a writer or two perhaps instead of a marketing person. And start writing and start getting people to listen to what you are saying. And you can't talk about yourself all the time, because no one is going to come back for that. Talk about things that are relevant for your industry or ideas that you have, and start building up an audience.*
>
> **Jason Fried** – Basecamp

For somebody aspiring to take things to the next level or even surpass their wildest dreams, there is always going to be an element of luck. But I think even more important is putting yourself in a business that can be ubiquitous; that really doesn't have limits. There is always going to be a grind to it, but if it can't be something you can visualize every business using or every consumer using, it is going to be tough to scale up to be big enough or to have the perceived value.

Mark Cuban – Cyber Dust

6. **FinanSourcerer:** Identifying potential investors and providers of other essential resources and creatively getting their interest and commitment to support your venture.

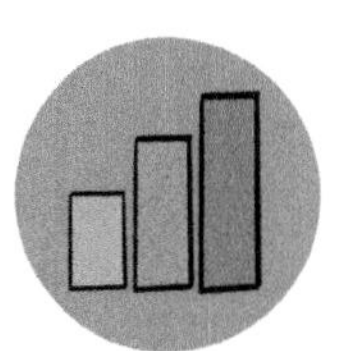

The priority of the *FinanSourcerer* mindset is to identify sources of funds and other essential resources (Stakeholders and Investors) and creatively connect them to the ambitions and strengths of the venture.

> *But understand that naturally no one is interested in your ideas. The world couldn't care less. And you have to persuade them and you have to show that you are the one person out there that can do it.*
>
> **Robert Greene** – 'Mastery'
>
> *So when we see a kid with a lemonade stand its different than when we see a vending machine selling lemonade; even if it is exactly the same product. Because the story around it is what people are paying for. So when I meet small business people, all I ask them is, not what's their balance sheet, but what's their story. Why should I pick you? Why should I care about what you are doing? And if you start giving me all this inside baseball statistics about why you are 2% better than some other competitor I am already glazed over because that's not part of the way I see the world.*
>
> **Seth Godin** – Tribes

7. **VentureBuilder:** Creating and developing a sustainable infrastructure and a path for growth and scalability of your venture.

The *VentureBuilder* mindset concentrates on establishing a sustainable infrastructure and a path to growth and scalability for the venture in order to create value for Investors and other Stakeholders.

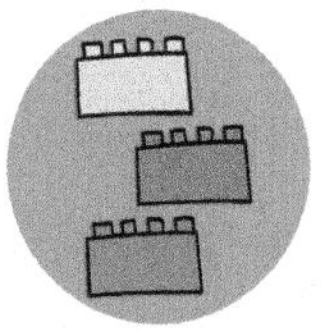

Often times the best methodology is to start with the perfect experience of just one person, get that right and then figure out how to scale something great; instead of scaling something not so great and then trying to improve it. That's really hard to do.

Brian Chesky – Airbnb

There is almost this expectation that you have to have in your mind this sort of "I am going to change the world or make a dent in the universe" kind of ambition. But its actually okay early on to just kind of solve small problems in layers until you actually have the capacity to do that.

Anthony Casalena – Squarespace

Don't think about "how do I get big really fast?" That will happen if you build something super meaningful and super important. So don't think about "What's the quickest way to success?" Think about "What's the best way to build something important that the world really needs?"

Danae Ringelmann – Indiegogo

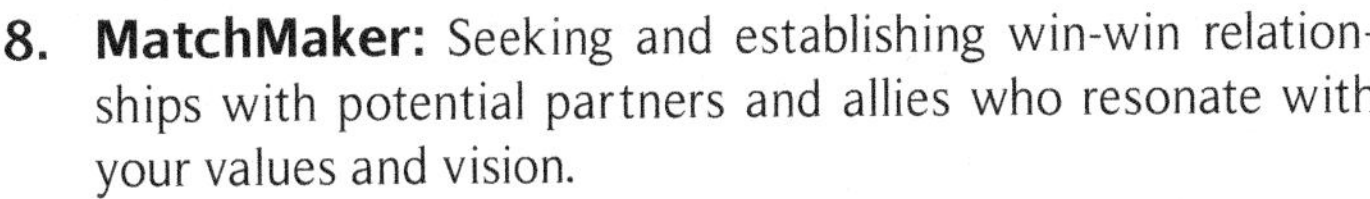

8. **MatchMaker:** Seeking and establishing win-win relationships with potential partners and allies who resonate with your values and vision.

The focus of the *MatchMaker* mindset is to seek other ventures (Partners/Alliances) that share common visions and values and complement one another's roles and strengths (through sharing, combining or exchanging) in order to build win-win relationships.

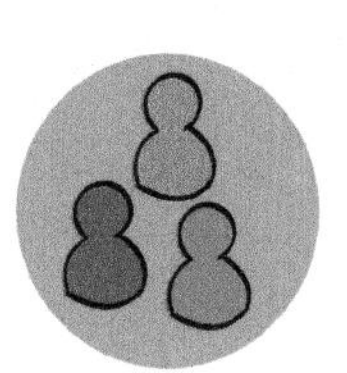

You should find a great partner, no matter what it is that you are doing. And you should look for someone who has very high intelligence, very high energy and very high integrity. You need all three of those and you can't compromise on any one of them. Otherwise, you will end up with someone who is not smart, which does you no good. Or someone who is not hardworking which also does you no good. Or the worse case is you end up with a smart hard-working crook who winds up working against your interests. And integrity is something that takes a lot of time spent with someone to figure out.

Kamal Ravikant – AngelList

The most important thing when you are working with people early on is that you guys line up what your goals are. That sounds really basic. But you can want to run a small business that makes money and you don't have to go to an office every day. Or you can want to build a huge company. You can want to build Google. But I think you have to be really aligned on that.

Ben Silbermann – Pinterest

If you are not utilizing an online community then you are at a disadvantage to those who are. You can be asking an online community if they have any ideas or if they have any advice for what you are working on. Not only will you hear from people who are passionate about the subject, but you will be hearing from people all around the world, each with their own experiences and stories who can help you.

Alan Schaaf – Imgur

9. **ReSourcerer:** Identifying and leveraging synergies between what you are doing and the products, services or competences of other ventures

The primary concern of the *Resourcerer* mindset is to recognize, explore and implement significant synergies with the products, services, competences, etc., of other complementary ventures (Partners/Alliances) in order to enrich and leverage resources.

The most important thing is the individual—whether or not you feel the individual is capable of doing the idea. There are many, many people who have similar ideas and great ideas . . . it's just whether they can actually deliver that idea. So try to work out whether that person will put in all the hours needed, whether they can motivate people. A company is simply a group of people and you want to be actually sure that the person who is coming to you with the idea is somebody that you feel can deliver, and everything else flows from that.

Richard Branson – The Virgin Group

As with the Meta Mindset and Macro Mindset distinctions, we are frequently more competent and comfortable with some of these mindsets than others. Thus, to build our Circle of Success, we need to either develop some of these mindsets more fully or partner with others who are more naturally inclined to the mindsets we lack in order to complement our areas of weaknesses.

For instance, the ProductCreator and TeamMaker mindsets are essential for making a *meaningful contribution*. The CompetenceBuilder and Resourcerer mindsets are necessary in order to produce *innovation and resilience*. The MatchMaker and VentureBuilder mindsets are what make it possible to achieve *scalable growth*. The MarketMaker and FinanSourcer mindsets are required to attain *financial robustness*. The Self-Motivator mindset is the foundation for achieving *personal satisfaction*.

Assessing Your Micro Mindset

Assess your Micro Mindset by rating the statements on the following page by putting an "X" in the columns that most fit for you.

Action	I enjoy it	I am good at it	I am spending time doing it
Setting aside the time to explore and reconnect with what you love to do, what is important to you and what you are good at doing – i.e., your passion, your sense purpose and your excellence.			
Creating opportunities for ongoing dialog with customers and prospects.			
Brainstorming and implementing products and services that antici-pate and fulfill customer needs.			
Attracting and providing direction and support to team members and encouraging team cooperation.			

Action	I enjoy it	I am good at it	I am spending time doing it
 *Encouraging and providing opportunities for team members to learn and grow.*			
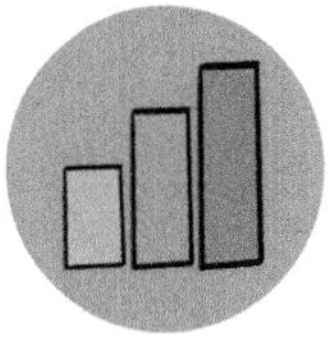 *Identifying potential investors and providers of other essential resources and creatively getting their interest and commitment to support your venture.*			
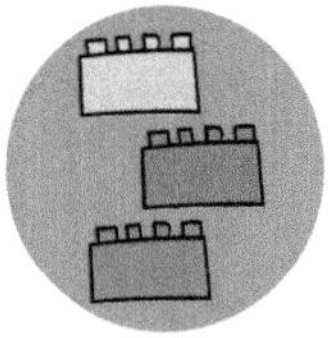 *Creating and developing a sustainable infrastructure and a path for growth and scalability of your venture.*			
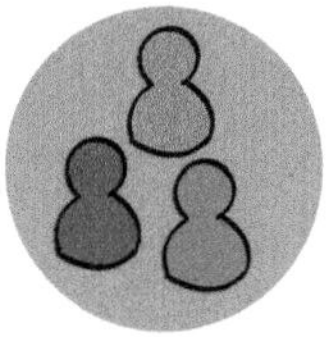 *Seeking and establishing win-win relationships with potential partners and allies who resonate with your values and vision.*			
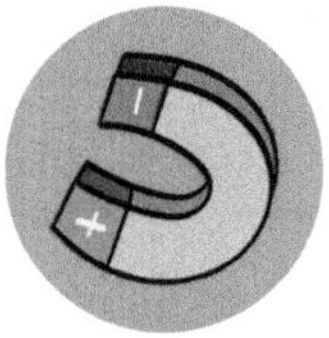 *Identifying and leveraging synergies between what you are doing and the products, services or competences of other ventures.*			

Assessing your Meta, Macro and Micro mindset helps you to identify your areas for development.

This time, as you reflect on the answers that you have given on the previous pages, be aware of the different aspects of mindset that your various responses represent.

- If you enjoy the activity, are good at it and spend time doing it then it is clearly a strength for you. That could, however, be an asset or a limitation depending upon whether or not it is the most important thing for you to be doing to reach your current goals for your venture.
- If you enjoy the activity and are good at it but don't spend time doing it then it means that you are probably giving priority to other actions. In this case, the main question is whether or not it is something you should spending time with in order to reach the goal of your project or venture.
- If you enjoy the activity and spend time doing it but are not good at it then it is likely that it is a source of some frustration for you. It is something that would be good for you to get some training or coaching with.
- If you are good at the activity and spend time doing it but do not enjoy it then you probably experience it as something necessary but as tedious and boring. It would be useful to explore ways to increase your motivation. It can be helpful, for instance, to spend time with and model someone who genuinely enjoys doing it.
- If you enjoy the activity, but are not good at it and don't spend time doing it then, even though you get pleasure from it, it probably does not add much value when you do. It is definitely something you will want to invest the time to learn more about and improve upon, depending upon your goals for your venture.

- If you spend time doing the activity but do not enjoy it and are not good at it then it is likely that you frequently feel overwhelmed and find that you are "spinning your wheels" or wasting your time, even if you think it is something that is important for you to do. It is clearly an area that you will want to get support developing both your capability and motivation for.
- If you are good at the activity but neither like it nor spend time doing it then it clearly an issue of motivation rather than one of competency or priority. It would be useful for you to spend some time better understanding the reasons why it is important and exploring how you might increase your interest and pleasure in doing it.
- If you do not enjoy activity, are not good at and do not spend time doing it then it is an obvious area for development, as it is likely that you will need some serious support to develop your motivation and capability in that area, or find a good partner that you can trust who has competence in that activity.

Again, Make note of your areas for development. As with the other areas of the Success Mindset Map, in the coming chapters, you will have an opportunity to develop these various aspects of your Micro Mindset.

Meta Goals

The final distinction needed to complete your Mindset Compass is to identify your Meta Goal. Your *Meta Goal* is your *current focus* for your project or venture. Even though there are many important goals you are probably working on, your meta goal is the most important one.

Your Meta Goal or current focus will relate to one of the five *core outcomes* associated with building your Circle of Success.

1. **Increasing your personal satisfaction in what you are doing.** To symbolize this goal we have chosen a person standing with arms outstretched on the bow of a ship (like the famous scene from the movie *Titanic*). It represents a sense of joy, excitement and pleasure in one's ongoing actions and activities. You would choose this goal if things are going fairly well in your venture, but you are not enthusiastic or excited about what you are doing.

2. **Establishing financial robustness/stability.** We have selected a treasure chest to represent this goal as it symbolizes a robust financial state. You would choose this goal if it is essential for your venture to achieve profitability.

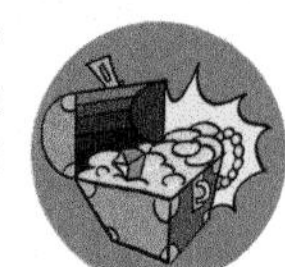

3. **Building a scalable business.** We have chosen a fleet or armada to represent this goal as it symbolizes an expanding group of units operating together and sharing a common origin, purpose and mode of coordination. You would choose this goal if it is important for your venture to grow.

4. **Making a genuine and meaningful contribution.** We have selected a rescue helicopter to represent this goal as it symbolizes a clear focus on serving others. You would choose this goal if it is important for your venture to clarify and/or enhance the benefit you are bringing to or creating for your customers and community.

5. **Achieving greater innovation and resilience.** We have chosen a tree house (like that of the Swiss Family Robinson) to represent this goal as it symbolizes ingenuity and the ability to creatively adapt to new and challenging situations. You would choose this goal if you need to increase your capabilities or creativity in order to get through a crisis, deal with a big change or stay competitive.

Assessing Your Meta Goal

Which of the Meta Goals described above is your current focus? What would you most like to accomplish in the next six to twelve months? Select the one you most want to give priority.

1. **Increase my personal satisfaction in what I am doing.** ☐

2. **Establish financial robustness/stability.** ☐

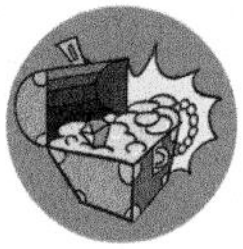

3. **Build a scalable business.** ☐

4. **Make a genuine and meaningful contribution.** ☐

5. **Achieve greater innovation and resilience.** ☐

Applying the SFM Mindset Compass

The SFM Mindset Compass specifies which elements of the three areas of mindset are most important and relevant for achieving your Meta Goal or current focus for your venture.

Putting all of the pieces—Meta Mindset, Macro Mindset, Micro Mindset and Meta Goals—together with respect to the Circle of Success, we can summarize the overall *SFM Success Mindset Map*™ in the diagram on the following page.

As I pointed out earlier in this chapter, the three areas of mindset, Meta, Macro and Micro, may be integrated together to make up a type of *Mindset Compass* with respect to your Meta Goal. This Mindset Compass specifies which elements of the three areas of mindset are most important and relevant for achieving your Meta Goal or current focus, providing you an *Ideal Mindset Map* for that Meta goal.

By having gone through the various mindset assessments in this chapter you will be familiar with your own particular aptitudes and tendencies with respect to your current mindset, skills and habits. By comparing them with the Ideal Mindset Map for your Meta Goal, you will discover which ones you need to prioritize and strengthen in order to take your project or venture to the next level.

The following pages summarize the Ideal Mindset Map for each of the Meta Goals. Compare the Ideal Mindset Map with what you have learned about your own current Meta, Macro and Micro mindset to identity the most important area of development for yourself.

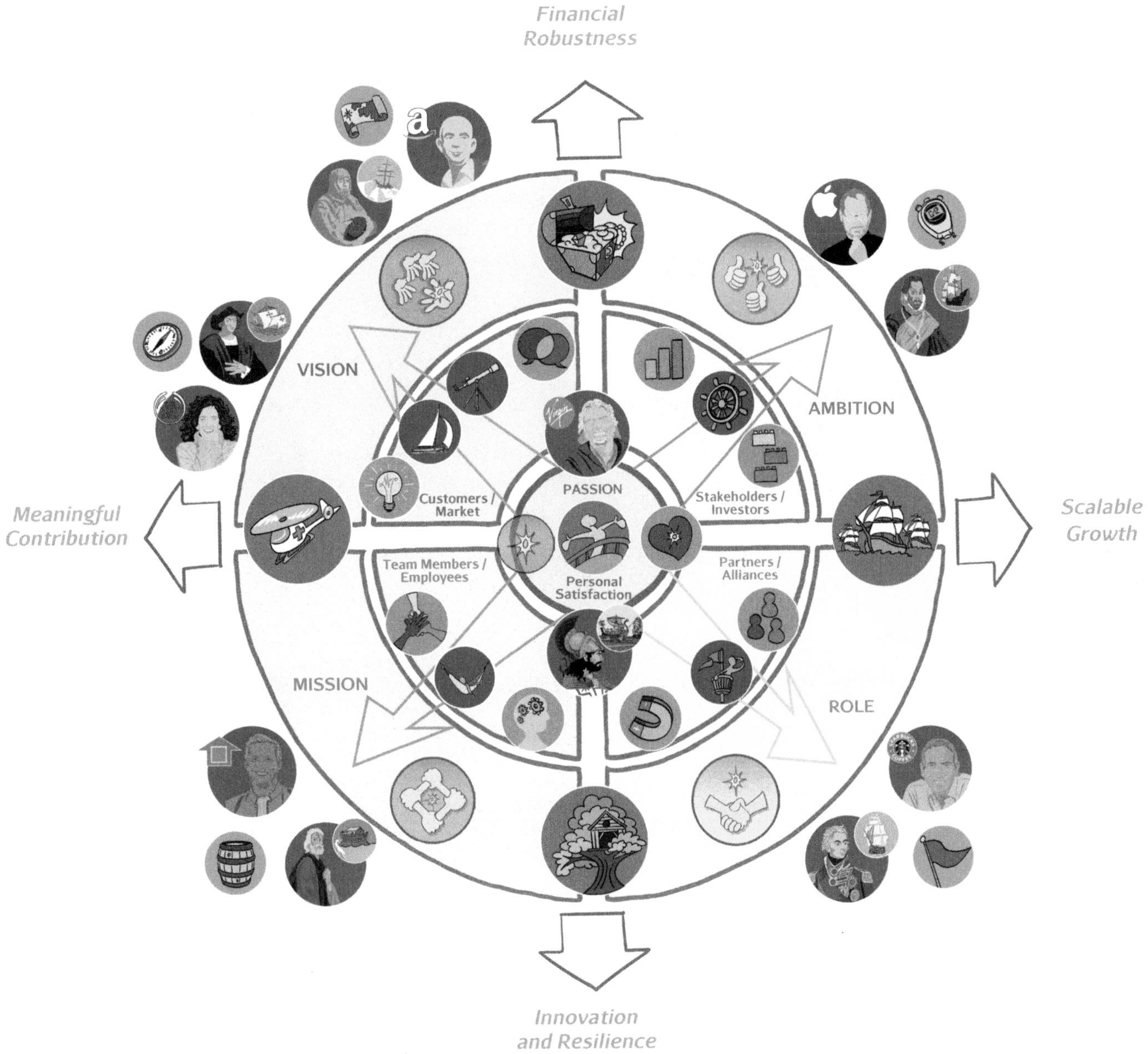

Financial Robustness

VISION

AMBITION

Customers / Market

PASSION

Stakeholders / Investors

Meaningful Contribution

Scalable Growth

Team Members / Employees

Personal Satisfaction

Partners / Alliances

MISSION

ROLE

Innovation and Resilience

The SFM Success Mindset Map™

Ideal Mindset Map 1:
Increase My Personal Satisfaction In What I Am Doing

- In order to increase your personal satisfaction in what you are doing you need to adopt a mindset like **Richard Branson** of the Virgin Group. You need to "follow your passions – in a way that serves the world and you."

- You also need to have a "lust for adventure" like the mythical traveler **Ulysses** and feel the desire "to strive, to seek, to find and not to yield."

- You need to be totally in touch with that **spark** that comes from connecting with your passion.

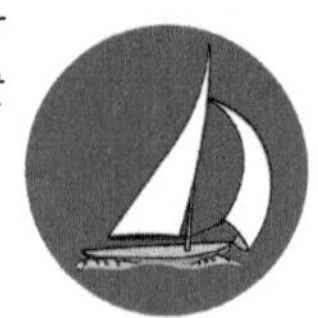

- This will give you the energy and motivation for your venture and help you ready to *go "full sail" for what you want.*

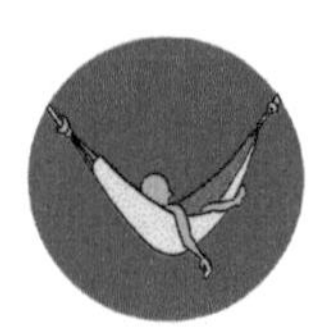

- You will also need to have the means and the discipline to be able to *take care of yourself* and not become overly stressed or burned out.

- To accomplish all of this, you need to *set aside the time to explore and reconnect with what you love to do, what is important to you and what you are good at doing* – i.e., your passion, your sense purpose and your excellence.

Ideal Mindset Map 2: Establish Financial Robustness / Stability

- In order to establish financial robustness and stability you need to adopt a mindset that combines the characteristics of **Jeff Bezos** of Amazon and **Steve Jobs** of Apple. You need to have a clear vision of your destination and the ambition to "put a dent in the universe."

- You also need to have the determination of explorer **Ernest Shackleton**, who persevered against all odds to reach the South Pole, and the boldness of adventurer **Sir Francis Drake** who was one of the first people to circumnavigate the globe.

- You will need to have a clear **map** of the destination you want to reach and *the will to achieve something within a defined period.*

- You need to have the routine set up to consistently *scan your horizon for possibilities* and "weak signals" that may indicate important opportunities.

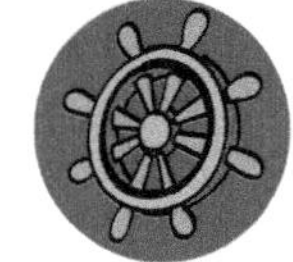

- You need to have the tools and resources to *remain in control and "stay the course"* under challenging and changing conditions.

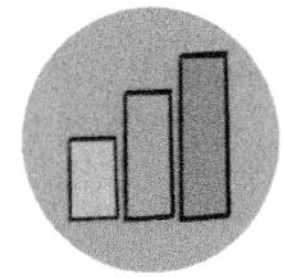

- To accomplish all of this, you will need to (1) consistently create opportunities for *ongoing dialog with customers* and prospects and (2) to *identify potential investors and providers of other essential resources* and creatively get their interest and commitment to support your venture.

Ideal Mindset Map 3:
Build a Scalable Business

- In order to build a scalable business you need to adopt a mindset that combines the characteristics of **Steve Jobs** of Apple and **Howard Shultz** of Starbucks. You will need to have a strong ambition to "put a dent in the universe" and a sense of a role that creates a meaningful relationship with customers and potential partners.

- You also need to have the boldness of adventurer **Sir Francis Drake**, who was one of the first people to circumnavigate the globe as well as the sense of reputation and duty of **Admiral Nelson**.

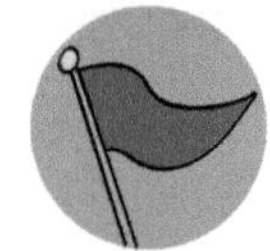

- You will need to have the *will to achieve something within a defined period* and a *clarity of the status and position* you have with respect to your customers, competitors and partners.

- You will need the energy and motivation for your venture and be ready to *go "full sail" for what you want*.

- You will need the means in place to *get ongoing and relevant feed-back* in order to avoid problems and obstacles and make necessary course corrections.

- You will also require the tools and resources to r*emain in control and "stay the course"* under challenging and changing conditions.

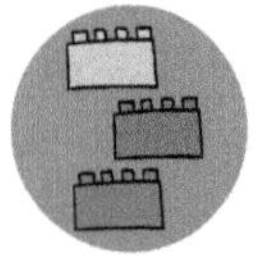
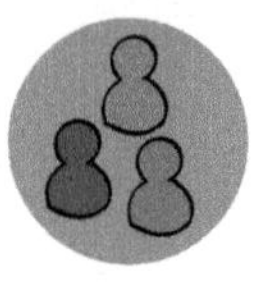

- To accomplish all of this you will need to (1) *spend time creating and developing a sustainable infrastructure* and a path for growth and scalability of your venture and (2) *seek and establishing win-win relationships with potential partners* and allies who resonate with your values and vision.

Ideal Mindset Map 4: Make a genuine and meaningful contribution

- In order to make a genuine and meaningful contribution you need to adopt a mindset that combines the characteristics of **Anita Roddick** of The Body Shop and **Muhammad Yunus** of the Grameen Bank. You need to have the desire to create "an honorable livelihood, where you take your skills and use them and you earn a living from it," in a way that "gives you a sense of freedom and allows you to balance your life the way you want." You also need the deep desire to empower others and help them to be happy.

- In addition, you will need the conviction and clear sense of direction of **Christopher Columbus** and the unwavering commitment to your calling of **Noah**.

- You will need to have a type of inner **compass** that lets you which you know which direction you want to go, even if you do not know where you will end up. You will also need to be *clear about your purpose and the unique gift and contribution that you bring* to other through your venture.

- You will need the energy and motivation for your venture and be ready to *go "full sail" for what you want*.

- You have to have the means in place to *get ongoing and relevant feedback* in order to avoid problems and obstacles and make necessary course corrections.

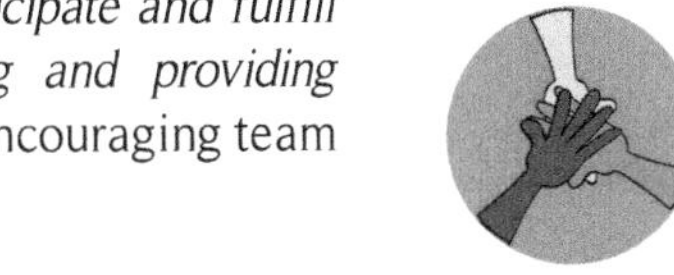

- Accomplishing all of this requires *brainstorming and implementing products and services that anticipate and fulfill customer needs*. It also requires *attracting and providing direction and support to team members* and encouraging team cooperation.

Ideal Mindset Map 5:
Achieve greater innovation and resilience

- In order to achieve greater innovation and resilience you need to adopt a mindset that combines the characteristics of **Howard Shultz** of Starbucks and **Muhammad Yunus** of the Grameen Bank. You will need a sense of a role that creates a meaningful relationship with customers and potential partners. You will also need the deep desire to empower others and help them to be happy.

- Additionally, you will need to have the sense of reputation and duty of **Admiral Nelson** and the unwavering commitment to your calling of **Noah**.

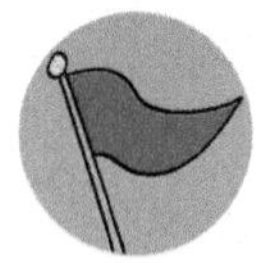

- You will need *clarity regarding the status and position* you have with respect to your customers, competitors and partners. You will also need be *clear about your purpose and the unique gift and contribution* that you bring to others through your venture.

- You will need the energy and motivation for your venture and be ready to *go "full sail" for what you want.*

- You have to have the means in place to *get ongoing and relevant feedback* in order to avoid problems and obstacles and make necessary course corrections.

- You will also need the routine set up to consistently *scan your horizon for possibilities* and "weak signals" that may indicate important opportunities.

- Accomplishing all of this will require *encouraging and providing opportunities for team members to learn and grow*. You will also need to *identify and leverage synergies between what you are doing and the products, services or competences of other ventures.*

The SFM Mindset Compass helps you to achieve the key outcomes necessary for you to establish and grow your venture.

Identifying Your Key Areas for Development

Reflect over what you have learned from this self-analysis. Compare the Ideal Mindset Map for your Meta Goal with your current strengths and tendencies with respect to your Meta, Macro and Micro mindsets. Make note of the areas you need to improve and develop. Mark them below.

Meta Mindset Areas for Development

- Know what I really love to do (what I am passionate about). ☐
- Know what I want to help create in the longer term future (be clear about my destination; and my longer term vision) ☐
- Clarify my direction, regardless of whether or not I know the ultimate destination. ☐
- Know my purpose – know what I stand for and why I am doing what I am doing. Be clear about my mission – the unique contribution I want to make through my venture. ☐
- Clarify my ambition – i.e., what I want to become and achieve in the next two to five years. ☐
- Clarify my role – i.e., the position I have with respect to others in my market/environment. ☐

Macro Mindset Areas for Development

- Do what I am passionate about and invest a lot of energy and focus into making what I want happen. ☐
- Seek feedback and establish ways to get honest and frequent feedback. ☐
- Constantly scan for opportunities and invest time to create them. ☐
- Be more internally grounded and resourceful, have ways of recharging and balancing myself and practice that on a daily basis. ☐
- Be more aware of risks and potential problems and don't get discouraged or distracted in the face of adversity and negative feedback. ☐

Micro Mindset Areas for Development

- [ ] Set aside the time to explore and reconnect with what I love to do, what is important to me and what I am good at doing – i.e., my passion, my sense purpose and my excellence.
- [ ] Create opportunities for ongoing dialog with customers and prospects.
- [ ] Brainstorm and implement products and services that anticipate and fulfill customer needs.
- [ ] Attract and provide direction and support to team members and encouraging team cooperation.
- [ ] Encourage and provide opportunities for team members to learn and grow.
- [ ] Identify potential investors and providers of other essential resources and creatively get their interest and commitment to support my venture.
- [ ] Create and develop a sustainable infrastructure and a path for growth and scalability of my venture.
- [ ] Seek and establish win-win relationships with potential partners and allies who resonate with my values and vision.
- [ ] Identify and leverage synergies between what I am doing and the products, services or competences of other ventures.

Success Factor Case Example:
Pike Place Fish Market

Be yourself and do what inspires you

The principles and practices of next generation entrepreneurship and conscious leadership are not limited to high-tech companies nor to high-tech products. Rather, they are about the mindset we bring to whatever we are doing. Consider the example of Pike Place Fish Market. Originally founded in 1930, Pike Place Fish Market is an open-air fish market located in Seattle, Washington. It was purchased in 1965 by John Yokoyama, a former employee of the fish market. According to Yokoyama, he bought the store hoping to make enough money to afford the payments on his new car.

Twenty years later, Yokoyama found himself bored and burned out, and his business was failing. As one might imagine, a fish market is quite a different venture than those established by people like Elon Musk and Steve Jobs. There is nothing inherently exciting or "world changing" about selling fish. The people who worked in the market did not need to be "the best and the brightest." In fact, they did not even need a high school education. For years, Yokoyama had simply run the business as a traditional "boss" as he had learned from his time working in the market.

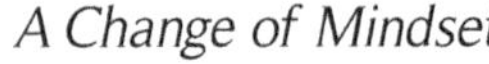

A Change of Mindset

John Yokoyama
Pike Place Fish Market

In 1986, unhappy and approaching bankruptcy, Yokoyama intuitively realized that he and his team needed a dramatic change in mindset. He brought in coach Jim Bergquist from bizFutures to help him and his team to conceive of ways to save the business. Bergquist assembled the team and asked a surprising question, one that Yokoyama had never thought to ask as a boss. That question was, "What do you want?" and more specifically, "Who do you want to be?"

Bergquist encouraged the team to explore who they were and what they were passionate about. "Your challenge is to 'just be' who you want to be," he told them, "...for free...just because you said so." This was to be a transformational exploration. As Yokoyama describes it:

In one of our early Pike Place Fish meetings with Jim we began an inquiry into "Who do we want to be?" We wanted to create a new future for ourselves. One of the young kids working for me said, "Hey! Let's be World Famous!" At first I thought, "World Famous...what a stupid thing to say!" But the more we talked about it, the more we all got excited about being World Famous. So we committed to it. We added "World Famous" to our logo and had it printed on our shipping boxes.

Exploring the questions "What do you want?" and "Who do you want to be?" helped the Pike Place Fish Market team clarify the passion, purpose and identity at the center of their Circle of Success.

Becoming "World Famous"

This decision at an identity level, of course, raised some other new, very important and equally challenging questions for the team at the levels of capabilities and behaviors: "How are we going to become world famous?" and "What does it mean to be 'World Famous'?" The company certainly did not have any money to put into advertising. Their coach, however assured them, "Your commitment to being world famous will naturally lead you to what to do." The important thing was that, as individuals, each team member needed to choose to align with the commitment. According to Yokoyama, "We took a stand that we were going to become world famous. We just said it and it became so."

Once they took a stand, the next big question, then, was "What does this mean – being world famous?" Yokoyama and his team decided to create their own definition. Instead of spending money on advertising (the company has never spent a dime), the team resolved that it would happen as a result of their being truly great with people. "For us it means going beyond just providing outstanding service to people. It means really being present with people and relating to them as human beings," they concluded. This meant "stepping outside the usual 'we're in business and you're a customer' way of relating to people and intentionally being with them right now, in the present moment, person to person. We take all our attention off ourselves to be only with them...looking for ways to serve them. We're out to discover how we can make their day."

As Yokoyama and his team put it:

We interact with people with a strong intention to make a difference for them. We want to give each person the experience of having been served and appreciated, whether they buy fish or not. We love them.

The Pike Place Fish Market team transformed their passion into the mission to provide outstanding service to their customers and "give each person the experience of having been served and appreciated, whether they buy fish or not."

Another part of being "World Famous," they all agreed, was that it would be fun. They would all be enjoying their work and having fun with each other so that customers would enjoy themselves and have fun as well. And, being "World Famous" would also mean that they would be creative and innovative.

A Big Change in the Way of Doing Business

These commitments organically led to big changes in the team's way of doing business. Because they wanted to have a stronger connection with customers, some of the staff would go out in front of the fish counter to interact with people. The challenge was that, if someone bought a fish, they would have to get the fish behind the counter to get wrapped and then back again to the customer. This lead to the tradition of the so-called "flying fish," in which the "fishmongers" hurl customers' orders across the shopping area. This habit has prompted them to post the sign, "Caution: Low Flying Fish."

Pike Place Fish Market's "Flying Fish" Tradition

A typical routine will involve a customer ordering a fish, with their fishmongers in an apron and boots calling out the order, which is loudly shouted back by all the other staff, at which point the original fishmonger will throw the customer's fish behind the counter for wrapping. All the while, the staff continually yell to each other and chant in unison while they throw the ordered fish. To show their gratitude to a customer who buys a fish, they may even sometimes sing to the customer.

Other times, the fish market staff will playfully throw a foam fish into the crowd to startle bystanders, or they will select a customer from the crowd to participate in the fish toss.

Another popular feature at the Pike Place Fish Market is the monkfish (an ugly fish with big teeth), which, thanks to a hidden device, can be made to "snap" at customers.

A Monk Fish at Pike Place Fish Market

It is important to note that the activity of the staff at the market is not simply a fixed performance. "It gets created by each one of us, newly every time," the team explains. "It comes out differently for different people. It also depends on who the customer is...how they react. It's about taking care of people. We're always on the lookout for how we can make a difference in people's lives." As the team points out:

> *People want to copy us – to do what we're doing. We keep telling them, "Your success isn't in doing what we do; it's in discovering your own way. Don't do what we do – we made it all up...do what inspires you...make it up!" You just have to be (yourself...what inspires you). And it means commit yourself to who you say you are: act like it, think like it, look like it, feel like it, speak it...be it! You will create your own way by just being yourself, doing what inspires you.*

A Role Model for Other Companies

The approach has been immensely successful. In time, a television news crew eventually discovered the fish market and its performances with customers, and filmed them. The news item went viral, leading to the market and its employees being filmed by various other film crews, and being featured in numerous magazines. Since then, they have been featured repeatedly in the national media and television shows.

Today, the store is a popular tourist destination and one of the most visited attractions in Seattle, attracting up to 10,000 visitors a day. In fact *Travel & Leisure* magazine ranked Pike Place Market as the 13th most visited attractions in the U.S. It has truly become "world-famous."

Just as importantly, the Pike Place Fish Market has been repeatedly named one of the "most fun places to work in America." The company has become a model of an empowered culture for other organizations and is used as a case study in business schools and universities. The employees of the fish market will often speak to businesses, civic groups, and schools on ways to be successful. There are at least four books that have been published about Pike Place Fish Market; one an international best-seller. They are also the subject of one of the best selling training videos and DVDs in the world.

The staff at Pike Place Fish Market has intentionally created a culture based on three core values:

- **Empowerment** – Supporting each person to be themselves and to do what inspires them.
- **Vision to Reality** – Setting ambitious goals and making them happen.
- **Making a Difference in the World** – The true purpose of being in business is to make a profound and lasting difference in the quality of life in the world.

These values are at the foundation of all conscious leadership and next generation entrepreneurship. As the Pike Place Fish Market team posts on their website:

> *At the World Famous Pike Place Fish Market, we know that it's possible for each of us as human beings to impact the way other people experience life. Through our work, we're out to improve the quality of life for everyone. We are working inside the possibility of world peace and prosperity for all people. This is our commitment – that's who we are – it's what we do.*

Through passionately living their mission and pursuing their ambition to become "world famous," the Pike Place Fish Market team has ended up attracting as many as 10,000 visitors a day and have been featured in national media and television shows as one of the "most fun places to work in America."

The Pike Place Fish Market team put their passion, ambition and mission in service of a new vision for their customers combining the best quality seafood with high quality (and entertaining) service.

I have personally visited the market myself and can verify that it is truly a unique, exciting and enjoyable experience. Crowds of people gather and wait in anticipation for someone to buy a fish so that they can discover what the staff is going to do next. The staff members are clearly not simply "performers." They interact personably, playfully and authentically with each other, their customers and the crowd.

Supporting a Sustainable Future

According to the team at Pike Place Fish Market:

> *Our vision is to see companies all over the world make it their business to improve the quality of life for people everywhere as well as for our planet, and we want to make this way of operating available to as many organizations as possible.*

This has translated for them into an expanded mission of "world peace and making a difference." As part of that mission, the company has made the commitment to "sell only 100% sustainable seafood." They have also partnered with the Monterey Bay Aquarium Seafood Watch program and joined in their mission to assist consumers and businesses in making better choices for healthy oceans. Seafood Watch raises consumer awareness through pocket guides, website, mobile applications and outreach efforts. It encourages restaurants, distributors and seafood purveyors to purchase from sustainable sources.

Pike Place Fish Market team decided to take on the Role of an "empowered culture" committed to "improve the quality of life for people everywhere as well as for our planet" and have partnered with the other organizations, such as Monterey Bay Aquarium, to assist consumers and businesses in making better choices for healthy oceans.

Reflections on Pike Place Fish Market's Journey to Being "World Famous"

Pike Place Fish Market provides a clear example of the power of mindset to transform a business. It is also a demonstration of many of the principles of next generation entrepreneurship and conscious leadership. It shows that if a clear direction is established, even if the destination is not yet certain, a path can be created leading to somewhere new that benefits all stakeholders.

In this regard, the case of Pike Place Fish Market illustrates a number of the key principles and elements of the SFM Circle of Success and the Success Mindset Map. In many ways, Yokoyama, his coach and his team intuitively applied the principles of the Mindset Compass presented in this chapter.

The journey clearly began in the center of the Circle of Success with an examination of Self, Identity and **Passion**. The first focus for Yokoyama and this team was to **increase their personal satisfaction in what they were doing**. With the help of their coach, they set aside the time to explore and reconnect with what they loved to do, what was important to them and what they were good at doing. Intuitively applying Richard Branson's advice, their coach encouraged the team to "follow your passions – in a way that serves the world and you." In the words of the team, this translated into "being yourself and doing what inspires you." This connection to their passion brought the team energy and motivation for the venture and helped team members to *go "full sail" for what they wanted*.

A next step in the journey was to establish **financial robustness and stability**. According to the Mindset Compass this requires having a strong **Ambition** to "put a dent in the universe" and the desire to create a meaningful relationship with customers and potential partners. As the Mindset Compass points out, achieving this outcome requires "the boldness of adventurer Sir Francis Drake" and "the will to achieve something." For the team at Pike Place Fish Market, this emerged as the desire to be "World Famous." As the Mindset Compass also suggests, their commitment to this ambition inspired them to "*consistently scan the horizon for possibilities* and 'weak signals' that indicate important opportunities" in order to figure out how to bring such a big ambition into reality.

In order to truly manifest the ambition of being "World Famous," the staff at Pike Place Fish Market had to **achieve greater innovation and resilience**. As the Mindset Compass indicates, this requires "encouraging and providing opportunities for team members to learn and grow" and helping them become "*clear about their purpose and the unique gift and contribution* that they bring to others through the venture." According to the Mindset Compass, increasing innovation and resilience also requires "a meaningful relationship with customers and potential partners" and "the deep desire to empower others and help them to be happy." The expression of these principles clearly shows up in the staff's definition of being "World Famous" which took the form of their **Vision** for their customers of "being present and relating to people as a human beings; making each person's day more positive; being of service and taking great care of customers; having the very best quality seafood; and serving not only customers, but the world."

The Pike Place Fish Market staff's desire to **make a genuine and meaningful contribution** brought them to a next phase requiring "*brainstorming and implementing products and services that anticipate and fulfill customer needs.*" According the Mindset Compass, in order to achieve this goal it is also necessary to "provide direction and support to team members and encourage team cooperation." The staff's implementation of these principles eventually led to their famous "flying fish" performance, their games with customers and the staff attitude of always enjoying their work. It also translated into their stated **Mission** of "providing outstanding service, promoting world peace and making a difference." The company's success in achieving their mission reflects Anita Roddick's comment that "You can create an honorable livelihood, where you take your skills and use them and you earn a living from it," in a way that "gives you a sense of freedom and allows you to balance your life the way you want."

Interestingly, **building a scalable business** in a traditional sense has never really been directly a part of the vision or ambition of John Yokoyama or the Pike Place Fish Market staff. They did not have the ambition to spread their market internationally like a Starbucks, Apple or Amazon. In their **Role** as "a model of an empowered culture" in business, however, they have managed to scale their contribution and influence on other companies. This is evidenced by their use as a case study in business schools and universities and as the subject of books and training videos. Their *partnership* with the Monterey Bay Aquarium Seafood Watch program has also allowed them to extend their range of influence regarding their vision and mission for a more sustainable future.

Pike Place Fish Market's Circle of Success

In summary, John Yokoyama and the Pike Place Fish Market staff built an effective Circle of Success by starting in the center of the circle, clarifying their Identity and **Passion** to "Be yourself and do what inspires you." This passion expressed itself in the **Ambition** to be "World Famous"; an ambition that ultimately led to their being featured in national media and television shows, attracting as many 10,000 visitors a day and becoming one of the "most fun places to work in America."

Manifesting the ambition to be "World Famous" meant establishing a new **Vision** for customers involving:

- Being present and relating to people as a human beings
- Looking for ways to make each person's day more positive
- Being of service and taking great care of customers
- Having the very best quality seafood
- Serving not only customers, but the world

This was an expression of an even bigger vision for a greater "holarchy" to: "See companies all over the world make it their business to improve the quality of life for people everywhere as well as for our planet." Implementing this vision led the Pike Place Fish Market staff to take on the **Mission** of "providing outstanding service, promoting world peace and making a difference" through the three principles of Empowerment, bringing Vision to Reality and Making a Difference in the World.

By doing so, Pike Place Fish Market took on the **Role** of—and became a model for—an "empowered culture" by demonstrating that "it is possible for each of us as human beings to impact the way other people experience life . . . and to improve the quality of life for everyone." Their use as a case study in business schools and universities as well as their being the subject of books and training videos is a powerful testament to their success in that role.

Pike Place Fish Market's Circle of Success

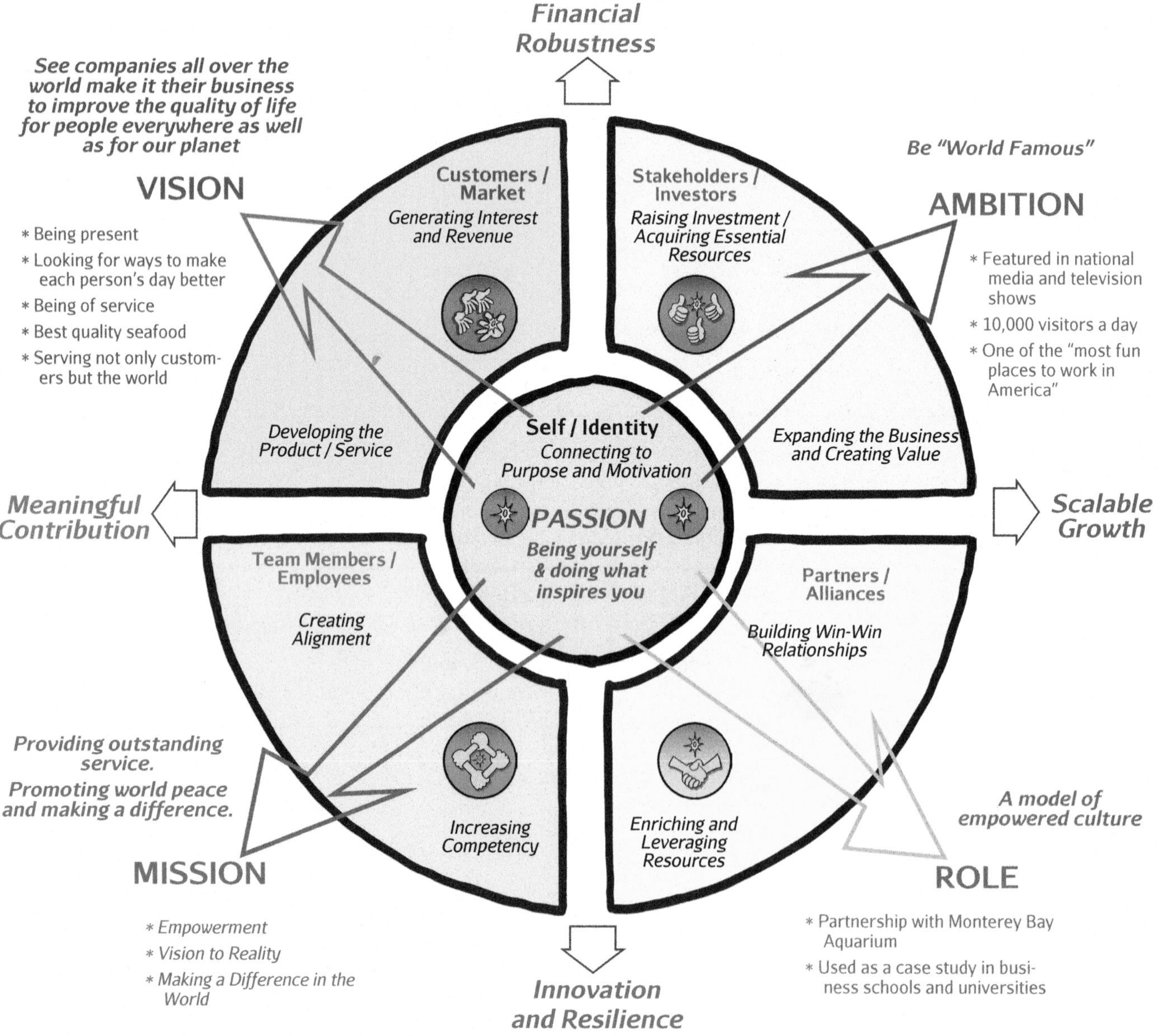

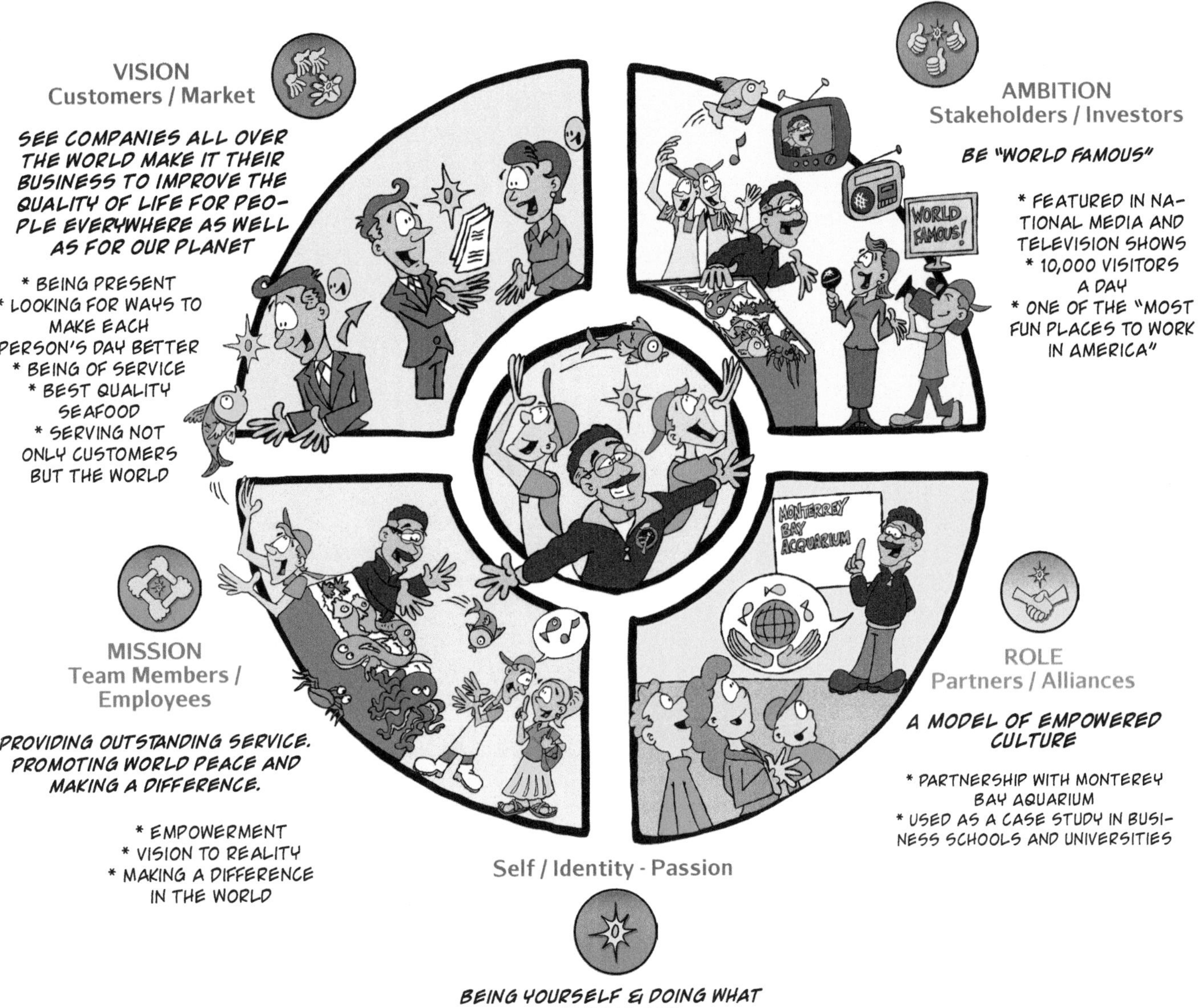
PIKE PLACE FISH MARKET'S CIRCLE OF SUCCESS
VISION
Customers / Market
SEE COMPANIES ALL OVER THE WORLD MAKE IT THEIR BUSINESS TO IMPROVE THE QUALITY OF LIFE FOR PEOPLE EVERYWHERE AS WELL AS FOR OUR PLANET
* BEING PRESENT
* LOOKING FOR WAYS TO MAKE EACH PERSON'S DAY BETTER
* BEING OF SERVICE
* BEST QUALITY SEAFOOD
* SERVING NOT ONLY CUSTOMERS BUT THE WORLD
AMBITION
Stakeholders / Investors
BE "WORLD FAMOUS"
* FEATURED IN NATIONAL MEDIA AND TELEVISION SHOWS
* 10,000 VISITORS A DAY
* ONE OF THE "MOST FUN PLACES TO WORK IN AMERICA"
WORLD FAMOUS!
MONTERREY BAY ACQUARIUM
MISSION
Team Members / Employees
PROVIDING OUTSTANDING SERVICE. PROMOTING WORLD PEACE AND MAKING A DIFFERENCE.
* EMPOWERMENT
* VISION TO REALITY
* MAKING A DIFFERENCE IN THE WORLD
ROLE
Partners / Alliances
A MODEL OF EMPOWERED CULTURE
* PARTNERSHIP WITH MONTEREY BAY AQUARIUM
* USED AS A CASE STUDY IN BUSINESS SCHOOLS AND UNIVERSITIES
Self / Identity - Passion
BEING YOURSELF & DOING WHAT INSPIRES YOU

Conclusion

The example of Pike Place Fish Market is a powerful demonstration that a company does not have to be a high-tech giant making computers, electric cars or rocket ships in order for its founders and team members to live more consciously and make a positive difference in the world and in other people's lives. Being a next generation entrepreneur and conscious leader does not need to be limited to or constrained by the product one is offering. Conscious leadership and next generation entrepreneurship first and foremost express themselves through the mindset that you bring to whatever you are doing.

Companies like Pike Place Fish Market, illy Café and Ben & Jerry's Ice Cream are examples of how the mindsets at the core of conscious leadership and next generation entrepreneurship can be applied to create and grow a meaningful, sustainable and successful venture regardless of the particular type of product or industry.

Companies like illy Café and Ben & Jerry's Ice Cream are other examples of how the mindsets at the core of conscious leadership and next generation entrepreneurship can be applied to practically any venture—whether it is selling fish, coffee or ice cream. Ventures like illy Café and Ben & Jerry's Ice Cream have reputations for being socially conscious and significantly contributing to a sustainable future while also providing a good atmosphere and working conditions for their employees and team members.

In the words of Andrea Illy of **illy Café**:

> *The perfect coffee is my mission, my passion and my obsession. So, peering into a cup of illy, I must ask myself: How can this be better? At illy, we pioneered the idea that a perfect cup of coffee needs to go beyond pleasing the palate. We believe it should build a better world. Since 1991, we purchase our coffee directly from the hands of growers. Illy selects the growers we work with based on the quality of their beans, then cultivates personal and exclusive relationships so that every cent we spend, and every bean we buy, contributes to a greater good. These farmers live and work in the remote cradles of coffee—Columbia, Costa Rica, Brazil, India. Here, the best of nature and humanity come together to give the precious coffee bean a meaningful life. By practicing responsible business from grower to trader to roaster, coffee is our conduit for improving the lives of 25 million families in over 70 countries.*

When Andrea Illy is looking at a cup of coffee, he is clearly seeing it in the context of a much larger holarchy.

Ben Cohen and Jerry Greenfield of **Ben & Jerry's Ice Cream** express a similar passion and vision for their venture. According to them:

> *Ben & Jerry's operates on a three-part mission that aims to create linked prosperity for everyone that's connected to our business: suppliers, employees, farmers, franchisees, customers, and neighbors alike.*
>
> - *Our Product Mission drives us to make fantastic ice cream – for its own sake.*
> - *Our Economic Mission asks us to manage our Company for sustainable financial growth.*
> - *Our Social Mission compels us to use our Company in innovative ways to make the world a better place.*

They have also established Ben & Jerry's Foundation, whose mission is "to engage Ben & Jerry's employees in philanthropy and social change work; to give back to our communities; and to support grassroots activism and community organizing for social and environmental justice around the country."

As I said in the Introduction to this book, *Conscious leadership* involves "building a sustainable venture and guiding yourself and your team from a state of centered presence, accessing multiple intelligences and living your highest values in service to a larger purpose to the benefit of all stakeholders." Pike Place Fish Market, illy Café and Ben & Jerry's Ice Cream provide compelling examples of the transformative potential of the mindset and skills of conscious leadership and next generation entrepreneurship for any type of venture.

Chapter Summary

Conscious Leadership shares many characteristics with Next Generation Entrepreneurship. A *next generation entrepreneur* is someone who creates a sustainable business or project to live his or her own dream, while delivering a product or a service that makes a positive difference in the world and personally growing through it.

The *SFM Circle of Success™* is a model that brings together the outcomes, actions and mindset needed to build a successful venture. The model is organized around five core outcomes necessary to create a truly successful venture:

1. Personal Satisfaction
2. Meaningful Contribution
3. Financial Robustness
4. Innovation and Resilience
5. Scalable Growth

In order to achieve these outcomes, successful entrepreneurs divide their focus of attention and their actions in a balanced way between five fundamental perspectives: 1) themselves and their sense of purpose and motivation for what they are doing, 2) their customers and their products or services, 3) their investors and stakeholders, 4) their team members or employees and 5) their strategic partners and allies.

According to the Circle of Success, creating a successful venture is ultimately founded upon an *entrepreneurial mindset* that produces and encourages the actions necessary to reach core outcomes. This mindset is a function of an entrepreneur's capacity to share his or her *passion*, in the form of his or her *vision*, *mission*, *ambition* and *role*.

The example of Elon Musk from the Introduction provides a good illustration of building an effective Circle of Success.

The *Success Mindset Map™* enriches the SFM Circle of Success by identifying three main areas of a successful entrepreneurial mindset:

1. Meta Mindset – Big-picture clarity
2. Macro Mindset – Habits of success
3. Micro Mindset – Ongoing priorities

The *Mindset Compass* specifies which elements of the three areas of mindset, Meta, Macro and Micro, are most important and relevant for achieving the various core outcomes defined by the Circle of Success. The Mindset Compass helps you to assess and identify your particular aptitudes and tendencies and to know which ones you need to prioritize and strengthen in order to take your project or venture to the next level.

The case of Pike Place Fish Market provides a clear example of the power of mindset to transform a business. It provides a powerful demonstration that a company does not have to be a high-tech giant making computers, electric cars or rocket ships in order for its founders and team members to live more consciously and make a positive difference in the world and in other people's lives. It shows that if a clear direction is established, even if the destination is not yet certain, a path can be created leading to somewhere new that benefits all stakeholders. By clarifying their identity and passion to "Be yourself and do what inspires you," and their ambition to be "World Famous" by "being present and relating to people as a human beings; making each person's day more positive" the company came back from the verge of bankruptcy and literally became world famous.

References and Further Readings

- *Success Factor Modeling, Volume I – Next Generation Entrepreneurs: Live Your Dream and Create a Better World through Your Business*, Dilts, R., Dilts Strategy Group, Santa Cruz, CA, 2015
- The SFM Mindset Compass™; Mindset Maps International, *http://www.mindsetmaps.com.*
- *50 Entrepreneurs Share Priceless Advice*; available at YouTube.com
- www.pikeplacemarket.org
- www.illy.com
- www.benjerry.com

04
Conscious Leadership and the SFM Leadership Model™

Leadership is lifting a person's vision to high sights, the raising of a person's performance to a higher standard, the building of a personality beyond its normal limitations.
Peter Drucker

If your actions inspire others to dream more, learn more, do more and become more, you are a leader.
John Quincy Adams

ANTONIO MEZA

Conscious Leadership and the SFM Leadership Model™

The need for the skills of leadership begins to emerge more and more clearly as our inner game expresses itself outwardly and we attempt to build a Circle of Success and deal with the potential obstacles in our way. As I wrote in Chapter 1, leadership is essentially about providing *direction* and bringing *energy* to our ventures. The basic skills of leadership involve expressing a vision, influencing others to achieve results, encouraging team cooperation and being an example. Conscious leaders enhance those skills through their capacity for authenticity, emotional intelligence and purposeful responsibility. Conscious leadership expresses itself through the abilities to:

1. Formulate and communicate a meaningful and inclusive vision for all stakeholders.
2. Focus on higher purpose.
3. Influence through inspiration.
4. Balance self-interest and the common good, in themselves and others.
5. Respect and integrate multiple perspectives.
6. Lead by example (walk the talk).
7. Exercise mindful self-leadership and reflect thoughtfully on the lessons gained from experience.

The mindset, abilities and actions of conscious leaders are an important complement to those of next generation entrepreneurship.

The mindset, abilities and actions of conscious leaders are an important complement to those of next generation entrepreneurship. We can say that all successful entrepreneurs are also effective leaders, though not all competent leaders are necessarily entrepreneurs (as we saw in the case of Dr. Lim Suet Wun of Tan Tock Seng Hospital at the end of Chapter 2). Thus leadership is a separate but overlapping and complementary set of abilities to the characteristics of next generation entrepreneurs explored in the previous chapter.

In this section, I will present how I have applied the principles and distinctions of Success Factor Modeling specifically to organizational leadership. We will then explore how the skills of exceptional leaders can powerfully synergize with and augment the other success factors we have presented so far in this volume.

The SFM Leadership Model™

From the late 1980s into the early 2000s, I applied the Success Factor Modeling process to conduct an in depth study of effective leadership, sponsored in large part by the Fiat Group based in Turin, Italy.* At that time Fiat was one of the world's largest industrial groups, operating in 61 countries with 1,063 companies that employed over 223,000 people. The Group ran 242 manufacturing plants and 131 research and development centers organized into 10 operating sectors: Automobiles, Agricultural and Construction Machinery, Commercial Vehicles, Metallurgical Products, Components, Production Systems, Aviation, Publishing and Communications, Insurance and Services.

The goal of the research was to produce a comprehensive and pragmatic model of organizational leadership derived from a combination of (a) interviews with CEOs and top managers from successful organizations around the world, (b) core values of world-class organizations, and (c) case examples and current literature on leadership.

The resulting SFM Leadership Model™ provides an important road map for helping ventures and organizations to be sustainable, resilient and fit for the future.

According to the model, effective leadership involves a dynamic relationship between the inner game and the outer game. The outer game is directed toward reaching key *organizational outcomes* necessary for the survival and growth of the venture. These outcomes are attained through behavioral *actions* involving others. The inner game of leadership is directed toward the development and expression of inner, *personal qualities* and capabilities that define the *mindset* necessary to generate and support the actions required to achieve the outcomes.

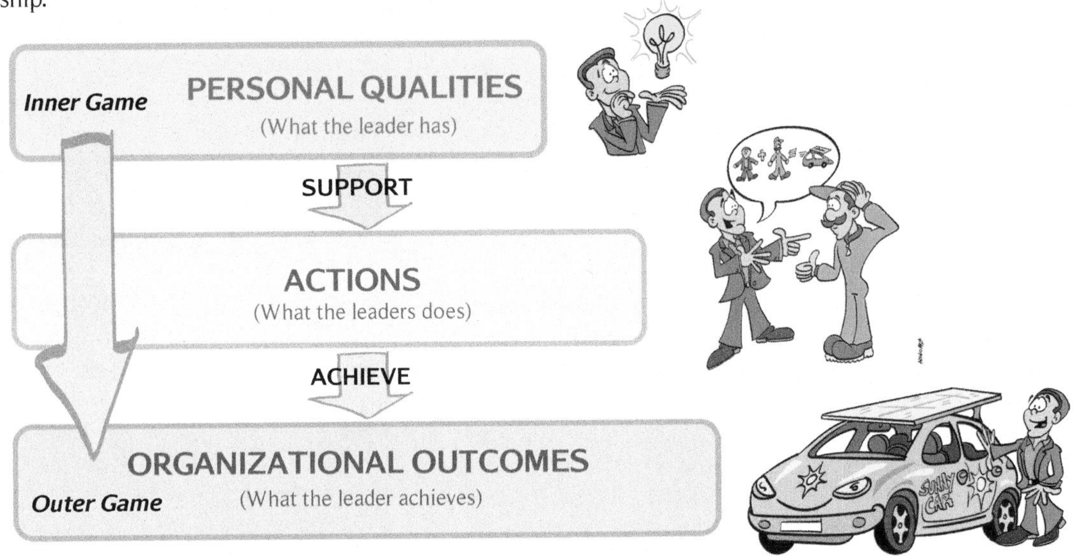

Key Elements of The SFM Leadership Model™

* A portion of this study is described in depth in my book *Modeling With NLP*, 1998.

The Four Essential Goals of Successful Ventures

To present the model, let's begin with the outer game. In a successful venture, leadership ability is directed towards four fundamental organizational outcomes: *achieving results, promoting change, developing people, and realizing values.*

1. Achieving Results:

All effective leadership is finalized in and measured with respect to achieving results of some type. Leadership is essentially about influencing others to achieve desired outcomes—that is, leaders lead others towards something. It has been said that "leaders communicate with other leaders through their accomplishments." Thus, true leadership is less about the authority of position than it is about the authoritativeness of capability. Achieving results comes from personal determination and the ability to empower others and seek continual improvement. As we have already established, for next generation entrepreneurs, these results fall into the basic categories of: Building a successful and sustainable venture; Contributing to society and the environment; Growing personally and spiritually; Supporting the emotional and physical well-being of oneself and others; Sharing visions and resources with a community of peers, igniting new possibilities.

2. Promoting Change:

Change is a fact of life. Change is both the source and the outcome of all interactions within a system. In fact, it has been argued that, in a dynamic system, "the only constant is change." Change, and the ability to promote and manage change, are necessary for both survival and growth. Thus, the ability to innovate, adapt and adjust are critical to the survival and growth of any venture or organization. This requires the development and reinforcement of vision and an entrepreneurial spirit within the venture. Promoting productive change requires the ability of the leader to form and express a vision, stretch to improve and to share knowledge and resources effectively.

3. Developing People:

Leaders and entrepreneurs achieve results and create positive changes through the efforts of the people they work with. People are the most valuable resource any venture has, but in order for them to consistently achieve results and manage changes they must grow and develop. Developing people comes from the leader's ability to motivate and empower them, encouraging them to work together collaboratively and drawing out their individual potential through some form of coaching.

4. Realizing Values:

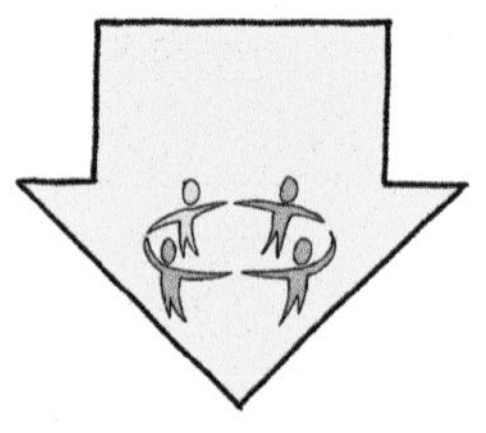

In an organization, values form a type of non-physical framework that surrounds all the interactions of the people within the system. Values, and related beliefs, determine how events and information are interpreted and given meaning. Thus, they are the key to motivation and culture. Shared values and beliefs are the "glue" which holds an effective organization or team together and form the "DNA" of the venture. (Consider Steve Jobs' comments that excellence, ease of use and "awesome design" were Apple's "reason for being.") The realization of values is fostered by the leader's ability to act coherently and be an example, and from consistently encouraging others to do so as well through sharing and coaching.

Fundamental Organizational Outcomes of Successful Ventures

The Four Fundamental Actions of Effective Leaders

Of course, desired results in the outer game are reached as a result of appropriate external actions. The most fundamental behavioral actions taken by successful leaders are: *empowering, coaching, sharing* and *stretching*.

A company is simply a group of people. And as a leader of people, you have to be a great listener; you have to be a great motivator; you have to be very good at praising and looking for the best in people. People are no different from flowers. If you water flowers they flourish and if you praise people they flourish. And that is a critical attribute of a leader.

Richard Branson – Founder Virgin Group

1. **Empowering** is a function of *promoting the expression of individual potential* (encouraging *autonomy*, assumption of *responsibility* and *authority*) in order to obtain more effective performance individually and in cooperation with others. Empowering requires the capacity to facilitate conditions which allow people to express themselves better, recognizing the *value* of their work and stimulating personal and professional growth as well as self-esteem. Empowering is necessary to *achieve results* and *develop people*.

   Everyone has an invisible sign hanging from their neck saying, 'Make me feel important.' Never forget this message when working with people.

   Mary Kay Ash – Mary Kay Cosmetics

Each person holds so much power within themselves that needs to be let out. Sometimes they just need a little nudge, a little direction, a little support, a little coaching, and the greatest things can happen.

Pete Carroll – NFL Head Coach

2. **Coaching** is an expression of the capacity to help people develop their capabilities and perform to the best of their abilities. Effective coaches help people to set clear goals and support them in reaching those goals by offering guidance and feedback, and by being a good example or role model. The purpose of coaching is to help people develop confidence and competence and to internalize and implement values and capabilities fully. Coaching is essential in order to develop people and realize values.

   To create a high-performance team, we must replace typical management activities like supervising, checking, monitoring, and controlling with new behaviors like coaching and communicating.

   Ray Smith – CEO, Bell-Atlantic

3. **Sharing** involves the *exchange of information and know-how*. It is based upon diffusing knowledge and promoting dialogue among people. An important part of sharing for leaders is delineating the venture's vision, values, and goals, and clarifying "the rules of the game." Sharing also engages the capacity to *involve* people with respect to objectives, including them in meetings in which ideas and information are exchanged, in order to achieve true collaboration and reach genuine consensus with respect to goals, outcomes and actions. Effective sharing results from expressing a clear vision and permitting easy access to resources that support the changes necessary to reach the vision. Sharing is required for *realizing values* and *promoting change*.

   Share your knowledge. It is a way to achieve immortality.

   Dalai Lama XIV

Information sharing is power. If you don't share your ideas, smart people can't do anything about them, and you'll remain anonymous and powerless.

Vint Cerf – Developer of DARPA Net, "Chief Internet Evangelist" for Google, Inc.

4. **Stretching** involves the ability to challenge established habits and to *innovate and take risks in order to continually improve*. Stretching also requires the willingness to try to do more with limited resources and to reach results more quickly, less expensively and with better quality. Thus, stretching is about "pushing the edge of the envelope," inspiring others to action, striving towards doing more and going beyond the status quo. Stretching is needed in order to *promote change* and *achieve results.*

   When you're trying to differentiate, when you're trying to do something different, there's going to be that gut moment, that gut sense, "Is this right? Is this not right?" If you are not having doubt, you are not pushing the boundaries far enough.

   Tony Fadell – Nest

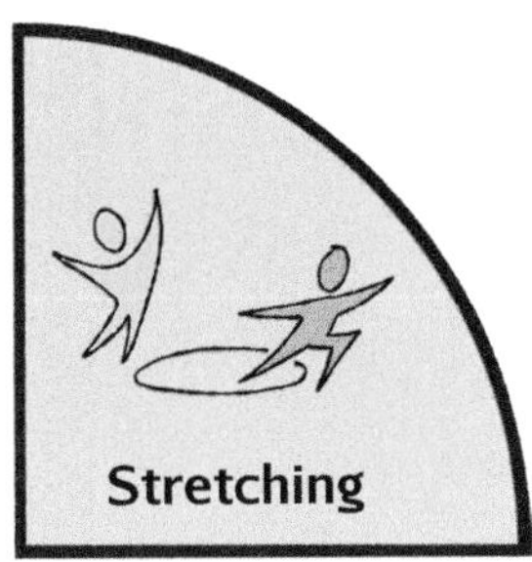

The passion for stretching yourself and sticking to it, even (or especially) when it's not going well, is the hallmark of the growth mindset.

Carol S. Dweck – Author of *Mindset: the New Psychology of Success*

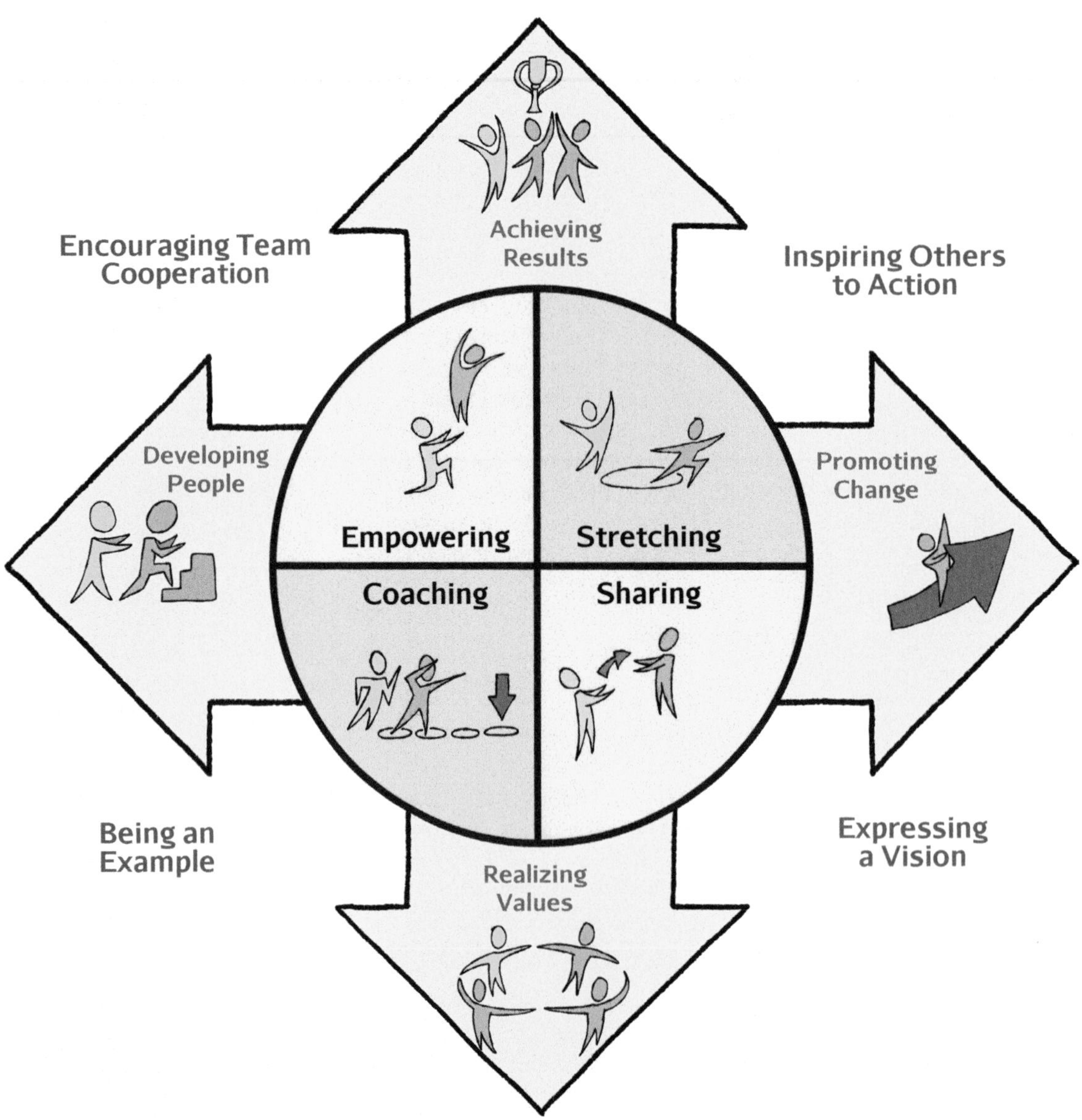

Combinations of key leadership Actions support the achievement of Organizational Outcomes

The Nine Key Inner Qualities of Good Leaders

In order for the four basic leadership actions to become expressed in relation to organizational outcomes, they must be supported by the leader's mindset and inner qualities and capabilities. While the four leadership actions relate to what leaders *do* with respect to others to reach outer goals and outcomes, leadership qualities are about what a leader *has* or *is* internally as a person. That is, the leadership actions define outer behaviors of *what* leaders do; leadership qualities define the inner processes and mindset behind those actions

The inner qualities of effective leadership relate to the attributes of mindset that drive the outer actions of empowering, coaching, sharing and stretching.

According to the SFM leadership model, there are nine core *inner qualities* that make up the mindset of successful leaders. Not surprisingly, these qualities overlap to some degree with the mindsets of successful next generation entrepreneurs. However there are a number of other qualities that are essential and unique to conscious and successful leadership. Effective leaders carry out the four actions of empowering, coaching, sharing and stretching through their *passion*, *vision*, *ambition*, *determination*, *openness*, *consistency*, *motivation* and *generosity* and by presenting a good *example*. We can define each of these qualities in the following way:

1. **Passion:** To *find what it is that you care deeply about and for which you have talent and pursue it with all of your heart.* Passion comes from connecting fully with one's self and one's deepest identity and discovering what brings us enthusiasm and energy. It involves connecting what you care about to what you do. Similar to its role in next generation entrepreneurship, passion is the foundation for all of the other key qualities of leadership.

> *People say you have to have a lot of passion for what you are doing and its totally true. And the reason is because it is so hard that, if you don't, any rational person would give up. Its really hard and you have to do it over a sustained period of time. So if you don't love it and you are not having fun doing it and if you don't really love it, you are going to give up.*
>
> **Steve Jobs** – Apple Inc.

> *Without passion, you don't have energy. Without energy, you have nothing.*
>
> **Warren Buffet** – Berkshire Hathaway

Good business leaders create a vision, articulate the vision, passionately own the vision, and relentlessly drive it to completion.

Jack Welch – Former CEO, General Electric

Your work is going to fill a large part of your life, and the only way to be truly satisfied is to do what you believe is great work. . .

We're just enthusiastic about what we do.

Steve Jobs – Apple Inc.

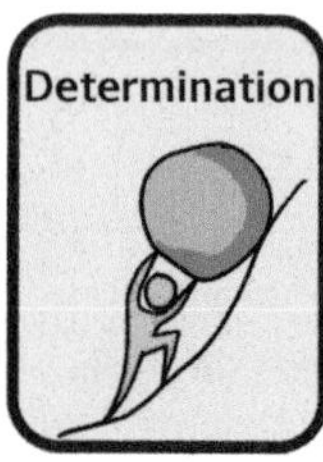

Whenever you see a successful business, someone once made a courageous decision.

Peter Drucker – Author of *The Practice of Management*

I don't ever give up. I mean, I'd have to be dead or completely incapacitated.

Elon Musk – SpaceX, Tesla Motors

2. **Vision:** To *set and stay focused on the bigger picture and longer-term goals.* As we have already established, vision is about seeing beyond the present, imagining future possibilities and clearly defining one's ambitions, adopting long-term plans and a holistic view. Vision provides the motivation for stretching and sharing in the service of *promoting change*.

    All successful people men and women are big dreamers. They imagine what their future could be, ideal in every respect, and then they work every day toward their distant vision, that goal or purpose.

    Brian Tracy – The Psychology of Achievement

3. **Ambition:** To have *"a strong desire to do or to achieve something."* Ambition is about directing one's actions towards particular results; maintaining a high level of *involvement* toward their attainment. Ambition comes from our innate desire for growth and mastery and is the commitment to work concretely and efficiently, aiming to reach a level of excellence. Ambition unites the actions of stretching and empowering and focuses them towards *attaining results*.

    High expectations are the key to everything.

    Sam Walton – Walmart

    Keep away from people who try to belittle your ambitions. Small people always do that, but the really great make you feel that you, too, can become great.

    Mark Twain

4. **Determination:** To *be resolute* and *firm in one's mission and purpose.* Determination fosters the willingness to take risks and try new solutions. It is an expression of emotional involvement in reaching the desired outcome; i.e., the act of "putting one's heart into it." The quality of determination is essential for stretching.

    The two things we really zero in on in people sound simple but they end up being very difficult: courage and genius. Courage is the one we talk about a lot because it's the one that people can learn. Courage which is not giving up in the face of adversity and just being absolutely determined to succeed is something you can force yourself into. It can be very painful but you can force yourself to do it. The genius part is more difficult to force yourself to do. Courage without genius might not get you where you want to go, but genius without courage almost certainly won't.

    Marc Andreessen - Andreessen Horowitz

5. **Openness:** To *communicate in order to share*. Openness comes from being curious and available to new ideas. It requires having faith in others and, building reciprocal esteem and respect. Openness is the key quality necessary for sharing.

   A classic entrepreneurial impulse is to hold your idea close to you and not tell anyone because it is so special. That's almost always a mistake. It's a mistake because your real competitive advantage is not that you have this great idea that is locked away in your closet, which may or may not be accurate and you have no idea which it is. Your actual competitive advantage is that you are assembling the intelligence around does this idea work, what is the right team, what are the right learnings and we are essentially in motion.

   Reid Hoffman – LinkedIn

Another quality [of good leaders and entrepreneurs] that I think is important is being flexible minded, or open minded. I am not saying you shouldn't have a vision for your idea or product, but you need to be open to changes.

Jessica Livingston - Y Combinator

6. **Consistency:** To be *faithful to one's words with one's actions* (i.e., "walk the talk"). Consistency is about adhering to one's values and beliefs and acting ethically and coherently through time. Consistency is a core quality for both coaching and sharing and is essential for *realizing values*.

   To think is easy. To act is difficult. To act as one thinks is the most difficult.

   Johann Wolfgang Von Goeth

   Leadership is doing what is right when no one is watching.

   George Van Valkenburg

Those who are blessed with the most talent don't necessarily outperform everyone else. It's the people with follow-through who excel.

Mary Kay Ash – Mary Kay Cosmetics

7. **Motivation**: To invest *energy into action*. Motivation is the drive to move forward, to "be there," and involve oneself with passion. It is about connecting with core values and devoting oneself to what one has chosen to do. Motivation, when put into practice through empowering and coaching is the essential quality for *developing people*.

   To be successful, you have to have your heart in your business, and your business in your heart.

   Thomas Watson – Founder of IBM

   You have to work hardest for the things you love most.

   Carol S. Dweck – Author of Mindset: the New Psychology of Success

Leadership is the art of getting someone else to do something you want done because he or she wants to do it.

Dwight Eisenhower

8. **Generosity**: To *dedicate time and personal involvement* in order to contribute to the recognition and development of other people's potential. It is the quality of readiness to give more of something, such as time or other resources, than is strictly necessary or expected. Generosity is the primary quality required for *empowering*.

You have not lived today until you have done something for someone who can never repay you.

John Bunyan

> *My goal is to live my life in such a way that when I die, someone can say, she cared.*
>
> **Mary Kay Ash** – Mary Kay Cosmetics

> *We live in an interdependent world. Every time you cut off somebody else's opportunities, you shrink your own horizons.*
>
> **Bill Clinton**

9. **Example:** *To provide a believable and trustworthy point of reference*—i.e., *a model to follow*. Being an example has to do with the congruency between "message" and "messenger," offering suggestions demonstrating how to learn from experience. The desire to provide a good example is the foundation for the action of *coaching*.

Leadership is a matter of having people look at you and gain confidence, seeing how you react. If you're in control, they're in control.

Tom Landry – NFL Head Coach

> *If you know exactly what you want to be, you need to spend as much time as possible with people who are actually that already.*
>
> **Gary Vaynerchuk** – Wine Library

> *It's better to hang out with people better than you. Pick out associates whose behavior is better than yours and you'll drift in that direction.*
>
> **Warren Buffet** – Berkshire Hathaway

The outer actions needed for success are supported by key inner qualities that make up a leadership mindset.

Summary of the Model

The overall SFM Leadership Model may be summarized in the diagram on the following page, which illustrates the relationships between the nine core leadership qualities, the four leadership actions and the organizational outcomes that they produce.

As the diagram illustrates, **passion** and **purpose** are the core of effective leadership. As we have emphasized numerous times, without passion and purpose it is easy to get lost or give up.

- **Generosity** is the primary inner quality needed to *empower* others.
- **Motivation** is the foundation for *developing people* and supports the actions of both empowering and coaching.
- Providing a good **example** is the underlying basis for effective *coaching*.
- **Consistency** is necessary for *realizing values* and is essential for effective coaching and sharing.
- **Openness** is the essential inner quality at the basis of productive *sharing*.
- **Vision** is the inner quality most associated with *creating and promoting change*. Vision is also the common stimulus for the actions of stretching and sharing.
- **Determination** is the primary inner driver for *stretching*.
- The **ambition** for achievement is the key motivator for *achieving results*, providing the focal point for the actions of both stretching and empowering.

The SFM Leadership Model™

Connections Between the SFM Leadership Model™ and the Circle of Success

There are a number of parallels between the SFM Leadership Model and the Circle of Success, though the two were developed independently of one another and were not intended to have any direct correspondence. The main links start with **outcomes**.

1. **Achieving Results** can be strongly correlated with reaching *Financial Robustness.*
2. **Developing People** is a necessary condition for making a *Meaningful Contribution* (both for customers and team members).
3. **Promoting Change** is a prerequisite for *Scalable Growth*
4. **Realizing Values** has major implications for supporting both *Innovation and Resilience.*

With respect to **actions**, we can make some fairly strong connections between:

1. **Empowering** as a means to *Develop the Product or Service* as well as *Generate Interest and Revenue*
2. **Coaching** in order to *Increase Competency* as well as *Create Alignment*
3. **Sharing** as a way to *Enhance and Leverage Resources* as well as *Build Win-Win Relationships*
4. **Stretching** in order to *Expand the Business* and *Create Value* as well as *Raise Investment* and *Acquire Essential Resources*

There are also parallels that can be made at the level of **mindset**:

- The qualities of **generosity**, **ambition** and **motivation** support empowering people to bring the venture's *vision* of what to create in the world into action.
- **Motivation, consistency** and providing an **example** are necessary for coaching team members to fulfill their *mission* and successfully make their unique *contribution* to the vision.
- **Openness**, **vision** and **consistency** are key qualities to help people share and clarify their *roles* in order to establish win-win partnerships.
- **Determination, vision** and **ambition** are what help ventures stretch, *expand and achieve* what they want to accomplish for investors and key stakeholders.

There is the obvious overlap between the inner qualities of passion, vision and ambition in the two models. Certainly, passion and ambition play a similar role in the mindset of both leaders and entrepreneurs. Vision, while always directed toward future possibilities, can have a different focus in leadership. In fact, while an entrepreneur's vision is primarily directed outward toward the customer, market and larger "holon," the leader's vision is focused equally on the growth of the venture and the value created for investors and partners. This creates a very important balance that sometimes creates problems for people who are too "entrepreneurial."

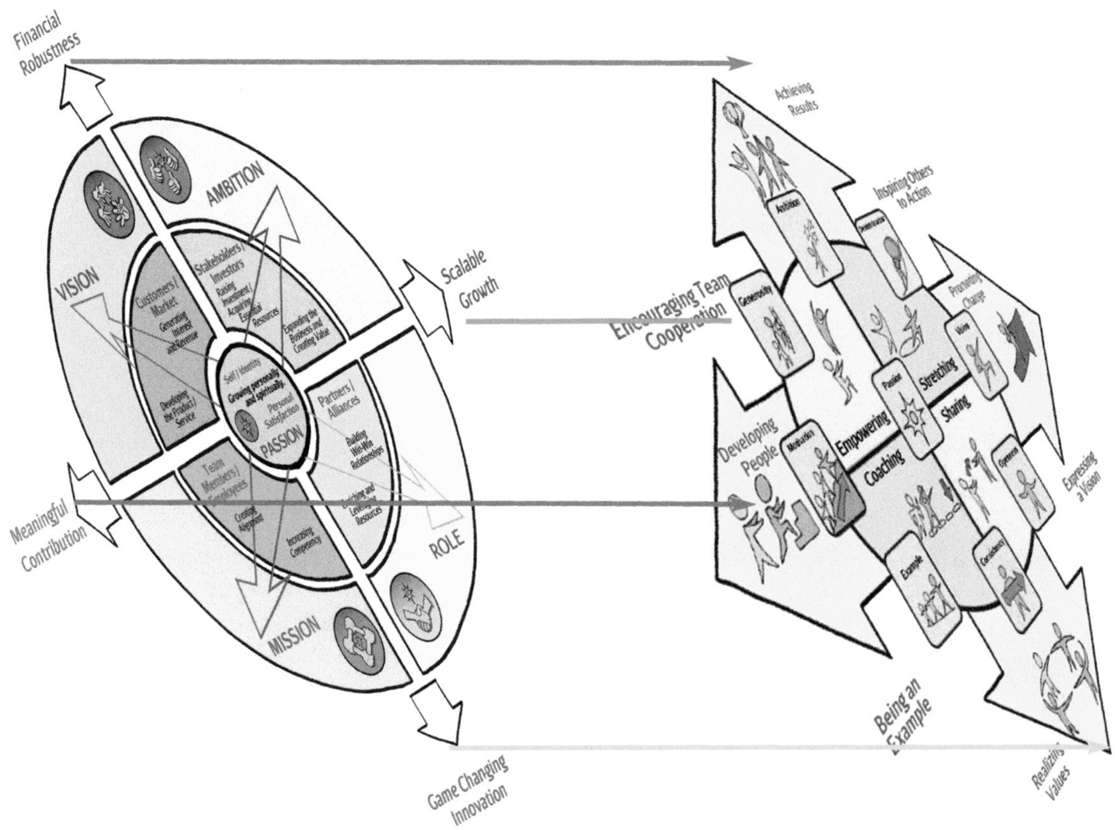

The SFM Leadership Model™ Complements the SFM Circle of Success in a Number of Ways

As an interesting observation, when Steve Jobs was forced out of Apple in the mid 1980s by the company's board of directors, it was primarily because his vision was always focused on the customer and what he wanted to create in the world. Board members were afraid this would come at the expense of investors and other key stakeholders. When Jobs returned take charge of Apple in the late 1990s, his vision was much more balanced, leading the company to an unprecedented period of growth and success.

This becomes an important question for your own venture. Is your vision primarily focused on what you will create for your customers and how it will benefit them, or on how your venture will grow and benefit the stakeholders who have supported you? Clearly a balance is essential.

This difference is highlighted in the following Success Factor Case Example illustrating some of the key elements of the SFM Leadership Model and its relevance for resilience and rebounding from adversity.

Success Factor Case Example:
Charles Matthews - Rolls Royce

Give people a toolkit of practical problem solving techniques and then empower them.

Charles Matthews
Former Managing Director of Rolls Royce Motors

According to Charles Matthews, "Large organizations require a combination of strong direction and leadership but then as much empowerment from top to bottom as possible."

When Charles Matthews was appointed Managing Director and Chief of Operations at Rolls-Royce Motorcars in late 1992, he was facing quite a challenge. The company had just completed a major downsizing of the business and was in a difficult phase of renewal.

In order to deal with the changes and get the business back on track, Matthews knew he would have to clearly communicate a vision for the future, facilitate easy access to resources, encourage the sharing of information and know-how, create an open environment for interaction and build authentic consensus. "People need to be able to do it *and* want to do it," Matthews claims.

He laid out a vision for how the factory operation would change and set out to engage as many people as possible. He knew he would need to improve the design and availability of parts, so he involved logistics people in materials flow (i.e., getting the right parts to the right places at the right time). He also provided for an "immense amount of training in total quality management," in order to "give people a toolkit of practical problem solving techniques and then empower them."

At the beginning, Matthews found himself at the pinnacle of a reporting hierarchy that began on the shop-floor, and moved up through team leaders, zone managers, senior production managers and then to the manufacturing director. By the time information reached him, it had been heavily filtered. His "feel" for what was happening in the factory was blunted by distance.

One of Matthews first steps was to "de-level" the business, taking certain levels of management out. He got the engineers out onto the shop floor, working alongside of people who were building the cars and established problem solving teams. Previously, operators could not get the technical support of engineers. Now, they could put names to faces and could call on them when they needed input or assistance, creating a greater sense of empowerment.

Perhaps the major issue that Matthews faced was defusing the tremendous amount of hostility that had built up during downsizing and restructuring. He knew he would need to "recapture the hearts and minds of people" because he "couldn't take the business forward without it."

Matthews took to walking around the factory with his coach, honing his listening and observational skills. He learned how to listen with attention and make shop-floor staff feel at ease with him, how to read non-verbal signals, and how to corroborate his understanding by saying: "So your view is that . . ." He learned to assume there was something useful or important in everything he heard. On a number of occasions, staff subjected him to strong verbal attacks on issues close to their hearts. But, people knew they could talk to him because, even when he disagreed with, or did not act on their input, he listened and responded. This served to build trust and grow a sense of team spirit.

Matthews also established internal communication and rapport building forums in order for people to share their feelings, opinions and ideas for change. As an example, Matthews instituted regular Friday lunchtime "open forums." People were notified in advance that there would be a one-hour open session, usually held in a conference room or an open area of the factory. People could bring their lunches and talk about anything they wanted.

In the beginning, people mostly complained, expressing hostility toward management relating to the downsizing. For months each session began by people airing their hostility. Over time, however, these outbursts transformed to more constructive comments and suggestions. "It takes a while for people let their guard down," Matthews comments.

During these forums, Matthews was constantly seeking people's views and recruiting them into change teams or at least engaging them in the change. "We (top management) had to keep 'walking the talk' and consistently plug away. Long-term change is a matter of consistency. Where there were particularly difficult areas where people were unconvinced, we took the debate to them."

Matthews' efforts paid off. By the beginning of 1996, the company had transformed dramatically. Not only had their been significant improvement in car quality and reduced costs and complaints, but the staff was more confident and working together as members of a winning team. The hostility about the changes had completely disappeared and shop floor operators became factory tour guides for new customers

"Large organizations require a combination of strong direction and leadership but then as much empowerment from top to bottom as possible," states Matthews. "It is a constant balance. The key is engaging people as much as possible."

By walking around the factory and listening with attention to people's concerns and complaints, Charles Matthews diffused their hostility and fostered a sense of trust.

Reflections on the Case

It is clear that Charles Matthews gave balanced attention to each of the four fundamental organizational outcomes:

- *Promoting Change* – Like IBM's Samuel Palmisano (profiled in *SFM Vol. I*, pp. 116-121), Matthews de-leveled the business and got people working alongside each other in problem solving teams.
- *Realizing Values* – He refocused the business on the values of quality and working cooperatively.
- *Developing People* – Matthews provided training in total quality management and supported his team to be more confident and working together.
- *Achieving Results* – He produced significant improvement in car quality and reduced costs and complaints.

De-leveling the business, seeking people's views and recruiting them into the change process is an illustration of

By de-leveling the business, seeking people's views and recruiting them into the change process, Matthews engaged in the action of **empowering**. In addition to exhibiting the leadership qualities of *generosity* and *motivation*, his interactions with people display a number of other characteristics of empowering including:

- Recognizing individuality
- Supporting the development of people's potential
- Promoting self-esteem
- Encouraging autonomy
- Stimulating motivation for growth

Walking around the factory, listening to people with attention and equanimity and providing training in quality management illustrate key aspects of Coaching.

As Matthews pointed out, "The key is engaging people as much as possible."

Matthews' behavior of walking around the factory and listening to people with attention and equanimity illustrates some of the key aspects of action of **coaching** and the leadership qualities of *example* and *consistency*. His activities, such as providing training in total quality management in order to "give people a toolkit of practical problem solving techniques" also show several other key aspects of coaching such as:

- Developing people's experience and competencies
- Building trust
- Listening with attention
- Guiding people in their learning process
- Growing team spirit

Matthews' establishment of communication forums and open lunchtime sessions are clear examples of the action of **sharing** and the qualities of *vision* and *openness*. His approach also demonstrates a number of key dimensions of sharing including:

- Describing clear vision
- Facilitating easy access to resources
- Sharing information and know-how
- Creating an open environment for interaction
- Looking for authentic consensus

In striving to improve the quality of both his company's products and people with fewer resources at his disposal, Matthews' case provides a classic example of **stretching** and the leadership qualities of ambition and determination. His actions with his team also demonstrate other important aspects of stretching such as:

- Raising expectations
- Stimulating innovation
- Looking for continuous improvement
- Encouraging the willingness to stretch oneself
- Challenging consolidated habits

These key steps can be summarized in the following diagram.

Laying out a vision for how the factory operation would change and establishing communication forums and open lunchtime sessions are an example of the action of Sharing.

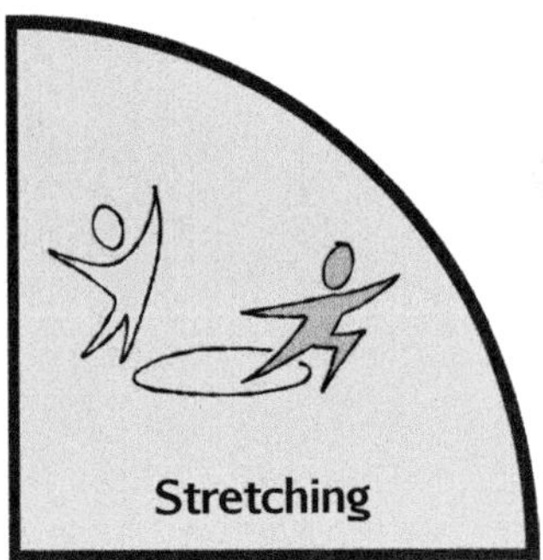

Striving to improve the quality of both the company's products and people with fewer resources is an example of Stretching.

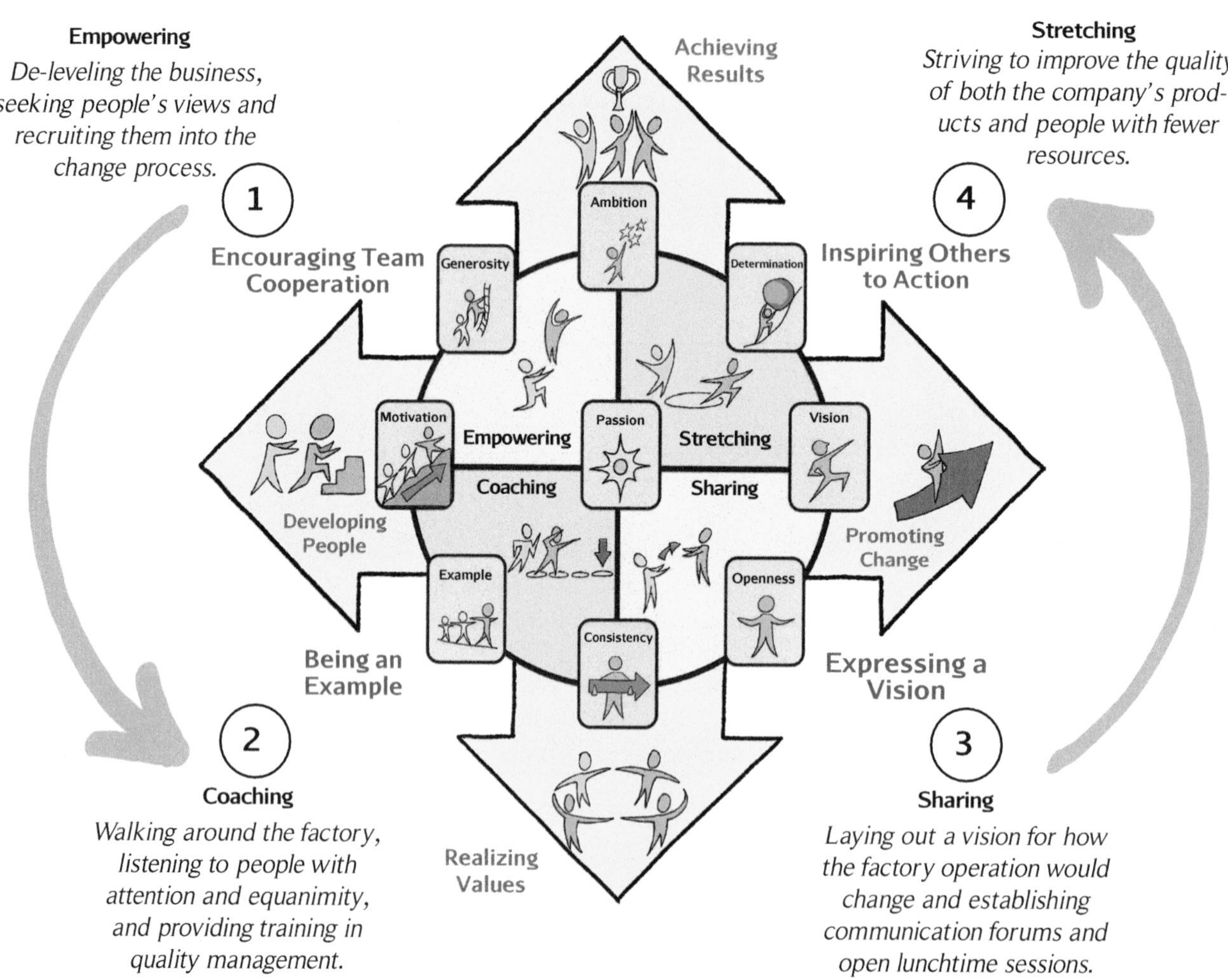

How Charles Matthews used Empowering, Coaching, Sharing and Stretching to help Rolls-Royce Motorcars recover and become more fit for the future.

The Necessity of Emotional Intelligence and Mastering the Inner Game

Matthews' responses to people's hostility and verbal attacks also provide a powerful illustration of *emotional intelligence*. Matthews was able to recognize, acknowledge and welcome (make a "guest house" for) strong emotions without judgment and make the space to hold their expression with equanimity. In doing so, the positive intention of these emotions was able to surface and ultimately his staff found the resources to transform and integrate them; instead of allowing them to become "the elephant in the room nobody is talking about."

To accomplish this, mastering his *inner game* was as important as his tactics in pursuing the outer game. Matthew's success required all of the inner qualities of vision, openness, consistency, example, motivation, generosity, achievement and determination.

The ability to recognize, acknowledge and welcome strong emotions without judgment and make the space to hold the expression of those emotions with equanimity is an illustration of emotional intelligence.

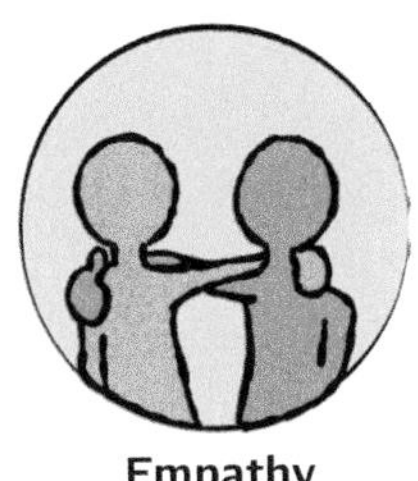

Empathy

A Critical Path for Conscious Leaders

There is another important and potentially subtle lesson in "conscious" leadership in Charles Matthews' example. His actions followed a particular sequence, beginning with Empowering, then moving to Coaching, followed by Sharing and ending with Stretching. This implies a type of critical path of actions to reach a successful and sustainable result. There is a deep but not necessarily obvious wisdom in this sequence.

Charles Matthew's actions followed a particular sequence, beginning with Empowering, then moving to Coaching, followed by Sharing and ending with Stretching. This implies a type of critical path of actions needed to reach a successful and sustainable result.

If people are not first empowered, then coaching makes no appreciable impact. What difference does it make if you have an increase in experience and competence but have no opportunity or authority to put it into practice?

If people are not empowered and coached, then sharing will probably be fairly ineffective. As Matthew's noted, it will probably mostly consist of complaining, blaming or superficial and non-innovative "chatter." This generally stems from a feeling of helplessness. As people are empowered and coached to become more responsible, accountable and skillful, their sharing becomes more productive and innovative.

The mistake, unfortunately, that many companies and business leaders make is to begin by stretching their teams and employees, without empowering them, coaching them and creating opportunities for them to share and amass their collective intelligence. Stretching without the support of the other leadership actions simply creates stress, overwhelm and other forms of CRASH for team members.

Empowering people first is as critical to promoting innovation as it is to developing resilience as is illustrated in the following Success Factor Case Example of William McKnight and 3M.

Success Factor Case Example
William McKnight - 3M

Encourage people's initiative, tolerate their mistakes and trust them.

The Minnesota Mining and Manufacturing Company (3M) was founded in 1902. It struggled in its early years, like most new businesses, before assuring its future in 1914 with the launch of an abrasive cloth, called "Three-M-ite," made with aluminum oxide. It was much better than natural mineral emery for cutting metal, and was used in huge quantities in World War I. The company paid its first dividend in 1916 and has not missed a quarterly cash payment to shareholders ever since. Such longevity clearly demonstrates a strong and sustainable capacity for innovation, resilience and fitness for the future.

William McKnight
President and Chairman of 3M

William L. McKnight joined the firm as an assistant book-keeper in 1907 and rose through the ranks, becoming president in 1929 and chairman in 1949. He is still revered as the firm's great "philosopher-leader" and the principal architect of 3M's famously innovative corporate culture, a culture that has been described by management writers Christopher Bartlett and Sumantra Ghoshal as "an organizational climate that stimulates ordinary people to produce extraordinary performance."

There are many examples of the innovations nurtured by 3M's capacity to recognize individuality, promote the development of people's potential, develop autonomy and stimulate people's motivation for innovation and growth. In *SFM Vol. II*, for instance, I presented the case example of how the highly successful product Post-it® Notes was developed in the 1970s as a generative collaboration between two 3M scientists (p. 190). Another story of empowerment and innovation begins in 1922, when 3M employee Dick Drew paid an afternoon visit to an autobody shop to test a new batch of sandpaper. 3M's patented Wetordry sandpaper was at the time the standard product in auto paint and repair shops because of its smooth finish and reduced dust hazard.

Empowerment fosters "an organizational climate that stimulates ordinary people to produce extraordinary performance."

Drew heard a group of workers cursing vehemently. Two-tone cars had recently become popular, but painters hated them because they had to mask parts of the autobody with heavy adhesive tape and butcher paper, and when they later removed the masking, some of the new paint often came away with it. As he watched the craftsmen repair the torn paint, Drew might have thought of all that extra Wetordry he could sell them. But instead he thought of a solution to the problem: a tape with a less aggressive adhesive. He also realized 3M was ideally placed to develop such tape, because it would be like sandpaper without the sand.

Drew returned to the laboratory, and began a long and frustrating quest for the right combination of adhesive and backing. After several fruitless years, 3M President McKnight told Drew to drop the project and get back to work on improving sandpaper. Drew duly complied, but a day later he thought of a new way to handle the backing problems and resumed his experiments. In the middle of one of them, McKnight paid another visit to the lab, saw Drew hard at work on his supposedly abandoned project, but said nothing.

The story of the development of masking tape at 3M illustrates the important relationship between empowerment and innovation,

Drew finally found the right combination of materials and asked McKnight to approve funding for a paper-making machine to manufacture the new tape. His request was rejected, but Drew wasn't about to give up now. As a researcher, he had authority to approve purchases of up to $100, so he began writing a series of $99 purchase orders. He later confessed his strategy to McKnight while showing him the new machine.

And in this way, masking tape was born. Its launch marked the start of a new chapter in 3M's evolution, which would lead to the launch of Scotch Cellophane tape (also invented by Drew) in 1930, and to 3M's current range of over 700 tapes for medical, electrical, construction, and dozens of other applications.

These exchanges between McKnight and Drew, Drew's insubordinate purchase of the paper-making machinery, and McKnight's relaxed response to his defiance, are an expression of the inner quality of *generosity* and the leadership action of *empowerment*. "They set forth a clear ethic for managers," the company states in its literature, "If you have the right person on the right project, and they are absolutely dedicated to finding a solution, leave them alone. Tolerate their initiative and trust them."

In 1948, McKnight articulated a set of Management Principles that underpin the organizational culture within which 3M's innovations flourish:

> *As our business grows, it becomes increasingly necessary to delegate responsibility and to encourage men and women to exercise their initiative. This requires considerable tolerance. Those men and women to whom we delegate authority and responsibility, if they are good people, are going to want to do their jobs in their own way.*
>
> *Mistakes will be made. But if a person is essentially right, the mistakes he or she makes are not as serious in the long run as the mistakes management will make if it undertakes to tell those in authority exactly how they must do their jobs.*
>
> *Management that is destructively critical when mistakes are made kills initiative. And it's essential that we have many people with initiative if we are to continue to grow.*

As William McKnight points out, "Management that is destructively critical when mistakes are made kills initiative."

Reflections on the Case

McKnight's statements clearly indicate an organizational culture based on empowerment. Empowerment creates a culture of innovation and self-leadership, in which the success of the organization is based on the combined energy and creative efforts of many people aligned toward a common vision. In a leadership culture, people are essentially viewed as equals who are in different roles. Roles are based on the development of individual capabilities and are not a reflection of the intrinsic value of the person. As a result, people at all levels are acknowledged and valued as individual members and contributors—even those who break the rules in order to deliver value to the organization as a whole.

1. Delegating responsibility and encouraging people to exercise their initiative.

Three Key Steps for Orchestrating Innovation

William McKnight's set of management principles and the example of the creation of masking tape also present a simple yet powerful prescription for "orchestrating innovation."

1. **Delegating responsibility and encouraging people to exercise their initiative.** This serves to develop autonomy and stimulate people's *motivation for innovation* and growth. It is also essential for *developing people* and supporting them to "invest energy into action."
2. **Letting people do their jobs in their own way and tolerating mistakes.** This relies on the leader's *generosity* and serves the purpose of recognizing and acknowledging people's individuality and promoting the development of their potential.
3. **Trusting that the right person on the right project will be "absolutely dedicated to finding a solution."** This helps to promote people's self-esteem and increase their capacity for *ambition* by supporting their innate desire for growth and mastery and acknowledging their commitment to work concretely and efficiently toward *achieving results*.

2. Letting people do their jobs in their own way and tolerating mistakes.

We can see these same principles at work in the case example of Pike Place Fish Market presented in the previous chapter. People's commitment to "Be yourself and do what inspires you," and their ambition to be "World Famous" by "being present and relating to people as a human beings; making each person's day more positive" creates a culture of empowerment in which team members tap into their own motivation and innovate in order achieve results.

3. Trusting that the right person on the right project will be "absolutely dedicated to finding a solution."

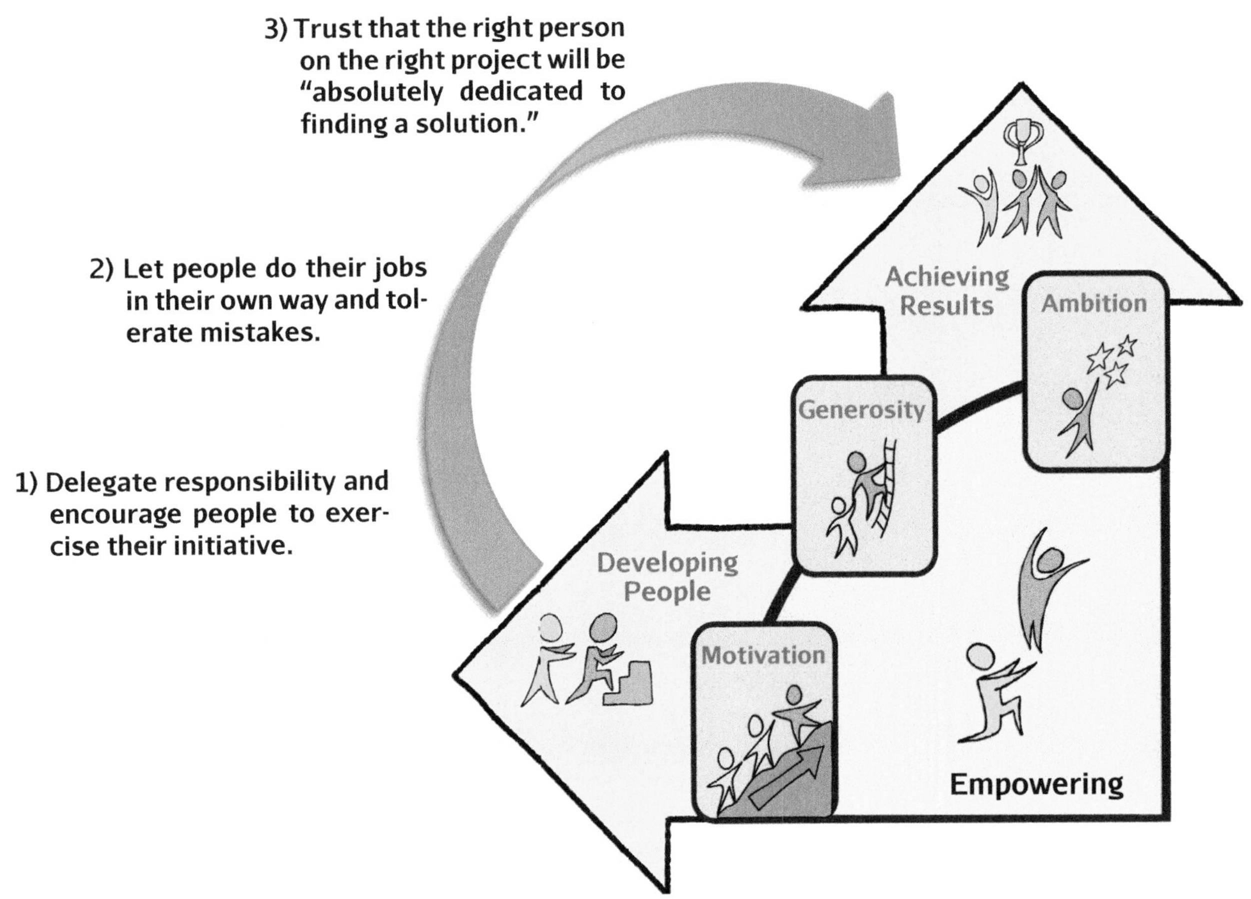

3M's Three Key Steps for Orchestrating Innovation

McKnight's statement that "if a person is essentially right, the mistakes he or she makes are not as serious in the long run as the mistakes management will make if it undertakes to tell those in authority exactly how they must do their jobs" also indicates that empowerment is also a crucial aspect of developing fitness for the future. An organizational culture based on empowerment that fosters innovation and self-leadership will inherently be more fit for the future in a dynamic and changing world than one hampered by rigidity and hierarchy

Chapter Summary

The *SFM Leadership Model* provides a rich road-map for building a venture, rebounding from adversity and becoming more fit for the future. The model is organized around personal qualities (what the leader has internally), actions (what the leader does) and organizational outcomes (what the leader achieves).

According to the SFM Leadership model, there are four essential *organizational outcomes* of successful ventures – promoting change, realizing values, developing people and achieving results. These outcomes are achieved as a result of four fundamental *leadership actions* – empowering, coaching, sharing and stretching. *Empowering* is necessary in order to develop people and achieve results. *Coaching* is also necessary for developing people and helping them to realize values. *Sharing* is also key to realizing values as well as to promote change. *Stretching* is essential to both promoting change and achieving results.

These four leadership actions emerge from and are supported by nine key *inner qualities* – passion, vision, determination, ambition, openness, generosity, motivation, consistency and example. Different qualities are more related to particular actions and outcomes than others.

There are a number of parallels between the SFM Leadership Model and the *Circle of Success*. The four leadership outcomes complement the entrepreneurial outcomes of achieving financial robustness, making a meaningful contribution, increasing innovation and resilience, and attaining scalable growth. Similarly, the leadership actions of empowering, coaching, sharing and stretching support the entrepreneurial actions develop the product or service and generating interest and revenue; increasing the competency of the team and creating alignment; enhancing and leveraging resources and build win-win relationships; expand the business and creating value and raising investment and acquiring essential resources.

There are also complementary relationships between the inner qualities of effective leaders and the mindset of successful entrepreneurs. The mindset of an entrepreneur primarily directed outward toward customers, the market and the larger "holon." The leader's mindset is focused equally on the growth of the venture and the value created for investors and partners. The complementary emphasis of the two mindsets creates and important balance that is sometimes missing in both start-ups and larger organizations.

The Success Factor Case Example of *Charles Matthews and Rolls Royce Motorcars* provides a good illustration of these skills in action. Matthews' application of Empowering, Coaching, Sharing and Stretching – supported by his emotional intelligence and ability to welcome and make space for people's difficult feelings – helped the company and its employees through a difficult time of renewal. The sequence of actions intuitively followed by Matthews illustrates an important critical path followed by conscious leaders that begins with Empowering first and then Coaching before Sharing and ultimately Stretching their team members. Stretching first without the support of the other leadership actions simply creates stress and overwhelm.

The Success Factor Case Example of *William McKnight and 3M* illustrates the importance of founding the organization's culture in empowerment. 3M has developed a long history of innovation and fitness for the future by implementing three key steps for orchestrating innovation: (1) delegating responsibility and encouraging people to exercise their initiative, (2) letting people do their jobs in their own way and tolerating mistakes, and (3) trusting that the right person on the right project will be "absolutely dedicated to finding a solution."

References and Further Readings

- *Modeling with NLP*, Dilts, R., Meta Publications, Capitola, CA, 1998.
- *Alpha Leadership: Tools for Leaders Who Want More From Life*, Deering, A., Dilts, R. and Russell, J., John Wiley & Sons, London, England, 2002.
- *Visionary Leadership Skills: Creating a World to Which People Want to Belong*, Dilts, R., Meta Publications, Capitola, Ca., 1996.

05 Applying the SFM Leadership Model™

A true leader has the confidence to stand alone, the courage to make tough decisions, and the compassion to listen to the needs of others. He does not set out to be a leader, but becomes one by the equality of his actions and the integrity of his intent.

Douglas McArthur

All of the great leaders have had one characteristic in common: it was the willingness to confront unequivocally the major anxiety of their people in their time. This, and not much else, is the essence of leadership.

John Kenneth Galbraith

Leadership is a potent combination of strategy and character. But if you must be without one, be without the strategy.

Norman Schwarzkopf

ANTONIO MEZA

The SFM Leadership Model was the basis for *ISVOR DILTS Leadership Systems*, a joint venture between Dilts Strategy Group and ISVOR Fiat – the organizational development branch of the Fiat Group.

"Leadership Moments" are natural decisions points, critical milestones or challenging events that have the potential to make a significant impact on people's perceptions and motivation.

Applying the SFM Leadership Model™

As I pointed out in the beginning of Chapter 1, the objective of the Success Factor Modeling™ process is to make an *instrumental map*—one supported by a variety of exercises, formats and tools that allow people to apply the factors that have been modeled in order to reach key outcomes within their chosen context.

In the early 2000s, my brother John and I used the SFM Leadership Model as the basis for our company *ISVOR DILTS Leadership Systems*, a joint venture between our Dilts Strategy Group and ISVOR Fiat – the organizational development branch of the Fiat Group during that period. We developed a 360% leadership assessment tool and a comprehensive leadership development program consisting of workshops, an online leadership portal, assisted self-development programs and individual coaching sessions. The program provided 65 different tools to support all of the different dimensions of the model.

For the purposes of this book and this chapter, however, I will present in depth only some of the most relevant tools and formats relating to rebounding from adversity, increasing resilience, improving innovation and enhancing your venture's fitness for the future.

Identifying "Leadership Moments"

To begin to apply the skills of leadership to your own venture, it is a good idea to identify some common "leadership moments" that you encounter. *Leadership Moments* are natural decisions points, critical milestones or challenging events that occur as part of a leader's or entrepreneur's daily reality. These are significant and often symbolic situations that have the potential to make a significant impact on people's perceptions and motivation.

Customers, co-workers, stakeholders and partners constantly present us with leadership moments through their relationships and interactions with us. Within any project or venture, there are a series of such leadership moments. These situations require initiative, intuition, courage, emotional intelligence and congruence. In these periods it is important to *express a vision*, *influence others to action*, *encourage team cooperation* and to *be an example*. In the words of one the leaders in my study, leadership moments are situations in which "you have to let people look you in the eye and read your body language."

The notion of a "moment," of course, is a relative term that could refer to literally a few minutes in time (such as making an important announcement) or to a time period extending into days, weeks or months (as when Elon Musk's companies were in danger of failing or when Steve Jobs returned to Apple when it was on the verge of bankruptcy). In the example of Charles Matthews, for instance, there were many leadership "moments." Some were brief exchanges when staff expressed hostility. Others related to the necessity for a consistent course of action extending over a long period of time.

Leadership moments are an obvious test of the mindset and inner qualities of the leader – i.e., his or her passion, motivation, determination, vision, openness, generosity, ambition, consistency and ability to be a good example. They are also situations that require some type of action—empowering, coaching, sharing or stretching—in order to reach the outcomes of developing people, putting some value into action, promoting change or getting results.

Elon Musk had an important "leadership moment" when his three companies were all facing bankruptcy at the same time.

Developing People to Achieve Results

When the situation is one that requires developing *people* and focusing them on getting *results*, the most important action is ***empowering***. This brings to the forefront the leadership qualities of *generosity*, *motivation* and *ambition* for achievement. The leader needs to dedicate time and personal involvement, invest energy into action and demonstrate and encourage a strong desire to achieve something. The situation facing John Yokoyama to salvage the Pike Place Fish Market and save it from bankruptcy would be an example of this. He was able to transform his team's mindset by encouraging them "to be themselves and to do what inspires them."

William McKnight's relaxed response to Dick Drew's insistence on tying to develop a tape with a less aggressive adhesive (instead of his job of improving sandpaper) and Drew's insubordinate purchase of paper-making machinery is another example of an empowerment mindset.

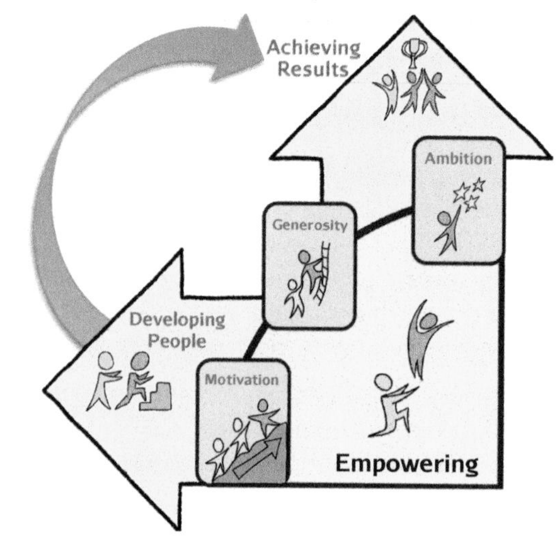

Guiding People to Enact Values

If the leadership moment is one that requires developing *people* and focusing them on enacting key *values*, then the most relevant action to take is ***coaching***. In this case, it is the leader's *example* that is most important supported by the qualities of *consistency* and *motivation*. This means the leader needs to "walk the talk," staying faithful to his or her words with his or her actions, and to "be there," involving himself or herself with passion in order to provide a believable and trustworthy point of reference. The example of how Dr. Lim Suet Wun of Tan Tock Seng Hospital in Singapore responded during the SARS epidemic is an illustration of this. By visiting all of the hospital staff and patients everyday during the crisis and shaking their hands, he built the necessary level of connection and trust essential for dealing with such a highly charged situation.

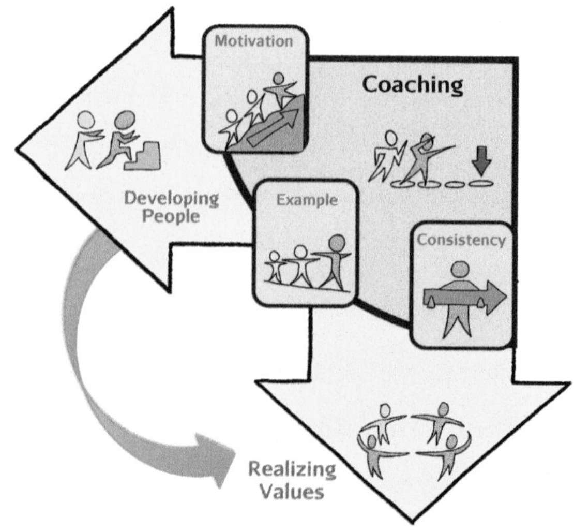

Maintaning Key Values During Times of Change

If the situation calls for promoting *change* and ensuring that key *values* are put or kept in place, then the most useful action is ***sharing***. This brings to the forefront the leadership qualities of *openness*, *vision* and *consistency*. This requires the leader to stay curious and available to new ideas and to have faith in others, building reciprocal esteem and respect. It also involves seeing beyond the present and imagining future possibilities, while remaining resolute and firm in one's mission and purpose. Charles Matthews' handling of the difficult transition at Rolls Royce provides a powerful example of how he employed sharing to defuse the tremendous amount of hostility that had built up during downsizing and restructuring of the company.

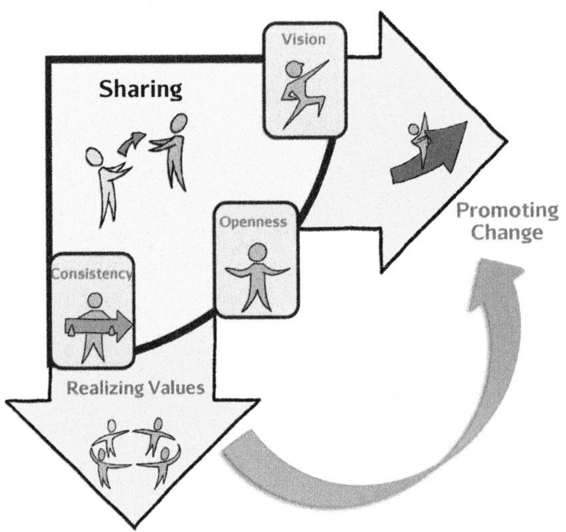

Promoting Change to Get Results

When the leadership moment demands *promoting change* in order to get *results*, the most critical action to take is ***stretching***. This brings to the forefront the leadership qualities of *vision*, *ambition* for achievement and *determination*. The leader must set and stay focused on the bigger picture and longer-term goals, and at the same direct actions towards particular results, maintaining a high level of involvement toward their attainment and devoting himself or herself to what he or she has chosen to do. Elon Musk's tenacious commitment to his vision and higher purpose during the time that all three of his ventures were failing epitomizes the qualities of mindset associated with stretching.

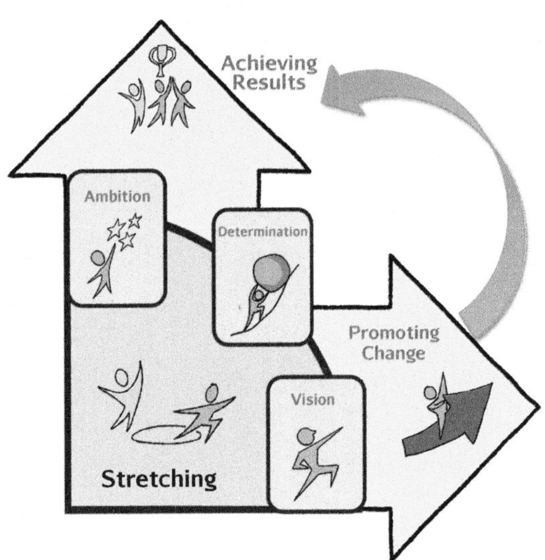

Anticipating Your Own Leadership Moments

As you reflect on your own project or venture, what are some of the "leadership moments" you are currently facing? Think in terms of the outcomes you need to achieve, the actions you need to take and challenges you face.

Are there some common or recurring "leadership moments" that you must address or anticipate facing in the future? Be sure to consider those involving both brief and extended periods of time. Take a moment and list some of your leadership challenges below.

Leadership Moments/Challenges:

____

____

____

____

____

____

Anticipating your own leadership moments helps you to prepare the necessary mindset and actions to address them in the best way possible.

As you reflect on your list of upcoming leadership moments, consider which outcomes are most important for you to accomplish? Are you wanting or needing to achieve a particular result? Develop people? Promote change of some sort? Realize or maintain certain values? A combination of these? Your desired outcome(s) will determine the actions you need to take and the mindset you need to adopt in order to be successful.

In the following pages, I will be presenting exercises that can be applied to the leadership moments that you have identified above. One of the goals of Success Factor Modeling is to support you in addressing these challenging moments more proactively, intelligently, confidently and consciously.

Empowering People to Achieve Results

As we have seen in cases such as 3M, Rolls Royce and Pike Place Fish Market, *Empowering* involves the ability to promote the *expression of individual potential*, permitting *autonomy* and the assumption of personal *responsibility* and *influence*, in order to better achieve results. Empowering requires the capacity to facilitate conditions which allow people to express themselves better, and recognize the value of their work, stimulating personal and professional growth as well as self-esteem.

In summary, the leadership action of Empowering involves:

- Stimulating motivation for growth
- Recognizing individuality
- Promoting self-esteem
- Encouraging autonomy
- Supporting the development of people's potential

The action of empowering is supported by three key personal qualities: *ambition, motivation* and *generosity*. Generosity is the quality most associated with empowerment. *Generosity* involves dedicating time and personal involvement in order to contribute to the development of the potential of others. It requires the capacity to maintain individual aims of growth with altruism, faith, and a sense of participation.

Support the development of people's potential
Encourage autonomy
Promote self-esteem
Recognize individuality
Stimulate motivation for growth
Achieving Results
Ambition
Generosity
Developing People
Motivation
Empowering

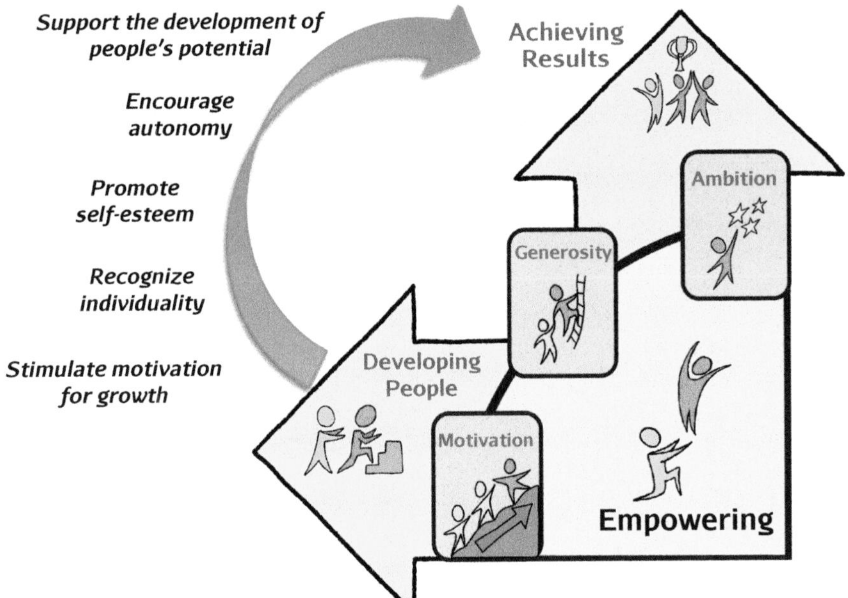

Empowering requires generosity, motivation and ambition and is necessary in order to develop people and achieve results.

Before you are a leader, success is all about growing yourself. When you become a leader, success is all about growing others.

Jack Welch – CEO General Electric

Outstanding leaders go out of their way to boost the self-esteem of their personnel. If people believe in themselves, it's amazing what they can accomplish.

Sam Walton – Founder Walmart

Empowerment, Resilience and the Power of Beliefs

In his book "Start with Why", Simon Sineck shares a simple model to help you explore your own WHY, or the purpose that can inspire you in situations when you need resilience.

This little idea explains why some leaders and some organizations are able to inspire while others aren't. Let me just define the terms really quickly. Every single person, every single organization on the planet knows what they do; one hundred percent. Some know how they do it; whether you call it your "differentiating value proposition" or your "proprietary process" or USP. But very, very few people or organizations know why they do what they do. And by "why" I don't mean "to make a profit," That's a result. It is always a result. By why I mean "what is your purpose?" "What is your cause?" "What is your belief?" "Why does your organization exist?"

Simon Sinek – *'Start With Why'*

When it comes to changing the world, what I learned from Steve Jobs is, if you believe in a Macintosh, if you believe in iPhone, iPod, iPad, if you believe enough, then you will see it. Because other people will believe in it; other people will create software; other people will create products. So you need to foster the belief in what you are dreaming, so it becomes a reality. Which is very different than saying, "I don't expect anybody to believe it until they see it." You need people to believe it before they can see it.

Guy Kawasaki – Apple Inc.

One of the most influential success factors for empowering ourselves and others is our belief. Beliefs determine how events are given meaning, and are at the core of motivation and culture. Our beliefs and values are a key part of our mindset and "inner game" and provide the reinforcement (*motivation* and *permission*) that supports or inhibits particular capabilities and behaviors. Beliefs and values relate to the question, "*Why*?"

The power of beliefs to enhance or inhibit people's capabilities was demonstrated in an enlightening study in which a group of children who were tested to have average intelligence was divided at random into two equal groups. One of the groups was assigned to a teacher who was told that the children were "gifted." The other group was given to a teacher who was told that the children were "slow learners." A year later the two groups were retested for intelligence. Not surprisingly, the majority of the group that was arbitrarily identified as "gifted" scored higher than they had previously, while the majority of the group that was labeled "slow" scored lower! The teachers' beliefs and resulting expectations about the students had affected their ability to learn.

Beliefs and values relate to the question, "Why?" They are a key part of our mindset and "inner game" and provide the reinforcement (motivation and permission) that supports or inhibits particular capabilities and behaviors.

In another study, 100 cancer "survivors" (patients who had reversed their symptoms for over 10 years) were interviewed about what they had done to achieve success. The interviews showed that no single treatment method stood out as being more effective than any other. Some patients had taken the standard medical treatment of chemotherapy and/or radiation, some had used a nutritional approach, others had followed a spiritual path, while others concentrated on a psychological approach and some did nothing at all. The only thing that characterized the entire group was that they all *believed* in what they were doing. They all believed that the approach they took would work for them.

Another good example of the power of beliefs to both limit us and empower us is that of the "four minute mile." Before May 6, 1954, it was believed that four minutes was an unbreakable barrier to the speed with which a human being could run a mile. In the nine years prior to the historic day in which Roger Bannister broke the four minute ceiling, no runners had even come close. Within six weeks after Bannister's feat, the Australian runner John Lundy lowered the record by another second. Within the next nine years nearly two hundred people had broken the once seemingly impenetrable barrier.

Our beliefs can influence, shape or even determine our degree of motivation, intelligence, health and performance.

Certainly, these examples demonstrate that our beliefs can influence, shape or even determine our degree of intelligence, health and performance.

Building a Winning Belief System

Increasing innovation, rebounding from adversity and enhancing our fitness for the future requires the establishment of a "winning belief system." In *SFM Vol. II* (pp. 211-215) I stated that a *winning belief* system produces a field of empowerment by creating:

- An expectation of a positive future
- A feeling of capability and responsibility
- A sense of self-worth and belonging

A winning belief system produces a field of empowerment necessary for increasing innovation, rebounding from adversity and enhancing our fitness for the future .

The *expectation of a positive future* is produced by having desirable outcomes that are believed to be within reach. The *feeling of capability and responsibility* come from the confidence that we have a good plan and possess the necessary capabilities to take the behavioral steps necessary to reach desired outcomes successfully. The *sense of self-worth and belonging* is a result of the degree to which it is believed that we deserve and have the permission and the support to mobilize the capabilities and qualities required to be successful.

Winning beliefs are directly related to the five fundamental components of the cause-and-effect chain required to achieve change. These five components include:

1. The *outcomes* the individual, team or organization is trying to achieve.
2. The *path* of steps that leads to those outcomes.
3. The *behaviors* or actions required to successfully travel the path.
4. The *plan* specifying the capabilities and qualities needed to in order to execute those behaviors and actions effectively.
5. The *people* or team who must possess the capabilities and qualities needed to take the actions and successfully complete the path leading to the desired outcome.

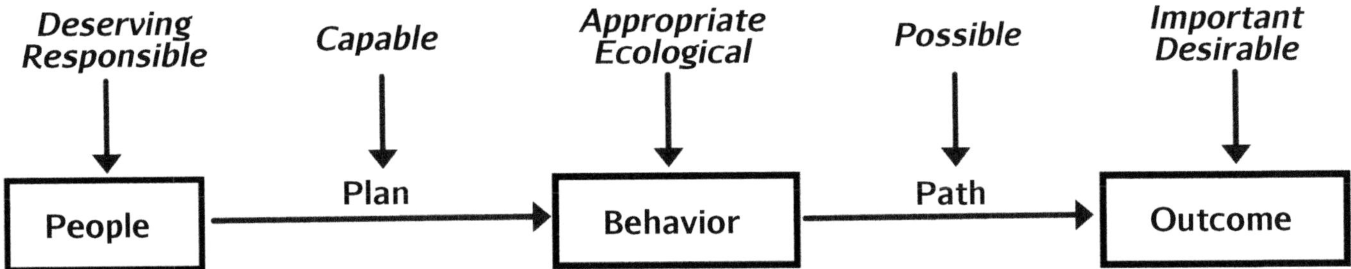

Belief Issues Related to Achievement and Change

People form key beliefs that affect their perception with respect each of these five elements of change. These beliefs have to do with:

1. The *importance* and *desirability* of the outcome (the strength of its link with vision, mission, ambition and values).
2. The conviction that it is *possible* to reach the outcome via some path of appropriate steps.
3. The judgment of how *appropriate* and *ecological* (i.e., effective, ethical, practical, etc.) the behaviors and actions required to reach the outcome are.
4. The confidence that the involved individuals, team or company is/are *capable* to follow the plan and perform the appropriate actions required to successfully reach the outcome.
5. The sense of *responsibility*, *worthiness* and *permission* that the involved individuals, team or company perceive with respect to using their capabilities, following through with the plan and reaching the desired outcome.

Creating a winning belief system involves establishing congruent and empowering beliefs relating to five fundamental components of change.

Each belief in a winning belief system is like a link in a chain. The chain is no stronger than its weakest link.

The overall degree of empowerment and motivation people experience is a result of their level of confidence with respect to this entire system of beliefs. If the goal, outcome or vision is perceived as unimportant and not desirable, for instance, it clearly makes no sense to put out any effort at all to try to achieve it. Even if the outcome is perceived as worth it, if it seems impossible to achieve, it would also feel like a waste of time to try to reach it. If the outcome is worth it and possible but inappropriate, or the means to achieve it is perceived as inappropriate, then it will create resistance and "push back." If the outcome is worth it, possible and appropriate but the individual or team who must achieve does not believe they have the ability or support to do what is necessary, they will lack the confidence to take risks, try something new or stick with it when things are challenging or difficult. And even if the outcome is believed to be worth it, possible and appropriate, and the person or team perceives themselves to be capable to reach it, if the individual or team does not consider themselves to be responsible, deserving or as having the permission to achieve the outcome, they will not be inclined to take action or do what needs to be done.

Thus, one of the most important and powerful success factors in enhancing innovation, rebounding from adversity and being fit for the future is the degree of belief one has in the vision one is pursuing, in oneself and in what one is doing. As successful entrepreneur Cindana Turkatte (profiled in *SFM Vol. I*, pp. 163-171) stated so clearly, "You have to believe in what you are doing. If you don't believe in what you are doing, you should be doing something else."

One of the most important and powerful success factors in enhancing innovation, rebounding from adversity and being fit for the future is the degree of belief one has in the vision one is pursuing, in oneself and one's team, and in what one is doing.

The Example of Elon Musk's Mars Mission

Elon Musk's surprising progress on his vision to colonize Mars is a good example of how beliefs can catalyze people to take action. While many would have considered establishing a human colony on Mars a far-fetched and even silly or meaningless fantasy, Musk has been able to get people to begin to regard and even pursue it as an actual possibility.

To do so, Musk has worked to establish the belief that the outcome of establishing a colony on Mars is *desirable* and *important*, arguing that it is necessary for human survival. "I think there is a strong humanitarian argument for making life multi-planetary in order to safeguard the existence of humanity in the event that something catastrophic were to happen," he states. Musk goes on to point out, "One option is to stay on Earth forever, and eventually there will be an extinction event...and the alternative is to become a spacefaring and multi-planetary species—That's what we want."

Elon Musk's ability to promote the belief that it is desirable and possible to colonize Mars, and that we capable to create the technology necessary to do so, has catalyzed surprising progress toward the vision of humans as a spacefaring and multi-planetary species.

Musk has also made a lot of progress in building the belief that such a thing is *possible*. At a conference in Mexico in September 2016, for the International Astronautical Congress, for example, the SpaceX founder and CEO unveiled the company's Interplanetary Transport System (ITS). The system will combine the most powerful rocket ever built with a spaceship designed to carry at least 100 people to the Red Planet. "What I really want to do here is to make Mars seem possible," he said. "To make it seem as though it's something that we could do in our lifetimes, and that you can go."

In addition, Musk claims that if SpaceX's plans to get to Mars do succeed, it could soon be possible to make trips even further out into space. "If we have a propellent depot, you can go from Mars to Jupiter, no problem," Musk said. "It means full access to the entire greater solar system." While this may sound "far fetched" to us today, it is probably not much different that our ancestors of 500 years ago musing about ocean travel between continents or of those 100 years ago thinking about the possibility of air travel around the world.

To show that it is not only possible, but that there is an *appropriate* path to reach and colonize Mars, Musk has posted computer-animated videos that paint a vivid and seemingly realistic picture of humans journeying to the planet. They illustrate specific technologies that could be used in a human mission to Mars, including a launch from Earth and on-orbit spaceship refueling, the use of solar arrays to power the human space capsule, and a booster-powered descent onto the Red Planet.

To accelerate the creation of the technologies needed to reach Mars, Musk has been building powerful partnerships with people in both the private sector and with governments.

Musk would like to make the trip to Mars himself—but only after putting together a Plan B for his company, in case of disaster.

In one such video, we see a rocket lift-off from SpaceX's Launchpad with 28,730,000 pounds of thrust behind it. After stage separation, the spaceship parks in orbit while the booster returns to Earth—where it lands. A propellant tanker is loaded onto the booster to refuel the spaceship in orbit for its trip to Mars. The tanker returns to Earth and the spaceship heads for Mars. The solar arrays deploy and the ships coasts until it finally enter Mars' orbit. The ship lands on the Martian surface and then we get a glimpse of the astronauts looking out onto the Martian plains. [See: *http://www.space.com/34211-spacex-mars-interplanetary-transport-concept-video.html*]

Part of Musk's whole purpose for creating SpaceX has been to show that we are *capable* of creating the technologies needed to get to Mars. He has already demonstrated the capacity to build re-useable rocket ships. To increase confidence in the capability to raise the estimated $10 billion needed to fund the project, Musk is developing powerful partnerships. "I know there's a lot of people in the private sector interested in funding a trip to Mars," he says, "hopefully there will be interest in the government side as well. Ultimately this will be a huge private-public partnership." NASA, for instance, is expected to launch its next Mars rover by 2020. The ExoMars mission, a joint initiative from the Roscosmos and European Space Agency (ESA) is also planned to take place before the end of the decade. There's also talk of the United Arab Emirates sending an orbiter to the Red Planet by then, along with China who has expressed its intent to reach Mars by 2020.

To support the belief that we are *deserving* and *responsible* to take the journey, Musk takes the lead by saying that he'd like to make the trip to Mars himself—but only after putting together a Plan B for his company, in case of disaster. "I would definitely like to go to orbit and visit the space station and then ultimately go to Mars," he said. "I have to make sure if something goes wrong on the flight and I die there's a good succession plan and the mission of the company continues."

Assessing Our Degree of Belief

As the Example of Elon Musk's Mars Mission shows, creating a winning belief system involves communicating and justifying confidence in each of the five key areas of belief defined earlier – (1) the importance and desirability of the outcome, (2) the possibility to achieve it, (3) the appropriateness of the path to accomplish it, (4) the capability to implement that path and (5) that the people involved are deserving and responsible to reach the outcome.

Beliefs come from and create an intimate connection between language and our experiences. The most direct way of building a winning belief system is to create a connection between the words expressing the beliefs and people's experience, coming from both memory and imagination. To create a strong belief, it is important that this connection involve all of the senses (seeing, hearing and feeling) if possible so that it resonates not only in one's "head," but in one's heart and "gut" as well.

Steve Jobs advised people to "have the courage to follow your heart and intuition." In addition to our cognitive, rational assessment (the "head"), we need to connect our motivation to achieve our visions and ambitions to our passion (the "heart") and our intuition (our "gut" feelings). Sometimes, for instance, our heart feels "yes" but our head says "no." Other times, we rationally know that something is possible, but have a "gut feeling" to beware. A strong belief requires head, heart and gut alignment.

Belief is also not generally an "all or nothing" process. We can "sort of" believe in something, believe in it "somewhat" or "mostly"; that is, we can believe something a little or a lot. The key for rebounding from adversity and being fit for the future is to believe in it "enough." To do this, we must reach a certain threshold of confidence.

In order to build and reinforce our belief and motivation to achieve our visions and ambitions, we need to engage not only our cognitive, rational understanding (the "head"), but also our passion (the "heart") and our intuition (our "gut" feelings).

Belief Assessment Process

You have to have a sense of confidence about what you're doing. You have to be a salesman, and you have to get your players, particularly your leaders, to believe in what you're trying to accomplish.

Phil Jackson – NBA Head Coach

The purpose of the following assessment process is to help an individual or group to make a comprehensive assessment of their degree of resonance and confidence with respect to the key beliefs needed to successfully rebound from adversity and pursue the vision, ambition and calling. It will assist in identifying both areas of strength and weakness and bring focus to the areas of belief that need to be fortified or reinforced. Keep in mind that, as we have seen in all of the case examples presented in this book, the strength of belief of the team starts with the strength of the leader's belief.

As a preparation for the assessment, it is a good idea to begin by recalling some past situations in which you were able to accomplish a difficult goal, rebound from adversity or get through a challenging situation due to your belief in yourself, your vision and what you were doing. Put yourself back into those situations and pay attention to how you experienced the level of belief that made it possible to get through the situation and rebound successfully. How did you experience that situation with respect to your inner game? How did you experience the alignment between your head, heart and gut? What did you see, hear and feel that allowed you to persevere and succeed?

The ability to make an accurate assessment of your own and other's belief in the vision and venture is an essential competence for effective leaders and entrepreneurs.

To begin the assessment process, choose a leadership moment where it is important to increase your belief in order to empower people and get results. Write the vision for the project or venture below (in ten words or less):

Vision: ____

Make sure that you can connect these words to the experience of what you will see, hear and feel in relation to the achievement of the vision — i.e., What will there be more of? What will there be less of?

Enter your COACH state and say each of the following statements aloud, paying attention to the degree of resonance or congruence you experience in your head, heart and gut. Rate your degree of belief in relation to each of the statements on a scale of 0 to 10, with 0 being the lowest and 10 being the highest degree of confidence or resonance. Be honest with yourself. It doesn't help to try to fool yourself. Accurate self-analysis is a key skill of conscious leadership.

1. "The vision is desirable, important and worth it. *I/We want to achieve it*."

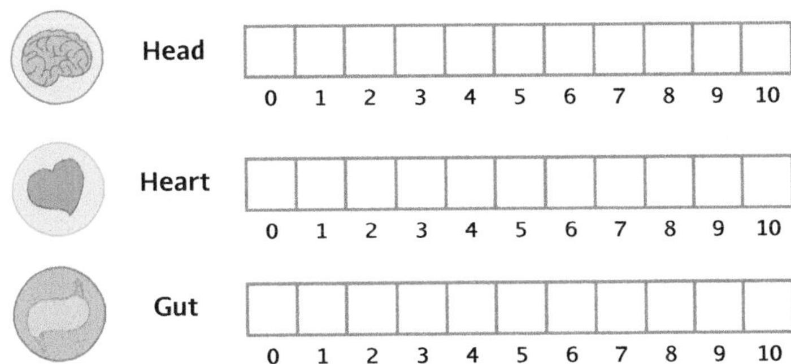

2. "It is *possible* to achieve the vision. *There is a way to get there*."

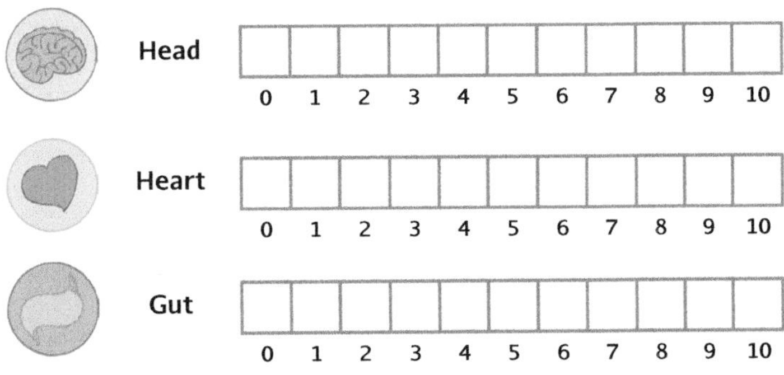

3. "It is *appropriate* to achieve the vision. *What I am/we are doing will work*."

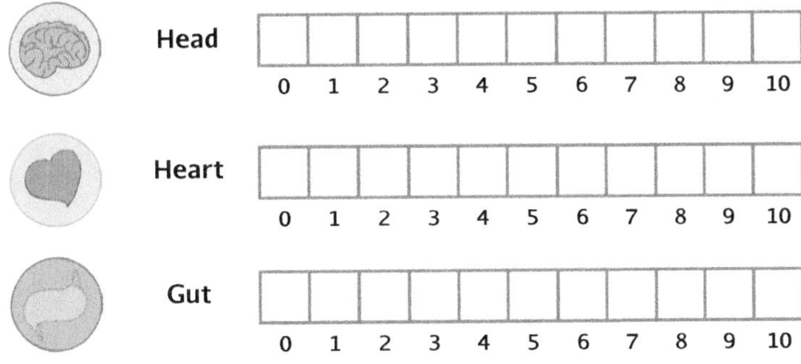

4. "I/We *have the capabilities* and support necessary to achieve the vision. I/We can do it."

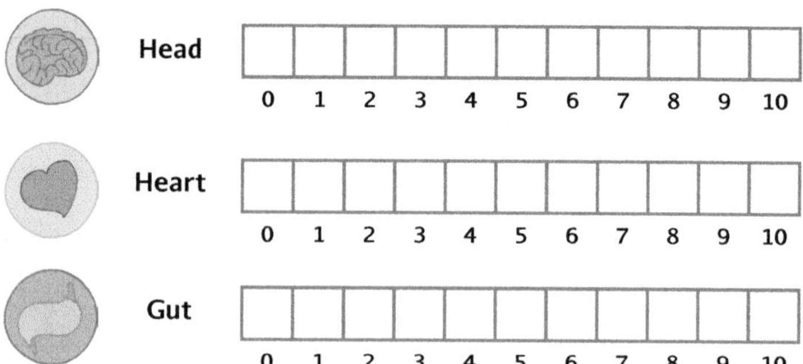

For a belief to be strong and congruent, it must resonate in the head, heart and gut.

5. "I/We *deserve and take responsibility* to achieve the vision. I/We have permission to achieve the vision and it is up to me/us."

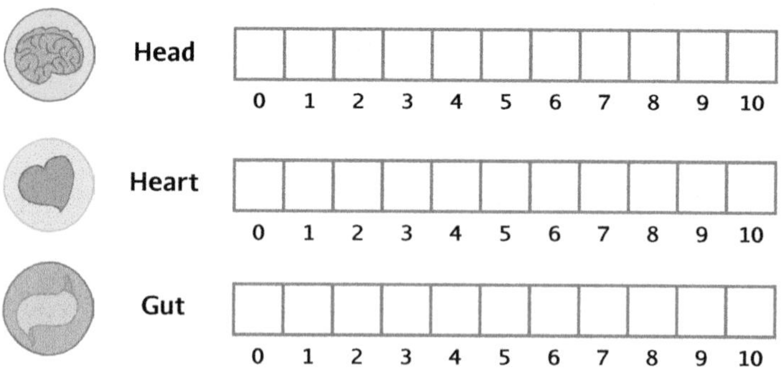

Reflect on the ratings for each statement. Which are the strongest? Where are there areas of doubt, uncertainty or conflict? What does the assessment bring to your attention with regard to areas requiring acknowledgment or focus? Can you think of other resources or reference experiences that would help you strengthen your belief in the areas where you are unsure?

Using Mentors and Role Models to Build Confidence and Strengthen Belief

Empowering beliefs are often built in relation to feedback and reinforcement from significant others. Our sense of identity and mission, for instance, is usually defined in relation to significant others who serve to connect us to our higher purpose.

Because identity and mission form the larger framework that surrounds our beliefs and values, establishing or remembering significant relationships can exert a strong influence on beliefs. Thus, clarifying key relationships, and messages received in the context of those relationships, often spontaneously facilitates changes in beliefs. Key relationships that strengthen our sense of confidence and our beliefs often come in the form of role models and mentors.

Mentors are generally significant others who have helped us to discover our own unconscious competencies, and to strengthen beliefs and values—usually through their own example. Mentors are typically individuals who have helped to shape or influence our lives in a positive way by "resonating" with, releasing, or unveiling something deep within us. Identifying such mentors with respect to the beliefs in the Winning Beliefs Assessment process can help to spontaneously strengthen our confidence and congruence.

You can do this on a personal level by going through the following steps:

1. What inner resource or knowledge would you need to have in order to be more congruent or confident? Where would you most need to experience that resource or knowing (head, heart or gut)?
2. Who would be your mentor or role model for that knowledge or resource?
3. Put yourself into the shoes of your mentor or role model and look at yourself through his or her eyes (second position). What message or advice would that person have for you?
4. Return to your own perspective (first position) and receive the message. How does it increase your degree of confidence and congruence?

Identifying personal mentors can help you to spontaneously strengthen your confidence and congruence.

Assessing and Building a Winning Belief System in a Group

When working with a group or team, the same statements can be used to assess the degree of belief of all of the group members with respect to the vision and ambition of the venture. Identifying common areas of doubt between individuals would point to key areas of concern for the team as a whole. When there are differences in the rankings of the various beliefs, the individuals who have greater confidence may have resources, knowledge or experiences that can help to raise the confidence level of others. These individuals can become internal mentors to the rest of the team, helping to increase their sense of assurance and conviction.

The CrossKnowledge co-founders understood the importance of building a winning belief system in their company and organized an inspiring event for their employees and partners.

As an example, in *SFM Vol. II* (pp. 101-113) I presented some key elements of the intervention I made for the e-learning company CrossKnowledge. As I explain, CrossKnowledge was launched by four founders in the early days of online learning. In their first years, the company was essentially in the role of being a pioneer and their challenge was to convince organizations that e-learning was a viable training method. They were able to do this and build a niche in the growing industry.

After some years of enjoying considerable growth and success, however, in 2009 the company encountered a challenging time of transition. In addition to the consequences of a global financial crisis, the industry had matured and the marketplace had evolved. More and more larger players had begun to enter the e-learning market; including big organizations who had much larger marketing budgets. So the company's founders realized that in order to stay competitive, they had to clarify their mission (specifying their unique contribution) and adjust their ambition to fit the changing marketplace. This meant that they had to anticipate the direction the e-learning industry was heading, readjust their business focus and shift their priorities, and then align their whole team to the new path. Furthermore, they needed to do this quickly or be left behind.

We organized an event for all 160 members of the company at a large conference center. I had coached the founders and Michael Ohana, the CEO, about how to clarify and communicate the updated vision, mission, ambition and role of the venture. All 160 people were provided with papers and drawing supplies, and each drew his or her image of what that vision meant for him or her as an individual within his or her role in the company. People formed groups comparing and looking for resonance and synergy with respect to their perception of the revised vision, mission, ambition and role of the company. Then we put all of the pictures on the walls of the conference room so the team was surrounded by the images the CEO's presentation had generated. It was quite an inspiring "field."

The next step was to do a collective *belief assessment*. We took the entire team through the five belief statements presented in the *Belief Assessment Process* with respect to vision that they had projected onto the walls through their own drawings. People were asked to be honest with themselves about their degree of belief that this evolving future was possible.

If people had a low rating with respect to one or several of the beliefs, they were not put on the spot to admit or explain why they doubted (and potentially fired). Rather, those who had given a high rating to one or more of the statements were invited, as mentors and role models, to share why they had so much confidence. Each time an individual shared his or her reasons for believing in the future of the venture, the confidence level of the whole room seemed to palpably increase creating a field of energy and excitement.

The final part of the event involved each of the 160 people making commitments to their own team members regarding specific actions they would take in the coming days, weeks and months to support creating the future of the company.

The CrossKnowledge founders shared their vision, mission and ambition for the company and invited the team to do the Belief Assessment Process with respect to co-creating the company's future.

The event was a great success and the company was able to achieve a whole new period of expansion and growth. Years later, the people who were at the event still talked about it as a high point in their time at the company. And new employees heard about the event as a key reference point in their introduction to the company and its culture.

As I explain in *SFM Vol. II*, the steps taken by the four founders of CrossKnowledge led to an ongoing path of success. By 2014 the company had grown to more than 200 employees, was bringing in $37 million in revenue and had expanded to 5 million end-users (and had grown to 8 million by 2016) in over 80 countries. They were acquired by publishing giant Wiley in April of 2014 for $175 million in cash, making each of the four founders a multimillionaire.

Coaching to Develop People and Embody Values

A good coach supports his or her team members in their personal and professional development and provides an example of how to be effective and trustworthy.

Coaching is one of the most important leadership actions required to stimulate innovation, increase resilience and enhance fitness for the future. *Coaching* involves the ability to be a *guide* and a *trainer*. A good coach knows his or her team, and helps the team grow through constantly monitored development which promotes integration and cohesion. He or she promotes continuous development, providing occasions for instruction which evaluates both positive and negative experiences.

Coaching is based on the capacity to *respect* people and to *listen* attentively, willingly, and considerately. It requires the recognition of individual potential and taking responsibility for the development of these competencies as assets in order to harvest underutilized potential. Thus, a coach gives equal attention to the individuals and the team. Coaches are able to communicate personably, consider the emotions of others, and offer support during times of uncertainty.

People buy into the leader before they buy into the vision.

John Maxwell – *The 21 Indispensable Qualities of a Leader*

Coaching is necessary to develop people and to realize values. Effective coaching requires the ability to create reference experiences for collaborators, which anchor knowledge to their everyday reality. It also requires the capacity to supervise and give feedback. A good coach is also skilled in team building and promoting a common culture and shared values amongst team members.

In matters of style, swim with the current; in matters of principle, stand like a rock.

Thomas Jefferson

The action of coaching is supported by three key personal qualities: *consistency*, *motivation* and *example*. Example is the quality most associated with coaching. To be a good *example* is to be a believable and trustworthy point of reference — i.e., a model to follow. It also involves the ability to offer suggestions and to demonstrate how to learn from experience. Being an example has to do with the congruency between "message" and "messenger."

In summary, Coaching, as an action of leadership, involves the capacities to:

- Develop people's experience and competencies
- Guide people in their learning process
- Listen with attention
- Build trust
- Grow team spirit

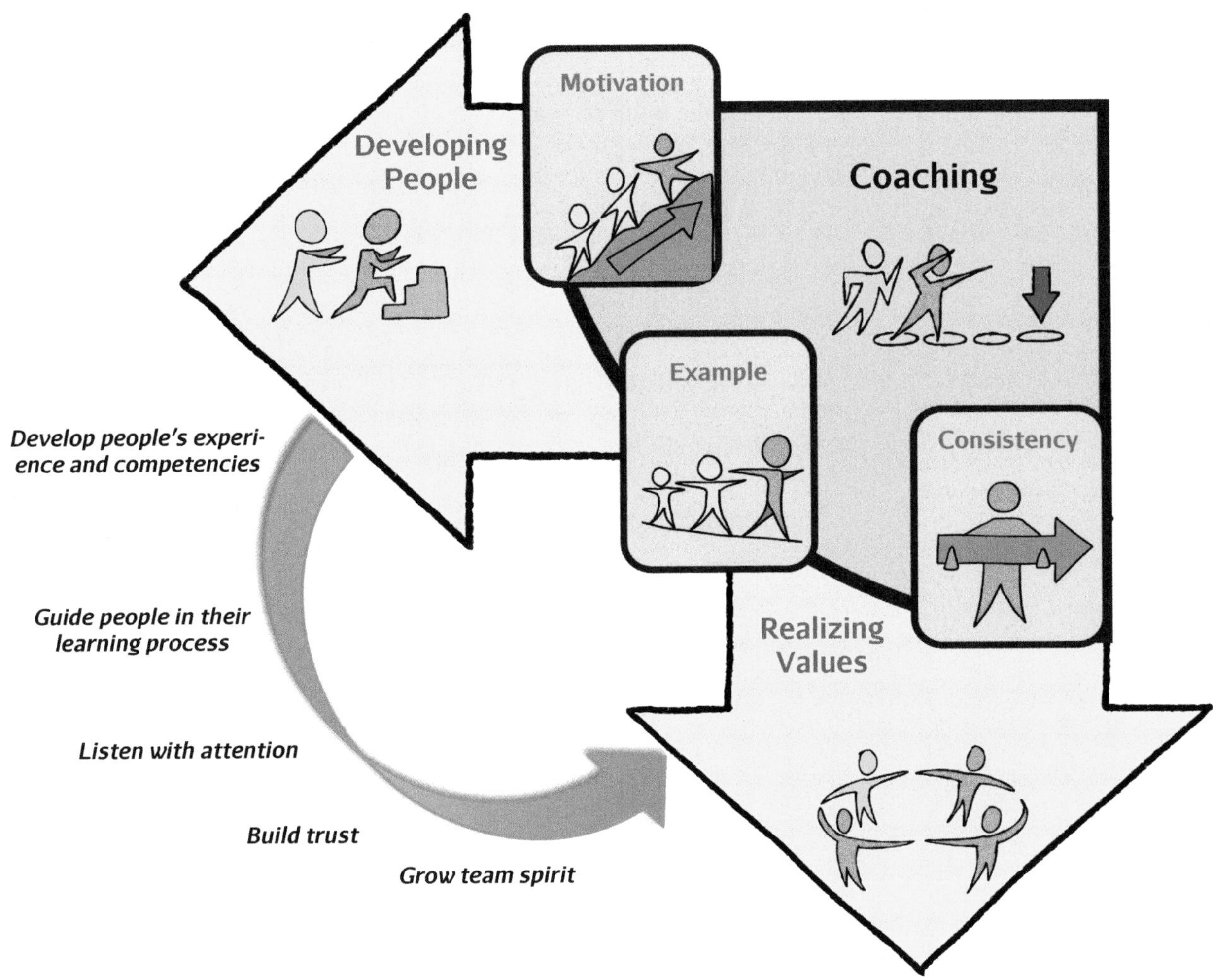

Coaching requires being an effective example, demonstrating consistency and motivation, and is necessary in order to develop people and realize values.

Realizing Values

A lot of corporations have what they might call core values or guiding principles or so on. But the problem is they are very lofty sounding, they kind of read like a press release the marketing department put out. They sound just like your competitors' values. And maybe you hear about it on day one of your job, but it becomes this meaningless plaque on the lobby wall. Well, we wanted to come up with commitable core values. And by commitable meaning we are willing to hire or fire people based on those values completely independent of their actual job performance.

Tony Hsieh – Zappos

The definition of values is that they are the behaviors or principles that you religiously adhere to within your company. And when I say "religious" I mean that no amount of data will sway you from those principles. And the degree you have the courage to maintain your conviction around those ideas is the degree to which you are going to be successful in the long term.

Andrew Mason – Groupon

Our goals are the tangible expression of our values.

A fundamental goal of coaching is to help people embody critical values. According to Webster's Dictionary, *values* are "principles, qualities or entities that are intrinsically valuable or desirable." Because they are associated with worth, meaning and desire, values are a primary source of motivation in people's lives – they are another key answer to the question *why*? When people's values are met or matched, they feel a sense of satisfaction, harmony, or rapport. When their values are not met or matched, people often feel dissatisfied, incongruent, or violated.

As an exploration of your own values, consider for a moment how you would respond to the following questions: "In general, what motivates you?" "What is most important to you?" "What moves you to action, or 'gets you out of bed in the morning'?"

Some possible answers might be:

Fulfilling My Responsibilities

Proving Myself

Getting Recognition

Having Fun

Achieving Something

Connecting with Others

Making a difference in the world

Values such as these greatly influence and direct the outcomes that we establish, the choices that we make and the actions into which we put greatest effort. The goals that we set for ourselves are, in fact, the tangible expression of our values. A person who has a goal to "create an effective team," for instance, most likely values "working together with others." A person whose goal is to "increase profits" probably values "financial success." Similarly, a person who has a value of "security" will set goals related to achieving stability and safety in his or her personal or professional life. Such a person will seek different outcomes than a person who values "flexibility," for example. A person who values security may be content with a 9 to 5 job that has consistent pay and involves well established tasks. A person who values flexibility, on the other hand, may try to find work involving a range of tasks and a variable time schedule.

Types of Values

In philosophy, a distinction is commonly made between **instrumental values**—what is good as a *means* to an end ("sustainability" or "wealth," for example)—and **intrinsic values**—what is good as an *end in and of itself* ("happiness" or "harmony"). Our **core values** are typically "intrinsic values." They are related to our identity. Instrumental values are those that we take on, often on a temporary basis, in order to achieve something (in order to support our core values). They are related to our goals.

Clarifying and prioritizing the values that will lead us to "the next level" in our lives and ventures are often about bringing focus to instrumental values that are the "means" to that end. Conflicts, however, can emerge when instrumental values produce actions that are not aligned with our core values – i.e., the "means" and the "ends" are not aligned. For example, the instrumental value of "focus" may come into conflict with a core value of "harmony" if the value of focus produces actions that disturb our sense of harmony.[1]

Bridging and aligning (or "dovetailing") values is an important skill for leaders. I will be presenting several ways to do that in the coming pages of this book

"Harmony" is a core value of our venture. It is the guidepost for everything we make and do. It is what we want to bring more of t o the world.

Fairness is an instrumental value. It helps us to stay in good harmony.

1. In such cases it can be useful to processes such at the Tetralemma (described in *SFM Vol. II*, pp. 306-309).

Clarifying Values

In order to be successful in our lives or ventures, it is useful to clarify and prioritize both our intrinsic (core) and instrumental values; and be sure that they complement one another. Start by listing your top five core values and the top five values you need to adopt or strengthen to get to the next level in your life or venture. Be sure that they complement each other.

Core Values	**Instrumental Values**

Putting Values Into Action

Values themselves cannot produce actions. Their function is to bring focus and energy to particular classes of behaviors. Putting values into action in a concrete form involves connecting them to the supporting *capabilities* and specific *behaviors* that would be a congruent expression of a particular value in a particular *environment*.

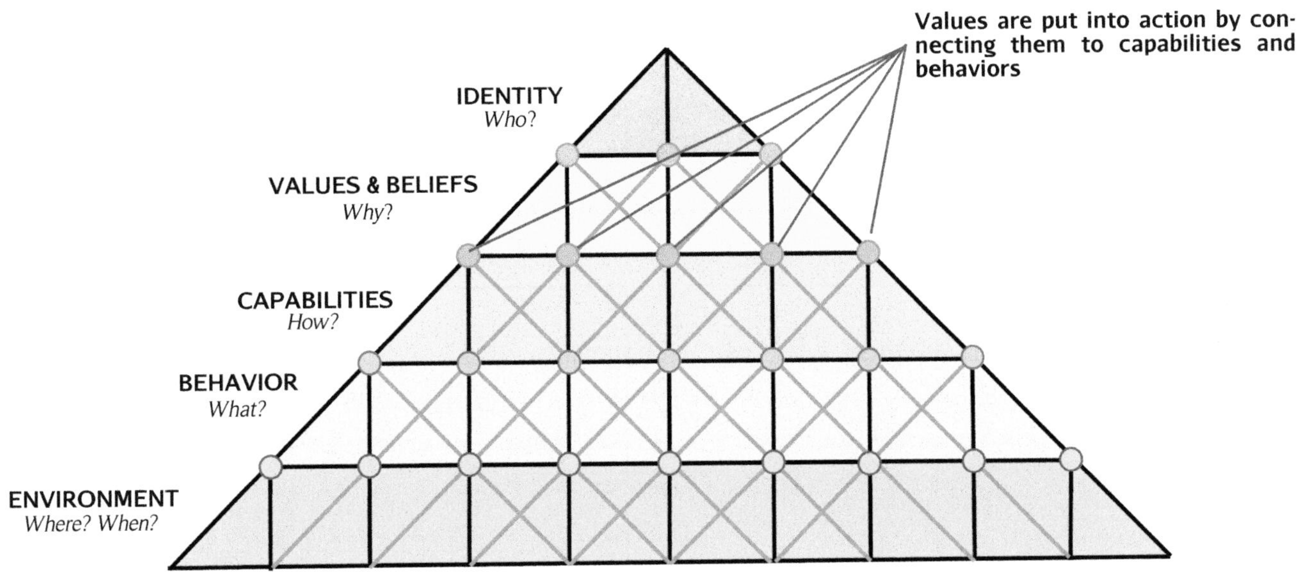

The purpose of the following exercise is to define the other levels of factors needed to effectively establish the values we want to put into practice. To authentically and congruently live his or her values, a person must have the supporting skills and capabilities necessary to assess situations and make decisions about which actions are in line with those values. Specific skills and capabilities are needed to be able to select and implement the behaviors which express particular values in widely differing environments.

The specific expression of values is usually represented by a portfolio of behaviors to be selected and enacted in key environments. The purpose of the following exercise is to help you to define and align the other levels of processes necessary to bring values congruently and consistently into action in your personal and professional life.

Choose a leadership moment where it is important for you to "walk your talk" and provide a consistent example of a core value for your venture.

1. What is the value (the why) to be implemented (e.g., "focus," "balance," "connection," etc.)?

 ____

2. What are the key capabilities (the how) necessary to establish and implement that value (e.g., communication, creativity, rapport, etc.)?

 ______________________ ______________________

 ______________________ ______________________

 ______________________ ______________________

3. What 'portfolio' of activities and behaviors (the what) best expresses and manifests this value (e.g., listening, acknowledging contributions, setting aside time for myself, etc.)?

 ______________________ ______________________

 ______________________ ______________________

 ______________________ ______________________

4. What are the significant environments or contexts (where and when) in which it is most important to express this value (e.g., team meetings, in front of the computer, interactions with customers, etc.)?

 ______________________ ______________________

 ______________________ ______________________

 ______________________ ______________________

Creating an Aligned State

The inner quality most associated with coaching is *example*. This involves "*being the change you want to see*" in others in the words of Mahatma Gandhi. As we have seen time and again in our various Success Factor Case Examples, being an effective entrepreneur or conscious leader involves connecting strongly to our passion and acting in line with our vision, mission, ambition and role. As the old adage points out, "Actions speak louder than words." Our greatest influence as an entrepreneur or leader is our own example.

Truly successful entrepreneurs and conscious leaders are those whose actions are aligned with their capabilities, beliefs, values and sense of identity in relation to their mission or purpose, their role within the system in which they are participating and their vision for the larger system of which they are a part (the "holarchy").

The actions of successful entrepreneurs and conscious leaders are aligned with their capabilities and in support of their beliefs and values, their sense of identity, and their higher purpose.

The concept of different "levels" of success factors provides us with a powerful road map for bringing the various dimensions of ourselves into alignment in order to manage leadership moments and realize our ambitions and visions.

Level Alignment Process

One of the most common and effective coaching processes I do with myself and my collaborators and clients is the Level Alignment Process. The *Level Alignment Process* provides a way to systematically access and connect experiences and resources associated with each of these different levels of success factors that we have been exploring in this book. By considering resources at each of the different levels of change, a person can bring all these levels into alignment in the service of his or her vision and mission. This allows us to stay connected with our higher purpose and provide a powerful and effective example to others.

Level Alignment Worksheet

To go through the process, choose one of the leadership moments you identified earlier in this chapter. Enter into your COACH state and fill in the statements provided below by answering the corresponding question.

1. "What is the *environment* in which you want to stay connected with your higher purpose and provide a good example?"

   "*When* and *where* do you want or need to be an effective example? What will be the external context surrounding the situation?"

   In the context of ______________________________

2. "What are your specific goals and actions in that context?

   "*What*, specifically, do you need to do in that context? What is the behavior associated with being a good example in that situation?"

   I want to ______________________________

3. "What *capabilities* are needed to stay connected with your higher purpose and provide a good example within the chosen context?"

   "*How* will you be a good example? What capabilities, in terms of inner game and outer game, are needed to guide your actions in that context? Which inner qualities (vision, openness, consistency, motivation, generosity, ambition, determination, etc.) are needed to support the actions you have defined?"

   I will use my capabilities of ______________________________

4. "What *beliefs* and *values* are expressed by or will be validated by reaching your goals in that context?"

   "What values are expressed by your actions and capabilities?"

   I want to do this because I value ______________________________

"*Why* will you use those particular inner qualities and capabilities in order to accomplish those goals? What beliefs provide the motivation for your thoughts and activity?"

I believe ____

5. "What is your *identity* or role with respect to the goals and the beliefs and values associated with them?" (Think in terms of a symbol or metaphor to answer this question.)

   "*Who* are you if you engage those particular beliefs, values, capabilities and behaviors in that particular context?"

   I am (or am like): ____

   "What is your mission in that context?"

   My mission is to ____

6. What is your *vision* with respect to the larger system in which you are operating?"

   "What is the world you are trying to create to which people will want to belong?"

   My mission is in the service of the larger vision of ____

   ____

The Level Alignment Process can also be applied to groups and teams. In fact, in *SFM Vol. II* (pp. 282-283) I present a Team Alignment process and worksheet. The process starts by having each team member identify his or her understanding of the vision and mission of the entire team. Each individual is then to define his or her understanding of his or her role, values and priorities, beliefs and assumptions, capabilities, tasks, and the contexts in which he or she will operate in order to support the team vision and mission.

Sharing to Enact Values and Promote Change

As the case examples of Charles Matthews and Roll Royce and Dr. Lim Suet Wun at Tan Tock Seng Hospital showed, the leadership action of Sharing can be one of the most critical success factors during times of adversity and uncertainty. *Sharing* involves the *exchange of information* and *know-how*. It requires diffusing knowledge and promoting dialogue among people. Another important part of sharing for entrepreneurs and leaders is to delineate the vision and goals of the project or venture, and to clarify core values and "the rules of the game"; like Steve Jobs' expectation of excellence from everyone he worked with.

Sharing is the foundation for collective intelligence and generative collaboration.

Sharing is founded upon the capacity to *involve* people in the process of solving problems and achieving goals by including them in meetings in which ideas and information are exchanged. This supports the development of collective intelligence, generative collaboration, wisdom and genuine consensus with respect to goals and outcomes (as opposed to "group think"). Effective sharing results from permitting easy access to resources and ensuring that they are available to everybody. It also requires the assurance that the same values and rules apply to everybody.

Effective sharing requires the capacity to involve people in the process of solving problems and achieving goals by including them in meetings, welcoming multiple perspectives and creating a safe environment for authentic exchange

Sharing is the core activity for both promoting change and realizing values. The ability to share is founded upon the capacity to promote open *communication* and the *exchange* of ideas, visions and energy. This requires creating a safe environment for authentic exchange and then, as Charles Matthews put it, "giving people a toolkit of practical problem solving techniques and empowering them." It also involves the ability to present ideas in different ways and incorporate *multiple perspectives.*

The action of sharing is supported by three key inner qualities: *consistency, vision* and *openness*. Openness is the quality most associated with sharing. *Openness* is a product of being curious and receptive to new ideas. It also requires that one is able to have faith in others; thus building reciprocal trust, esteem and respect. Some other characteristics related to openness include being clear and straightforward, willing to be challenged and recognizing and acknowledging one's mistakes.

To summarize, the leadership action of Sharing requires the capabilities to:

- Create an open environment for interaction
- Share information and know-how
- Look for authentic consensus
- Describe a clear vision/direction
- Facilitate easy access to resources

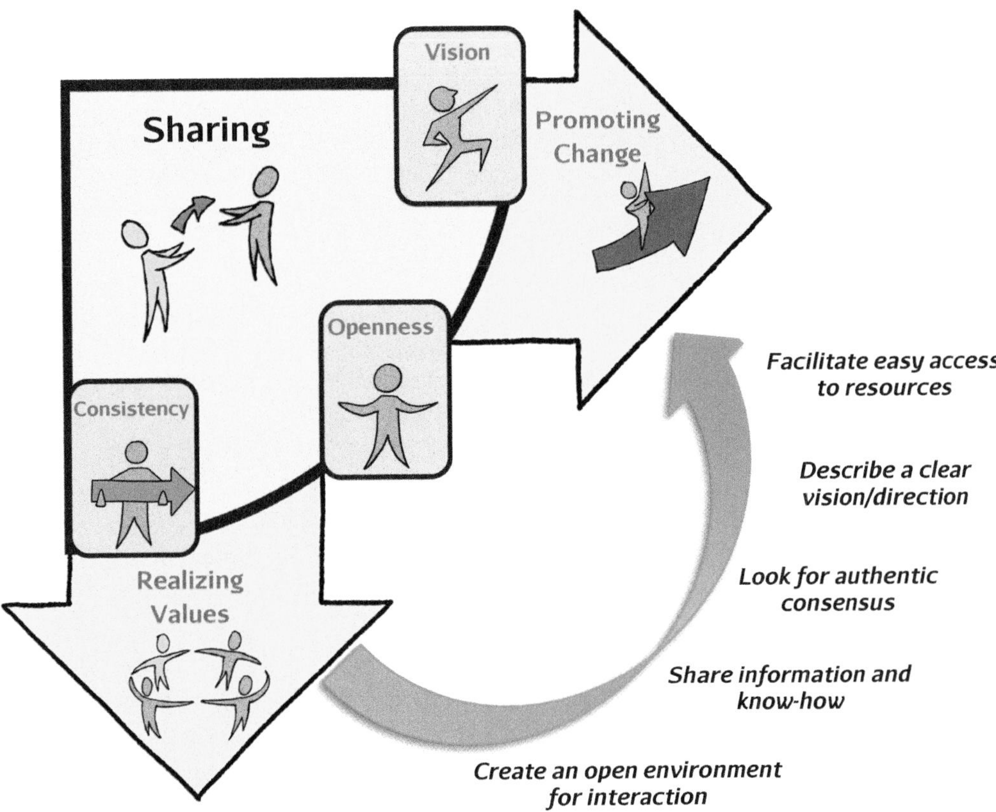

Sharing requires openness, vision and consistency and is necessary in order to promote change and realize values.

The second volume of the Success Factor Modeling series, *Generative Collaboration: Releasing the Creative Power of Collective Intelligence*, is essentially devoted to the action of Sharing. It provides many formats and exercises to promote open communication, facilitate the exchange of ideas, visions and energy, to incorporate multiple perspectives, and to involve people in the process of solving problems and achieving goals. For this volume, I will primarily focus on the application of Sharing to promoting change through collective problem solving.

Applying Sharing to Collective Problem Solving

Leaders think and talk about the solutions. Followers think and talk about the problems.
Brian Tracy

Leadership is solving problems. The day people stop bringing you their problems is the day you have stopped leading them. They have either lost confidence that you can help or concluded you do not care. Either case is a failure of leadership.
Colin Powell

A "problem" can be defined as the difference or gap between the present and desired state.

In order to solve a problem, it is necessary to find a "solution space" that contains alternatives and resources that allow us to either overcome, transform or avoid the problem.

Promoting change and realizing values are often a function of solving problems. One of the main purposes for sharing is to catalyze and direct collective intelligence and generative collaboration between team members. Charles Matthews mentioned the importance of "giving people a toolkit of practical problem solving techniques" as key to his success in helping Rolls Royce Motorcars rebound from its crisis situation.

One of the great strengths of Success Factor Modeling lies in the tools and methods it provides for practical problem solving. To explore some ways to direct the process of sharing toward collective problem solving, we must first ask, "What is a problem? What makes something a problem? What are the important elements to define in regard to the problem?"

From an SFM perspective, if you have no outcome, you have no problem. That is, if you don't want to be anywhere other than where you are, you have no problem. In fact, often the process of establishing a goal actually creates a problem. The problem is the gap between your present state and your desired state, and the issues that have to be dealt with in order to get to the desired state.

Thus, in SFM, a "problem" is typically defined as the difference or gap between present and desired state. If you congruently do not want to be anywhere other than you are now, you do not have a problem. But as soon as you set a goal or an outcome you have created a problem, because you want to change something about your present state in order to reach a desired state. Resources are the actions, operations and maps that allow you to move from a present state to a desired state. A "solution" is the identification and application of the appropriate resources to a present state that leads you to the desired state.

A key element of effective problem solving is defining the entire *problem space*. Problem space is not just the physical space associated with a problem. Relationships, values, perceptions and beliefs might all contribute to the problem space. The problem space is defined by the elements, both physical and non-physical, which create or contribute to the problem.

In order to solve a problem, it is necessary to find a "solution space." A *solution space* contains alternatives and resources that allow us to either overcome, transform or avoid the problem. If, however, the alternatives and resources available in the solution space are not enough to address all of the elements of the problem space, an insufficient solution will arise. The solution space needs to be broader than the problem space. It is possible to implement inadequate solutions because they don't address all of the elements of the problem.

Thus, effective problem solving methods need to serve two basic functions: 1) to enrich and clarify our perception of the problem space, and 2) to define or create some area of solution space that is broad enough to address all of the relevant aspects of the problem space.

Before we can find a solution, we have to first comprehend the variables that are creating the problem space. The basic principle of finding a solution space is that *you can't solve the problem with the same kind of thinking that is creating the problem.* In the words of Albert Einstein, "Our thinking creates problems that the same type of thinking cannot solve." A map that leads us into a problem space may not show us the way out. The whole goal in creative problem solving is to find a way of thinking that is not the same type of thinking that is creating the problem.

The goal of creative problem solving is to find a way of thinking about the problem that is not the same type of thinking that is creating the problem in the first place.

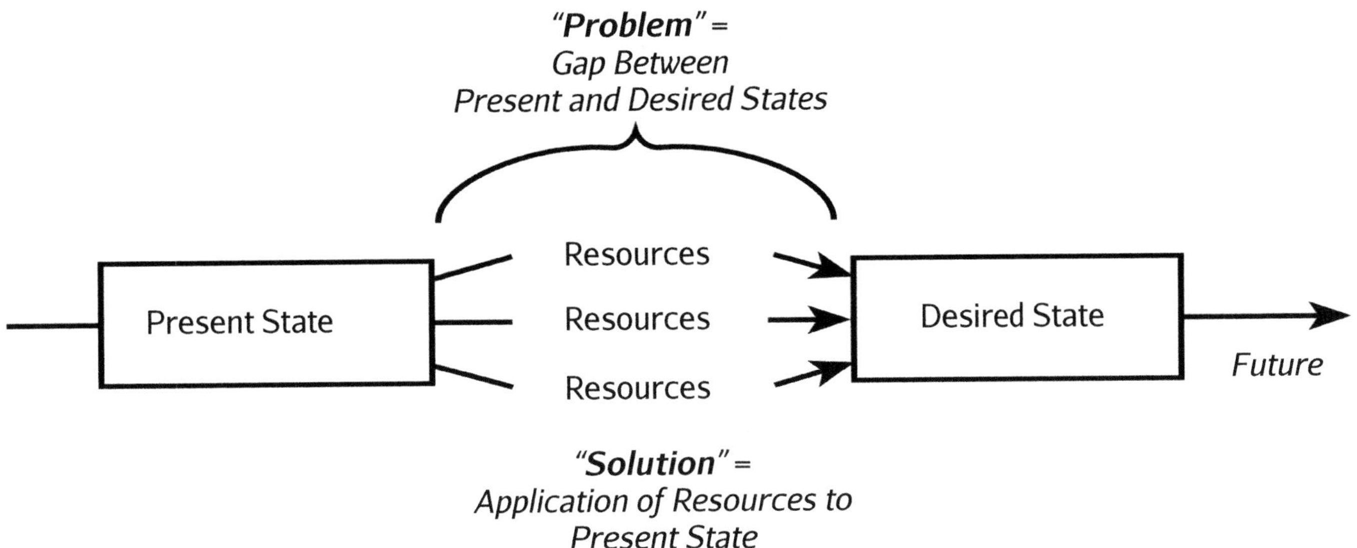

A "Problem" Is the Gap Between One's Present State and Desired State

The S.C.O.R.E. Model

Fundamentally, a "problem space" is defined by the relationship between the goal or *outcome*, the type of *symptoms* that are getting in the way of achieving the outcome, the *causes* of those symptoms, the longer range desired *effects* of reaching the outcome and the *resources* that will help to transform the causes of the symptoms and support reaching the outcome. These are the elements of the *S.C.O.R.E. Model:*

The S.C.O.R.E Model provides a structure for defining the key elements needed to understand and solve a problem.

1. **S***ymptoms*— typically the most noticeable and concrete aspects of a present problem or problem state.
2. **C***auses*— the underlying elements responsible for creating and maintaining the symptoms. They are usually less obvious than the symptoms they produce. Symptoms in the "outer game," for example, are sometimes caused by limitations in people's "inner games."
3. **O***utcomes*— the particular state or behaviors that will take the place of the symptoms.
4. **R***esources*— the underlying elements (actions, skills, tools, beliefs, etc.) responsible for removing the causes of the symptoms and for reaching and maintaining the desired outcomes.
5. **E***ffects*— the longer-term results of achieving a particular outcome. Effects are the expression of the vision and ambition of the project or venture.

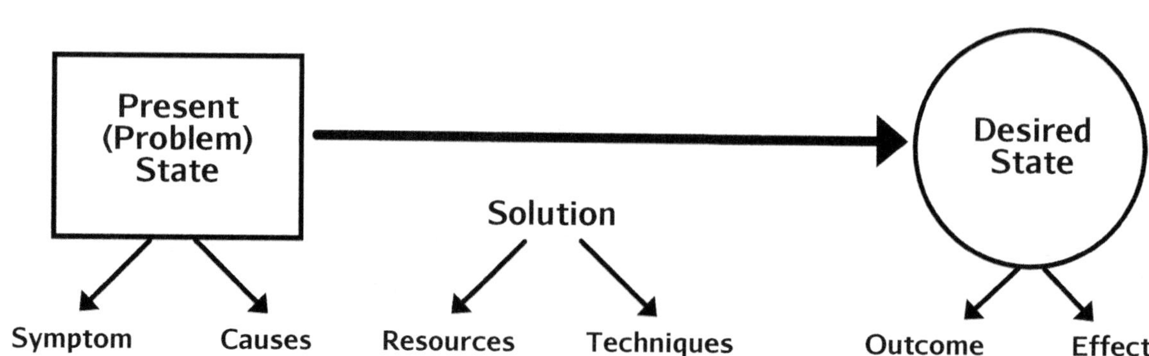

The S.C.O.R.E. Model Defines the "Problem Space" of Promoting Change

Specific outcomes are generally stepping stones to get to a longer-term desired effect, which is generally the underlying reason or motivation for establishing a particular outcome to begin with. It is also important to keep in mind that there is generally a type of "mirror image" between symptoms and outcomes. If I want more motivation, for instance, I will need to reduce inertia and resistance. If I want more efficiency, I will need to simultaneously reduce waste. If I want greater quality, I will have to decrease the number of defects, and so on.

In order to produce an effective solution for a particular problem or challenge, it is necessary to find resources that effectively address the causes of the symptoms, as well as those that promote the achievement of the outcome and the ultimate desired effect to be reached. Some solutions may require a number of different resources applied over a space of months or years. The situation may evolve over time as well. Thus, defining symptoms, outcomes, causes and potential effects is an ongoing process requiring constant sharing.

In order to produce an effective solution for a particular problem, it is necessary to find resources that effectively address the causes of the symptoms, as well as those that promote the achievement of the outcome and the longer-term desired effect to be reached.

According to the S.C.O.R.E. Model, effective problem solving ability involves defining the "problem space" and identifying potential areas of "solution space" by continually exploring the following questions:

1. What is the *symptom* in this problem?
2. What is the *cause* of the symptom in this problem?
3. What is the desired *outcome* or goal that will replace the symptom?
4. What would be the longer-term *effect* of reaching that goal (i.e., what is the bigger vision and ambition)?
5. What *resource* could help address the cause?
6. What *resource* would help achieve the outcome?

Multiple S.C.O.R.E.s

Complex, systemic problems often manifest themselves in terms of more than one symptom; and any particular symptom may have multiple causes. Both projects and problems may involve several different desired outcomes and effects. In gathering information about a particular problem or 'problem space', it is often necessary to identify and synthesize multiple symptoms, outcomes, etc.

For instance, in a large organization, the problem may present different symptoms to different parts of the organization. That is, the symptoms of a "quality" problem may show up in terms of "product defects" to a production manager, but in terms of "customer returns" to a marketing manager. The symptom may reach a financial manager in terms of budget constraints due to reduced profitability.

Effective problem solving in an organization involves the recognition of such symptoms and their interrelationships. Sometimes, in order to successfully diagnose a problem, its causes and potential solutions, it is necessary to look at the relationship between several symptoms.

In interdependent systems, the S.C.O.R.E. elements which effect each member of the system often "complement" those of other members—like a type of "problem space" jigsaw puzzle. That is, one person's "symptom" is often the "cause" of another person's problem. A "defective product," for example, may be the symptom to a manufacturing manager, but the cause of a marketing manager's problem of "customer returns." Customer returns, on the other hand, itself becomes the cause of "lower profitability," which is the symptom perceived by a manger in the planning division.

The same type of complementary relationship can take place for the S.C.O.R.E. elements relating to the desired state. A sales manager's outcome of "increased sales" may be the desired effect of a marketing manager's outcome of "an effective marketing plan." Similarly, the longer term effects of the outcome of "increasing sales" for the sales manager might be something like "greater profitability for the company"; which may be the desired outcome of the finance manager.

The Various S.C.O.R.E. Elements Which Make Up a Problem Shift as a Result of Different Perspectives and "Punctuations"

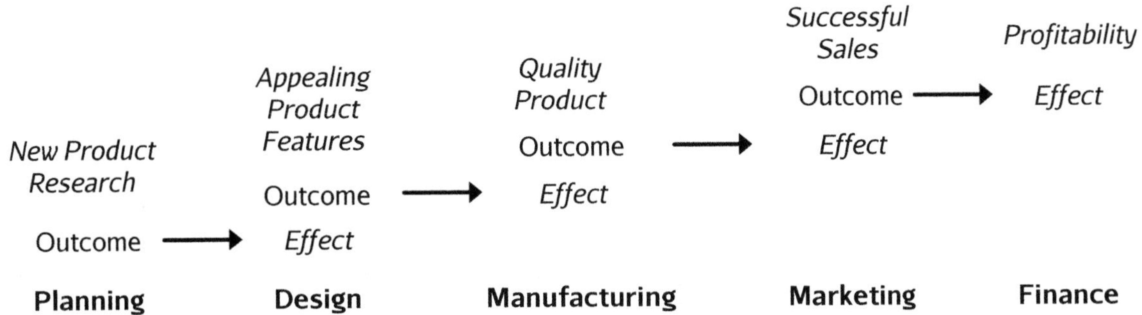

In an Interdependent System, the Outcome of One Part May Be the Desired Effect of Another

In healthy teams and ventures, the S.C.O.R.E.s of the various members complement one another in such a way that solutions may be found which create a type of "positive domino effect" which spreads the solution throughout the group.

Problems and conflicts emerge when the S.C.O.R.E.s of the various members become misaligned. In this situation, one person's (or function's) outcome becomes the "cause" of another's symptoms. The planning manager's outcome of "downsizing," for instance, could become a cause of stress for the production manager, who must lay off some of his or her work force. Confusion arises in a system when one person's outcome is another person's desired effect, yet simultaneously the cause of someone else's symptoms. While this may be unavoidable in some circumstances, it can be more effectively addressed by the team (and sometimes avoided altogether) by being able to have all members "get outside the problem space" and reflect on the way in which their S.C.O.R.E.s overlap.

Multiple S.C.O.R.E. Worksheet

Thus, when working in teams, it is often useful to gather *Multiple S.C.O.R.E.s* in order to have a more complete overview and appreciation for all of the team members' perspectives of the problem situation. The various perspectives may then be explored and aligned to produce the most encompassing and ecological solution. Such information can be gathered and considered using a tool like the following Multiple S.C.O.R.E. worksheet:

	Person A	Person B	Person C	Person D	Person E
Symptoms					
Causes					
Outcomes					
Effects					
Resources					

In gathering information from a team, and considering the possible 'solution space' with respect to a Multiple S.C.O.R.E., it is important to distinguish between 'resources' and 'solutions'. In the situation regarding the quality problem, for example, the marketing manager may view the *solution* as "fixing the product so that it is no longer defective." However, this is not a *resource* that the marketing manager can mobilize directly. It is an outcome required of the manufacturing function. The actual resource that the marketing manager can contribute to the solution of the problem may be his or her ability to get input from customers on what they need and suggestions they have for change or improvement. Similarly, the design manager may perceive the "solution" as "having a bigger budget for research"; again, this is not a "resource" that is available to the design manager. His or her resources are in the area of technical know-how.

Examples of the resources of other team members are provided in the following hypothetical Multiple S.C.O.R.E. worksheet.

	Marketing	Manufacturing	Design	Finance	Planning
Symptoms	*Customer Returns*	*Defective Products*	*Design Flaws*	*Budget Reductions*	*Lower Profitability*
Causes	*Defective Products*	*Design Flaws*	*Budget Reductions*	*Lower Profitability*	*Customer Returns*
Outcomes	*Satisfied Customers*	*Quality Products*	*New Product Features*	*Profitability*	*Organizational Success*
Effects	*Profitability*	*Satisfied Customers*	***Quality Products***	*Organizational Success*	*Growing Market Share*
Resources	*Customer Input*	*Product Knowledge*	*Technical Know-How*	*Predictive Tools*	*System Overview And Models*

Hypothetical Multiple S.C.O.R.E. Worksheet Related to a Team Addressing a Quality Problem

The goal of the team would be to use the Multiple S.C.O.R.E. worksheet to map the entire problem space and then identify the resources that can be contributed by each member of the team to the overall solution. It is another useful process to be able to orchestrate innovation.

This type of collective problem solving can be greatly enhanced by applying the *Intervision* process that I describe in *SFM Vol. II* (pp. 120-127). This process encourages people to apply visual and metaphorical thinking as well as rational analysis. This can make it easier to discover and visualize the entire problem space and more readily discover resources and solutions.

Stretching to Promote Change and Achieve Results

You gain strength, courage and confidence by every experience in which you really stop to look fear in the face. You must do the thing you think you cannot do.
Eleanor Roosevelt

It is clear that times of crisis, uncertainty and adversity call upon us to stretch ourselves and our resources. Effective *stretching* involves the ability to *challenge* consolidated habits and take risks in support of greater innovation and experimentation. Stretching also involves the capacity to set challenging goals, to call success into question and to push towards doing more—*to go beyond*. Stretching is a result of the ability to gradually increase performance, to aim for excellence with accumulated success, achieving continuous improvement. Stretching is needed for both promoting change and achieving results.

Effective stretching requires the ability to *think strategically*—to identify and contrast one's present state with one's desired state, and to define the chain of actions that lead from one to the other. It also requires the practical use of *imagination*—constantly moving toward new possibilities; stretching the boundaries of current thoughts and actions.

Stretching involves the ability to aim for excellence, set challenging goals, take risks and question consolidated habits in order to achieve greater innovation and continuous improvement.

The action of stretching is supported by three key personal qualities: ambition, vision and determination. *Determination* is the quality most associated with stretching and is connected to the capacity to make decisions rapidly and with timeliness, to take risks, and to try new solutions. Determination is characterized by resoluteness and emotional involvement with the will to "put one's heart in it." Some other leadership characteristics related to determination include being resolute, taking risks and taking prompt action.

In summary, stretching is about:

- Challenging consolidated habits
- Encouraging the willingness to stretch oneself
- Looking for continuous improvement
- Stimulating innovation
- Raising expectations

Stretching, especially during times of uncertainty and adversity, is one of the most challenging leadership actions. It requires that we stay closely connected to our higher purpose. It can be very useful to have a road-map that helps us to do this while thinking strategically about the overall "problem space." One of the road-maps most often use in my coaching and consulting work is that of the *Hero's Journey.*

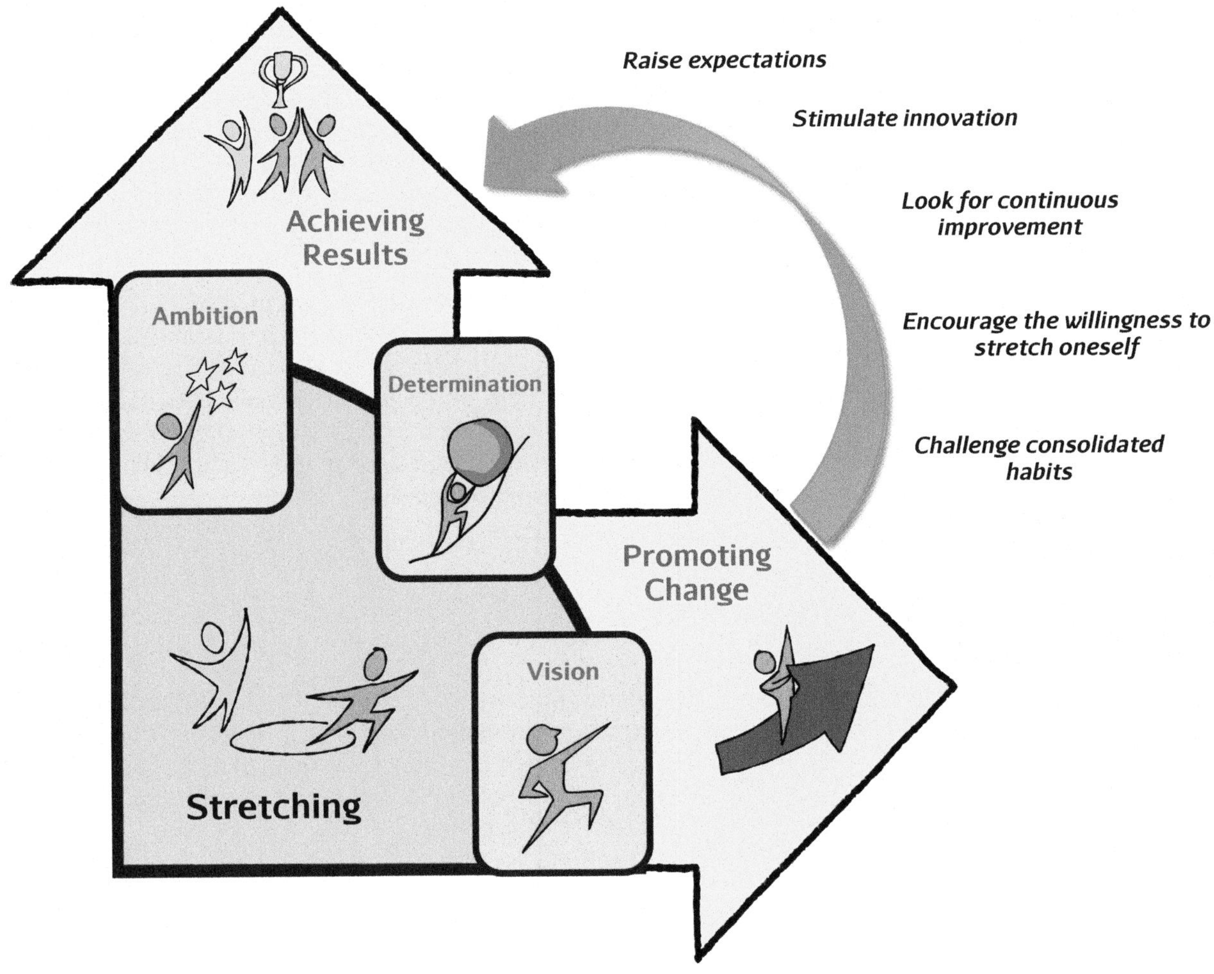

Stretching requires vision, ambition and determination
and is necessary in order to promote change and achieve results.

The Hero's Journey

In the cave you fear to enter lies the treasure that you seek.
Joseph Campbell

The Hero's Journey provides a powerful road map for leaders and entrepreneurs to deal with the challenges of growing and guiding a venture.

Dealing with adversity, crisis and change can be likened to what Joseph Campbell called the "Hero's Journey" (The Hero With A Thousand Faces, 1949). Heroes are individuals who have a vision and a calling that compels them to take risks, face uncertainty and attempt to surmount seemingly overwhelming obstacles. Campbell examined stories of heroes, historical and mythical, spanning all ages, cultures, religions and genders; performing a type of success factor modeling.

Campbell described the common features of all of these different stories and accounts in terms of the steps of the "Hero's Journey"—the sequence of events that seem to be shared in the epic myths and stories and achievements of every culture. These same steps also apply to the sometimes arduous demands that we face in our own lives and businesses today. Campbell's notion of the hero's journey provides a powerful road map for leaders and entrepreneurs to deal with the challenges of growing and guiding a venture.

According to Campbell, the fundamental steps of the hero's journey are comprised of:

1. HEARING A CALLING

2. COMMITTING TO THE CALLING

3. CROSSING THE THRESHOLD

1. *Hearing a calling* (a "call to adventure") that touches in some way the level of our identity, life purpose or mission. These callings can come in many forms and frequently represent major transition points. Such callings generally arise as a result of changing circumstances and are typically quite challenging (otherwise it would not need to be a "hero's" journey). They typically involve an expansion or evolution of identity.

2. *Committing to the calling* leads us to confront a boundary or threshold in our existing abilities or map of the world. We can choose to either accept or try to ignore the calling. Attempting to refuse or disregard the calling, however, frequently leads to the formation or intensification of problems or symptoms in our lives, precipitating crises that we cannot ignore.

3. *Crossing the threshold* propels us into some new heretofore unknown "territory" outside of our current comfort zone; a territory that forces us to grow and evolve, and requires us to find support and guidance. According to Campbell, this threshold is generally a "point of no return," meaning that, once we are across it, we cannot go back to the way things used to be. We must move forward into the unknown.

4. *Finding guardians*, mentors or sponsors is something that often comes naturally from having the courage to cross a threshold. (As it has been said, "When the student is ready, the teacher appears.") "Guardians" are the key relationships we develop that support us to build skills, believe in ourselves and stay focused on our objectives. Although a hero's journey is a very personal journey, it is not something that we can do alone. We need to be open and willing to receive support.

   Because the territory beyond the threshold is new for us, we cannot necessarily know what type of guardianship we will need ahead of time or who those guardians will be. Sometimes guardians will come from surprising places. Thus, we must stay open and available to receiving guidance and support at every step on our journey.

4. FINDING GUARDIANS

5. *Facing challenges* (or "*demons*") is also a natural result of crossing a threshold. A demon is generally something that appears to oppose, tempt or negate us as heroes. "Demons," however, are not necessarily evil or bad; they are simply a type of "energy" that we need to learn to contend with, accept and redirect. Often, demons are simply a reflection of one of our own inner fears and shadows (parts of ourselves that we are disconnected from and try to suppress, avoid or deny). It is here that we confront "negative sponsorship"—messages, coming from either inside of us or from significant others, that imply, "You will not succeed," "You should not even try," "You do not deserve success," "You are incapable," "You will never be good enough," etc.

5. FACING CHALLENGES

6. *Developing new resources* is necessary in order to deal with uncertainty and transform the "demons." A hero's journey is ultimately a path of learning and self-evolution. The resources that help us to cross the threshold into new territory and transform the demon are the beliefs, capabilities, behavioral skills and tools we are able to put into action in order to deal with complexity, uncertainty and resistance. This is the area where we ourselves must grow in order to develop the flexibility and increased competence necessary to navigate new territory (internal and external) successfully and overcome the obstacles that arise along the way.

6. DEVELOPING NEW RESOURCES

7. COMPLETING THE TASK

8. RETURNING HOME

7. Completing the *task* for which we have been called, and *finding* the *way* to fulfill the calling is ultimately achieved by creating a *new map of the world* that incorporates the growth and discoveries brought about by the journey.

8. *Returning home* as a transformed person, and sharing with others the knowledge and experience gained as a result of the journey. It is also important that you be seen and acknowledged as your new identity. This is necessary in order to complete the cycle of personal transformation.

Sometimes the return home is also a very challenging part of the journey. In fact, according to Campbell there are frequently obstacles and sometimes a refusal to the return as well, which often involves crossing another type of threshold. The remarkable journey and transformation that has occurred can make it difficult to reintegrate with life and key relationships as they used to be. There can be a fear on our own part of getting stuck in our own previous "mundane" existence. And there can be desire on the part of significant others for us to stay as we were before so that they don't have to change in response to our movement and growth. Our return can disrupt the status quo.

There is also a natural vulnerability that accompanies transitions of any type that can bring up difficult feelings and shadows. Remaining connected with our guardians and staying rooted in the center of our Circle of Success and the new resources that we have gained on our journey are key to the success of the return home.

THE HERO'S JOURNEY

8. RETURNING HOME

1. HEARING A CALLING

7. COMPLETING THE TASK

2. COMMITTING TO THE CALLING

6. DEVELOPING NEW RESOURCES

3. CROSSING THE THRESHOLD

5. FACING CHALLENGES

4. FINDING GUARDIANS

Applying the Hero's Journey in a Venture

While the hero's journey is clearly a metaphor, it captures a good deal of the reality facing people and ventures as they seek to build a path to a successful future and contend with the uncertainties of change. The notion of a "calling," for instance, clearly symbolizes the vision and mission that the entrepreneur, team or organization is pursuing – i.e., the higher purpose.

In times of adversity and uncertainty, the details of the journey's destination are frequently unclear. This does not mean, however, that there is no clear direction in which to go. In these times, the direction may come more as a felt sense. In fact, the notion of a "calling" implies something more heard or felt than seen. As Steve Jobs pointed out, "You can't connect the dots looking forward . . . you have to trust that the dots will somehow connect in your future. You have to trust in something – your gut, destiny, life, karma. . . ."

The "threshold" represents the new territory, and unknown and uncertain elements that a person must confront in order to put the vision and mission into action. To achieve transformation and awakening, our mental maps of who we are and what is possible in the world must become broader, and we must perceive old limitations in a completely new way. This requires that we break through our old mindset and "get outside of the box," learning at the level of what anthropologist Gregory Bateson called *Learning IV*—the creation of something "completely new." Such a generative state both "transcends and includes" our previous knowledge and awareness, and is a key part of the Hero's Journey.

The symbol of the "demon" reflects the challenges of upheaval, competition, internal politics and other obstacles and crises that emerge from circumstances beyond our control. As pointed our earlier, what makes these external circumstances and challenges become "demons" is that they catalyze our own inner fears and *shadows*; the difficult feelings and parts of ourselves that we do not know how to welcome, hold with equanimity and integrate. The demon is transformed by making a "guest house" for our difficult feelings in order to welcome and transform our own inner shadows.

The resources that help us to cross the threshold into new territory and transform our demons and shadows are the values, behavioral skills and business practices we are able to put into action in order to deal with complexity, uncertainty and resistance. This is the area where we ourselves must grow in order to develop the flexibility and increased requisite variety necessary to successfully navigate the new territory and overcome the obstacles that arise along the way.

"Guardians" are the sponsors and relationships we develop (which can include our team members, stakeholders and partners) that support us to build skills, believe in ourselves and stay focused on our long-term objectives.

THE HERO'S JOURNEY IN A VENTURE

Mapping Your Hero's Journey

In our book *The Hero's Journey* (2011) my co-author Stephen Gilligan and I provide a number of principles and exercises for navigating the various aspects of the hero's journeys that emerge in our lives and ventures. For the purposes of our exploration of the success factors of entrepreneurship, the main value of this model is to explore and prepare yourself for some of the key challenges you confront in your project or venture. Consider some of the leadership moments that you have identified with respect to your project or venture and explore the following questions:

1. **The calling:** What is the situation calling me/us to become or become more of? What needs to be clarified or committed to with respect to my/our vision? Mission? Ambition? (It is often useful to answer this question in the form of a symbol or metaphor; e.g., "I am/We are being called to become eagles/warriors/magicians, etc.")
2. **The threshold:** What is the threshold I/we must go beyond or the risk I/we must take? What is the unknown territory, outside of my/our comfort zone, that I/we must enter in order to achieve the calling?
3. **The demon:** What is the "demon" or "shadow" (challenge, danger, difficulty, etc.) I/we must face? What am I/are we afraid of? (What are the consequences that I/we fear will occur if I/we go over the threshold?) What seems to be against me/us?
4. **The resources:** What resources do I/we have and which do I/we need to develop more fully in order to face the challenge, cross the threshold and accomplish the calling?
5. **The guardians:** Who are my/our inner and outer guardians (past and present; physical and non-physical) for these resources? What is their message or advice for me/us?

When you have identified your guardians, it is interesting to imagine what messages or advice they might have for you and/or your team if they were actually present.

As in the Strengthening Belief process described earlier in this chapter, you can put yourself into the shoes of each of the guardians, and look at yourself and your situation through their eyes (second position). What message or advice does each guardian have for you?

How can the messages and support of your guardians help you to address the situation or challenge you are facing?

In the next chapter, we will explore how you can apply Empowering, Coaching, Sharing and Stretching in order to take on the Hero's Journey of *doing the impossible!*

Conclusion: Preparing for Leadership Moments

In conclusion, rebounding from adversity, developing resilience and enhancing fitness for the future involve adequate preparation. A simple formula for preparing for inevitable leadership moments is expressed in the following steps:

1. Select a leadership moment and reflect upon the situation? What is the external context? What is the S.C.O.R.E.? (Symptom, cause, outcome, available resources and desired effect.)
2. What are your goals? Think in terms of the four organizational outcomes: promoting change, realizing values, developing people and achieving results.
3. What Actions do you need to take? Empowering, Coaching, Sharing, Stretching?
4. What inner qualities are most important to support those actions? Vision, openness, consistency, example, motivation, generosity, ambition?
5. What is the Hero's Journey that you are on? What is the threshold you must cross? What "demons" are you facing? Which resources and guardians do you have to support you?
6. Where will you need emotional intelligence? What difficult feelings will you encounter in yourself or others? What resources will you need in order to hold them?
7. What will be your (inner and outer) feedback that you are progressing/ succeeding?

Chapter Summary

Putting effective leadership into practice with respect to our own ventures involves first identifying "*leadership moments*," symbolic or challenging situations that will strongly influence the perception of key collaborators and require us to be the best of ourselves.

Creating a successful venture that is innovative, resilient and fit for the future requires *Empowering* all of those involved to give their best. This entails supporting the development of people's potential by recognizing individuality and promoting self-esteem, encouraging autonomy and stimulating motivation for growth. *Building a Winning Belief System* is one of the most profound and powerful ways entrepreneurs and leaders can empower themselves, their teams and collaborators. A winning belief system is one that creates an expectation of a positive future, a feeling of capability and responsibility, and a sense of self-worth and belonging. *Assessing our degree of belief* in each of these core areas and *using mentors and role models to build confidence and strengthen belief* are key skills to building a winning belief system within an individual or group.

Coaching is one of the most important leadership actions in order to increase resilience and enhance fitness for the future. Coaching involves developing people's experience and competencies, building trust, listening with attention, guiding people in their learning process and growing team spirit. The core leadership quality for effective Coaching is that of being a consistent example. Realizing *core values* in different contexts is one of the keys to resilience and fitness for the future. Clarifying and distinguishing core values from instrumental values is important in order to know how to prioritize actions and avoid confusion and conflicts. *Putting values into action* involves defining the other levels of factors (cognitive, behavioral and environmental) needed to effectively establish the values we want to put into practice. *Creating an Aligned State* allows entrepreneurs and leaders to stay connected to the best of themselves and be an effective example in order to increase trust and resilience in challenging situations.

Sharing stimulates innovation and strengthens resilience through the exchange of information, ideas, resources and energy. Sharing involves the capacity to promote open communication and dialogue between people. One of the main contexts in which Sharing is important is for effective *problem solving*. The *S.C.O.R.E. Model* offers a simple yet comprehensive template for defining a *problem space* and *solution space* by helping to identify *symptoms*, their *causes*, the *outcomes* that will replace the symptoms and the *resources* necessary to transform the causes of the symptoms and achieve the outcomes that will bring the desired *effects*. Multiple S.C.O.R.E.s emerge in complex and interdependent systems where different people's behaviors, resources and limitations can complement or compound those of others with whom they interact. *Defining Multiple S.C.O.R.E.s* is an application of the discipline of systems thinking that helps to orchestrate innovation by promoting collective intelligence and generative collaboration.

Many leadership moments require some degree of *Stretching* in which a leader and his or her teams must raise expectations, stimulate innovation, look for continuous improvement and challenge consolidated habits. *The Hero's Journey* provides a powerful roadmap for successfully Stretching by helping to define the *call to action* the situation requires from us, the *threshold* into the new territory we must cross, the *demons and shadows* we must confront and transform and the *resources and guardians* we will need to successfully travel the journey.

The various methods and distinctions that support effective Empowering, Coaching, Sharing and Stretching can be effectively integrated and used for Preparing for Leadership Moments.

Once you are prepared to handle a variety of leadership moments, you are ready to do the impossible!

References and Related Readings

- *From Coach to Awakener*, Dilts, R., Meta Publications, Capitola, CA, 2003.
- *Beliefs: Pathways to Health and Well-Being*, Dilts, R., Hallbom, T. & Smith, S., Metamorphous Press, Portland, OR, 1990; 2nd Edition: Crown House Publishers, London, 2014.
- *Changing Belief Systems with NLP, Dilts*, R., Meta Publications, Capitola, Ca.,1990.
- *Skills for the Future, Dilts, R.*, Meta Publications, Capitola, CA, 1993.
- *Tools for Dreamers*, Dilts, R. B., Epstein, T. and Dilts, R. W., Meta Publications, Capitola, CA, 1991.
- *NLP II: The Next Generation*, Dilts, R. and DeLozier, J. with Bacon Dilts, D., Meta Publications, Capitola, CA, 2010.
- *Alpha Leadership: Tools for Leaders Who Want More From Life*, Deering, A., Dilts, R. and Russell, J., John Wiley & Sons, London, England, 2002.
- *Visionary Leadership Skills: Creating a World to Which People Want to Belong*, Dilts, R., Meta Publications, Capitola, Ca., 1996.
- *The Hero With A Thousand Faces*, Campbell, J., Fontana Press., London, UK, 1993.
- *The Hero's Journey: A Voyage of Self-Discovery*, Gilligan, S. and Dilts, R., Crowne House Publishers, London, 2009.

06
Doing the Impossible

Living in dreams of yesterday,
we find ourselves still dreaming of impossible future conquests.
Charles Lindbergh

It's tough to make predictions, especially about the future.
Yogi Berra

Do not confuse lack of imagination with logical impossibility.
Tom Gruber – Cofounder of Siri

ANTONIO MEZA

Entrepreneur Cindana Turkette maintains that the greatest satisfaction for an entrepreneur is helping clients and customers achieve "something they did not know was possible."

Doing the Impossible

In addition to orchestrating innovation, enhancing fitness for the future and rebounding from adversity, conscious leaders and next generation entrepreneurs are also frequently called upon to "do the impossible." As entrepreneur Cindana Turkette (see *SFM Vol. I*, pp. 163-171) so eloquently pointed out, the greatest satisfaction for an entrepreneur is helping clients and customers achieve "something they did not know was possible" but which has become possible "because of the tools you provided them." As Cindana's comment implies, *impossible* usually means that the path to achieve a particular outcome does not currently exist (which does not mean that it will never exist). Thus, the entrepreneur's job is to create a path that does not yet currently exist.

In the Silicon Valley, there is a term known as the BHAG. BHAG is an acronym for "**B**ig **H**airy **A**udacious **G**oal." It implies a bold and daring undertaking or "impossible dream" that is a combination of both vision and ambition. BHAGs are the drivers at the basis of the ventures of next generation entrepreneurs.

As entrepreneur Don Pickens (see *SFM Vol. I*, p. 137) advises, in order to succeed, it is essential for leaders and entrepreneurs to "stay focused and understand that your vision will differ from others who are looking at the same map." He adds that, "By definition, an entrepreneur has a vision that is moving forward—beyond what people are currently familiar or comfortable with." In fact, Pickens claims that if too many people are telling you that you have a good idea, and you are not getting enough doubters who think what you are proposing is "impossible," you may want to consider revisiting your goals for your venture and extend your imagination to make them even "bigger," "hairier" and more "audacious."

Impossible Dreams?

It is interesting to note that many of the technologies and other developments that we consider the bedrock of today's reality were at one time considered foolish, useless or "impossible." This is because, as Don Pickens pointed out, they are "beyond what people are currently familiar or comfortable with." Consider some of the following classic examples.

Computers

I think there is a world market for maybe five computers.
Thomas Watson, Chairman of IBM, 1943.

Computers in the future may weigh no more than 1.5 tons.
Popular Mechanics magazine, 1949.

I have traveled the length and breadth of this country and talked with the best people, and I can assure you that data processing is a fad that won't last out the year.
The editor in charge of business books for Prentice Hall, 1957.

But what is it good for?
Engineer at the Advanced Computing Systems Division of IBM, 1968, commenting on the microchip.

Personal Computers

There is no reason anyone would want a computer in their home.
Ken Olson, president, chairman and founder of Digital Equipment in 1977.

So we went to Atari and said, "Hey, we've got this amazing thing, even built with some of your parts, and what do you think about funding us? Or we'll give it to you. We just want to do it. Pay our salary, we'll come work for you." And they said, "No." So then we went to Hewlett-Packard, and they said, "Hey, we don't need you. You haven't got through college yet."
Steve Jobs on attempts to get Atari and HP interested in his and Steve Wozniak's personal computer prior to starting Apple Computer in a garage in 1976.

Entertainment

Who the hell wants to hear actors talk?
H. M. Warner, Warner Brothers, 1927.

I'm just glad it'll be Clark Gable who's falling on his face and not Gary Cooper.
Gary Cooper on his decision not to take the leading role for *Gone With The Wind* in 1939.

We don't like their sound, and guitar music is on the way out.
Decca Recording Co. rejecting the Beatles in 1962.

Steve Jobs and Steve Wozniak and their ideas for making a personal computer were initially rejected by established companies like Atari and Hewlett-Packard.

Many of the products and services that we take for granted and consider commonplace in today's world were at one time considered impossible or ridiculous.

Dealing with "critics" and "naysayers" is one of the primary challenges in doing the impossible.

The Last Century

Drill for oil? You mean drill into the ground to try and find oil? You're crazy.
Drillers who Edwin L. Drake tried to enlist in his project to drill for oil in 1859.

Louis Pasteur's theory of germs is ridiculous fiction.
Pierre Pachet, Professor of Physiology at Toulouse, 1872.

This "telephone" has too many shortcomings to be seriously considered as a means of communication. The device is inherently of no value to us.
Western Union internal memo, 1876.

Heavier-than-air flying machines are impossible.
Lord Kelvin, president, Royal Society, 1895.

Airplanes are interesting toys but of no military value.
Maréchal Ferdinand Foch, Professor of Strategy, Ecole Supérieure de Guerre, 1928.

The wireless music box has no imaginable commercial value. Who would pay for a message sent to nobody in particular?
David Sarnoff's associates in response to his urgings for investment in the radio in the 1920s.

Recent Developments

The concept is interesting and well-formed, but in order to earn better than a "C," the idea must be feasible.
A Yale University management professor in response to Fred Smith's paper proposing reliable overnight delivery service. (Smith went on to found Federal Express Corp.)

A cookie store is a bad idea. Besides, the market research reports say America likes crispy cookies, not soft and chewy cookies like you make.
Response to Debbi Fields' idea of starting Mrs. Fields' Cookies.

If I had thought about it, I wouldn't have done the experiment. The literature was full of examples that said you can't do this.
Spencer Silver on the work that led to the unique adhesives for 3M "Post-It" Notepads.

All of these comments reflect the natural resistance of our rational, "thinking" minds and egos to visions and ideas that are "beyond what we are currently familiar or comfortable with." Knowledge of "what is" is clearly a double-edged sword. On the one hand, it provides clarity, comfort and stability. On the other hand, too much confidence and investment in our knowledge of what is can make it difficult to see beyond what we already know. Perhaps the most classic example of this is the statement made by Charles H. Duell, the Commissioner of the U.S. Patent Office, in 1899: *"Everything that can be invented has been invented."*

The Skills and Disciplines of Doing the Impossible

Doing the impossible first and foremost requires the disciplines of using imagination to create the future and constantly being aware of, reflecting upon and questioning our mental maps and assumptions. This is important not only in our businesses but in other parts of our lives as well.

Consider the example of my mother who in the early 1980s had a recurrence of breast cancer. The recurrence was unexpectedly advanced. The doctors' diagnosis placed its progression at stage 4. There is no stage 5. The next stage is essentially death. Given that the first occurrence had been less than two years earlier and the cancer had spread so dramatically, the doctors pointed out that it was clearly a very aggressive variety. Based upon how quickly the cancer had progressed and how quickly it had spread to so much of her body (not only the other breast, but also her bladder, her ovaries and into the bone marrow of practically every bone in her body), they estimated she might live a few more months. Further, given the advanced stage of the disease, they claimed that there was nothing that could be done medically at that point to stop or even slow its spread. It was an impossible dream to think that my mother might live even a few more years. Rather than a business, my mothers project or "venture" and BHAG was related to her health.

Patricia Dilts

Patricia Dilts applied many of the skills covered in the Success Factor Modeling book series—including clarifying her vision, mission and ambition for her life—to "do the impossible" during her remarkable recovery from stage 4 breast cancer.

I have written about this situation in several other books (*Beliefs: Pathways to Health and Well-Being*, 2011 and *Changing Belief Systems with NLP*, 1989). Suffice it to say here that my mother did the impossible. She took charge of her life, had a remarkable recovery (with only limited medical support), and, to the great surprise of her doctors, ended up living 18 more years; symptom free for the vast majority of that time. Interestingly, to accomplish this, she applied many of the skills we have covered so far in this book series, beginning with clarifying her vision, mission and ambition for her life. (I have often considered it quite relevant that a common term for a remarkable recovery from a serious illness is "remission"; as reconnecting with one's mission is frequently a key success factor in rebounding from a health crisis.) My mother's belief in herself and in the possibility of a positive future were also essential factors in her success. [She has written her own account of this journey in her monograph *My Pathway to Wholeness*, 1991.]

In giving their poor prognosis, the doctors, of course, were doing their job with the very best of intentions; trying to avoid "false hope." They were viewing her future through the filters of what they knew at that time. Their perspective was important and valuable, but not necessarily complete nor ultimately accurate. When this type of perspective contradicts our visions and ambitions for the future it frequently comes in the form of criticism, creating obstacles in the form of doubt and resistance. Dealing with "critics" and "naysayers" is one of the primary challenges in doing the impossible.

This is no doubt why Steve Jobs advised us not to be "trapped by dogma" or "the consequences of other people's thinking" nor let "the noise of other's opinions drown out your own inner voice." On the other hand, it has been argued that Jobs' own arrogance led to his early demise from pancreatic cancer because he did not heed the advice of his doctors early enough. Thus, there is an important difference between not being "trapped" by other people's opinions and rejecting them outright. One of the key issues with respect to doing the impossible is how to incorporate the perspectives and positive intentions of our critics without either discounting them or becoming overly limited by them. This will be one of our major explorations in this chapter; how can we transform our critics into our supporters and advisors.

One of the key skills for doing the impossible is incorporating the perspectives and positive intentions of critics without either discounting them or becoming overly limited by them.

It is obvious that doing the impossible requires all of the skills we have explored so far relating to orchestrating innovation, enhancing fitness for the future and rebounding from adversity, but requires several others as well. Some of the skills we have covered up to this point include (1) having and expressing a direction in the form of a vision, mission and ambition and a role that aligns them; (2) taking a balanced, win-win approach to each part of the Circle of Success; and (3) developing and practicing emotionally intelligent, conscious leadership.

In the previous chapter, we emphasized the importance of "being an example" and "sharing" as key success factors for rebounding from adversity. In addition to these, doing the impossible requires particular emphasis on "encouraging team cooperation" and "influencing others towards results." This involves developing the abilities for effective persuasion and "meta leadership."

The Necessity of "Meta Leadership"

Meta leadership is the ability to promote and to lead other leaders. The founder of a new venture must be able to awaken the sense of purpose and vision in others in order to attract and choose team members, stakeholders and partners who can share a passion for the vision and who can become committed to making this vision a reality.

According to David Guo, former CEO of Display Research Laboratories and an avowed "serial entrepreneur," "A successful entrepreneur needs to be able to communicate his or her vision and ideas, and to understand people and their motivation." These abilities are essential features of "meta leadership." Meta leaders are those who lead other leaders, rather than simply direct or command followers. To do the impossible, everyone on the team has to be a leader in their own right.

According to "serial entrepreneur" David Guo, "A successful entrepreneur needs to be able to communicate his or her vision and ideas, and to understand people and their motivation."

As David Guo maintains, "My number one rule is always get people who are better than myself. Who ever you are hiring make sure they are better than you." This, of course, can create quite a challenge. Guo points out that he is often the youngest member of the team. Thus, he does not feel he can be their "boss" or "commander." "I respect my team," he says. "They have a lot more experience than I do, in many things. That's why I have them on my team. They know what I need better than I do. They don't need to come to me to ask for permission for things. My role as the leader of the company is to provide the necessary resources so they can best do their jobs." In this sense, meta leadership has much in common with "servant leadership." *Servant leaders* are those whose job it is to make other people's jobs easier.

David Guo
Former CEO
Display Research Laboratories

David Guo has founded several high-tech ventures in the Silicon Valley. As co-founder of MicropolisVideo/Multi-Media System Division, he pioneered in the fields of interactive television and digital video storage since the industry's inception. As CEO of Display Research Laboratories, he raised more than $20 million in venture financing. DRL developed next generation emissive flat-panel displays, pioneering "printable" thin-film semiconductors on plastic. DRL's display technology enabled low-cost and high-resolution displays for use in consumer and mobile electronics, internet appliances, video billboards and home theaters.

Guo claims, "The goal of the leader is to understand what motivates people and leverage that, not just show them a path." He points out that you cannot *make* other leaders do things. You have to get them to subscribe to your vision, and ask yourself, "What motivates them?"

As an example, when CEO of Display Research Labs, Guo needed extremely highly skilled people, such as experts in phosphor technology. There were only a few people on the planet who had the necessary background and experience to make the type of displays Guo envisioned. One of the people that Guo was pursuing was already highly successful, had made millions of dollars from a previous venture and retired to a mansion in the mountains hundreds of miles away. Guo had to try and figure out how to persuade this expert to come out of retirement and work for Guo's company. The man was not interested in more money and did not need to prove himself professionally, so Guo had to find what would be interesting enough for this person to want to go back to work.

Ultimately, the most powerful motivation was Guo's vision for the venture and the possibility for the phosphor expert to explore some of his own theories and ideas and see them applied to do what people thought was not possible. Guo's vision was of a high definition screen the size and thickness of a table cloth. He was able to convince the phosphor engineer that DRL was a great opportunity for the man to put his theories into practice. The engineer ended up joining the team and flying his own private aircraft to work several days a week.

Meta leadership involves "leading other leaders" by inspiring them through one's own sense of vision and mission.

As David Guo's example illustrates, *meta leadership* involves "leading other leaders" by inspiring them through one's own sense of vision and mission. It is an example of extreme empowerment. Meta leadership is probably one of the most important emerging forms of leadership for next generation entrepreneurs. As ventures become less hierarchical and more "flat," and as people's jobs require increasing autonomy and "discretionary space," the fundamental relationships between people working together in teams and companies are changing. Rather than the traditional "leader–subordinate" relationship, companies and organizations of the future will need to rely more on "leader–leader" interactions, in which each group member is also a leader in some way.

Ultimately, meta leadership is based upon envisioning the future, committing to that future, awakening that vision in others and working together with them to create it. Thus, rather than "power," meta leadership results from vision and the influence of authentic commitment. Meta leaders view others as valuable and interconnected parts of a larger, shared system.

To do the impossible, team members need to be empowered to act quickly and flexibly.

Meta leadership, for instance, involves the ability to negotiate with, empower and inspire others, as opposed to commanding them. In order to be successful in a dynamic environment, entrepreneurs need to work with others who are leaders in their own right and who are proactive and willing to take responsibility and action. An entrepreneur does not have the time to be constantly controlling other people and telling them what to do. As David Guo explains, "Our strategy changes every five minutes. Our vision and goal have not changed, but the strategy changes every time there is new information." To do the impossible, team members need to be empowered to act quickly and flexibly.

Success Factor Case Example
Jan E. Smith – Disney Interactive Studios

Coaching and empowering people to take hold of the vision.

When Jan Smith took over as President of Disney Interactive (now Disney Interactive Studios) in 2000 she knew she had quite a challenge on her hands. The gaming division of the entertainment giant was not doing well, and that was not supposed to happen at Disney.

The Disney empire had been growing steadily in the 1990s, piling up success after success in its core areas. Their new strategy was to diversify and innovate in order to extend the demographics of the Disney product line, leveraging Disney "equity" into other markets by extending the brand name into new areas. It had translated easily into education and the company was working to bring it into gaming and retail.

Jan E. Smith
Former President
Disney Interactive Studios

In fact, Jan first joined the Walt Disney Company in 1987 to help create and launch The Disney Store. The idea of the Disney Store was "retail in the form of entertainment," Jan explains. Its goal was the "transfer of the service level of the amusement parks to a retail environment." To accomplish this, they had to "do things in ways people had never done before." Jan and her team redefined typical roles of the store personnel, referring to people as "cast members," for example, instead of "employees." Rather than "selling," staff were encouraged to refresh the customers' memory; a type of marketing through storytelling and entertainment. This required that staff learn history, trivia and other facts about Disney's productions. Implementing this learning process meant creating a whole Disney University for the stores.

Jan Smith's turnaround of Disney Interactive Studios is a good example of applying the principles of Next Generation Entrepreneurship and Conscious Leadership in order to orchestrate innovation and do the impossible.

What they were doing was brand new and, as Jan points out, "New is exciting but risky." Getting initial internal "buy-in" for the venture from Disney top management was "very hard." There was concern the stores could negatively affect the Disney brand. Jan and her team were persistent, however. The project took off and Disney Stores became another flagship for the Disney organization.

Jan then served as President of Disney Publishing, where she was instrumental in the introduction and growth of several new book businesses.

Beginning the Journey

It was following this that Jan took over the interactive gaming division. Jan accepted responsibility for worldwide operations of Disney Interactive, including product development, marketing, finance and administration, business and legal affairs, and customer support. Her mission was to turn the business around; with a goal to be the #1 interactive entertainment company. However, an impending global recession was already beginning to grip many companies and Jan knew that she had to completely restructure the organization to accomplish the same result with fewer resources. The personal computer business was also declining, so they would need to shift gears to create content for different platforms, such as hand-held game devices. They also needed to internalize competencies that had previously been outsourced (such as manufacturing, sales and marketing) by bringing them in-house.

Jan Smith's *Ambition* was to make Disney Interactive the #1 entertainment company by "leveraging" the Disney brand and characters into a new market.

Oddly enough, though, one of Jan's biggest problems was the mismatch between computer gaming customers and the Disney brand. The typical demographic of Disney customers was children 8 years-old and under and families. The demographic for computer gaming, on the other hand, was young males 15 and older. While eight-year-olds were happy to play a game in which The Little Mermaid helped them to read or spell, fifteen-year-olds were more interested in shooting her.

Crossing the Threshold

In order to increase their market reach in the gaming area, Jan realized that they would have to stretch in two ways:

1. Creating products that brought the typical Disney customer into computer gaming.
2. Creating products that reached the older age group without a compromise in the company's values.

Jan Smith's *Vision* was of computer games that would appeal to the typical Disney customer and that reached an older age group without a compromise in the company's values.

A key challenge for Jan was maintaining the integrity and values of Disney and leveraging the positives, while extending the thinking about what was possible. Again, she needed to do things no one had ever done before at Disney. In this regard, the Disney brand was as much of a hindrance as a help. To make a move into new product areas was extremely dangerous for the company, and made top management nervous. Success would require breaking barriers both internally and externally.

Her task would not be easy. *"I knew I would be 'a hero or a zero',"* she says. *"If I didn't succeed, I would become the 'fall guy'."*

A Vision Emerges

In July 2000, Jan happened to see a pre-production version of a pilot for a new TV quiz show to be aired on one of the Disney television affiliates, titled *Who Wants to Be a Millionaire.* "I saw the show and had the vision of an interactive product." Jan says. "I had the intuition, 'This is going to be the right thing. We just have to find the way'."

Jan faced several major challenges, however. First, this type of product was not Disney Interactive's core competency. They would have to develop a whole new computer platform for a game based on the television show. Secondly, even popular TV programs have a short life cycle. It was July and, in order to have a high sales for a computer game, the game would have to be ready by Christmas.

Transforming Resistance

Jan ran into a lot of resistance when she first began to present her vision. "At first the CFO said 'No way'," Jan recalls. "People started laughing." The usual development cycle for a video game was 18 months, and they only had 3 months to make the Christmas market. Everyone told her, "What you are proposing is impossible."

Jan Smith had a *Passion* to look at problems from every angle.

But Jan did not give up. "I had the intuition it could work and felt up to the challenge," she explains.

To get buy-in from the CFO and upper management, she reminded them that there was a strategic goal at the corporate level to extend all Disney content into new markets. She told people, "This is what we want to be anyway. It is just earlier than planned."

A first task was to figure out how to "do the impossible" and develop the product in one-sixth of the typical time frame. Jan took her team off-site for several days to look at the project from every angle and "think outside of the box." "You have to show it is possible and then ask 'why wouldn't this work?'" she explained.

"First, I spent a lot of time talking to them and getting their views on the business," Jan says. Then she had to synthesize those views to get her own "picture of what is possible."

Jan describes her approach to finding a solution when there is no history or precedent as: "creating an open forum, encouraging different opinions, having heated discussions, refereeing, and at the end making a decision."

Jan's process for transforming resistance and achieving something unprecedented involved "creating an open forum, encouraging different opinions, having heated discussions, refereeing, and at the end making a decision."

Jan points out, "Ultimately the leader is responsible, whether it is good or bad news." She claims that the leader has to "Take all the responsibility personally if it goes wrong," and "Give all the credit to the team if it goes right."

Transcending the Constraints

As a result of these "ground-breaking" meetings, the team discovered that, applying the principles of open innovation, rather than developing the whole technology platform for the game from scratch, they could license one from another "trailblazing" company that did something similar and then adapt it. This would shorten development time considerably. The team also figured out a way that they could work "around the clock," by scheduling overlapping shifts.

A key for Jan was to stay "really focused on the vision." She set up meetings with key players and stakeholders (the show's host, the Producer, Production Executive, etc.) and built key distribution partnerships.

Jan was able to transcend major constraints by staying "really focused on the vision," setting up meetings with key players and stakeholders and building key distribution partnerships.

Jan points out with pride that, over time, people shifted from talking about "Jan's crazy idea" to "*our* project."

Achieving the Impossible

The result was a breakthrough in the existing time line of how to get a product to market. Jan and her team shipped a product in three months that would normally have taken eighteen months. Jan's intuition about the game show paid off. It attained widespread popularity with family television audiences and Disney Interactive ended up with a hit product that sold 3 million copies before Christmas!

Building from the foundation of this first success, Jan was able to continue to stretch and extend Disney Interactive's products into the game market and reach the older age video game playing group without a compromise in values. Using a similar strategy of taking her team off-site and thinking outside the box, they looked for models of any companies that had been successful in the gaming market that did not violate the Disney values. They realized that some Japanese video game developers had a history of making games that sold well in the US that were not simply the violent "shoot-em up" type. They identified a company in Japan that has several hit games in the US that were not objectionable and built a strategic alliance. The result was another hit game that changed the fortunes of Disney Interactive.

Jan went on to establish a superb track record at Disney Interactive and was responsible for establishing the business unit as a global leader.

Jan Smith took on the Role of a groundbreaker working with trailblazers, making key alliances and partnerships.

Meta Leadership in Action

Jan summarizes her recipe for success as "*Coaching and empowering people to take hold of the vision.*" This is the fundamental equation for meta leadership. As Jan puts it, "Leadership is about accelerating the process of the strategic plan and helping people see a new path." She explains, "The organizations I inherited had a group of smart executives who were stuck in looking at their strategy in a specific way." To be effective meta leaders and do the impossible, entrepreneurs need good communication skills and "the belief that people will rise to the occasion if the vision is clear."

Jan's case illustrates that effective leaders and entrepreneurs must, in her words, "Communicate, communicate, communicate" in order to "educate people about the vision." That is, leaders of new ventures need to "Establish the communication structure and help people see the destination." Jan explains that, in the beginning, it was necessary for her to "fly around the world and meet people so that they knew me . . . At first be more visible and present; setting the tone and example. After that, you need your people to lead."

Similar to Steve Jobs, Jan felt that once the team got "it" and shared a common vision, they would be able to follow through on their own. Jan had a strong belief in her team and their capabilities. "If you have the right people you can do anything," she says. Jan trusted that they would make the right decisions. When the bigger picture is shared, then "They will work within the constraint of the vision, even if they do it a different way."

Jan Smith motivated and aligned her team toward their Mission by coaching and empowering people to take hold of the vision.

In a Successful Venture, Execution Needs to Be Aligned with Vision

In order to promote generative collaboration and orchestrate innovation, Jan Smith worked to "develop both communication infrastructure and creativity infrastructure" for her team and encouraged them to "dedicate time to be creative."

Moving From Vision to Execution

Jan's case also demonstrates the importance of defining and aligning different levels of success factors to bring vision into action. She asserts that achieving success requires "Operational execution on key elements to attain the vision." This involves communicating the vision and then "having a plan and doing each step really well." In her words, you have to "start with a strategic plan tied to an operating plan."

Jan points out that "Creating without a box is not very creative." The challenge of the Disney Store, for example, was to "be creative in a box." That is, to understand the parameters of the vision and then, within the confines of those parameters, create something that had never before existed. The challenge of Disney Interactive, on the other hand, was "to get outside of the box" of a limited view of what was possible and into the "bigger box" of the vision. The vision is the larger box that contains the smaller "box" of the strategic plan and within that the smaller "box" of an operating plan – like Russian dolls nested inside of one another.

Promoting Generative Collaboration

To be successful, Jan advises that ventures need to "develop both communication infrastructure and creativity infrastructure." She says that it is also important to "dedicate time to be creative." Otherwise, "people get caught up in executing." This requires the discipline for "creative dialog on a regular basis."

Clearly, one of Jan's key success factors was her ability to "put a number of people in a room with different backgrounds and stretch." For her off-site meetings, she established what we have called a "COACH container," creating an "open forum" within which "everyone debated and argued," but with a space big enough to hold different perspectives and with a strong focus on the vision. According to Jan, in order to do the impossible, "the dream needs to outweigh criticism." She points out that Walt Disney went bankrupt three times before the first Disneyland park was built.

Mastering the Inner Game

Jan's basic "inner game" resources were her vision, intuition and the belief "I can accomplish that." "If you don't believe in yourself, you cannot stand in the ring," she contends. Another key aspect of her inner game was the determination to "drive to the finish line." "If you can dream it, you can do it," she claims. She complemented her belief and determination by having "creative ways of looking at problems" and "trusting" her intuition.

Building a Circle of Success

To summarize, it is clear that Jan systematically built a powerful Circle of Success. In the center of that Circle were her qualities of purposefulness and intuition, and her belief "I can accomplish that." She applied her *passion* for looking at problems in creative ways to each of the four quadrants.

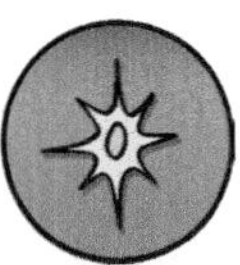

Passion

She started by applying that passion to the *vision* to "transfer the Disney level of quality to other products." This involved creating video games that would bring typical Disney customers into computer gaming and that reached an older age group without a compromise in the company's values.

Vision

To reach that vision she had to apply her passion for creative ways of looking at problems to establish a "communication infrastructure and creativity infrastructure," and then "coach and empower people to take hold of the vision." To support the team in increasing their competency and to create alignment regarding their *mission*, Jan had to establish a forum for open, honest dialog in order to find new solutions and to identify and transform obstacles.

Mission

Applying her passion to the *ambition* to become the #1 interactive entertainment company, Jan had to creatively leverage Disney "equity" into other markets and fully engage her determination to "drive to the finish line."

Ambition

Taking on the *role* of a ground-breaker working with trailblazers, Jan was able to apply her passion for creative ways of looking at problems to promote "open innovation" and license an existing platform and adapt it in order to dramatically reduce the software development cycle. She went on to establish a powerful strategic alliance with a Japanese game company and build key distribution partnerships.

Role

We can represent the key elements of Jan's Circle of Success in the following diagram:

Jan Smith's Circle of Success

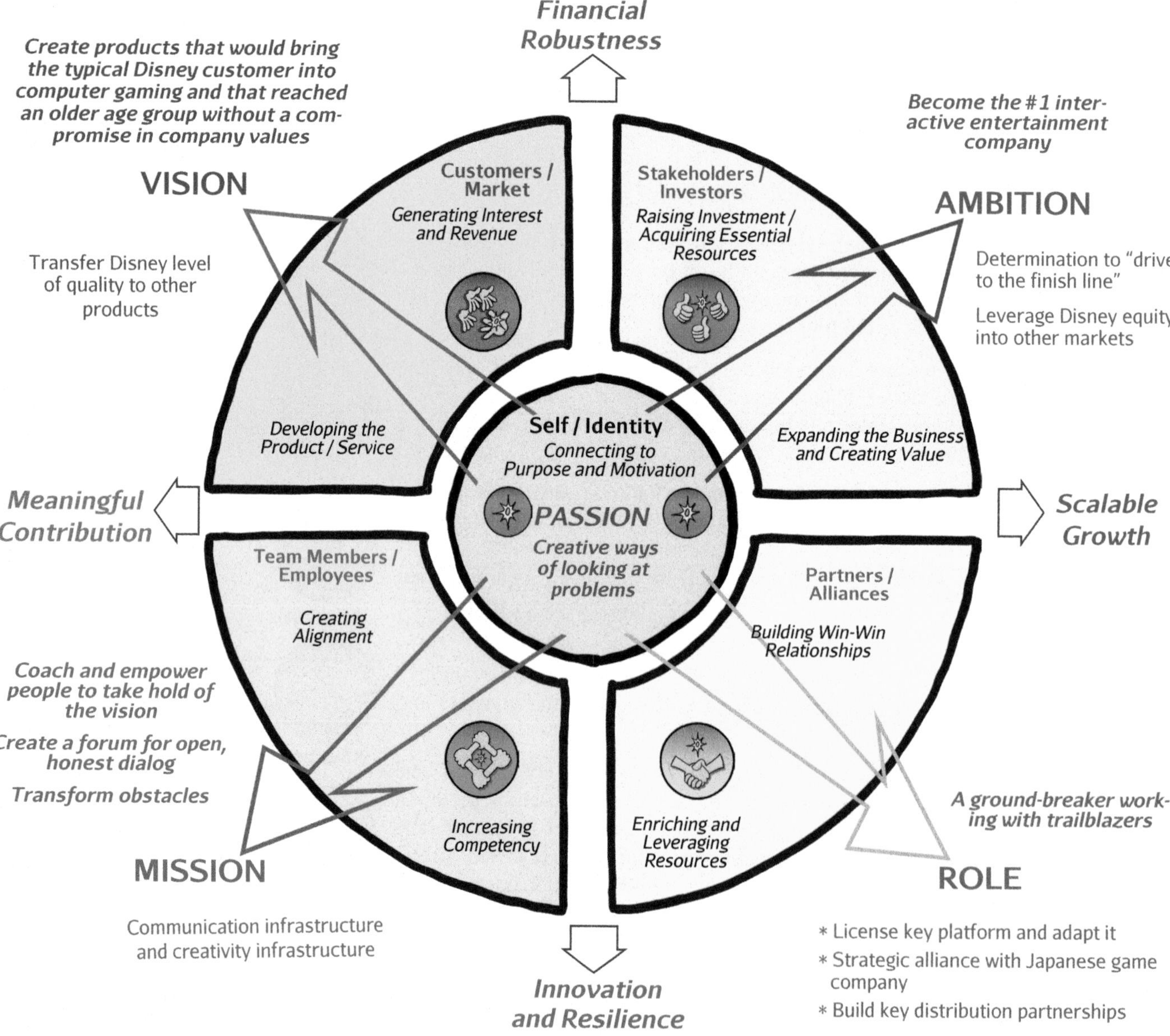

JAN SMITH'S CIRCLE OF SUCCESS
VISION
Customers / Market
CREATE PRODUCTS THAT WOULD BRING THE TYPICAL DISNEY CUSTOMER INTO COMPUTER GAMING AND THAT REACHED AN OLDER AGE GROUP WITHOUT A COMPROMISE IN VALUES
TRANSFER DISNEY LEVEL OF QUALITY TO OTHER PRODUCTS
GAME ON!
AMBITION
Stakeholders / Investors
BECOME THE #1 INTERACTIVE ENTERTAINMENT COMPANY
DETERMINATION TO "DRIVE TO THE FINISH LINE"
LEVERAGE DISNEY EQUITY INTO OTHER MARKETS
MISSION
Team Members / Employees
COACH AND EMPOWER PEOPLE TO TAKE HOLD OF THE VISION
CREATE A FORUM FOR OPEN, HONEST DIALOG
TRANSFORM OBSTACLES
COMMUNICATION INFRASTRUCTURE AND CREATIVITY INFRASTRUCTURE
ROLE
Partners / Alliances
A GROUND-BREAKER WORKING WITH TRAILBLAZERS
* LICENSE KEY PLATFORM AND ADAPT IT
* STRATEGIC ALLIANCE WITH JAPANESE GAME COMPANY
* BUILDING KEY DISTRIBUTION PARTNERSHIPS
Self / Identity – Passion
CREATIVE WAYS OF LOOKING AT PROBLEMS

Jan Smith's success with Disney Interactive Studios demonstrated a remarkable balance of leading from the head, heart and gut.

Leading From Head, Heart and Gut

As a leader, Jan's actions are clear example of our basic definition of conscious leadership. She was able to "build a sustainable venture, guiding herself and her team from a state of centered presence, accessing multiple intelligences and living her highest values in service to a larger purpose and to the benefit of all stakeholders." Jan demonstrated authenticity, emotional intelligence, purposefulness and responsibility. She also exemplified each of the key practices of conscious leadership:

1. Formulating and communicating a meaningful and inclusive vision for all stakeholders.
2. Focusing on a higher purpose.
3. Influencing through inspiration.
4. Balancing self-interest and the common good.
5. Respecting and integrating multiple perspectives.
6. Leading by example (walking her talk).
7. Exercising mindful self-leadership and reflecting thoughtfully on the lessons gained from experience.

Jan demonstrated a remarkable balance of leading from the head, heart and gut. She clearly had a cognitive (head) understanding of the business issues and strategic goals she needed to address. This allowed her to formulate a strategic plan tied to an operating plan and move from vision to execution. She also had the emotional intelligence (heart) to connect with people, acknowledge their concerns and understand their motivations. This allowed her to identify and transform their resistances and motivate them to "take hold of the vision." She also applied a great deal of intuition (gut) to select a project worth risking her credibility and career on. This allowed her to fully and congruently commit to putting her vision into action and "do things no one had ever done before at Disney."

Orchestrating Innovation

Last, but not least, Jan Smith's journey to successfully "do the impossible" provides us with some other key steps for orchestrating innovation.

1. *Empowering:* **Believe in yourself, your team and your vision. Take all the responsibility personally if things go wrong and give all the credit to the team if things go right. Show it is possible and then ask, "why wouldn't this work?"**

   Jan's case emphasizes the crucial importance of building a *winning belief system* based on her own belief in herself, her team and in her vision.

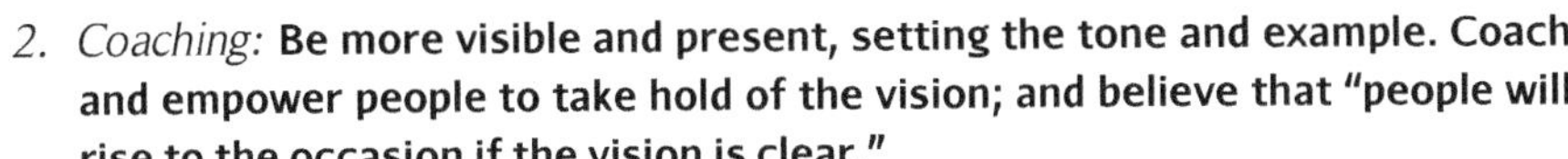

2. *Coaching:* **Be more visible and present, setting the tone and example. Coach and empower people to take hold of the vision; and believe that "people will rise to the occasion if the vision is clear."**

   Clearly, one of the main challenges Jan faced was to create new video games that transferred the Disney level of quality without a compromise in values. This required the skills of *putting values into action* and *creating an aligned state* for herself and her team in order to move from vision to execution.

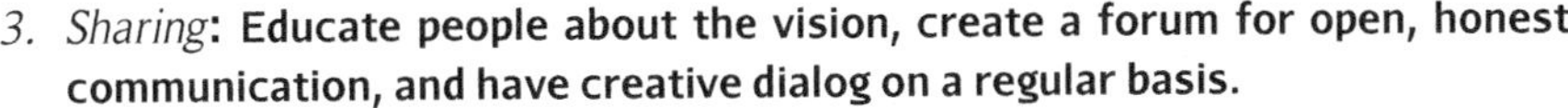

3. *Sharing*: **Educate people about the vision, create a forum for open, honest communication, and have creative dialog on a regular basis.**

   Jan was masterful at promoting *collective problem solving* and generative collaboration. One of her areas of excellence was engaging *Multiple S.C.O.R.E.s* by "creating an open forum, encouraging different opinions, having heated discussions, refereeing, and at the end making a decision."

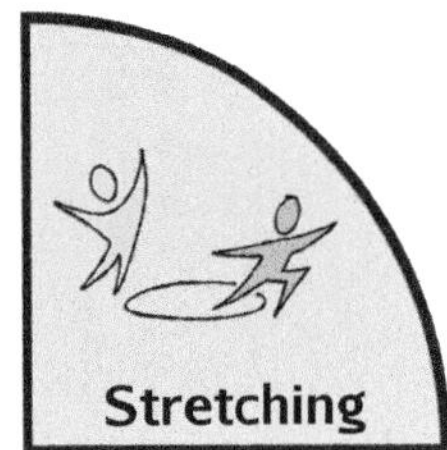

4. *Stretching:* **Do things no one has ever done before. Put a number of people in a room with different backgrounds and stretch.**

   Jan understood that turning around the business would be a Hero's Journey for her and her team. As she said herself, "I knew I would be 'a hero or a zero.'" By embracing the calling, crossing the threshold, finding guardians and facing and transforming the "demons," Jan was able to "do the impossible" and ship a product in 3 months that would normally have taken 18 months to develop.

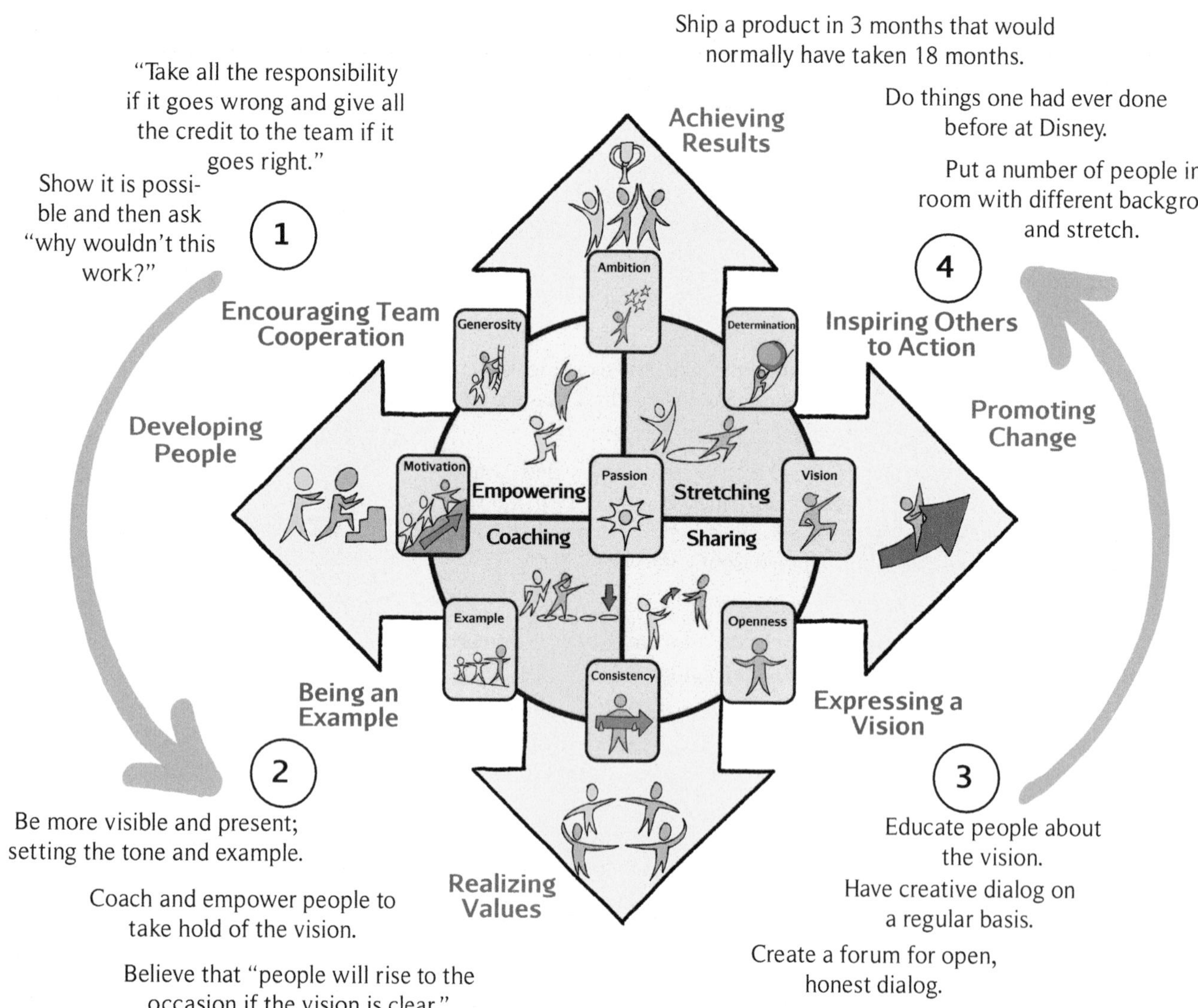

Jan Smith's Formula for Orchestrating Innovation

In the remainder of this chapter, I will be presenting methods that will help you to implement Jan Smith's formula for building a Circle of Success, leading from the head, heart and gut, and orchestrating innovation in your own venture.

"Imagineering" the Impossible

As most of the successful entrepreneurs and leaders I have studied and interviewed have pointed out, in a dynamic and changing world it is not possible to predict the future. Instead, the future must be created. To do this, you must continually "make successive approximations until you reach a point of 'no return'." Like the metaphor of the Russian dolls I used in reflecting on Jan Smith's process of moving from vision to execution, creating the future requires first defining the larger box in the form of a vision that contains the smaller "box" of the strategic plan and within that the even smaller "box" of an operating plan that ultimately leads to "operational execution on key elements to attain the vision."

Walt Disney

It is quite fitting that Jan Smith's example involves the Walt Disney Company since her process for creating successful ventures and doing the impossible completely parallels the strategy for "Imagineering" that I modeled from Walt Disney (*Strategies of Genius Volume I*, 1995). *Imagineering* is a term coined by Walt Disney (by combining the words "imagination" and "engineering") to describe the process he used to "create the future" by forming dreams and then turning them into realities. The imagineering process essentially involved chunking the dream into all of the steps that were necessary to manifest it.

I have written extensively about Disney's creative process in a number of my books and it is now used by managers, coaches and entrepreneurs throughout the world as a key part of developing new ideas and projects for their clients, organizations and new ventures. It still deserves mention, however, in this book as it is such an essential process for the success of leaders and entrepreneurs.

Imagineering is a term coined by Walt Disney (by combining the words "imagination" and "engineering") to describe the process he used to "create the future" by forming dreams and then turning them into realities.

Coordinating Dreamer, Realist and Critic Mindsets

The essence of the imagineering process is best reflected in the comment, made about Walt Disney by one of his co-workers, that "there were actually three different Walts: *the dreamer, the realist*, and *the spoiler*" (which I have relabeled as *critic*) and the question was always: which one would be coming to the meeting? As the example of Jan Smith (as well as so many of the other entrepreneurs mentioned in this book series) demonstrates, creating the future, rebounding from adversity and doing the impossible involves the coordination of these three fundamental mindsets: Dreamer, Realist and Critic.

The process of imagineering involves the coordination of three fundamental mindsets: Dreamer, Realist and Critic.

The *Dreamer* is necessary to form new ideas and goals. The *Realist* is required in order to transform ideas into concrete expressions. The *Critic* is crucial as a filter and as a stimulus for refining the result into something "insanely great" (in the words of Steve Jobs).

A Dreamer without a Realist cannot turn ideas into tangible expressions. A Critic and a Dreamer without a Realist just become stuck in a perpetual conflict. A Dreamer and a Realist might create things, but they might not reach the necessary level of excellence without a Critic. The Critic helps to evaluate and refine the products of creativity. There is a humorous example of a boss who prided himself on his innovative thinking abilities but lacked some of the realist and critic perspective. The people who worked in the company used to say, "He has an idea a minute . . . and some of them are good."

In summary:

- A Dreamer without a Realist and Critic is just that: only a Dreamer.
- A Realist without a Dreamer and Critic is a Robot.
- A Critic without a Dreamer and a Realist is a Spoiler.
- A Dreamer and a Realist without a Critic are a research & development department—they make a lot of prototypes but lack the quality standards for success.
- A Realist and a Critic without a Dreamer are a Bureaucracy.
- A Dreamer and a Critic without a Realist are a roller coaster of Manic-Depression.

Effective meta leadership and entrepreneurship involve a balance and synthesis of these different mindsets. As David Guo points out, "An entrepreneur has to be an eternal optimist, but also a pragmatist. The optimist says, "I can always do this," but the pragmatist says, "If I don't do this by a certain time, I'll miss the window, so I'd better move on." The entrepreneur must also heed the critic, and welcome feedback. Respecting the critic also means to "learn from mistakes of others, not just yourself."

Steig Westerberg (see *SFM Vol. I*, pp. 82-83), Founder and CEO of StreamTheory, Inc., a pioneer of cloud-based gaming and application streaming, describes the entrepreneur's balancing act between Dreamer, Realist and Critic in the following way:

> *The dream is something that can never die. The dream quite literally is part of me. It is something that I think about all the time. It is something that permeates everything that I do.*
>
> *On the other hand, the realist aspect comes in equally strongly. You end up with a multiple personality. It's weird. So by having the realist, and also the critic, you are sitting there analyzing what you are doing—you're analyzing the directions that the company is taking at all times—realizing perhaps that even as you start to execute, you can see that that's not the appropriate one, based on other things that can happen in the marketplace and the forces that come in and interact with the company. Of course, that's part of the dream. Realizing that reality can impact the dream, and then what do you do? The two play out together. You make a change and you keep on going as rapidly as you can.*
>
> *So all three (dreamer, realist and critic) play equally important roles. However, if you lose the overall dream and you allow the everyday realities and the problems that you face to become too overwhelming or too strong, then you are in trouble.*

Steig Westerberg
Founder and CEO
Stream Theory

According to entrepreneur Stieg Westerberg, the dreamer, realist and critic mindsets "play equally important roles." However, "if you lose the overall dream and you allow the everyday realities and the problems that you face to become too overwhelming or too strong, then you are in trouble."

Steig's comments reflect Jan Smith's approach with the Disney Store and Disney Interactive in which the dream or vision provides the larger "box" for the strategic plan, the operational plan and execution. This makes it possible to align *efficiency* ("doing things right") with *efficacy* ("doing the right things"). Steig's account also echoes Jan's insistence that it is important to "dedicate time to be creative" so that people don't "get caught up in executing." This requires the discipline for "creative dialog on a regular basis" and being sure that the dream outweighs any "criticism."

Imagineering Questions

Most people have natural strengths in one area: Dreamer, Realist or Critic. The tools and methods of Success Factor Modeling™ can be applied to help entrepreneurs and their teams to develop all three mindsets and ensure that they are used in a balanced way. For instance, the processes of Dreamer, Realist and Critic can be associated with particular types of questions. One way for an entrepreneur to ensure that he or she and his or her team are taking a wise and balanced approach to a particular project or initiative is to be sure that he or she, and the team, have clear answers to each of these questions. The following is a summary of the fundamental questions required to effectively "imagineer" a project or vision into being.

Reflect upon your project or venture (either individually or as a team) and see if you can answer all of Dreamer, Realist and Critic questions.

The "Dreamer" mindset is a crucial part of Disney's imagineering process.

Dreamer:

What is the long-term vision for the project/venture?

What is the purpose of the project/venture?

What is the "Big, Hairy, Audacious Goal" for the project/venture?

What are the potential benefits to possible customers? investors/stakeholders? partners? team members?

What other possibilities could the project/venture lead to in the future?

The "Realist" mindset involves planning the steps to reach the dream.

Realist:

What is the time frame for the project/venture?

Who are the key actors (customers, investors/stakeholders, partners, team members)?

What are the specific next steps (operational plan) necessary to make progress?

What is evidence or feedback that you are making progress?

What resources are available to assist in the success of the project/venture?

Critic:

Who might be positively or negatively affected by the project/venture? (Be sure to consider all possible stakeholders in the holarchy.)

What are their needs or expectations?

Why might someone (customer, investor/stakeholder, partners, team members) object to the project/venture?

What is missing from the vision, strategy or plan?

Under what circumstances would you not proceed with the project/venture?

It should be pointed out that these questions are not something to simply consider once at the beginning of a project or venture, but should, as Steig Westerberg's earlier commentary indicates, be constantly revisited throughout the launching and the life of the project or venture.

The "Critic" mindset is necessary to ensure that the plan is both effective and ecological.

"Storyboarding" the Steps to the Dream

Key to doing the impossible is moving from the Dreamer to the Realist. This involves creating both a strategic plan and an operational plan by defining a set of steps, or a *path*, which will lead from some present state to a desired state. *Storyboarding* is a process for defining such a path that was also developed by Walt Disney. Disney's primary imagineering strategy, and his major strength as a realist, was the ability to chunk and sequence his dreams into pieces of a manageable size. Disney was the innovator of the process of storyboarding (a process now used by all major film developers). In the story room (the "Dreaming" room) of his studios Disney had set aside a wall where anyone could tack up an idea or suggestion. One day, after he had just had the wall repainted, he came in and a group of animators had tacked pictures all over the newly painted wall. After recovering from his initial shock, Disney noticed that he could easily follow the flow of the story just by looking at the sequence of pictures. So he put up cork board all over the walls of the room and established "storyboarding" as his primary form of idea development.

A storyboard is like a visual table of contents that maps the sequence of critical events necessary in order to move from a present situation to a desired outcome.

A storyboard is like a visual table of contents—it is a set of still drawings that represent the sequence of critical events to take place in order to move from one's present situation to the desired outcome. The "story-boarding" process is a very powerful way of organizing and planning that is particularly important for launching a new project or venture and doing the impossible. An effective PowerPoint presentation is form of storyboard.

Making Your Own Storybaord

To make your own storyboard for your venture, review the answers you and/or your team have made to the Realist questions in the previous pages. How could you organize those answers into a sequence of steps? We generally recommend working with seven plus-or-minus two steps (i.e., 5-9 steps) at a time. This is because psychological tests show that this is the number of "chunks" people can easily hold in short-term memory.

To practice, use the following frames to draw pictures representing the key steps of the path necessary to reach your desired state or dream. Write any titles or comments in the spaces below the frames.

It is often useful to start by filling the final frame representing the dream or desired state first. Then fill in the first frame representing the present or starting state. This helps to create "bookends" for the plan and makes it easier to get a sense for the key steps required to link them. Then, think in terms of the S.C.O.R.E. model. The symptom and cause frequently make up the present state. The effect is the ultimate desired state. Identifying the resources and applying them to create the solution that leads to the outcome (or outcomes) are the steps of the storyboard.

A powerful way to fill in the key steps is the process of Reverse Planning. In this process, you put yourself fully into the desired state in the future and imagine as fully as possible what it would be like to have already achieved it. From that position in the future, you look back over the most important actions that you have taken to get there.

Looking back, what were the key steps that I took to reach this desired state?

Looking back, what were the most important decisions and choices that I made to reach the desired state?

At this stage, just focus on the "big chunks" or major steps that will be necessary to move from the present state to the desired state.

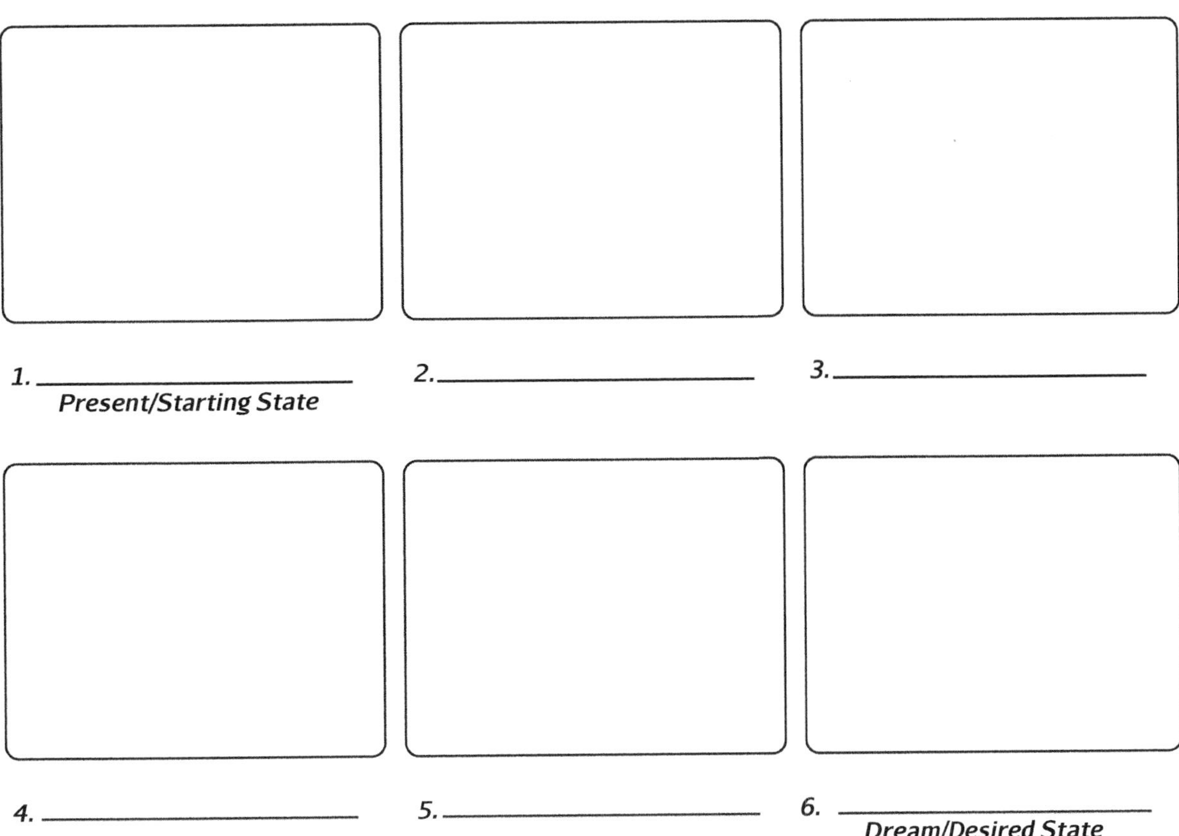

When you have made your storyboard, present it to another person or a group and describe the steps in your plan. What questions or suggestions do they have about the sequence and path you have defined?

Example Storyboard: Jan Smith's Intervention at Disney Interactive

As an example, we could storyboard Jan Smith's intervention at Disney Interactive into several key steps. The present state of the venture was declining revenue due to a conflict between the values of the Disney organization and those of typical teenage video game players. The desired state was to become the #1 interactive entertainment company. In order to make this transition, Jan had to first come up with a vision for a new type of video game that would bring the typical Disney customer into computer gaming. Once she had the vision, it was necessary to "fly around the world and meet people," educating the various stakeholders about the vision and getting their buy in. Next, Jan needed to empower her team to "take hold of the vision," establishing a "communication infrastructure and creativity infrastructure."

Another key part of Jan Smith's storyboard was to identify the key barriers and obstacles to moving forward with the vision and then to tackle them; especially the ones that made it seem "impossible." To do this, she took her team off-site for several days to look at the project from every angle and "think outside of the box." This allowed them to find solutions to shorten the development time and accelerate the development process of producing the game. The result was the creation of a hit video game that was a major step to becoming the #1 interactive entertainment company.

Present State: **Declining revenue due to conflict between Disney values and interests of typical video game players**

Step 1: **Form a vision for a new type of video game that would bring typical Disney customers into computer gaming**

Step 2: **Become more visible and present; educate stakeholders about the vision and get their buy in**

Step 3: **Empower team members to "take hold of the vision"**

Step 4: **Identify key barriers and obstacles to moving forward with the vision**

Step 5: **Take the team off-site for several days to look at the project from every angle and "think outside of the box"**

Step 6: **Find solutions to shorten development time and accelerate the development process**

Desired State: **Create a hit game on the way to becoming the #1 interactive entertainment company**

Example Storyboard of Jan Smith's Intervention at Disney Interactive

"Chunking Down" the Storyboard

Moving to an operational plan and execution involves "chunking" your storyboard down into successively more detailed steps in order to define the "box within the box" as in the metaphor of the Russian dolls. For instance, take a moment and focus just upon frames 1 and 2 in the storyboard that you have defined for your project. Reflect on the seven plus-or-minus two smaller steps it would take to move from what you have defined in frame 1 to what you have put in frame 2.

You can then repeat this chunking down process for each of the smaller steps that you have defined between frame 1 and frame 2 as illustrated in the following diagram.

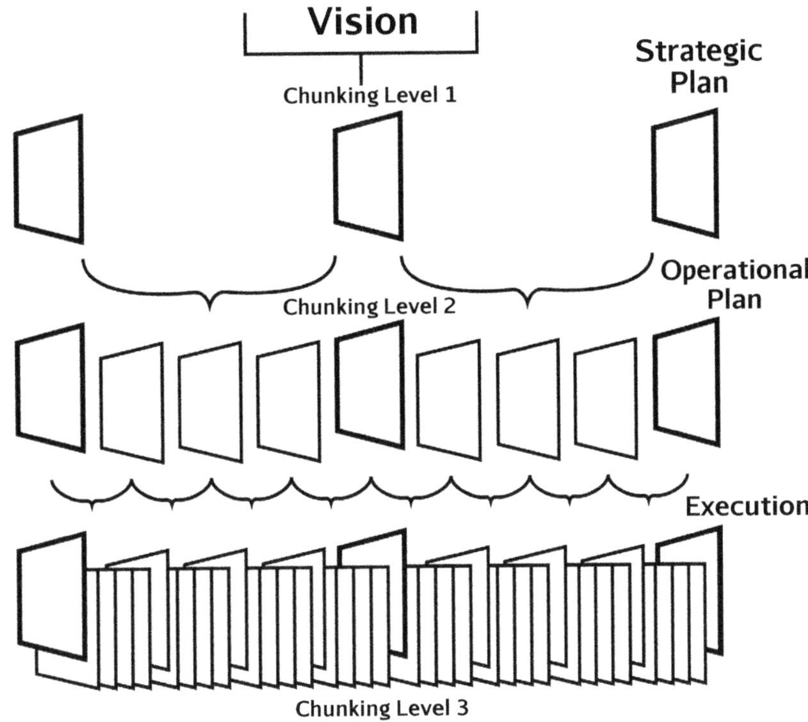

From Vision to Execution
Different Chunking Levels in the Storyboarding Process

For example, let's say that one of the key steps in your storyboard is to *organize a conference* on a particular topic. Some of the sub-steps could be to (1) complete the schedule, (2) contact the key presenters and (3) to assemble the event materials.

In order to *complete the schedule*, the more specific steps would involve (a) clarifying the objectives for the conference, (b) coordinating the various events and (c) sequencing the activities.

Contacting the key presenters would involve (a) identifying the key roles, (b) defining the presentations and (c) verifying the commitment of the potential presenters.

Assembling the event materials would entail (a) determining the sequence of presentations, (b) gathering possible materials for each presentation and (c) organizing and formatting those materials into a booklet.

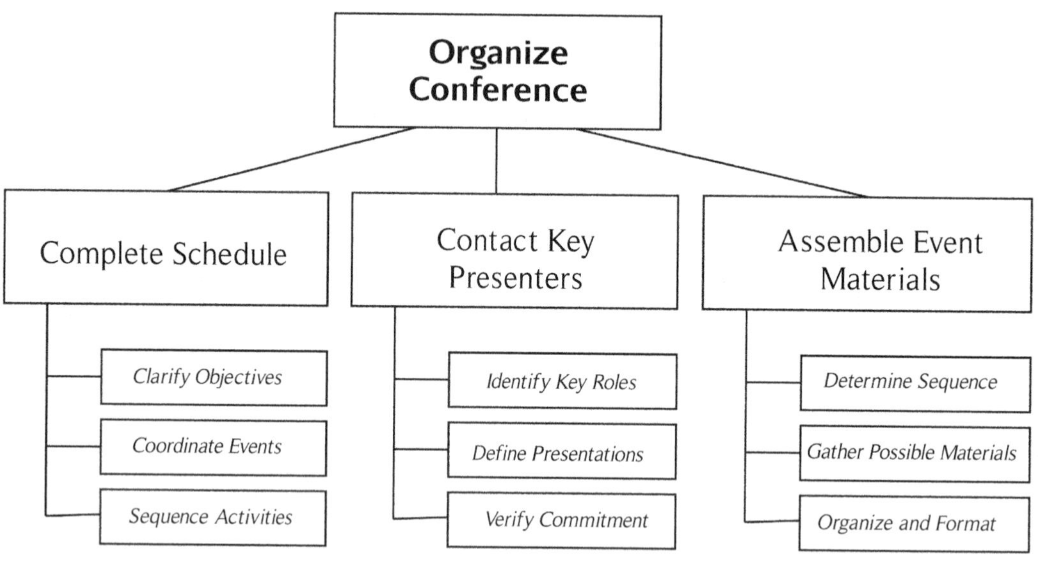

Example of Chunking Actions Into Sub-Actions

This type of chunking down is precisely the process that animators go through to create an animated film; moving from the overall story to the various scenes that make up the story and eventually to the specific actions bring each scene to life.

It is the same process that successful entrepreneurs go through to create their ventures.* Such an approach helps to keep everything in perspective and not "lose sight of the forest because of the trees."

* Another valuable process and set of distinctions to help chunk down your vision for your venture into an operational plan is the "business model generation" format defined in the books *Business Model Generation* (2010) and *Business Model You (2012).* The Nine Building Blocks of the Business Model Generation Canvas (see *Appendix A*) help entrepreneurs to define the "logic" by which their project or venture can earn its livelihood and sustain itself financially. This is done by identifying and exploring the value their project or venture provides for customers in terms of solving problems or satisfying needs and the revenue that can be generated from that. The key channels, resources, activities and partners required to provide value to customers are explored along with the costs associated with acquiring necessary resources, performing key activities, and working with key partners.

Example of Storyboarding Leadership at Microsoft

As an example of how to apply this "chunking down" process in a venture, in 2007 I participated in a major leadership development project for Microsoft. The project, spearheaded by corporate vice president Vahé Torossian, involved more than 30 country leaders for Microsoft in Central and Eastern Europe. My part of the program consisted of designing a series of activities whose overall objective was to produce a practical leadership development plan for each participant.* These activities included:

Dilts Strategy Group's Storyboarding process for Microsoft's leadership development program provides a good example of chunking down vision into actions.

1. Forming a long-term vision for themselves and their business (a Big, Hairy, Audacious Goal)
2. Establishing the critical path and the key challenges to reaching that vision
3. Identifying key leadership moments and on-the-job development opportunities
4. Aligning themselves for change
5. Defining leadership practices
6. Committing to their course of development

These activities provide a good illustration of how to practically apply a number of the principles and processes we have covered so far in this book.

Each activity produced an output (such as drawings, questions, descriptions, etc.) that contributed to the overall plan which were recorded and arranged on a piece of flip chart paper (as illustrated in the following diagram). In this way, participants were able to keep track of and integrate the results of each activity and have a record that they could take with them at the end of the workshop in order to transfer their efforts to their working realities.

This project provides a useful summary of many of the principles we have been exploring in this and the previous chapters. The following is a brief description of the key development activities.

---

* It is interesting to note that this particular geographical division of Microsoft was the company's most profitable division during this period.

Creating a Strategic Vision for the Future

Exploring the long-term vision and the question, "What is the future you want to create?"

1. Participants were instructed to reflect upon their long-term vision, mission and ambition, exploring the question, "What is the future you want to create?"
2. Each participant then drew a picture representing their future and wrote down some key elements in short sentences or phrases. This image was placed on the top of a flip chart page.
3. *Intervision* (see *SFM Vol. II*, pp. 120-123): Each person described his or her vision to a group of 3 to 4 others. As they listened, each person drew their own picture of that vision. The listeners then shared their picture of the presenter's vision with the group and made the following contributions:
   a) a word or short phrase reflecting how he or she felt about the presenter's vision
   b) a question for the presenter about the vision
   c) a resource (article, book, contact, website, etc.) that could help the presenter to reach his or her vision
4. The presenters affixed the various drawings of their visions to the top of their flip chart paper.

Storyboarding the Critical Path and Key Challenges

Storyboarding the five to nine key steps necessary to reach the vision.

1. Applying Disney's storyboarding technique, each person was given a set of cards on which to describe the five to nine key steps (7 plus or minus 2) of the critical path and key challenges that would have to be overcome, and the order in which they needed to be addressed to reach the leadership vision. Participants attached the cards to their flip chart page underneath the drawings of their visions.
2. Participants then paired up with a partner. Each reviewed his or her vision and storyboard. The partner formulated and wrote down questions and concerns on post-its which were placed beneath the storyboard.

Defining Leadership Moments

Defining challenges and "leadership moments" with respect to the storyboard.

1. Each participant was provided with a worksheet upon which to identify upcoming situations and events (leadership moments) where they could start to exercise new leadership approaches.

2. Participants attached the list to their flip chart page beneath their storyboard and got together with a partner to specify what would be required to deal effectively with that situation and to share and exchange thoughts.

Aligning Yourself for Success

1. Participants were given an alignment worksheet and guided to fill in the different levels of change and experience that would need to be mobilized in order to successfully manage their leadership moments: environment, behavior, capabilities, beliefs, values, identity and purpose. (See the *Level Alignment Process* described on pages 209-211.)
2. When finished, participants attached the worksheet to the bottom of their flip chart pages.

Aligning the key levels of success factors needed to effectively address significant leadership moments.

Establishing Ongoing Leadership Practices

1. Each participant was instructed to define the core leadership values, principles and abilities that he or she would need to consistently bring into his or her working reality in order to reach the vision he or she had created.
2. Participants were then to come up with a number of practices that would put those values, principles and abilities into action in a way that would move him or her toward reaching his or her vision. Each person was to define the *What* and the *Why*; i.e., "the things I'm going to do and the rationale behind them." (See the *Putting Values Into Action* process described in the previous chapter.)
3. Participants attached their lists of practices to the bottom right of their flip chart pages.

Establishing the leadership practices needed in order to enact the necessary abilities, principles and values within one's working reality.

Committing to the Path

Finally, each person contracted with at least one other person, an "accountability partner," regarding his or her commitments to the leadership practices and the overall change process he or she has defined in his or her storyboard. Specific contact times were established as well as the consequences or contingencies if commitments were not kept.

Contracting with an "accountability partner" to follow through on the plan.

Example of Different Chunking Levels in the Microsoft Leadership Development Storyboards

Welcoming Critics and Criticism

The final, and generally the most challenging, component of the Imagineering process is to engage the Critic. As Elon Musk advises:

> *Constantly seek out criticism. A well thought out critique of whatever you are doing is as valuable as gold. And you should seek that from everyone you can . . . Take as much feedback from as many people as you can about whatever idea you have.*

A Critic mindset is essential in order to effectively "imagineer" a high quality plan and outcome.

In fact, seeking feedback and establishing ways to get honest and frequent feedback is one of the five *habits of success* identified in Chapter 3 as part of an effective "Meta Mindset." As I have pointed out, getting honest and frequent feedback is important in order to avoid problems and obstacles and make necessary course corrections.

On the other hand, while good criticism is necessary to achieve results effectively and ensure high quality, Critics are often considered "difficult" people to handle in an interaction because of their seemingly negative focus and their tendency to find problems with the ideas and suggestions of others. Critics are frequently perceived as "spoilers," because they operate from a "problem frame" or "failure frame."

Resistance to Change

As we saw in the cases of Charles Matthews and Jan Smith, criticism frequently comes as a negative reaction and resistance to change, even if the change is necessary. Generally, people resist change for one of four reasons – new behaviors and ways of doing things are:

Understanding and addressing resistance to change is a crucial capability for leaders and entrepreneurs.

- *Different* – Anything new is inherently unfamiliar. There is a natural inertia created by old habits.
- *Difficult* – Change generally requires additional effort and can create an increased sense of pressure.
- *Disruptive* – New ways of doing things can disturb the status quo, bring instability and create uncertainty.
- *Dangerous* – Doing things differently is in many ways risky. There is no guarantee of success or that things will be better than before.

Criticism and resistance to change often reveal perspectives of key stakeholders that have not been taken into account or sufficiently acknowledged and considered.

While some of these challenges are inevitable, it is important to apply emotional intelligence and acknowledge people's concerns and, as Elon Musk counsels, "constantly think about how you could be doing things better." Criticism often reveals perspectives of key stakeholders that have not been taken into account or sufficiently acknowledged and considered. People become even more intensely critical when they feel left out and unacknowledged, contracting more strongly into their own perspective rather than experiencing themselves as part of a larger holon.

It is important to keep in mind that criticism, like all other behavior, is positively intended. The purpose of the Critic is to evaluate the output of the Dreamer and Realist. An effective Critic makes an analysis of the proposed plan or path in order to find out what could go wrong and what should be avoided. Critics find missing links by logically considering "what would happen if" problems occur.

Good Critics often take the perspective of people not directly involved in the plan or activity being presented, but who may be affected by it, or influence the implementation of the plan or activity (either positively or negatively). That is, they help to ensure ecology of the larger holarchy that is involved. To effectively and ecologically achieve the fundamental organizational outcome of promoting change, leaders need to authentically welcome Critics and criticism.

Destructive criticism **is presented in a "failure frame," focusing on what is wrong.** ***Constructive criticism*** **is offered in a "feedback frame" and offers suggestions on what could be improved.**

Making a Stakeholder Analysis

A key function of a constructive Critic is being sure that all stakeholders have been taken into account and that their concerns have been addressed or at least genuinely acknowledged. In fact, the first Critic question in the Disney Imagineering process described earlier is "Who might be positively or negatively affected by the project/venture?" A more complete definition of a stakeholder would be any individual or group who:

- impacts decisions;
- is affected—positively or negatively—by the effects of decisions and the intended results;
- can either hinder or facilitate reaching the expected results;
- has resources or skills which can significantly influence the quality of results.

We have already established that one of the critical characteristics of conscious leadership is "living your highest values in service to a larger purpose to the benefit of *all* stakeholders." One of the challenges of truly achieving this is being sure that you have identified all of the significant stakeholders in the holarchy surrounding your project or venture.

It is then important to be sure that you understand their needs and expectations, and if there is any reason that they might object to the project or venture. This lets you know where there might be gaps or missing links in your overall vision, storyboard or strategic plan. It also helps you to determine what needs to be clarified, improved, added or enriched in order to increase the stakeholders' level of support.

Making a Stakeholder Analysis helps you to be sure that you have identified all of the significant stakeholders in the holarchy surrounding your project or venture.

Identifying Key Stakeholders and Their Current Level of Support

The purpose of the following exercise is to help you to develop a detailed map of the major stakeholders related to your project or venture, to highlight their current opinions with respect to the initiative and define the support level that is required for the project or venture to succeed. We will then examine how to use various strategies to help increase their level of support where needed.

Making a Stakeholder Analysis helps you to develop a detailed map of the major stakeholders related to your project or venture, to highlight their current opinions with respect to the initiative and define the support level that is required for the project or venture to succeed.

This process assumes that:

1. A "critical mass" must either exist or be formed to undertake and succeed in a particular project or venture.
2. One or more stakeholders may be taken to a higher support level.
3. Some stakeholders simply need to be "neutral" or only "moderately unfavorable" for the project or venture to be successful.

The first step is to explore the following questions:

"Who is involved in and who is interested in or affected by my project or venture?"

"What do they currently think or feel about my project or venture?

"What position do they need to take in terms of their level of support with respect to my project or venture in order for it to be successful?"

Using the chart on the opposite page, go through the following steps:

1. Identify the key collaborators to include in your map and list them in the left-hand column of the chart. Again, a stakeholder is a person who controls critical resources, or can directly or indirectly influence the progress or success of the project or venture.
2. Reflect upon the current position of each stakeholder with respect to the project or venture. Using either direct feedback, objective evidence or intuition derived from taking "second position" with the person, make an "X" in the column that best represents that key collaborator's current level of support.
3. Consider what level of support the various key collaborators would need to reach in order for you be able to undertake and succeed in your project or venture. Draw an arrow from the current state of support to the desired state of support.

	Level of Support				
Stakeholder	*Very Unfavorable*	*Moderately Unfavorable*	*Neutral*	*Moderately Supportive*	*Very Supportive*

Chart for Making a Stakeholder Analysis

The following is an example of a chart representing some of the key stakeholders in Jan Smith's situation with Disney Interactive. The arrows indicate their starting versus needed level of support.

	Level of Support				
Stakeholder	*Very Unfavorable*	*Moderately Unfavorable*	*Neutral*	*Moderately Supportive*	*Very Supportive*
SHOW'S HOST					X
PRODUCER			X →	→	→
CFO	X →	→	→		
DEVELOPMENT TEAM		X →	→	→	
DISNEY BOARD		X →	→	→	

Example Stakeholder Analysis for Jan Smith's Intervention at Disney Interactive

It is important to consider your group of stakeholders as an entire system. Sometimes the attitude of one stakeholder influences the position of another, either positively or negatively. For instance, if one stakeholder increases his or her support, it may influence another stakeholder to become more favorable. It could also have the opposite effect. If one person is overly enthusiastic, another stakeholder may become more negative. At times it may even be necessary to persuade a stakeholder to pull back on his or her level of support.

Strategies for Transforming Criticism and Increasing a Stakeholder's Level of Support

In the remainder of this chapter, I will be presenting several strategies for increasing a stakeholder's level of support. The deeper structure underlying all of these strategies essentially involves two steps:

1. Understand people and their motivations.
2. Create a mental and emotional bridge that connects (or reconnects) them and their motivation to the larger holarchy – that is, to help them move from a "me" perspective to a larger "we" perspective in which there is a common purpose.

One of the essential skills of emotional intelligence for understanding people and their motivations is the ability to look beyond the "content" of their criticism or resistance to the deeper intention behind their concerns.

The Principle of "Positive Intention"

One of the most important and useful principles for dealing with Critics and criticism relates to the notion of "positive intention." This principle is especially valuable when dealing with resistance and objections. The principle essentially states that: *At some level, all behavior is intended or has been developed for some "positive purpose."* According to this principle, for instance, resistances or objections would actually emerge from some underlying positive intention or purpose. For example, the positive purpose behind the objection, "It is not desirable to try something new," may be to "protect" the speaker from oversaturation or failure. The positive intention behind a resistance such as, "It is not possible for things to change," might be to prevent "false hope" or to avoid unrewarded effort.

Transforming criticism involves looking beyond the objection of the stakeholder to the positive intention behind the criticism or resistance to change.

The principle of positive intention implies that, in order to successfully address resistance or criticism, these underlying concerns, or positive purposes, must be acknowledged and addressed in some way. The positive intention behind a resistance or criticism may be addressed directly or by expanding the person's map of the situation such that they are able to see choices for satisfying their positive intent other than resistance or objection.

In fact, resistances created by positive intentions often arise from other limiting (and frequently unrecognized) assumptions. For instance, the reason that a person may feel threatened by "change" may be because that person does not feel he or she has the skills or support to deal with the personal or social impact brought about by the change. This concern may be addressed by providing the appropriate coaching and guidance for developing the necessary resources. Another way to address this might be to help the person realize that he or she already has the capabilities necessary and is going to be supported.

The principle of positive intention is derived from the deeper assumption that people make the best choices available to them given the possibilities and capabilities that they perceive to be accessible within their model of the world. One of the goals of conscious leadership is to help people enlarge their map of a situation and perceive other choices and options.

In dealing with objections or resistance, an effective strategy is to first acknowledge the person or their positive intent and then respond to the issue or problem the person is raising as a separate issue.

Thus, when managing an objection or resistance, it is useful to begin by acknowledging its positive intent and then lead to a wider space of perception or thinking. It is especially important to separate a person's identity and positive intention from their behaviors. In dealing with resistance or reticence, an effective strategy is to first acknowledge the person or their positive intent and then respond to the issue or problem as a separate issue.

It is important to realize that you can acknowledge another person's point of view without having to agree with that person, i.e. it is different to say "I understand that you have this perspective", than to say, "I agree with you". As the example of Charles Matthews at Rolls Royce in Chapter 4 illustrates, saying, "I appreciate your concern", or "That is an important question" is a way to acknowledge the person or their intention without necessarily implying that their map of the world is the right one.

In summary, according to the principle of positive intention, when dealing with resistance or objections it is important and useful to:

1. Presuppose that all behavior (including resistance and limiting beliefs) is positively intended.
2. Separate the negative aspects of the behavior from the positive intention behind it.
3. Identify and respond to the positive intention of the person with the resistance.
4. Offer the person other choices of behavior to achieve the same positive intention.

Getting Positive Statements of Positive Intentions

One of the problems with many criticisms is that, in addition to being "negative" judgments, they are stated in negative terms linguistically—that is, they are stated in the form of a verbal negation. "Avoiding stress," and "becoming more relaxed and comfortable," for example, are two ways of verbally describing a similar internal state, even though they use quite different words. One statement ("avoiding stress") describes what is not wanted. The other statement ("becoming more relaxed and comfortable") describes what is wanted.

Similarly, many criticisms are framed in terms of what is not wanted, rather than what is wanted. As an example, the positive intent (or criterion) behind the criticism, "this is a waste of time," is probably the desire to "use available resources wisely and efficiently." This intention is not easy to ascertain from the "surface structure" of the criticism however, because it has been stated in terms of what is to be avoided. Thus, a key linguistic skill in addressing criticisms, and transforming problem frames to outcome frames, is the ability to recognize and elicit positive statements of positive intentions.

This can be challenging at times, because Critics operate so much from a problem frame. For example, if you ask a Critic for the positive intention behind a criticism such as, "This proposal is too expensive," you are likely to get initially a response like, "The intention is to avoid excessive costs." Notice that, while this is a "positive intention," it is linguistically stated or framed negatively—i.e., it states what is to be "avoided" rather than the state to be achieved. The positive statement of this intention would be something like, "To make sure it is affordable" or "To be certain we are within our budget."

To elicit the positive formulations of intentions and criteria, one needs to ask questions such as: "If (stress/expense/failure/waste) is what you do not want, then what is it that you do want?" or "What would it get for you (how would you benefit) if you were able to avoid or get rid of what you do not want?"

The following are some examples of positive reformulations of negative statements.

Negative Statement	Positive Reformulation
too expensive	*affordable*
waste of time	*use available resources wisely*
fear of failure	*desire to succeed*
unrealistic	*concrete and achievable*
too much effort	*easy and comfortable*
stupid	*wise and intelligent*

Turning Criticisms Into Questions

Another major problem with criticisms, on a linguistic level, is that they are typically asserted in the form of generalized judgments, such as: "This proposal is too costly," "That idea will never work," "That's not a realistic plan," "This project requires too much effort," etc. One problem with such verbal generalizations, is that, given the way they are stated, one can only agree or disagree with them. If a person says, "That idea will never work," or, "It is too expensive," the only way one can respond directly is to say, either "I guess you are right," or "No, you are wrong, the idea will work," or, "No, it is not too expensive." Thus, criticism usually leads to polarization, mismatching and, ultimately, to conflict if one does not agree with the criticism.

One of the most helpful ways of responding to criticism is to transform it from a judgment into a question. This opens up many more options for addressing the positive intention behind the criticism.

Once the positive intention of such criticisms have been identified and stated in positive terms, however, the criticism can be turned into a question. When a criticism is transformed into a question, the options for responding to it are completely different from those available when it is stated as a generalization or judgment. Say, for instance, that instead of saying, "It is too expensive," the Critic asked, "How are we going to afford it?" When asked this question, the other person is given the possibility of outlining the details of the plan, rather than having to disagree with, or fight with the Critic. This is true for practically every criticism. The criticism, "That idea will never work," can be transformed into the question: "How are you going to actually implement that idea?" "That's not a realistic plan," can be restated as: "How can you make the steps of your plan more tangible and concrete?" The complaint, "It requires too much effort," can be reformulated to, "How can you make it easier and simpler to put into action?" Typically such questions not only serve the same purpose as the criticism, but are actually more productive.

Notice that the questions above are all "how" questions. These types of questions tend to be the most useful. "Why" questions, for instance, often presuppose other judgments, which can lead back into conflict or disagreement. To ask, "Why is this proposal so expensive?" or "Why can't you be more realistic?" still presupposes a problem frame. The same is true with questions like, "What makes your proposal so expensive?" or "Who is going to pay for it?" In general, "how" questions are most effective for refocusing on the goal and turning potential problems into feedback.

Helping Critics to be Advisors

In summary, in order to be a "constructive" Critic, or an advisor, it helps to: 1) find the positive purpose behind the criticism, 2) make sure the positive intention is stated (framed) positively, and 3) turn the criticism into a question – and in particular, into a "how" question.

This can be accomplished by using the following sequence of questions:

1. *What is your criticism or objection?*

   e.g., "What you are proposing is too risky."

2. *What is the value or positive intention behind that criticism? What is it that you are attempting to achieve or preserve through your criticism?*

   e.g., "Security and stability."

3. *Given that that's the intention, what is the HOW question that needs to be asked?*

   e.g., "How can we be sure that the project or venture will not threaten the security and stability that we have achieved?"

Ultimately, the objectives of the Critic are to ensure that a new project or venture is sound and preserves any positive benefits or by-products of the current way(s) of doing things. When a Critic asks *how* questions, then he or she shifts from being a "spoiler" or "killer" to being an "advisor."

It is useful to practice this process of transforming criticisms into questions by trying it out on yourself first. For example, think of a presentation you are planning or have made regarding your project or venture to a stakeholder or potential stakeholder and go into a "Critic" position with respect to it. What objections or problems do you find with your presentation? Is it too long? Is it not passionate enough? Does it make sense? Is it appealing to potential stakeholders?

When you have identified some potential problems or objections, go through the three steps defined above by yourself or with a partner, in order to turn your criticisms into questions.

Once the criticisms have become questions, you can take them to the "Dreamer" or "Realist" within you in order to formulate appropriate answers to the questions.

Next, try out this process with respect to one of the stakeholders you identified on your chart that needs to be taken to a higher level of support. Put yourself into "second position" with that stakeholder and intuitively sense what his or her objections or resistances might be.

To help a Critic become an advisor it is useful to: 1) find the positive purpose behind the criticism, 2) make sure the positive intention is stated positively, and 3) turn the criticism into a question.

When you have identified a potential objection, go through the three steps defined above, in order to turn the objection into a question. Find the positive intention and the "how" question related to the objection or resistance. Again, once the objections have become questions, you can go back to the "Dreamer" or "Realist" mindsets in order to explore other possibilities and choices.

The Art of Principled Persuasion

Principled persuasion involves influencing others to take action in a manner that is ethical, emotionally intelligent and in service of a higher purpose.

Once key stakeholders' resistances or criticisms have been acknowledged, their positive intentions identified and their verbal expressions transformed into questions, increasing the stakeholders' level of support is a matter of persuasion. At the very beginning of this book, we established that one of the four main capabilities of all leadership is the ability to *influence others towards results*. Conscious leaders do this in an ethical and emotionally intelligent way that is in service of something bigger than themselves. Rather than use threats, pressure or manipulation, conscious leaders are skilled in artful and principled persuasion.

The term *persuasion* comes from the Latin *persuadere*, which is derived from per (meaning "thoroughly") and *suadere* (meaning "to advise or urge"). Thus, "persuasion" literally means to "thoroughly advise." The modern usage of the word has come to mean, "to move by argument, entreaty, or expostulation to a belief, position, or course of action" (Webster). Put simply, persuasion is essentially the attempt to use language (and non-verbal communication) to influence the thoughts and actions of others by appealing to their values, beliefs and motivations.

The great Greek philosopher Aristotle identified three means of persuasion:

1. the appeal to **reason** (*logos*)
2. the appeal to **emotion** (*pathos*)
3. the appeal of the speaker's **character** (*ethos*)

Engaging the Head, Heart and Gut

From the view of Success Factor Modeling, reason (or *logos*) is directed to the level of mental *capability* – it is an appeal to the *head*; *pathos* or emotion arises from connecting with the level of *beliefs and values* – an appeal to the heart; character (*ethos*) is at the level of identity – it appeals to the intuition and *gut* feelings.

Steve Jobs' famed ability to create a so-called "reality distortion field" through what was described as "a mix of charm, charisma, bravado, hyperbole, marketing, appeasement, and persistence" is an example of effective persuasion that involves a combination of all three of these factors. Jan Smith's successes at The Disney Store and Disney Interactive also demonstrate the power of persuasion for effective meta leadership and "doing the impossible."

Building from Aristotle's definitions, we can say that *logos* (reason) is the primary channel for giving *direction. Pathos* (emotion) is the source of *energy. Ethos* (the leader's character and example) is the "secret sauce" for persuasion needed to convince people to *risk* attempting the impossible. As Aristotle points out:

> *Persuasion is achieved by the speaker's personal character when the speech is so spoken as to make us think the speaker credible. We believe good people more fully and more readily than others: this is true generally whatever the question is, and absolutely true where exact certainty is impossible and opinions are divided.*

"Doing the impossible" is clearly a situation where "exact certainty is impossible and opinions are divided." This is why the conscious leadership characteristics of being authentic, purposive and responsible, and the qualities of consistency and example, are so crucial. In the words of John Maxwell (quoted earlier), "People buy into the leader before they buy into the vision."

Aligning Motivations in the Service of a Higher Purpose

The primary goal of principled persuasion is to align people's motivations with one another and focus them toward the vision and higher purpose. David Guo's success in getting the phosphor engineer to come out of retirement and join his venture described at the beginning of this chapter is a great example of this capacity for persuasion.

Effective persuasion involves appealing to reason (the head), emotion (the heart) and intuition (the gut).

Principled persuasion is grounded in emotional intelligence and the ability to hold multiple perspectives with equanimity. A key to effective persuasion as a meta leadership skill is to avoid ending up in an ego battle about who is right and who is wrong. The most important thing for an entrepreneur or leader is not winning an argument, but rather to support progress toward the bigger vision and purpose.

Principled persuasion begins by building and/or strengthening the bridge between the motivations and values of your stakeholders and your own motivations and values.

Motivation as an Expression of Values and Beliefs

Our values and beliefs provide the internal reinforcement that supports or inhibits what we think and do.

Motivation is primarily driven by *values and beliefs* – i.e., the level of success factors related to *why* we think and act the way we do. Values and beliefs shape how an individual "punctuates" and gives "meaning" to his or her perception of a situation. This, in turn, determines which kinds strategies and behaviors the person selects and commits to in order to approach that situation. Thus, our beliefs and values provide the internal reinforcement that supports or inhibits particular capabilities and behaviors. This makes them an important influence on people's degree of effort and quality of performance.

You can increase a stakeholder's level of support by finding a way to align your project or venture with their key values and motivations.

As I pointed out in the previous chapter, a person's values and beliefs will greatly influence the way that person acts in the world. Our values, for instance, determine the degree of importance or meaning we attach to various actions and experiences. A person who values "relationships," for instance, will structure his or her life more around maintaining good connections and interactions with others. A person who values "achievement" over "relationships," on the other hand, would focus more on completing tasks and outcomes. He or she might sacrifice his or her relationships in order to achieve these outcomes.

The most direct way to increase a stakeholder's level of support is through finding a way to align your project or venture with their key values and motivations.

Eliciting "Meta Outcomes" to Find Core Values

In the previous chapter, I brought up the distinction between "core values" and "instrumental values." Principled persuasion involves discovering, respecting and creating bridges between significant core values shared by you and your stakeholders. This frequently first requires a clarification of values and their priority. One effective method for doing this is through the elicitation of "meta outcomes."

A *meta outcome* is the "outcome of an outcome." Any specific outcome or task can be framed within the context of a higher order outcome; i.e., an organizing principle or "meta outcome." A meta outcome is one that organizes the behavior of the system in terms of general, long term goals, like the "preservation and survival," "growth and evolution," "protection," "betterment," "adaptation," etc., of the system, individual or organization. Meta outcomes are the source of what were referred to previously as "positive intentions." They are often the desired effects of a particular outcome or goal. To be ecological, any particular objective or strategy must contribute to the basic meta outcomes of both the individual and the holarchy.

A meta outcome is the "outcome of an outcome"—the longer-term desired effect of achieving a more immediate outcome or goal. It is often an expression of core values.

Thus, identifying the meta outcome of a particular behavior, task or project, and checking whether or not the behavior or task is in fact supporting the higher level meta outcome, is important for maintaining the integrity and ecology of a system. Identifying meta outcomes is also important for effective and principled persuasion. People will often disagree about specific goals and objectives, but find consensus about higher-level meta outcomes. The meta outcome of seemingly conflicting objectives, such as "expansion" and "downsizing," for instance, may be the same: "adaptation and survival in a changing world."

People will often disagree about specific goals and objectives, but find consensus about higher-level meta outcomes.

For example, to transform resistance and persuade the Disney CFO and upper management to increase their support for her project at Disney Interactive, Jan Smith reminded them that there was a strategic goal at the corporate level (i.e., a "meta outcome") to extend all content in Disney. She explained to them, "This is what we want to be anyway. It is just earlier than planned."

Usually the reason people have differences of opinion about the specific strategies or paths that lead to mutually acceptable meta outcomes is because they have different mental maps and assumptions related to the situation. By finding the shared meta outcome, it is easier to identify and communicate about the places in which their mental maps and assumptions diverge.

Finding meta outcomes also creates the possibility of having more choices in both decision making and negotiation. This is due to the fact that the same meta outcome can frequently be reached through diverse paths. Because the meta outcome is the deeper, more important goal, defining the meta outcome of a particular behavior or position opens up the possibility of finding more options, which may achieve the same meta outcome, but in a different manner. New paths and strategies can be explored, which are just as effective in reaching the meta outcome, but avoid other problems and challenges.

As an example, let's say a person has the outcome of "winning the lottery." The chances of actually attaining such an outcome may be small, setting the person up for disappointment. The "meta outcome" of this outcome, however, may be discovered by asking, "What will it do for you to win the lottery?" The answer might be something like, "Then I'll have a lot money, and won't have to worry about paying my bills." If you ask again, "And what will it do for you to have a lot of money and not have to worry about paying your bills?," you might get the answer, "Then my life would be easier and more stress free." Thus, the deeper meta outcome of "winning the lottery" is to have "an easier, more stress free life." Winning the lottery is only one means to achieve this meta outcome. There are many other strategies and outcomes (such as practicing stress management techniques, making sound investments, learning effective financial planning and money management skills, etc.) that can also help to reach the same meta outcome; and which may be more easily achievable. Knowing about them and pursuing them does not require giving up on the initially stated outcome ("winning the lottery"), but can add more options that make it much more likely that the meta outcome will ultimately be attained.

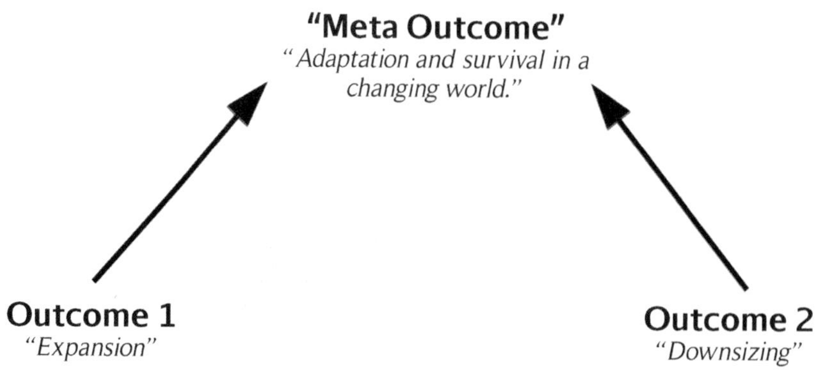

Conflicting Outcomes Can Share the Same Meta Outcome

The Meta Outcome Question

Meta outcomes are elicited by asking the question, "What will getting that outcome do for you?" The answer to this question will be the anticipated outcome of the outcome. Asking this question several times typically leads to successively higher-level meta outcomes. For example, let's say that a person has an outcome of "punishing someone else." The meta outcome of "punishment" might be "to teach them a lesson." The meta outcome of "teaching them a lesson" might be to "change their behavior." The meta outcome of "changing their behavior" might be to "make me feel more safe." The meta outcome of "feeling more safe" might be "the freedom to be myself"; and so on.

To explore meta outcomes for yourself, try the following exercise:

1. Think of a particular goal or outcome that you would like to achieve. (Let's call this outcome "A.")
2. Ask yourself the question, "If I achieve that outcome, what will it do for me? What will it get for me?" (Let's call the outcome of outcome A —or the "meta outcome" of A— outcome "B.")
3. Now ask yourself, "If I achieve this outcome (B), what will it do for me?" (Let's call the meta outcome of B, outcome "C.")
4. Continue to ask this question several times, using the "meta outcome" you identified in your previous answer as your new outcome. Where does it lead you? What new understandings do you get about your own values and criteria?

Filling in the blanks below can help you discover some of your own meta outcomes.

What do you want?

I want ____

What will getting that do for you?

If I get that, then I will ______________________________________

What will getting that do for you?

If I get that, then I will ______________________________________

What will getting that do for you?

If I get that, then I will ______________________________________

David Guo applied this strategy in order figure out how to persuade the phosphor expert to come out of retirement and work for Guo's company. The man was not interested in more money and did not need to prove himself professionally, so Guo had to find what would be interesting enough for this person to want to go back to work. He was able to discover that the phosphor expert's "meta outcome" was to explore some of his own theories and ideas and see them applied to do what people thought was not possible. Guo was then able to convince the phosphor engineer that his vision of a high definition screen the size and thickness of a table cloth was a great opportunity for the man to put his theories into practice.

Verbal Reframing as a Tool for Aligning Values

Another way to create resonance and alignment of key values and motivations is through what is known as "verbal reframing." *Verbal reframing* involves taking a word or phrase expressing a particular idea or concept and finding another word or phrase for that idea or concept that puts either a more positive or negative slant on the concept. As the philosopher Bertrand Russell humorously pointed out, "*I* am firm; *you* are obstinate; *he* is a pig-headed fool." Borrowing Russell's formula, we could generate some other examples, such as:

> *I* am righteously indignant; *you* are annoyed; *he* is making a fuss about nothing.
>
> *I* have reconsidered it; *you* have changed your mind; *he* has gone back on his word.
>
> *I* made a genuine mistake; *you* twisted the facts; *he* is a damned liar.
>
> *I* am compassionate; *you* are soft; *he* is a "pushover."

Verbal reframing involves taking a word or phrase expressing a particular idea or concept and finding another word or phrase for that idea or concept that overlaps its meaning and then puts either a more positive or negative slant on the concept.

Each of these statements takes a particular concept or experience and places it in several different perspectives by "re-framing" it with different words. Consider the word "money," for example. "Success," "tool," "responsibility," "corruption," "green energy," etc., are all words or phrases that put different "frames" around the notion of "money," bringing out different potential perspectives. Try forming some of your own one-word reframes for some of the following values words:

- *responsible* (e.g., stable, rigid)
- *playful* (e.g., flexible, insincere)
- *stable* (e.g., comfortable, boring)
- *frugal* (e.g., wise, stingy)
- *friendly* (e.g., nice, naive)
- *assertive* (e.g., confident, nasty)
- *respectful* (e.g., considerate, compromising)
- *global* (e.g., expansive, unwieldy)

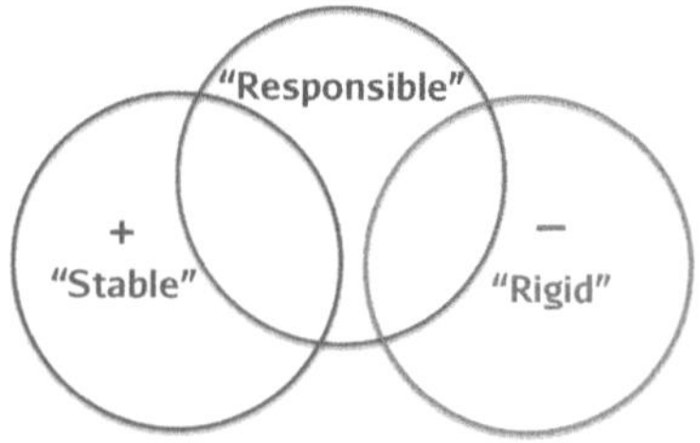

Verbal reframes can be used to help create a bridge between seemingly incompatible values and motivations.

These types of verbal reframes can be used to help create a bridge between seemingly incompatible values and motivations. An entrepreneur, for example, may desire "growth" while an investor is looking for "security." The investor may believe that the steps necessary to promote growth, however, threaten his or her sense of security. These types of seemingly fundamental incompatibilities can create conflict and resistance if not properly addressed.

Applying Verbal Reframing to Build a Values Bridge

One way to create more alignment between seemingly conflicting values is to use verbal reframing to create a "bridge" linking them. As an example, an entrepreneur may have a core value of "contribution" while a potential investor may have a core value of "control." These initially appear to be potentially in conflict. "Contribution," however, could be easily reframed to "satisfying needs." "Control" could be reframed to "taking care of business." In many ways, "satisfying needs" and "taking care of business" are quite similar. Thus, the simple verbal reframes have closed the gap between the two seemingly incompatible values.

As another example, let's say a stakeholder has a core value of "quality;" but the entrepreneur is keen on "creativity." Again, these two values might initially seem at odds with one another ("quality" is about "keeping to standards" but "creativity" is about "changing things"). "Quality," however, could be verbally reframed as "continual improvement." "Creativity" could be reframed as "producing better alternatives." The simple reframes can help close the gap and begin to create a bridge between the two seemingly disparate values.

A Values Bridge Closes the Gap Between Seemingly Incompatible Motivations

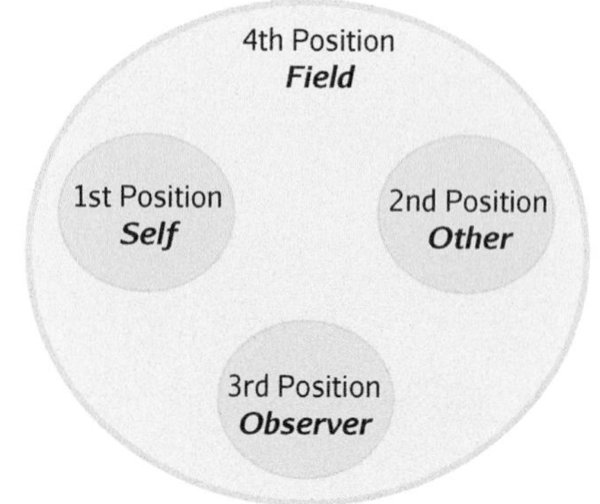

There are four fundamental perceptual positions from which we can perceive a leadership moment.

The Importance of Multiple Perceptual Positions to Principled Persuasion

In *SFM Volume II* (pp. 164-167) I presented the skill of integrating multiple "perceptual positions." *Perceptual positions* refer to the fundamental points of view you can take concerning a relationship between yourself and another person or group of people in any situation.

- **1st Position:** Associated in your own point of view, beliefs, values and assumptions, seeing the external world through your own eyes—an "*I*" position or *self* position.
- **2nd Position:** Associated in another person's point of view, beliefs, values and assumptions, seeing the external world through his or her eyes—a "*you*" position or *other* position.
- **3rd Position:** Associated in a point of view outside of the relationship between yourself and the other person as a witness to the interaction—a "*they*" position or *observer* position.
- **4th Position:** Associated in the perspective of the larger system (the holarchy)—a "*we*" position or *field* position.

In order to create effective and ethical values bridges, it is important to take all of these perspectives with respect to the leadership moment you are addressing. *1st* Position helps you to be clear about your own values and meta outcomes. *2nd* Position supports you to understand your stakeholders and their motivations. It is one of the foundations of emotional intelligence. *3rd* Position allows you to reflect thoughtfully on your relationship with the stakeholder and find areas of resonance. *4th* Position is necessary to have a sense of how your interaction with the stakeholder(s) can serve the higher purpose of the larger system.

4th Position is one of the most important perspectives for conscious leadership and meta leadership as it involves an identification with the larger system, producing the experience of being part of a collective, characterized by language such as "we" (first person plural). Many of the leaders in my study would often refer to the process of taking a "company position" or a "system position" in order to make key decisions, for instance. Fourth position is essential for producing a "group mind" or "team spirit." This is the ultimate goal of principled persuasion. As Jan Smith pointed out, she knew she was succeeding when, over time, people shifted from talking about "Jan's crazy idea" to "*our* project."

Engaging the Somatic Mind in Principled Persuasion

It is also useful and important to engage your somatic mind and emotional intelligence in values bridging and principled persuasion. A good way to do this is to first build the bridge between yourself and your stakeholder somatically. Applying the principles we explored in Chapter 2, this can be done by physically making two positions, as you would do in a role play exercise.

1. Starting in your own first position, find the value that is important for you and your venture – for example "growing." Make a physical gesture or movement that represents that value. Then, in a different location, step into second position with the stakeholder whose support you would like to increase. Put yourself in his or her perspective and identify what is the most important value for that person – to be "secure," for example. Make a physical gesture or movement that represents that value. Usually, you will find that these gestures are quite different from one another as the adjacent illustration suggests.

2. To build a somatic bridge, return to your first position and make the gesture or movement associated with your value. Then, literally take one step closer to the location representing the stakeholder's position. Adjust your posture or movement so that it is a little closer to the gesture or movement of the stakeholder whose support you want to increase. Reflect on what type of inner state or value that posture would represent. As the adjacent illustration shows, perhaps it would be something like "open to possibilities."

3. Repeat the same process with the stakeholder's position. Standing in the location representing your stakeholder, make the gesture or movement associated with his or her value. Then, take one step closer to the location representing your own position. Adjust your posture or movement so that it is a little closer to your own gesture or movement. Reflect on what type of inner state or value that posture would represent. Perhaps it would be something like "careful."

4. As a final step, complete the somatic bridge by finding the gesture or movement that is in between the two new gestures you have just created, as shown in the adjacent illustration. What type of inner state or value that posture would that posture represent? Perhaps it would be something like "grounded." You now have a somatic bridge that can form a powerful source of intuition and the foundation for a very fruitful conversation with your stakeholder.

Values Bridging Exercise

The following exercise puts together the three skills of perceptual positions, somatic intelligence and verbal reframing to help you to create a powerful potential values bridge

1. Select one of the stakeholders in your chart whose level of support you would like to increase. Establish two locations for yourself and the stakeholder.

2. Start in your own perspective (1st position) and consider what values and motivations are important to you regarding your project or venture. What do you want to get support for? Choose the most important one and express it as a gesture or movement. Write the word or phrase that best describes your value or motivation in the space above **Value #1** in the form below (e.g., *Innovation*).

3. Now put yourself fully into the shoes of that stakeholder (2nd position). As you enter the perspective of your stakeholder, consider what is important to you as that stakeholder? What are your primary values or motivations for making decisions? Which one seems most in conflict with the value or motivation that you have listed in the space above **Value #1?** Express the stakeholder's value as a gesture or movement. Write the word or phrase that describes that value on the line above **Value #2** in the form below (e.g., *Prestige*).

4. View the relationship between yourself and the other person/part as if you were an observer watching the two people (3rd position). Where is there resonance in their perspectives and values? Where do the two connect?

5. Take the perspective of the field between you (4th position) and consider the two of you as a team in service of a higher purpose (a "we"). Physically step in between the two positions and consider, "What do we both want? What is our shared meta outcome?" Express that as a gesture or movement and write the word or phrase in the space under ***Meta Outcome*** in the form below (e.g., *Do Something Special*).

   - What word or phrase could you use to "reframe" your value or motivation so that it seems closer to the other person's and your shared meta outcome? Write the word or phrase in the space above **Reframe #1** in the form below (e.g., *Accomplishment*).

   - What word or phrase could you use to "reframe" the other person's value or motivation so that it seems closer to yours and your shared meta outcome? Write the word or phrase in the space above **Reframe #2** in the form below (e.g., *Recognition*).

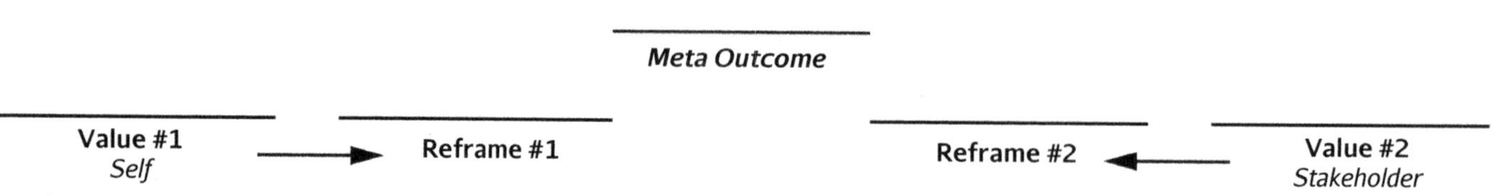

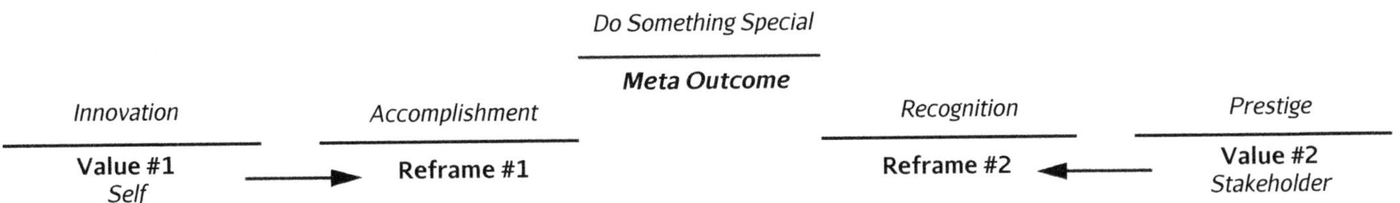

Example Values Bridge

6. Finish by going back into your stakeholder's perspective. How do you experience the bridge created by this somatic and verbal reframing? How does it influence your perspective of the project or venture? How does it affect your level of support?

Continue trying different somatic postures and verbal reframes, and moving through the different perceptual positions, until you find the somatic gestures and verbal reframes that bring the seemingly incompatible values closer together in a way that makes them more harmonious or complementary.

The Example of Disney and the Banker

There is a fascinating anecdote about Walt Disney that illustrates how this process can be applied. Apparently, during the time that he was making *Snow White*, Disney ran out of money and was about to go bankrupt. He knew he would need to go to the manager of the bank—his "investor"—and ask for yet another loan. Given that it was in the middle of the Great Depression of the 1930s and no one had ever made a feature length animated film before, there was likely to be a great deal of resistance by the banker to lend more money because of the high level of uncertainty.

Before going to see the bank manager, Disney engaged in a role-playing game with his brother Roy (who was the company's financial officer). One of them would put himself in the shoes of the banker. The other would then try to persuade the one role-playing the banker to lend the company more money. The brother in second position with the banker would bring up concerns and questions from the perspective of the bank manager. After a while, they would switch positions—the one who had been attempting to get the loan would become the banker and vice versa—and then continue the dialog.

By repeating this a number of times, they found ways to build a bridge between their vision and motivations of the banker. The result is history. They got the loan, finished the picture and *Snow White* became a tremendous success.

Belief Barriers and Belief Bridges

Effective and principled persuasion is about finding resonance between values, but it is also equally about addressing beliefs. Frequently a stakeholder withholds support due to limiting beliefs they have regarding a particular project, venture or vision. In addition to building values bridges, conscious leaders and entrepreneurs will need to create belief bridges.

In the previous chapter, we explored the notion of a "winning belief system," which is characterized by:

- An expectation of a positive future
- A feeling of capability and responsibility
- A sense of self-worth and belonging

Belief Barriers Interfere with Progress Toward the Vision

Belief barriers are limiting beliefs or assumptions that interfere with or undermine our motivation and progress toward the successful achievement of our projects or ventures.

Limiting beliefs, or "belief barriers," produce the opposite of these experiences: i.e., fear about the future, doubt and lack of confidence, and self-negating judgments. Belief barriers are beliefs or assumptions that interfere with or undermine our motivation and progress toward the successful achievement of our projects or ventures. The example of the four-minute mile cited in the previous chapter is a good illustration of a belief barrier. It created an artificial limit about what was possible to achieve.

Limiting beliefs are essentially those which assert or imply that your vision, mission and/or ambition is (1) not desirable or worth it (2) not possible, (3) not appropriate, (4) that you are not capable to achieve them, (5) you are not responsible, not deserving, or don't have permission.

Belief bridges transform or bypass limiting beliefs and belief barriers by reconnecting people to a larger perspective and focusing them on the higher purpose of the project or venture.

Belief Bridges Reconnect People to the Higher Purpose of the Project or Venture

To motivate stakeholders and key collaborators and "do the impossible," effective entrepreneurs and leaders need to have the skill to create "belief bridges" that transform or bypass such limiting beliefs and belief barriers. The most effective belief bridges are those that accomplish this by reconnecting people to a larger perspective and focusing them on the higher purpose of the project or venture.

As an example, Jan Smith's reminder to the CFO and upper management of the Disney Company that "there was a strategic goal to extend ALL content in Disney" and that her ideas for the Disney Store and Disney Interactive were "what we want to be anyway . . . just earlier than planned," created a belief bridge around their concerns and resistance. The belief barrier came in the form of the concern that her project was not pertinent to the business (given the unprecedented nature of the Disney Store and the poor financial history of Disney Interactive) and therefore not worth the risk. Jan created a bridge by connecting her project to a major strategic goal of the larger organization (its meta outcome on an identity level), clearly showing that it was pertinent, and adding that it was worth it because it would actually accelerate the achievement of this higher purpose.

Jan Smith created a belief bridge by connecting her project to a major strategic goal of the larger organization and adding that it was worth the risk because it would actually accelerate the achievement of this higher purpose.

Practicing Creating a Belief Bridge With Your Own Belief Barriers

A good place to start practicing creating belief bridges is with yourself. If you don't believe in your project or venture it will be difficult to convince anyone else to. Take a few moments and explore making belief bridges to get around some of your own belief barriers. The following is a format for this that we use in our conscious leader and entrepreneur coaching sessions.

1. Think of a challenging situation in which it is difficult for you to stay motivated, clear and confident in relation to your project or venture. Create a physical location for that situation and put yourself into it. Similar to the *Holding Difficult Feelings* exercise in Chapter 2, bring awareness to how you experience the situation now; seeing what you see, hearing what you hear and feeling what you feel. Notice the quality of your inner game in response to the outer game you are facing.
2. Step out of that situation and into a new location. Reflect upon the situation and ask yourself, "What beliefs prevent me from being naturally clear and confident in that context? What are the "belief barriers" that block me from experiencing clarity and confidence in that situation?" You may use the list of beliefs we explored in the previous chapter to help search for belief barriers: i.e., Is there a belief that is not desirable or worth it? Not possible? Not appropriate? That you are not capable? Not responsible? Not deserving? That you don't have permission?

   For example, perhaps you have the belief that "M*y vision and ambition are so big. I am too small/ inexperienced/unprepared to make it happen*." This would essentially come down to the belief that "I am not capable or good enough."

Belief Barriers Frequently Arise When We Encounter a Challenging Situation

3. Once you have identified the belief barriers, center yourself in your COACH state, connect to your vision and use the anchor or trigger that you established in the *Finding Your Connection to the Larger "Holarchy"* exercise in Chapter 1. From this position of clarity and confidence, ask yourself the question, "What beliefs would I need in order to naturally feel clear and confident in that situation? What are the possible "belief bridges" that would allow me to bring more clarity and confidence into that context, even in the face of the belief barriers?" What beliefs would help me to stay connected with my higher purpose? Rather than trying to figure it out cognitively, let it come to you through your COACH state. For instance, it may something like, *"My vision is inevitable and my higher purpose is worth taking a stand for. Whatever amount of progress I make is worth it."*

   Apply the *Belief Assessment Process* and the steps for *Using Mentors and Role Models to Build Confidence and Strengthen Belief* from the previous chapter to be sure the belief bridge is strongly aligned in your head, heart and gut.

4. Staying centered and present, hold the beliefs associated with the "belief bridge" in your head, heart and gut. Step back into the challenging situation, maintaining your attention on these beliefs. Notice how your experience of that situation changes.

Creating a "Belief Bridge" Can Help You to Get Around "Belief Barriers" that Stop You From Being Clear and Confident in Challenging Situations.

Applying the "As If" Frame to Create Belief Bridges

The "as if" frame is another powerful tool for creating belief bridges. The *"as if" frame* is a process by which an individual or group acts "as if" a desired state or outcome has already been achieved. The "as if" frame is a powerful way to help people identify and enrich their perception of the world, and of their future desired states. It is also a useful way to help people overcome resistances and limitations within their current map of the world. As Jan Smith maintained, "you have to show it is possible and then ask 'why wouldn't this work?'"

For example, if a person says, "We can't do X" or "It is impossible to do X," the "as if" frame would be applied by asking, "What would happen if we could do X?" or "Let's act as if we could do X. What would it be like?" or "If we were (already) able to do X, what would we be doing?" For instance, if a company executive were unable to describe what his or her desired state for a particular project is going to be, an SFM coach or consultant might say, "Imagine it is five years from now. Looking back, what has changed? What have you accomplished? What resources and beliefs have allowed you to do that?"

Acting "as if" allows us to drop our current perception of the constraints of reality and use our imagination more fully. It utilizes our innate ability to imagine and pretend. It also allows us to drop the boundaries of our personal history, belief systems, and "ego." Acting "as if" was one of Steve Jobs' primary methods for creating what people referred to as a "reality distortion field."

In order to reach our visions and ambitions, we must first act "as if" they are possibilities. We create pictures of them visually in our minds' eyes, and give those pictures the qualities we desire. We then begin to bring them to life by acting "as if" we were experiencing the feelings and practicing the specific behaviors that fit those dreams and goals.

Creating a "Belief Bridge" Can Be Facilitated by Acting "As If" Something is Possible and Looking Back from a Future Perspective

"As If" Exercise for Creating Belief Bridges

The "as if" frame is one of the key tools for conscious leaders and next generation entrepreneurs. The following exercise shows how to use the "as if" frame as a means to help people create belief bridges.

1. With your team, stakeholders or partners, identify the issue about which you have doubt. Express the limiting belief verbally — i.e., "It is not possible for us to . . .," "We are not capable of . . .," "We don't deserve...," etc.

2. As a group, explore the "as if" frame. Ask, "What would happen if (it was possible/we were capable/we did deserve it)? What would it be like?"

   Imagine that you had already dealt with all of the issues relating to your belief that (it is not possible/you are not capable/you do not deserve it). What would you be thinking, doing or believing differently?

3. If other objections or interferences arise, continue asking:

   "Act 'as if' we have already dealt with that interference or objection. How would we be responding differently?" Explore the following questions:

   Going into the future and now looking back . . .

   - *What has happened or changed as a result of your actions?*
   - *How do you/others recognize it?*
   - *What are you most proud/excited about?*
   - *What new awareness do you have?*
   - *What is your advice to the earlier/present self?*
   - *How have you transformed the belief barrier? What other belief moved you beyond the belief barrier?*

Acting "as if" helps to create belief bridges by allowing us to drop our current perception of the constraints of reality and use our imagination more fully.

The Example of Barney Pell

Successful entrepreneur Barney Pell (profiled in *SFM Vol. I*, pp. 102-115) provides a powerful example of how he applied this method to himself when he was considering launching his own natural language search engine. Barney mapped out his belief barriers by making "a list of all the reasons not to do it." One of the main reasons was his fear that some other bigger company would be in a better position to carry out his idea than he would. So he thought to himself, "Let me confront that fear."

Barney reports, "I started supposing 'what if they did?' Then it validates my idea," he thought. "I have 'moved the giants.' The world is a better place and that is what is most important to me." In fact, "If it is not you, it is all the better," he thought to himself, "Its about the power of the idea to make a better world." Besides that, there would be other big companies competing for search technologies and, he figured, "in a fierce battle, others will be desperate for what I have."

Entrepreneur Barney Pell applied the "As If" frame to transform his major belief barrier to launching his company Powerset, which he sold to Microsoft for more than $100 million after less than three years.

Ultimately, Barney concluded that "there was an unlimited upside and almost no downside," "In the worst case," he reasoned, "we would have assembled an awesome team and technology that would probably be acquired for more than was put into it."

Interestingly, this is exactly what happened. Barney ended up selling his company Powerset to Microsoft for more than $100 million after less than three years since starting the company. Barney himself became a multi-millionaire. Parts of the technology and the framework were integrated into the Bing search engine used by Microsoft and Yahoo and were also adopted by Google. Powerset's developments significantly changed users' experience in a number of key areas and has had a wide impact on the information search industry. For example, Powerset's technology became the basis for Apple's Siri voice guidance system used on the iPhone and iPad.

Other Resources for Principled Persuasion

Identifying meta outcomes and practicing verbal reframing, building values bridges and creating belief bridges are only a few of the possible techniques for principled persuasion. Another group of resources are known as Sleight of Mouth patterns (see Appendix B).

Sleight of Mouth patterns (see Dilts, 1999) are a form of verbal persuasion that leaders and entrepreneurs can use to help create belief bridges to address and either bypass or transform limiting beliefs in themselves or key collaborators and stakeholders. Sleight of Mouth patterns can be characterized as categories of "verbal reframes" which influence beliefs—and the mental maps from which beliefs have been formed—by bringing new perspectives and a greater awareness of mental maps and assumptions. *Sleight of Mouth questions* can help entrepreneurs, leaders and their collaborators to "Have open, honest dialogue about concerns" and "keep finding different ways to overcome or transform the obstacles."

Chapter Summary

Being a successful entrepreneur or leader frequently requires the ability to *do the impossible*. Vision and dreaming lead us to imagining future scenarios that have not existed before and that we do not know how to achieve with our current tools and knowhow. These new possibilities are often labeled "impossible," "unrealistic" or "irrelevant" because they are "beyond what people are currently familiar or comfortable with."

When our conscious cognitive mind and ego look into the future they can generally only project through the filters of what we already know. Extrapolating from what we know gives us only a very limited view of future possibilities. This is why Albert Einstein claimed, "Imagination is more important than knowledge." Doing the impossible requires a strong connection with the creative unconscious and the "field."

History is full of examples of how people have inaccurately and incompletely pictured the future due to the limitations of their own cognitive filters. It is also filled with instances of things that were thought to be impossible, unrealistic or irrelevant that turned out to be possible, achievable and valuable.

Doing the impossible requires the capabilities to "Create the Future," "Make the Pie Bigger" and "Rebound from Adversity," but requires several others as well. These include the skills of meta leadership, "chunking down" vision into execution and effective persuasion.

Meta leadership is the capacity to create and lead other leaders. This requires, in the words of successful entrepreneur David Guo, the ability to communicate one's vision and ideas, and to "understand people and their motivation" in order to support them to take responsibility and become leaders themselves.

The *Success Factor Case Example of Jan Smith* shows how the skills of conscious leadership and meta leadership work together to help do the impossible. Jan Smith's success with The Disney Store and Disney Interactive illustrate the power of "coaching and empowering people to take hold of the vision" and the capacity of people to "rise to the occasion if the vision is clear" and if the leader is committed and congruent.

Walt Disney's *Imagineering* process of a balanced cycling between the mindsets of *Dreamer*, *Realist* and *Critic* is a powerful method for creating the path from vision to execution. Imagineering questions help to guide an individual or team to consider key issues related to each stage of the process and to align *efficiency* ("doing things right") with *efficacy* ("doing the right things"). *Storyboarding* the steps to the dream is a procedure that allows leaders, entrepreneurs and their teams to capture the results of the Imagineering process and "*chunk down*" the vision into a critical path and ultimately an operational plan. The example of *Storyboarding Leadership at Microsoft* illustrates how a number of other formats we have covered in this book may be incorporated into the storyboarding and chunking down process.

Welcoming Critics and criticism is another important skill for doing the impossible. While good criticism is necessary to achieve results effectively and ensure high quality, Critics are often considered "difficult" people to handle in an interaction because of their negative focus and their tendency to find problems with the ideas and suggestions of others. Often times, criticism comes from the *resistance to change*. Criticisms also often reveal perspectives of key stakeholders that have not been taken into account or sufficiently acknowledged and considered.

It is important to keep in mind that criticism is ultimately positively intended. Good Critics often take the perspective of people not directly involved in the plan or activity being presented, but who may be affected by it (either positively or negatively). That is, they help to ensure ecology of the larger holarchy that is involved.

The process of making a *Stakeholders Analysis* provides a detailed map of the major stakeholders related to a particular project or venture, highlights their current opinions with respect to a project or venture and defines the support level that is required from the various stakeholders in order for the initiative to succeed. This information can be used to identify which stakeholders need to be brought to a higher level of support.

The objections and criticisms of key stakeholders can be addressed by identifying, understanding and responding to the *positive intentions* behind those criticisms or objections. This is accomplished by directing attention to those intentions, getting *positive statements of the positive intentions* at the base of a *criticism* and *turning the criticisms into "how" questions*. Identifying and honoring positive intentions in this way helps to turn critics into advisors.

The energy to execute and persist in strategies and plans once they are formed is intimately tied to the *motivation* of the people involved. Motivation is necessary to obtain willing cooperation to execute the operational plan effectively and reach results. Motivation is primarily driven by *values and beliefs*, which provide the internal reinforcement that supports or inhibits the application of capabilities and behaviors.

Principled persuasion is a key skill for entrepreneurs and leaders that involves using language to align people's values and motivations and focus them toward the vision. Identifying *meta outcomes* is a powerful way to elicit the higher purpose behind people's motivations and goals and bring focus to core values.

Once core values have been acknowledged and clarified, processes such as *verbal reframing*, *perceptual positions* and *somatic intelligence* can be applied in order create a *values bridge* between the motivations of the stakeholder and those related to the leader or entrepreneur and his or her project or venture.

Objections, resistance and criticisms are also frequently the result of *belief barriers*—limiting beliefs or assumptions that interfere with or undermine our motivation and progress toward the successful achievement of our projects or ventures. Another form of effective persuasion involves creating *belief bridges* that bypass or transform limiting beliefs and belief barriers by reconnecting people to a larger perspective that keeps the focus on the higher purpose. The *Belief Barriers* and *Belief Bridges* exercise a way for leaders and entrepreneurs to become aware of some of their own belief barriers and find potential belief bridges that help them to experience more clarity and confidence and stay connected with their higher purpose.

References and Related Readings

- *Skills for the Future*, Dilts, R., Meta Publications, Capitola, CA, 1993.
- *Strategies of Genius Vol. I*, Dilts, R., Meta Publications, Capitola, CA,1994.
- *Business Model Generation*, Osterwalder, A. & Pigneur, Y., John Wiley & Sons, Inc., Hoboken, New Jersey, 2010.
- Business Model You: A One-Page Method For Reinventing Your Career
- *The Lean Startup*, Reis, E., Crown Business, New York, NY, 2011.
- *NLP II: The Next Generation*, Dilts, R. and DeLozier, J. with Bacon Dilts, D., Meta Publications, Capitola, CA, 2010.
- *Dilts, R., Sleight of Mouth*: The Magic of Conversational Belief Change, Meta Publications, Capitola, CA, 1999.

Conclusion

I start with the premise that the function of leadership is to produce more leaders, not more followers.

Ralph Nader

Change will not come if we wait for some other person or some other time. We are the ones we've been waiting for. We are the change that we seek.

Barack Obama

ANTONIO MEZA

Conclusion

We live in a challenging and ever changing world. As the rate of change accelerates, it brings with it increasing instability, uncertainty and risk. Creating a successful and sustainable venture under such conditions requires a high degree of conscious leadership, innovation and resilience. Robust and durable individuals, teams and ventures are those that are "fit for the future"; i.e., able to ride the inevitable waves of change and to navigate the path of dangers and opportunities that comes with those waves.

The primary purpose of this book has been to provide principles, models, exercises and other resources to help you develop a greater proficiency and aptitude for *conscious leadership* – to build a sustainable venture and guide yourself and your team from a state of centered presence, accessing multiple intelligences and living your highest values in service to a larger purpose for the benefit of all stakeholders. Hopefully, with the support of these resources, you will become increasingly authentic, emotionally intelligent, purposive and responsible, and create teams and ventures that are more productive, ecological, sustainable and fun.

The purpose of this book has been to provide resources for developing a greater proficiency and aptitude for conscious leadership and for building a sustainable venture by guiding yourself and your team from a state of centered presence, accessing multiple intelligences and living your highest values in service to a larger purpose for the benefit of all stakeholders.

A Review of Key Themes

In *Chapter 1*, I made the assertion that truly conscious leaders perceive themselves to be a contributing member of a larger "holarchy," extending from the cells and organs in their own bodies to their families, professions, communities, societies and the larger environment. The primary measure of the "consciousness" of a conscious leader is how much of the larger *holarchy* he or she is able to hold in awareness as he or she is planning for the future, making decisions and taking action. Finding Your Connection to the Larger "Holarchy", Balancing Ego and Soul and Developing Wisdom are some ways of helping to enhance your capacity for conscious living, leading and decision-making.

Chapter 2 explored some of the personal leadership skills necessary to *rebound from adversity*. I emphasized the importance of *emotional intelligence* for conscious leadership and resilience. I presented some key processes and exercises for strengthening the five fundamental components of emotional intelligence – Self-Awareness, Self-Regulation, Self-Motivation,

Empathy and Social Skills. These included skills for *dealing with "negative" emotions, coordinating head, heart and gut, mastering your inner game* and distinguishing between a *COACH state and a CRASH state*. Some of these skills included Creating Resource Anchors, Managing your Energy, Finding Your "Inner Zone of Excellence," Holding Difficult Feelings in yourself and a group and Transforming CRASH States.

One of the key understandings for emotionally intelligent and conscious leaders is that promoting change in any direction will necessarily require welcoming and addressing its opposite or complementary quality. That is, if you want to bring more happiness into the world, you need to have a good relationship with sadness. If your intention is to bring more harmony into the world you will need to have a very good understanding of and relationship with dissonance and conflict.

Chapter 3 focused on developing a *Success Mindset* in order to build a *Circle of Success* for your venture. I identified three key areas of mindset: *Meta Mindset* (big picture clarity), *Macro Mindset* (habits of success), and *Micro Mindset* (ongoing priorities). By assessing your natural strengths in each of these areas and identifying your *Meta Goal*, or current focus for your venture, you can create a Mindset Map and Mindset Compass that helps you to *Identify Your Key Areas for Development*.

Chapters 4 and 5 covered the *SFM Leadership Model*. The model defines the four essential *Organizational Outcomes*, the four fundamental *Leadership Actions* and the nine key *Inner Qualities* shared by effective leaders from all over the world. In applying leadership actions to *orchestrate innovation*, conscious leaders begin with *Empowering* first and then *Coaching* before *Sharing* and ultimately *Stretching* themselves and their team members. Stretching first without the support of the other leadership actions simply creates stress and overwhelm.

Empowering entails supporting the development of people's potential by recognizing individuality and promoting self-esteem, encouraging autonomy and stimulating motivation for growth. *Building a Winning Belief System* is one of the most profound and powerful ways entrepreneurs and leaders can accomplish this. *Assessing our degree of belief* and *using mentors and role models to build confidence and strengthen belief* are key skills to building a winning belief system within an individual or group.

Coaching involves developing people's experience and competencies, building trust, listening with attention, guiding people in their learning process and growing team spirit. Supporting others to clarify and realize *core values*, especially through one's own example, is a key skill of coaching. *Creating an Aligned State* is a powerful way to stay connected to the best of yourself and be an effective example when coaching others.

Sharing stimulates innovation and strengthens resilience through the exchange of information, ideas, resources and energy. Sharing involves the capacity to promote open communication and dialogue between people. One of the main contexts in which Sharing is important is for effective *problem solving*. The *S.C.O.R.E. Model* offers a simple yet comprehensive template for defining a problem space and solution space by helping to identify *symptoms*, their *causes*, the *outcomes* that will replace the symptoms and the *resources* necessary to transform the causes of the symptoms and achieve the outcomes that will bring the desired *effects*.

When *Stretching*, a leader and his or her teams must raise expectations, stimulate innovation, look for continuous improvement and challenge consolidated habits. The *Hero's Journey* provides a powerful roadmap for successfully Stretching by helping to define the *call to action* the situation requires from us, the *threshold* into the new territory we must cross, the *"demons" and shadows* we must confront and transform and the *resources and guardians* we will need to successfully travel the journey.

The theme of *Chapter 6* was *doing the impossible*. This becomes necessary when our vision inspires us to attempt to create or achieve something that has not existed before and that we do not know how to accomplish with our current tools and knowhow. These new ideas and goals are often labeled "impossible," "unrealistic" or "irrelevant" because they are "beyond what people are currently familiar or comfortable with." In addition to the other leadership skills presented in this book, doing the impossible requires the skills of *meta leadership* – the capacity to create and lead other leaders.

All forms of leadership are founded on the ability to provide the necessary guidance and motivation (direction and energy) for oneself and one's team members. Meta leadership requires the ability to communicate one's vision and ideas, and to "understand people and their motivation" in order to support them to take responsibility and become leaders themselves. Skills such as moving from vision to execution through Walt Disney's *Imagineering* and *storyboarding* processes are important for meta leaders in order to empower team members to become better leaders themselves.

Welcoming Critics and criticism is another important skill for doing the impossible. The objections and criticisms of key stakeholders can be addressed by identifying, understanding and responding to the *positive intentions* behind those criticisms or objections and then *turning the criticisms into questions*. *Principled persuasion* is another key skill for doing the impossible that involves *verbal reframing* and other language patterns to build *values bridges* and *belief bridges* that align people's values and motivations and refocus them toward the bigger vision and purpose.

Leadership "Culture" Versus "Cult" of the Leader

Clearly, the main goal of conscious, meta leadership is to create other empowered leaders as opposed to simply obedient followers. This is not only important for achieving effective performance, it is ultimately essential for the survival of the venture. If a venture loses direction and motivation and falls apart after the founder or current leader departs, the subsequent ruin is an evidence of that leader's failure to nurture the conditions under which leadership can flourish.

Robust and sustainable ventures and organizations are built on an empowered leadership culture as opposed to a cult formed around a particular leader. A *cult* is a rudimentary, incomplete, inherently ephemeral social structure, that fades away when the personality that creates it departs. In a cult, the success of the group or organization is based primarily on the ego and personality of the leader. The leader is the principal source of the organization's vision, mission, values and motivation. Thus, the organization exists and succeeds almost entirely because of the leader's ideas, energy and charisma.

Cults are frequently based on the perception of fundamental inequality between people. They are founded upon a hierarchy in which people at the top are inherently "better than" those at other levels. As a result, people are viewed as dispensable entities that can be easily replaced by others.

A culture is much more durable and robust than a cult, because its survival and growth do not depend on the presence and personality of a single individual. "Culture" is generally something that arises from and is shared by all the members of an organization or social system. Merriam-Webster's Dictionary defines *culture* generally as "the integrated pattern of human knowledge, belief, and behavior that depends upon man's capacity for learning and transmitting knowledge to succeeding generations." Thus, a key aspect of a culture is its ability to pass on knowledge and competence to other members of the culture.

Because culture is shared, it can remain influential long after its creator has stepped aside. And, while culture certainly comes from the interrelations between people *within* an organization or social system, it is ultimately determined by that system's relationship to some larger holarchy.

In both start up ventures and existing organizations, it is important to distinguish between a *culture of leadership* and the *cult of the leader*. In the cult of the leader, there is typically one powerful individual who makes the decisions and determines the direction the company will take. The result is that the organization's actions and plans are controlled by a single charismatic figure. People's plans and actions within the organization are primarily motivated either by their fear or by their love of the leader. (A dictatorship, for example, is generally a fear-based leadership cult.)

In this type of situation, there is only room for a few people to be leaders, and the credit for success is confined to the leader or to a few key individuals at the top. There are no plans or ongoing efforts to develop future leaders. In fact, people who try to be proactive and enact leadership are likely to be suppressed and punished.

As a result, people wait to act until they are given permission by the leader or someone close to the leader, and are expected to follow orders and directives without question. Cults tend to be characterized by a lot of rhetoric. Leaders don't listen, and people are afraid to speak openly about what they think.

Characteristics of a Leadership Culture

In a leadership culture, on the other hand, everyone must develop and express key leadership actions and qualities to some degree. While there are still symbolic individuals who have key responsibilities, represent cultural values and provide an example of leadership, many others in the organization are also empowered to make decisions and encouraged to have their own visions in parallel with the larger vision driving the organization.

In a culture of leadership, the success of the organization is based on the combined energy and efforts of many people aligned toward a common vision. The organization's actions and plans are determined by the desire and efforts of people at all levels of the organization, and the credit for success is spread to many contributors.

People are essentially viewed as equals who are in different roles. Roles are based on the development of individual capabilities and are not a reflection of the intrinsic value of the person. As a result, people at all levels within the group or organization are acknowledged and seen as a valuable and indispensable contributors.

In a culture of leadership, many people are encouraged to lead and express their ideas and visions. There is genuine conversation—leaders listen to what people say. People at all levels are encouraged and supported to speak openly and honestly about what they think.

There is an authentic and sustained effort to train and develop future leaders. People at all levels are encouraged to be proactive and take leadership. Consequently, the organization will continue to run smoothly and effectively in the absence of the leader.

Thus, a leadership culture is a "winning" culture in that it:

- Promotes the contribution of all members
- Recognizes individuals and supports their growth and success, and each individual contributes to the success of the larger system
- Seeks continuous improvement—act to stay "ahead of the curve"
- Fosters an open environment in which everyone can provide input (feedback)
- Is one from which people benefit and to which they can contribute—i.e., is "a world to which people want to belong"
- Produces a whole which is greater than the sum of its parts

We can see these characteristics in action in the examples of the various leaders and ventures that I have profiled in this book: Elon Musk (SpaceX, Tesla, SolarCity), Dr. Lim Suet Wun (Tan Tock Seng Hospital, Singapore), John Yokoyama (Pike Place Fish Market), Charles Matthews (Rolls Royce Motors), William McKnight (3M), David Guo (Display Research Laboratories), Jan E. Smith (The Disney Store, Disney Interactive) and Vahé Torossian (Microsoft).

In summary, if a leader's success is based on the power of his or her personality, his or her job is only half done. As the American journalist Walter Lippmann said: "The final test of a leader is that he leaves behind him, in other men [and women], the conviction and the will to carry on." Effective leaders develop other leaders as their successors—and develop wide-ranging leadership within their organizations.

Because effective leadership becomes distributed throughout the entire population, leadership cultures are self-sustaining. Leadership cults frequently fall apart or disintegrate into power struggles and conflict when the leader can no longer be present.

To check whether your organization is more of a leadership culture or cult, go through the following checklist. Count the number of check marks you have in the "cult" column. If you check more than six items in the "cult" column, your organization is in serious danger of being or becoming a leadership cult.

Leadership Culture Versus Cult Assessment

Culture

__ Many people are encouraged to lead and express their ideas and visions.

__ The organization will continue to run smoothly and effectively in the absence of the leader.

__ The leader is a reflection and example of the vision, mission and values shared by people at all levels in the organization.

__ Values, goals and actions are determined and shared by the people at all levels of the organization.

__ The success of the organization is based primarily on the energy and efforts of many people aligned toward a common vision.

__ The credit for success is spread to many contributors.

__ People are encouraged to think for themselves and take responsible actions based upon what they understand to be important for the organization's success.

__ The organization's goals and values reflect those of people at all levels within the organization.

__ People act according to what they think and believe to be most important to the success of the organization.

__ People at all levels are encouraged and supported to speak openly and honestly about what they think.

Cult

__ There is only room for a few people to be leaders.

__ The organization will experience many problems (such as power struggles and conflicts) and may collapse if the leader were to leave.

__ The leader is the source of the organization's vision, mission and values.

__ Values, goals and actions are determined and enforced by a few people at the top.

__ The success of the organization is based primarily on the personality of the leader.

__ The credit for success is confined to the leader or to a few key individuals at the top.

__ People wait to act until they are given permission by the leader or someone close to the leader.

__ The organization's goals and values are primarily a reflection of the interests and ideas of the leader.

__ People are expected to follow orders and directives from the leader without question.

__ People are afraid to speak openly about what they think.

Culture	*Cult*
__ There is genuine conversation—leaders listen to what people say.	__ There is a lot of rhetoric—leaders don't listen.
__ The organization's actions and plans are determined by the desires and efforts of people at all levels of the organization.	__ The organization's actions and plans are controlled by a single charismatic figure.
__ The primary purpose for the actions of people within the organization come from some goal or service that is beyond the leader and the organization itself.	__ The primary purpose for the actions of people within the organization comes from what the leader says.
__ People's plans and actions within the organization are primarily motivated by their alignment with common values and shared vision.	__ People's plans and actions within the organization are primarily motivated by either their fear or their love of the leader.
__ The organization succeeds primarily because of the vision and empowerment of people at all levels of the organization.	__ The organization succeeds primarily because of the leader's vision and energy.
__ There is a genuine and sustained effort to train and develop future leaders.	__ There are no plans or ongoing efforts to develop future leaders.
__ People at all levels are encouraged to be proactive and take leadership.	__ People who try to be proactive and take leadership are suppressed and punished.

Closing Reflections

It seems quite clear that there is an increasing need for authentic and conscious leadership in the world today; including the way we lead ourselves, our families, our clients, our teams and our communities, as well as our ventures. The purpose of this book has been to provide principles, roadmaps and exercises to help you become a more conscious and effective leader of yourself and others and to create a resilient and sustainable venture.

As I pointed out in the Preface to this volume, to achieve more in the world around us we must first grow and evolve personally. In order to contribute more, we have to develop ourselves more. This involves increasing our emotional intelligence as much as our intellectual understanding and knowledge. By optimizing your mindset and connecting more with your somatic intelligence, you become more perceptive, innovative and fit for the future.

A major conclusion of Success Factor Modeling is that in order to achieve more in the world around you must grow and evolve personally.

As you finish reading this book, it is now time to begin to put the skills and resources you have been learning into practice. It is time for you to take the necessary steps to empower yourself and others, orchestrate innovation, rebound from adversity and take your projects and ventures from vision to execution. I wish you much success on your journey to live your dreams and make a better world through your projects and ventures. Let's create the future together!

Afterword

I hope you have enjoyed this exploration of Success Factor Modeling™ and the SFM Leadership Model™. If you are interested in learning about the principles and technology of Success Factor Modeling in more depth, other resources and tools exist to further develop and apply the distinctions, strategies and skills described within these pages.

Dilts Strategy Group

Dilts Strategy Group is an organization committed to providing training, consulting and coaching in the applications of Success Factor Modeling™, including Next Generation Entrepreneurship, Collective Intelligence, Leadership and Innovation. Dilts Strategy Group also sponsors research projects promoting the development of new models and the identification of evolving success factors in the dynamic social and economic world in which we live. Dilts Strategy Group offers trainings and certification programs in Success Factor Modeling throughout the world.

For more information please contact:

Dilts Strategy Group
P.O. Box 67448
Scotts Valley CA 95067-7448
USA
Phone: (831) 438-8314
E-Mail: info@diltsstrategygroup.com
Homepage: http://www.diltsstrategygroup.com

In addition to the training programs I offer through Dilts Strategy Group, I also travel extensively internationally, presenting seminars and workshops on a variety of topics related to personal and professional development.

For more information on scheduled programs, please consult my website: http://www.robertdilts.com or write for information to: rdilts@nlpu.com.

Journey to Genius

I have also written a number of other books and developed audio recordings based on the principles and distinctions of Success Factor Modeling™ and NLP. For example, I have produced several products based on my modeling of Strategies of Genius such as audio recordings describing the creative processes of geniuses such as Mozart, Walt Disney and Leonardo Da Vinci.

For more information on these and other products and resources, please contact:

Journey to Genius
P.O. Box 67448
Scotts Valley, CA 95067-7448
Phone (831) 438-8314
E-Mail: info@journeytogenius.com
Homepage: http://www.journeytogenius.com

NLP University

I am also a co-founder, director and trainer at *NLP University*, an organization committed to providing the highest quality trainings in basic and advanced skills of Neuro-Linguistic Programming, and to promoting the development of new models and applications of NLP in the areas of health, business and organizations, creativity and learning. Each summer, NLP University holds residential programs at the University of California at Santa Cruz, offering extended residential courses on the skills of NLP, including those related to business consulting and coaching.

For more information please contact Teresa Epstein at:

NLP University
P.O. Box 1112
Ben Lomond, California 95005
Phone: (831) 336-3457
E-Mail: Teresanlp@aol.com
Homepage: http://www.nlpu.com

Success Factor Modeling™ illustrations and products

Antonio Meza and I have created this series of books with the intention of offering you something different, fun and visually rich. Through the pages of this book and the following volumes you will find many memorable illustrations and characters that will help you create a deeper connection with the content of the book.

We have created a special online store where you can find a variety of products like posters, t-shirts, mugs, etc., that can help you to stay connected to the main concepts of Next Generation Entrepreneurship.

For more information on these and other products and resources, you can visit:

Success Factor Modeling website

Homepage: http://www.successfactormodeling.com

Success Factor Modeling product store

Homepage: http://society6.com/successfactormodeling

Antonio Meza illustrates books, articles, presentations and also performs as a graphic facilitator for conferences and seminars. He is also a business consultant, trainer and coach as well as a member of the Dilts Strategy Group.

If you are curious about Antonio's work as an illustrator, you can contact him at:

Antoons

E-Mail: hola@antoons.net

Homepage: http://www.antoons.net

Mindset Maps International

Co-founded by Robert Dilts and Miklos (Midkey) Feher, Mindset Maps International has applied the distinctions and discoveries of Success Factor Modeling™ to create the SFM Success Mindset Map™. This map identifies three main areas of a successful mindset:

1. *Meta Mindset* – Big-picture clarity
2. *Macro Mindset* – Habits of success
3. *Micro Mindset* – Ongoing priorities

Mindset Maps International has created an App that integrates these three areas of mindset together to create the "SFM Mindset Compass." The SFM Mindset Compass helps you to identify your particular aptitudes and tendencies and to know which ones you need to prioritize and strengthen in order to take your project or venture to the next level.

Homepage: http://www.mindsetmaps.com.

Conscious Leaders Mastermind

The Conscious Leaders Mastermind is an exclusive, accelerated growth program for successful entrepreneurs and business owners. Conscious Leaders Mastermind integrates the seven core strategies shared by the world's most successful people with the practices of conscious leadership. This provides participants with a clear roadmap for sustainable success, accelerated growth, and positive impact (see *SFM II*, Chapter 1, pp. 66-71). Current members include influential leaders from a variety of fields who have positively impacted the lives of hundreds of millions of people.

Conscious Leaders Mastermind was created by author Robert Dilts, Mitchell Stevko (a Silicon Valley growth expert who has helped over 150 entrepreneurs achieve their dreams, raising over $5 billion in capital) and Dr. Olga Stevko (a Russian MD and Belief Medicine expert who specializes in working with high level professionals). The Conscious Leaders Mastermind program is available only by approved application and interview or member referral.

If you are ready to take your business and your abilities to an entirely new level of impact and influence, you can learn more and apply for membership at:

E-Mail: mitchell@consciousleadersmm.com

Homepage: http://www.consciousleadersmm.com

Logical Levels Inventory

Logical levels inventory (***lli***) is an innovative online leadership profiling tool based on the various levels of success factors that we have been exploring in this book. ***lli*** identifies the key qualities that leaders need to possess in order take advantage of opportunities and remain successful in times of uncertainty and crisis. Developed as a direct result of the first Success Factor Modeling™ certification program, ***lli*** takes you through a self-assessment process that helps you uncover the driving forces behind your actions and provides insight into what you can change to be a more successful leader in any area.

E-Mail: info@lli.uk.com

Homepage: http://www.logicallevels.co.uk

Appendix A: Business Model Generation Canvas

The *Business Model Generation Canvas* provides a useful set of distinctions to help chunk down your vision for your venture into an operational plan. In the books *Business Model Generation* (2010) and *Business Model You*, the authors define a "business model" as the logic by which an enterprise sustains itself financially. Put simply, it's *the logic by which an enterprise earns its livelihood.*

They base their approach on what they refer to as *The Nine Building Blocks* for how organizations provide *Value to Customers*. The following is a brief summary of the nine building blocks and the questions to consider in order to identify and clarify each one of these building blocks in relation to your project or venture.

1. ***Customers***

   An organization serves Customers . . .

   For whom are you creating value?

   Who are your most important customers?

2. ***Value Provided*** ... by solving Customer problems or satisfying Customer needs.

   What value do you deliver to the customer?

   Which of your customer's problems are you helping to solve?

   What bundles of products and services are you offering to each Customer Segment?

   Which customer needs are you satisfying?

3. ***Channels***...Organizations communicate and deliver Value in different ways...

   Through which Channels do your Customer Segments want to be reached?

   How are you reaching them now?

   How are your Channels integrated?

   Which ones work best?

   Which ones are most cost-efficient?

   How are you integrating them with customer routines?

4. ***Customer Relationships***...and establish and maintain different kinds of relationships with Customers.

   What type of relationship does each of your Customer Segments expect you to establish and maintain with them?

Which ones have you established?

How are they integrated with the rest of your business model?

How costly are they?

5. ***Revenue***...Money comes in when Customers pay for Value Provided.

    For what value are your customers really willing to pay?

    For what do they currently pay?

    How are they currently paying?

    How would they prefer to pay?

    How much does each Revenue Stream contribute to overall revenues?

6. ***Key Resources***...The assets needed to create and/or deliver the previously described elements.

    What Key Resources do your Value Propositions require? Your Distribution Channels? Customer Relationships? Revenue Streams?

7. ***Key Activities***...The actual tasks and actions required to create and deliver the previously described elements.

    What Key Activities do your Value Propositions require? Your Distribution Channels? Customer Relationships? Revenue streams?

8. ***Key Partners***...Some activities are outsourced, and some resources are acquired outside the organization.

    Who are your Key Partners?

    Who are your key suppliers?

    Which Key Resources are you acquiring from partners?

    Which Key Activities do partners perform?

9. ***Costs***...The expenses incurred acquiring Key Resources, performing Key Activities, and working with Key Partners.

    What are the most important costs inherent in your business model?

    Which Key Resources are most expensive?

    Which Key Activities are most expensive?

The authors of the Business Model Generation process advise entrepreneurs to capture the answers to these questions in the form of what they call a "canvas." In contrast to a storyboard, which shows a critical path, the Business Model Generation canvas is more like a painting, providing a type of strategic overview for your project or venture. The recommended structure for the canvas is illustrated below:

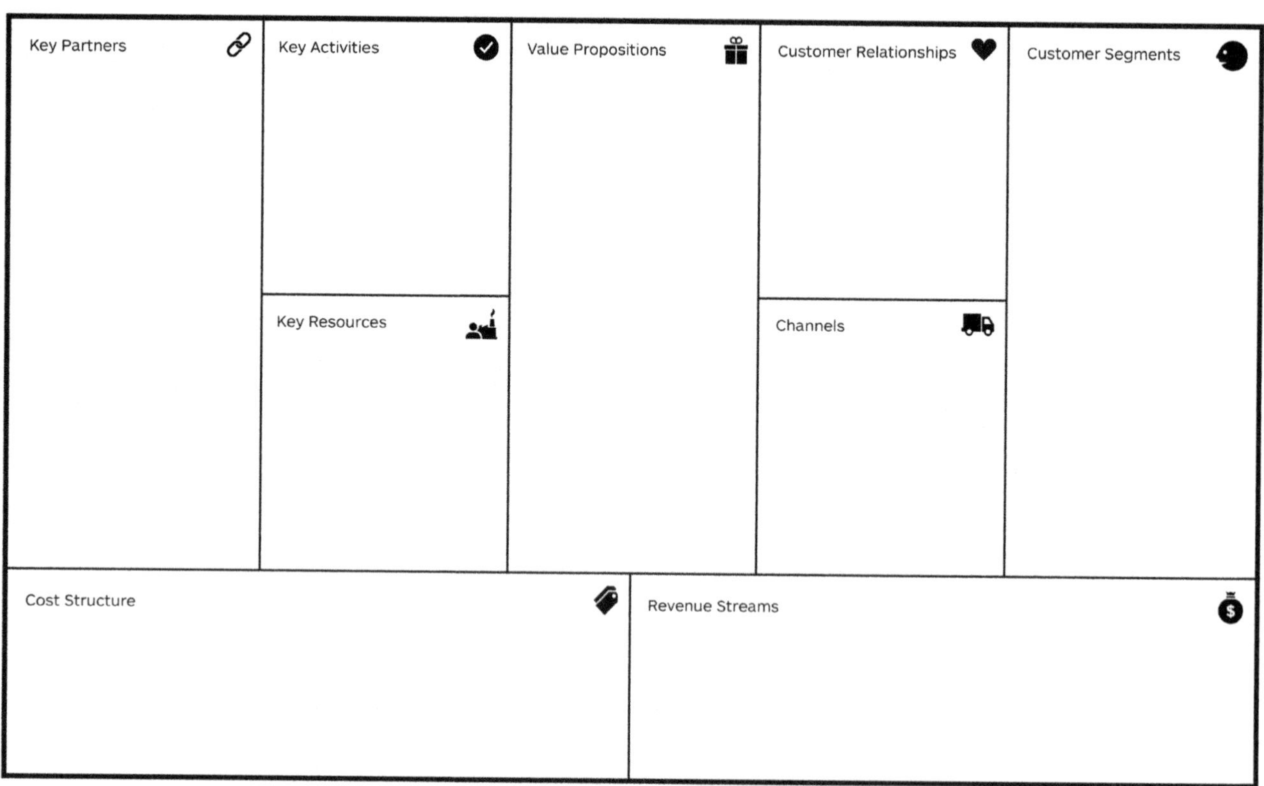

The Business Model Generation canvas is a very useful complement to the SFM Circle of Success and your successive levels of storyboards. It available to download for free at: BusinessModelGeneration.com/canvas.

The nine building blocks of the Business Model Generation canvas clearly are primarily focused on defining activities and resources with respect to customers and partners (as opposed to team members and stakeholders) in terms of the Circle of Success.

Appendix B:

Sleight of Mouth – Verbal Reframing, Persuasion and Conversational Belief Change

Effective and principled persuasion is a function of being able to create belief bridges that reframe belief barriers and build a winning belief system. My book *Sleight of Mouth: The Magic of Conversational Belief Change* (1999) describes the use of a particular group of language patterns that support the process of effective persuasion. The purpose of Sleight of Mouth patterns is to lead people to "punctuate" their experiences in new ways and take different perspectives as a means to establish, reframe, or transform beliefs.

Generally, Sleight of Mouth patterns can be characterized as categories of "verbal reframes" which influence beliefs and the mental maps from which those beliefs have been formed. The term "Sleight of Mouth" is drawn from the notion of "Sleight of Hand." The word sleight comes from an Old Norse word meaning "crafty," "cunning," "artful" or "dexterous." Sleight of hand is a type of magic done by close-up card magicians. This form of magic is characterized by the experience, "now you see it, now you don't." A person may place an ace of spades at the top of the deck, for example, but, when the magician waves his or her hand over the card, it has "transformed" into a queen of hearts. The verbal patterns of Sleight of Mouth have a similar sort of "magical" quality because they can often create dramatic shifts in perception and the assumptions upon which particular perceptions are based.

Sleight of Mouth patterns are categories of "verbal reframes" that can often create dramatic shifts in perception and the assumptions upon which particular perceptions are based.

There are a number of ways to apply Sleight of Mouth patterns to create the belief bridges necessary to take on the impossible. From the meta leadership perspective, however, it is better to stimulate collaborators to discover and create their own belief bridges. That is, rather than give people answers, it is more powerful to provide them with questions. Questions are a potent means to generate new realities that lead to doing the impossible. Gregory Bateson commented that many of today's problems have emerged from being too sure of our answers and too hesitant about asking questions. To do the impossible, we have to be more hesitant about our answers and more bold about asking questions. As Jan Smith pointed out, "You have to show it is possible and then ask 'why wouldn't this work?'"

Thus, one of the best ways to overcome or transform belief barriers is by asking questions related to the various Sleight of Mouth categories in order to lead people to consider different perspectives and perceptual positions. As you do, it is also important to keep in mind Jan Smith's comment that "the dream needs to outweigh criticism." In this regard, the key to effective persuasion is to continually bring the focus of attention back to the larger vision or dream.

Sleight of Mouth Questions

The following exercise is best done with other group or team members around issues relating to your project or venture. It involves exploring questions that can help create potential belief bridges that bypass or transform belief barriers. It is important that a strong COACH Container (see page 77) be created before exploring these questions in order to avoid getting caught in ego defenses or conflicts.

Identify a limiting belief or "belief barrier" coming from yourself, a stakeholder or key collaborator in relation to your project or venture that you would like to shift or transform.

Belief Barrier: *It is not possible to* ______________________________ *because* ______________________________.

Example: "It is not possible to *achieve the goal* because *we do not have enough time or resources.*"

Example Belief Barrier

*"**It is not possible to** achieve the goal **because** we do not have enough time or resources."*

With the help of other group members, explore the following frames and questions as a way to find or open possible new perspectives. Enter the COACH state and explore your answers to the following questions:

1. **Intention**: Directing attention to the positive intention or purpose of the belief barrier.

   Questions: *What is the positive purpose or intention of this objection?*

   ____

   How can you acknowledge and address the positive intention in a way that does not stop progress toward the vision?

   ____

Example **Intention** Responses:

Positive intention = "Not building false hope" and "Avoid wasting what few resources we have."

How can we proceed in a way in which we are being realistic and using our time and available resources carefully and wisely so that we can best continue our progress toward our bigger vision?

2. **Redefine**: Replacing or shifting some of the words used in the belief barrier statement with others that mean something similar but have more open ended implications.

   Questions: *What are the key words or phrases in the limiting belief statement?*

   ____

Example **Redefine** Responses:

Key words/phrases = "not possible," "achieve the goal," "time," "resources."

Example Belief Barrier

*"**It is not possible to** achieve the goal **because** we do not have enough time or resources."*

What is another word or phrase that could replace or be added to one of the key words or phrases that means something similar but has more open implications that do not stop progress toward the vision?

____

Instead of saying it is "not possible" we could say, "it is more difficult" or "we don't know yet how it could be possible."

Instead of saying it is not possible to "achieve the goal" we could say it is not possible to "take the next step in the way that we normally would."

Instead of saying "resources" we could say "the usual resources."

3. **Consequence**: Directing attention to a positive effect of the belief barrier or the relationship defined by the belief barrier.

Question: *What is a positive effect of the belief barrier or the relationship defined by the belief barrier that could actually support progress toward the vision?*

____

Example **Consequence** Response:

If it truly is not possible to achieve the goal, then it gives us the opportunity to just focus on doing our best and learning everything we can from the experience.

4. **Chunk Down:** Breaking the elements of the belief barrier into small enough pieces that it changes the relationship defined by the belief barrier.

Question: *What smaller elements or chunks are implied by the limiting belief but have a richer or more positive relationship than the ones stated in the belief that could actually support progress toward the vision?*

____

Example **Chunk Down** Response:

Maybe it is best to start by focusing on how much of the goal we can achieve with the time and resources we have. Exactly how much time and what resources do we have available? Could we achieve half? Two thirds? Three quarters?

5. **Counter Example:** Finding an example that challenges the rule defined by the belief barrier.

Question: *What is an example or experience that is an exception to the rule defined by the limiting belief that supports progress toward the vision?*

____

Example **Counter-Example** Response:

There are many examples of projects and ventures that succeeded even though they only had sparse resources and limited time. Apple and Hewlett-Packard, for instance, both started in garages. There are also many examples of ventures with more than ample time and resources that neither achieved much nor succeeded. Time and resources may not always be the differences that make the difference.

Example Belief Barrier

*"**It is not possible to** achieve the goal **because** we do not have enough time or resources."*

6. **Another Outcome**: Switching to another outcome or issue that is more relevant to reaching the vision.

Question: *What other outcome or issue could be more relevant than the one stated or implied by the limiting belief that actually supports progress toward the vision?*

____

Example **Another Outcome** Response:

Maybe achieving the goal is not so much the outcome we should focus on but instead become very curious about what is possible to achieve given the time and resources we have.

7. **Analogy**: Finding a situation or context analogous to that defined by the belief barrier, but which has different implications.

Question: *What is some other situation which is analogous to that defined by the limiting belief (a metaphor for the belief), but which has different implications that actually support progress toward the vision?*

____

Example **Analogy** Responses:

Consider the Bible story of "the loaves and the fishes" where a small number of loaves of bread and a couple of fishes ended up feeding 5,000 people (with 12 baskets left over). It is an interesting metaphor about how sometimes limited resources go much farther than we anticipate, and that there are resources within the larger system that we may not be taking into account. It illustrates the "miracle" of generative collaboration and synergy between resources; i.e., 1+1=3.

The "four minute mile" is another interesting analogy of something people believed could not be achieved for many years.

8. **Hierarchy of Criteria**: Re-evaluating the belief barrier according to a criterion (or value) that is more important than those addressed by the belief.

Question: *What is a criterion (value) that is potentially more important than those addressed by the limiting belief that has not yet been considered that could actually support progress toward the vision?*

____

Example **Hierarchy of Criteria** Response:

Achievement is not necessarily as important as our commitment to do our best to realize our values and move toward our vision. As Steve Jobs said, the most important thing is go to bed each night saying "we've done something wonderful."

Example Belief Barrier

*"**It is not possible to** achieve the goal **because** we do not have enough time or resources."*

9. **Change Frame Size**: Re-evaluating the implication of the belief barrier in the context of a longer (or shorter) time frame, a larger number of people (or from an individual point of view) or a bigger or smaller perspective.

Question: *What is a longer or shorter time frame, a larger number or smaller number of people, or a bigger or smaller perspective that would change the implications of the limiting belief to be something more positive that supports progress toward the vision?*

Example **Change Frame Size** Response:

Eventually, someone will accomplish it. If not us, whom? If not now, when? It is probably the people who believe they can do it regardless of the constraints that will achieve it first.

10. **Meta Frame**: Reflecting on the belief barrier as a "belief" in a way that brings awareness to the assumptions and other beliefs behind it.

Question: *What is a belief about this limiting belief that could change or enrich the perception of the limiting belief in a way that supports progress toward the vision?*

Example **Meta Frame** Response:

Maybe it only seems impossible because we are not considering all of the levels of success factors that contribute to achieving goals. It may be the belief that "it is not possible" that is limiting us more than reality.

As a practice, go through the same questions with a different belief barrier, such as: "It is impossible to do what you want because it has never been done before."

References:

* **Sleight of Mouth: The Magic of Conversational Belief Change**, Dilts, R., Meta Publications, Capitola, CA, 1999.

Photos

Page 12 – Elon Musk
twitter.com/elonmusk

Page 36 – Tom Chi
http://www.watsonuniversity.org/portfolio/tom-chi/

Page 54 – Tim Gallwey
https://www.bigspeak.com/speakers/tim-gallwey/

Page 59 – Barak Obama
http://www.ndtv.com/world-news/what-does-barack-obama-carry-in-his-pocket-find-out-on-youtube-1266454

Page 62 – Phil Jackson
https://www.alaturkaonline.com/wp-content/uploads/2014/03/13/Phil-Jackson.jpg

Page 80 - Dr. Lim Suet Wun
http://biomedicalengineeringconsultancy.blogspot.com/p/company-news.html

Page 136 – John Yokoyama
http://karenducey.photoshelter.com/gallery-image/Pike-Place-Fish-Market-for-Seafood-Business/G00004FIA25QFu-fA/I0000qOSsIpTWUL8

Page 138 – Pike Place Fish Market
https://www.pikeplacefish.com

Page 169 – Charles Matthews
http://www.offshoreenergytoday.com/african-petroleum-in-non-exec-chairman-change/

Page 174 – William McKnight
http://www.omagnatta.com/lideres-william-mcknight-3m

Page 239 – Patricia Dilts
photo courtesy of Robert B. Dilts

Page 241 – David Guo
photo courtesy of Robert B. Dilts

Page 243 – Jan E. Smith
http://www.hobknobrealty.com/p.php/hobknob/team

Page 257 – Steig Westerberg
twitter.com/steigw

Page 326 – Robert Dilts
photo courtesy of Susanne Kischnick

Page 327 – Antonio Meza
photo courtesy of Susanne Kischnick

Bibliography

Success Factor Modeling, Volume I – Next Generation Entrepreneurs: Live Your Dream and Create a Better World through Your Business, Dilts, R., Dilts Strategy Group, Santa Cruz, CA, 2015

Success Factor Modeling, Volume II – Generative Collaboration: Releasing the Creative Power of Collective Intelligence, Dilts, R., Dilts Strategy Group, Santa Cruz, CA, 2016

Alpha Leadership: Tools for Leaders Who Want More From Life, Deering, A., Dilts, R. and Russell, J., John Wiley & Sons, London, England, 2002.

Visionary Leadership Skills, Dilts, R., Meta Publications, Capitola, CA, 1996.

Modeling with NLP, Dilts, R., Meta Publications, Capitola, CA, 1998.

From Coach to Awakener, Dilts, R., Meta Publications, Capitola, CA, 2003.

Tools for Dreamers, Dilts, R. B., Epstein, T. and Dilts, R. W., Meta Publications, Capitola, CA, 1991.

Strategies of Genius Vols I, II & III, Dilts, R., Meta Publications, Capitola, CA,1994-1995.

Encyclopedia of Systemic Neuro-Linguistic Programming and NLP New Coding, Dilts, R. and DeLozier, J., NLP University Press, Santa Cruz, CA, 2000.

Effective Presentation Skills, Dilts, R., Meta Publications, Capitola, CA, 1994.

Skills for the Future, Dilts, R., Meta Publications, Capitola, CA, 1993.

NLP II: The Next Generation, Dilts, R. and DeLozier, J. with Bacon Dilts, D., Meta Publications, Capitola, CA, 2010.

The Hero's Journey: A Voyage of Self-Discovery, Gilligan, S. and Dilts, R., Crowne House Publishers, London, UK, 2009.

Innovations in NLP, Hall, M. and Charvet, S., Editors; Crown House Publishers, London, 2011.

Sleight of Mouth: The Magic of Conversational Belief Change, Dilts, R., Meta Publications, Capitola, CA, 1999.

Success Factor Modeling Volume III – Conscious Leadership and Resilience was created using:

- Aurulent Sans - by Stephen G. Hartke
- Roman Serif - by Mandred Klein
- COMIC GEEK - WWW.BLAMBOT.COM
- COMIC BOOK - WWW.PIXELSAGAS.COM
- BADABOOM BB - WWW.BLAMBOT.COM

Robert B. Dilts - Author

Photo by: Susanne Kischnick

Robert Dilts – Author

Robert Dilts has had a global reputation as a leading coach, behavioral skills trainer and business consultant since the late 1970s. A major developer and expert in the field of Neuro-Linguistic Programming (NLP), Robert has provided coaching, consulting and training throughout the world to a wide variety of individuals and organizations.

Together with his brother John, Robert pioneered the principles and techniques of Success Factor Modeling™ and has authored numerous books and articles about how they may be applied to enhance leadership, creativity, communication and team development. His book *Visionary Leadership Skills* draws from Robert's extensive study of historical and corporate leaders to present the tools and skills necessary for "creating a world to which people want to belong." *Alpha Leadership: Tools for Business Leaders Who Want More From Life* (with Ann Deering and Julian Russell) captures and shares best practices of effective leadership, offering approaches to reduce stress and to promote satisfaction. *From Coach to Awakener* provides a road map and set of toolboxes for coaches to help clients reach goals on a number of different levels of learning and change. *The Hero's Journey: A Voyage of Self Discovery* (with Stephen Gilligan) is about how to reconnect with your deepest calling, transform limiting beliefs and habits and improve self-image.

Past corporate clients and sponsors include Apple Computer, Microsoft, Hewlett-Packard, IBM, Lucasfilms Ltd. and the State Railway of Italy. He has lectured extensively on coaching, leadership, innovation, collective intelligence, organizational learning and change management, making presentations and keynote addresses for The International Coaching Federation (ICF), HEC Paris, The United Nations, The World Health Organization, Harvard University and the International University of Monaco. In 1997 and 1998, Robert supervised the design of *Tools for Living*, the behavior management portion of the program used by Weight Watcher's International.

Robert was an associate professor at the ISVOR Fiat School of Management for more than fifteen years, helping to develop programs on leadership, innovation, values and systemic thinking. From 2001–2004 he served as chief scientist and Chairman of the Board for ISVOR DILTS Leadership Systems, a joint venture with ISVOR Fiat (the former corporate university of the Fiat Group) that delivered a wide range of innovative leadership development programs to large corporations on a global scale.

A co-founder of Dilts Strategy Group, Robert was also founder and CEO of Behavioral Engineering, a company that developed computer software and hardware applications emphasizing behavioral change. Robert has a degree in Behavioral Technology from the University of California at Santa Cruz.

Email: rdilts@nlpu.com
Homepage: http://www.robertdilts.com

Antonio Meza - Illustrator

Antonio Meza has been drawing cartoons ever since he can remember, but his professional cartoonist work started more recently in his life.

A native of Pachuca, Mexico, Antonio is a Master Practitioner and a Trainer of Neuro-Linguistic Programming (NLP). He has a degree in Communication Sciences from Fundación Universidad de las Américas Puebla, a Masters degree in Film Studies from Université de Paris 3 –Sorbonne Nouvelle, a diploma in Cinema Scriptwriting from the General Society of Writers in Mexico (SOGEM), and a diploma in Documentary Films from France's École Nationale des Métiers de l'Image et du Son (La Fémis).

He was recently certified in Generative Coaching with Robert Dilts and Stephen Gilligan at the Institut Repère in Paris; and in Success Factor Modeling with NLP University and the Dilts Strategy Group.

Antonio's career includes work in marketing research, advertising, branding, corporate image, film production, and scriptwriting. His professional photography work has been exhibited in Mexico, Belgium, and France.

He participated in animated cartoons startups in Mexico before moving to France where he works as a consultant, coach, and trainer, specializing in creative thinking and collective intelligence. He offers his services under his brand: Akrobatas.

His NGO and Foundations clients include the European AIDS Treatment Group (EATG), OXFAM, the European HIV/AIDS Funders Group, the Open Society Foundations (OSF) and the European Public Health Alliance (EPHA). He has conducted training workshops for business schools such as the ESCP-Europe and international organizations such as the IABC (International Association of Business Communicators).

Antonio is also an experienced public speaker and member of Toastmasters International. In 2015 he was awarded best speaker at the International Speech Contest of District 59, covering South-West Europe, and reached the semifinals at the international level.

His cartoons and illustrations have been published by the Université Pantheon-Assas (Paris 2). He is co-author of three books (as illustrator); two with Jean-Eric Branaa: "English Law Made Simple" and "American Government Made Simple" published by Ellipses in Paris and "Les Vrais Secrets de la Communication" with Beatrice Arnaud.

He also uses his skills as a cartoonist and trainer to collaborate in seminars, conferences and brainstorming sessions as a graphic facilitator, and to produce animated videos to explain complex information in a fun way.

Antonio has illustrated the three volumes of the *Success Factor Modeling* series with Robert Dilts.

Antonio Meza – Illustrator

Photo by: Susanne Kischnick

Email: hola@antoons.net

Homepage: http://www.antoons.net

CPSIA information can be obtained
at www.ICGtesting.com
Printed in the USA
FSOW04n0728290717
36774FS

9 780996 200448